AFTER *LA DOLCE VITA*

Cultural Memory
    in
    the
    Present

Mieke Bal and Hent de Vries, Editors

AFTER *LA DOLCE VITA*

A Cultural Prehistory of Berlusconi's Italy

Alessia Ricciardi

STANFORD UNIVERSITY PRESS

STANFORD, CALIFORNIA

Stanford University Press
Stanford, California

©2012 by the Board of Trustees of the Leland Stanford Junior University. All rights reserved.

This book has been published with the support of a Research Grant from the University Research Grants Committee at Northwestern University.

No part of this book may be reproduced or transmitted in any form or by any means, electronic or mechanical, including photocopying and recording, or in any information storage or retrieval system without the prior written permission of Stanford University Press.

Library of Congress Cataloging-in-Publication Data

Ricciardi, Alessia, author.
  After la dolce vita : a cultural prehistory of Berlusconi's Italy / Alessia Ricciardi.
     pages cm
  Includes bibliographical references and index.
  ISBN 978-0-8047-8149-7 (cloth : alk. paper) — ISBN 978-0-8047-8150-3 (pbk. : alk. paper)
  1. Politics and culture—Italy—History—20th century. 2. Italy—Intellectual life—20th century. 3. Italy—History—1976- I. Title.
  DG581.R53 2012
  945.092—dc23
                         2011052268

Typeset by Bruce Lundquist in 11/13.5 Adobe Garamond

for Michele

Contents

Acknowledgments — xi

Introduction — 1
1 Sweetness — 19
2 Lightness — 81
3 Weakness — 125
4 Softness — 211

Notes — 241
Index — 297

Acknowledgments

The completion of this book was not an easy task, for a variety of reasons, some of which were intellectual and some more personal. Now that the work is done, I would like to thank properly everyone who has helped me along the way.

I am grateful to my colleagues in the Department of French and Italian at Northwestern University for their ongoing sympathy and camaraderie. In particular, I wish to thank Scott Durham, Michal Ginsburg (who I hope will never retire), Paola Morgavi, Nasrin Qader, Marco Ruffini, Tom Simpson, Domietta Torlasco, and Jane Winston. My appreciation is due as well to the graduate students who attended my seminars on Italy's anthropological mutation and on Pasolini at the University of California, Berkeley. Their sparkling conversation made the process of thinking and writing about several of the questions in this book seem a far less solitary endeavor. I wish specifically to thank Rossella Carbotti, Rebecca Falkoff, Janaya Lasker Ferretti, and Marina Romani for their incisive and amicable contributions. Warmth, delight, and encouragement were provided by a number of friends, including Kevin Bell, Patricia and Sophia Dailey, Laurent Debreuil, Laurent Ferri, Paola Marrati, Leonor Marrati-Guénoun, Mary Murrell, Armando Solis, Jared Stark, Mark Strand, and my brother, Alfonso.

An emphatic word of thanks to Penelope Deutscher, whose personal and intellectual vivacity, wise counsel, and general marvelousness have sustained me through difficult moments. I am indebted as well to Franca, Orsola, and Domenico Fraternali for their enduring friendship and affection.

My additional gratitude goes to everyone at Stanford University Press who has been involved in the publication of this book, most notably Emily Jane Cohen for her invaluable and gracious advice, Hent de Vries for his interest in the project, Sarah Crane Newman for her unfailing helpfulness, Tom Finnegan for his judicious copy editing, and my exceptionally kind and generous reader, Roberto Dainotto, whose suggestions and comments I shall treasure.

A portion of Chapter 1 appeared, in a much different form, in *Modernism/Modernity* 7, no. 2 (April 2000). A portion of Chapter 2 was delivered as a talk at the University of California, Berkeley, in 2006. I thank Albert Ascoli and Barbara Spackman for their observations and comments on the material.

The University of California, Berkeley, granted me a leave of six months in 2009 that was instrumental to the completion of the project. I acknowledge with great appreciation this assistance.

Two important presences in my daily life deserve special recognition. The first and most crucial is that of Chris Yu, to whom I give my love for all his support and for making continuous merriment of our time together. The second is that of my large and affable cat, Rocco.

Finally, I wish to acknowledge my father, Michele, whom I lost while writing this book. Kindness and courage were equally embedded in him; I was extraordinarily lucky to have him in my life. It is to his memory that I dedicate *After* La Dolce Vita.

AFTER *LA DOLCE VITA*

Introduction

The Italian filmmaker Michelangelo Antonioni's *La notte* captures the historical conditions of its moment with an incisive eye, indeed with an eerie prescience. Released in 1962, *La notte* depicts the discontent of a successful writer named Giovanni Pontano and his wife, Lidia. The action of the film begins on a day of celebration for the publication of his latest novel, the ominously titled *The Season*, and ends at dawn of the following day in the wake of an all-night party at the house of the Milanese industrialist Gherardini. As the party winds down to its conclusion, Gherardini, a member of the *nouveau riche* and a man with an astute grasp of the latest techniques of communication, offers Pontano a job as an executive in charge of telling the company's "story" to its employees. After refusing this proposition, the author departs with Lidia. As they wander away from the villa on foot, she reveals in conversation that she no longer loves him.

This final scene, however, is only the epilogue of a narrative that starts with the couple's visit to their friend Tommaso Garani, who is dying of cancer in a hospital. A colleague of Pontano and a former suitor of Lidia, Tommaso also enjoys the dubious distinction, in the milieu portrayed by the film, of being an Adorno scholar, whose latest article on the German philosopher Pontano praises in a passing remark. Translations of Theodor Adorno's writings, we should recall, began to appear in Italy in the mid-1950s and 1960s, starting with *Minima Moralia* in 1954. In roughly the same period, Silvio Berlusconi launched his career as a real estate developer in Milan, where he graduated from the Università Statale in 1961, raised the money for his first housing developments on via Alciati in 1962 and in the suburb of Brugherio in 1964, and went on to build the enormous gated community of Milano 2 for a residential population of more than 10,000 in the 1970s.[1] By rapidly expanding his investments to cable television outlets such as Telemilano; the daily newspaper *Il Giornale*; Italy's largest publishing house, Mondadori; and a vast array of corporate assets in media, finance, advertising, insurance, and other industries through holding companies such as Fininvest and Mediaset, Berlusconi succeeded in establishing a solidly conservative "counter-counterculture." This ethos could not be regarded as "clerical-fascist," to invoke Pier Paolo Pasolini's term, in the manner of the Democrazia Cristiana but rather coincided with growing acceptance of the most spectacular forms of consumerism. For Pasolini, such an attitude of conformism or acquiescence to the sameness of mass society was the hallmark of the "anthropological mutation" that he analyzed brilliantly in the late essays collected in his books *Corsair Writings* (1975) and *Lutheran Letters* (1976).

My purpose in *After* La Dolce Vita*: A Cultural Prehistory of Berlusconi's Italy* is not to try to add to the already substantial literature analyzing Berlusconi's rise to power. Rather, I am interested in exploring how the leftist intelligentsia, the Giovanni Pontanos of Italy, managed in a few decades, and most decisively from the mid-1970s through the 1980s, to lose the position of intellectual and social centrality that was handed to them after the defeat of Fascism and the end of the Second World War. The unique potential of the left in the postwar period ensued from two factors. The first was the critical legacy derived from publication of the celebrated Marxist philosopher Antonio Gramsci's corpus of writings over several decades, most notably the *Letters from Prison* (Platone edition 1947; Caprioglio and Fubini edition 1965) and *Prison Notebooks* (Platone edition 1948–1951; Gerratana edition 1975). The second was the de facto cultural hegemony of the Partito Comunista Italiano (PCI) from the 1950s through the mid-1960s.

Already in 1966, it was possible for Pasolini to envision the left's allegorical death in his film *The Hawks and the Sparrows* by inserting footage of the funeral of Palmiro Togliatti, a founding member of the PCI with Gramsci in the 1920s and the leader of the party from 1927 until his death in 1964. The film further enlarges the allegory by concluding with the bathetic tableau of a talking crow, which spouts Marxist rhetoric, being killed and eaten by Totò and Ninetto. Even more thoroughly in the 1970s and 1980s than in the day of Pasolini's requiem for the left, however, critical thought in Italy may be seen to have undergone a radical reorientation that made it possible, and even easy, for Berlusconi to become the purveyor of a new type of "national-popular" culture. As Alfonso Berardinelli points out in his preface to *Lutheran Letters*, Pasolini's jeremiads in his essays of the early to mid-1970s seem to have fallen on deaf ears and almost wholly to have been forgotten by the time of the so-called second economic miracle, which is to say the economic boom of the 1980s. A crucial cultural change took place, in other words, during the period that Massimo Panarari has dubbed "the long 1980s."[2] It was in fact the supposedly leftist Italian intellectual establishment that over this span of years prepared the way for Berlusconi's subsequent achievement of cultural and political hegemony.[3]

During the second economic miracle, Italy became the fifth largest industrial economy in the world. The anthropological mutation of the country that Pasolini decried in its incipient form in the mid-1970s had become by the end of the 1980s a fait accompli. In *After* La Dolce Vita, I criticize the development of this hegemonic order across the fields of film, literature, philosophy, and art criticism. Following the corruption scandals of 1992 that heralded the downfall of the Democrazia Cristiana and the Partito Socialista Italiano (PSI), Berlusconi's ascent to the office of prime minister in 1994 with the victory of his own party, Forza Italia, represented a seismic shift in the terrain of Italian politics. This upheaval could not have taken place without the squandering of its cultural capital by the Italian left, which until the end of the 1980s still retained a position of relative strength that it inherited from what was in the 1960s the largest Communist Party membership in Western Europe.

A number of commentators, including Alexander Stille, Perry Anderson, and Geoff Andrews, have observed that Berlusconi's monopolistic grip on the means of social organization has had a profoundly destructive effect on democracy in Italy. According to Stille, Berlusconi in effect conquered the nation twice: first on the cultural level through the media and then on the political level through the electoral process.[4] Yet little has been written about the specific ideological constellation revolving around the Italian appropriations of postmodernism and poststructuralism that helped to prepare Berlusconi's way.[5] As I argue in the chapters that follow, his conquest of Italian society was facilitated by intellectual contributions largely from the left: namely, the conservative belle-lettrism of Italo Calvino's *Six Memos for the Next Millennium*, which aspires to resuscitate a literary aesthetics of taste; Gianni Vattimo's poststructuralist doctrine of weak thought; and Achille Bonito Oliva's art historical movement of *Transavanguardia*.

Since Berlusconi's first election to office, he has governed the country through center-right coalitions with only a couple of brief interruptions, benefiting from the power vacuum that resulted from the lack of an organized opposition to win the elections again in 2001 and 2008. As Anderson notes, Forza Italia was the first political party to be structured like a corporation; in fact, it was formed and managed by Publitalia, the marketing agency owned by Fininvest.[6] Following the entrenchment of Forza Italia in the political establishment, observers such as the *Financial Times* and the *Economist* recurrently have described Italy as an anomaly insofar as Berlusconi's ownership of the most important private television and publishing outlets, together with his hold on political office, has created an unbearable conflict of interest and concentration of power.[7]

In the immediate aftermath of the Liberation, which is to say the fall of Mussolini's régime at the end of the Second World War, power devolved to the Democrazia Cristiana and culture to the PCI, as Anderson remarks. At least through the 1960s, the Communist Party in fact exerted widespread influence by means of publishing houses, the writings and teachings of intellectuals, and the cinema: "At its height, the PCI could draw on an extraordinary range of social and moral energies, combining both deeper popular roots and broader influence than any other force in the country."[8] However, the standing of the left declined over the following decades not because power inherently trumps culture, but rather because the populist right competed aggressively in the cultural domain as a prelude to pursuing its ambitions in the political. More damagingly, from the mid-1970s through the end of the 1980s, the left itself failed to articulate an effective critique of the emerging forms of capitalism and mass media in Italy and thus neglected to pursue the sort of analysis that might have resulted in productive change.[9] The intellectual community was of little help in questioning the new social conditions because this group by and large occupied itself with debates in history, philosophy, and literature rather than in disciplines such as sociology or economics.[10]

In other words, there was almost no place in Italy for thinkers of the Frankfurt School type. Not only were leftist critics unable to assess correctly the threat posed by mass culture, but for the most part they reiterated its triumphal view of consumerism. Leftist discourse in Italy, Carlo Freccero rightly points out, has withered to the point that it now plays by Berlusconi's rules.[11] To Freccero's point, it might be added that the capitulation of the left was in effect since well before the founding of Forza Italia. In defiance of a Supreme Court ruling that prohibited privately owned television stations from broadcasting nationally, Berlusconi successfully maneuvered in the early 1980s to establish a monopoly in private television under the protection of the leader of the so-called Socialist Party (i.e., the PSI) and then-prime minister, Bettino Craxi. Through the respective acquisitions of his two largest broadcast competitors, Italia 1 and Rete 4 in 1983 and 1984, Berlusconi dramatically expanded the corporate empire that eventually provided the base of operations for his political career.

If the populist consumerism of the right espoused by Berlusconi has set the terms of cultural discourse in the country, it has succeeded in doing so because in the 1980s the most prominent members of the ostensibly leftist intellectual class largely embraced the ideals of contemporary capitalism. The result was to deprive Italian society of the critical insights and vocabulary necessary to resist the forces of mass mediation and commodification. As Ernesto Galli della Loggia reminds us, thanks to its preoccupation with questions of individualism and familism, Italy has always been vulnerable to censure as a weak example of modernity, and not just in relation to industrial or technological problems. According to Galli della Loggia, whatever aspects of modernity in fact have been incorporated by the culture never acquired a truly Italian character, as they typically were direct appropriations of American lifestyles.[12] Yet there emerges in the 1980s a uniquely Italian brand of cultural currency that, in its most famous examples of Calvinian aesthetics, weak thought, and Transavanguardia, deliberately avoids any critical questioning of the dominant order of power and its relation to thought itself. The same certainly is not true, for example, of the philosophical contributions of Jacques Derrida, Michel Foucault, or Gilles Deleuze in the French context.

It may be true that the culture of the present day is identifiable with an ever-growing dependence on the technologies of mass communication and control. We should note nevertheless that certain modes of resistance have come to the fore in recent decades, through the voices of women, minorities, and the colonized in world literature, art, and criticism. In Italy, however, we confront a way of thinking that enlists the jargon of postmodernism and poststructuralism in the service of a relentlessly consumerist, spectacular, acritical aesthetics. With few exceptions, postmodernism in Italy has been discussed mostly in terms of style (e.g., Umberto Eco's definition of postmodernism in relation to his own *The Name of the Rose*, Omar Calabrese's notion of the "neo-baroque," etc.) rather than in terms of, say, the specific cultural logic of the contemporary forms of capitalism à la Fredric Jameson. To understand Italian contemporary culture in a meaningful way, it is thus helpful to pay attention to the theoretical or conceptual frames of reference that have prevailed within different disciplines. In assessing the place of weak thought in the domain of philosophy, I will read Vattimo's project in relation to the strategies of poststructuralism, particularly as they have been elaborated in France. By contrast, I will examine Calvino's *ars poetica* of *Six Memos for the Next Millennium* and Bonito Oliva's art theory in the light of their respective reinterpretations of postmodernism, although as both the category itself and Calvino's and Bonito Oliva's uses of it are in different ways problematically mystificatory, I intend to invoke the term sparingly and with some skepticism.[13]

Postmodernism, in other words, will not be granted in these pages any a priori synthetic or explanatory power as a theory. My goal is not to decide whether certain thinkers are "truly" postmodern or not, but rather to understand how some of the most important figures of the once-leftist intelligentsia in Italy came to celebrate the logic of the market, to enjoy in strikingly similar fashion the performative mobilization of the cultural ideals of sweetness, lightness, weakness, and softness.[14] Constant rehearsal of these terms has given rise in the country to a mind-set that is fundamentally hostile to the very notion of criticism. The triumph of this "anti-Frankfurt School" of discourse, as it might be called, has precipitated in turn the cultural defeat of the left, whose former hegemonic status (albeit mostly limited to high culture) had produced some genuine political gains in the 1970s.[15] By now it has become conventional to dismiss the idea that structure produces superstructure, particularly under the conditions of the so-called new economy, which supposedly values knowledge above all other commodities. However, the relevance of the "Italian case," as several critics from Carla Benedetti to Romano Luperini have recognized, consists precisely in the extent to which the culture's media-driven metamorphosis helped to consolidate Berlusconi's base of political power in the 1990s.[16]

From a certain perspective, my book may be viewed as something of an update of Giacomo Leopardi's treatise *Discourse on the Present State of the Customs of the Italians* (1824), in which he proposes a comparative analysis of the diverse conditions of modernity of European societies at the time of the birth of capitalism. Like Leopardi, I am interested in exploring Italy's public virtues and cultural forms of life at least to some degree in comparison with those of other Western societies, particularly France, at the time of the triumph of poststructuralism and postmodernism. A legendary pessimist, Leopardi concluded that, unlike the other nations of Europe, Italy lacked a "tight society," by which he meant an open, thriving, and ethically active civil society, where intellectually productive discussion would allow mutual understanding between discrete viewpoints to occur. Instead, the superficial distractions of strolling, spectacles, and churches in his opinion had come to dominate the entire life of the country. Of course, I do not wish to suggest that Italian mores have remained the same since Leopardi's day. However, I would contend that in Italy today we encounter a crippling deficiency of democratic and cultural life that in some sense represents the metastasis of the problem that Leopardi so cogently diagnosed. On a related note, it is no wonder that Mastrantonio and Bonami have argued that in contemporary Italy the society of spectacle has replaced civil society.[17]

To Agamben's observation that tragedy is not an Italian category, one thus might add that neither is criticism.[18] Since at least Dante's decision to call his masterpiece a comedy, we Italians have been convinced of the epistemological privilege of the comic and the need to renounce the tragic perspective. At the risk of swimming against the tide and of reminding readers of the litany of historical tragedies that Italy has endured since the Second World War, from Fascism to the violence of the Mafia and the terrorist acts of the extreme left, I wish to reflect in *After* La Dolce Vita on the nation's cultural conditions during the so-called *anni di bambagia* or "years of the cotton ball" from the mid-1970s through the 1980s, a period that immediately followed and to some extent overlapped with the *anni di piombo* or "years of lead," which were mordantly so named because of the prevalence of terrorist violence at the time. My intention is not to foster a sort of Spenglerian *Kulturpessimismus* about Italy, a country that from Antonio Negri to Giovanni Arrighi has given rise to the most critical approaches to globalization, as Anderson has remarked. It may be argued after all that, since the significant accomplishments in the Western world of social welfare, civil rights, and economic equality through the beginning of the 1970s, the international political left seems merely to have fallen asleep for a couple of decades.[19] Yet in Italy the traditional network of alliances between the various constituencies of the family, labor unions, educators, etc. that make up civil society, engagement of which was Gramsci's cultural and political objective throughout his life, has unraveled in an especially dramatic and rapid fashion. In this respect, the nation's intellectual life has been the key to the historical process. Italian poststructuralism has centered neither on the more promising notion of difference à la Derrida nor on those of archeology, genealogy, and problematization à la Foucault, but rather on the intellectual litotes of "weakness." Notwithstanding Vattimo's belated political career and recent political conversion, this theoretical school consequently has shown nothing but indifference to questions of social inequality or justice and has managed to dissolve the critical capital of the greatest Communist Party in Europe.

. . .

Italy is "not a normal country," to cite Geoff Andrews, and indeed it represents something of an extreme-limit case with respect to the degradation of contemporary cultural and political conditions. Perry Anderson has suggested that Gramsci's insistence in the *Prison Notebooks* on the importance of hegemony as a cultural consensus to be achieved through the operations of civil society made it possible to think of the rebirth of Italy in cultural rather than economic or political terms. Hegemony thus was a consoling thought for a nation dominated for centuries by foreign powers, yet ennobled by its cultural inheritance. Gramsci reinforced his thinking on hegemony by means of the principle of the "national-popular," meaning an ethos that would abandon Italy's elitist and spiritualist traditions to imagine more vital, democratic, and unconventional forms of life. Yet at the moment of the triumph of mass media in the 1980s, Gramsci's concepts proved useless to the left as tools of resistance and may be said to have transformed into their perverse doppelgängers under Berlusconi's influence.

In *After* La Dolce Vita, I set out to show how Italy has failed to live up to the dream of a culture that responds to the life of the political collective as a whole, including such typically disempowered groups as the poor. What Italy has achieved instead of this Gramscian ideal is a society subjugated at every level to the benumbing power of the mass media.

The book consists of four chapters, titled "Sweetness," "Lightness," "Weakness," and "Softness." I argue that these four nouns name the coordinates of contemporary Italian culture under the condition of "integrated spectacle," to invoke Guy Debord's term. Debord introduces this concept in *Comments on the Society of Spectacle* to designate what happens when spectacle becomes a totalizing form of life. Indeed, he argues that only in Italy was this phenomenon fully achieved, thus attributing to the nation a unique symbolic position. Remarkably, he arrived at this conclusion even before Berlusconi's election to Parliament and the prime ministership in the 1990s.

Sweetness, lightness, weakness, and softness function in the Italian context as key tropes of belonging and self-identification. The terms constitute the linguistic basis for the ideological reimagination of a country that is dominated by consumerism and identified with the label "Made in Italy." The four categories delimit the "good temperament" of the typical Italian in accordance with a cliché idea of national identity. Perhaps not surprisingly, given its stubborn persistence into the present, this stereotype has deep historical roots and the generally uncontroversial status of received wisdom. In this connection, we might recall Nietzsche's blithe declaration in *Human, All Too Human* that the Italian exhibits "a secure, mild, and basically cheerful soul."

Cinema, which at first glance might be regarded as one of the media most vulnerable to spectacularization, has given life in Italy to some of the most exemplary critiques of the status quo, from the films of Neorealism to those of Fellini and Moretti. In "Sweetness," I examine the hostility that Fellini encountered during the production and distribution of his last motion pictures. The chapter focuses in particular on *Ginger and Fred*, which elaborates a bitter appraisal of Berlusconi's brand of media empire building. Financiers and critics turned against the celebrated director of *La dolce vita* when he stopped offering a mythical narrative that glamorized the country's spectacular life. Moreover, the sharp political attacks that Fellini mounted against the cable television industry, presided over by Berlusconi, continue to meet with utter lack of recognition from commentators in Italy and the United States, despite the historical record of the director's three separate lawsuits against the media tycoon. I question this silence regarding Fellini's project in the face of the critical challenge of his last works as exemplified by *Ginger and Fred*. Whereas the later chapters of my book tell the disheartening story of the surrender of the Italian left to the logic of the market, this first chapter provides a contrasting example of creative acuity and courage in Fellini's resistance to Berlusconi during the 1980s. Although the director was never a member of the Communist Party, his awareness of the severity of the intellectual corruption spreading through society at the time makes his final productions, especially *Ginger and Fred*, representative of a cinema of critique that had been a saving grace of Italian culture since the days of Neorealism.

The next chapter explores the problematic of lightness, the first and symbolically most important of the values that Italo Calvino identified in *Six Memos for the New Millennium* as relevant for contemporary society (lightness, rapidity, exactitude, visibility, multiplicity, consistency). Of the cases explored in these pages, Calvino's is certainly the most complicated. Although he began his career in the mid-1940s as a member of the PCI and as an author of realist fiction who was committed to exploring Italy's social and political problems in the post-War era, he gradually withdrew from this position and by the early 1960s had become an advocate for the idea that literature ought to be "predictable and reassuring," to cite his own words. Yet he continued to be troubled by the degrading influence of the mass media until the end of his life. Unlike Vattimo or Bonito Oliva, then, Calvino betrays a deeply ambivalent, even anguished, sense of his own role as an intellectual. At the same time, he becomes so vehement in his rejection of his youthful leftism that, as the culmination of a kind of immunodeficiency, he appears to incubate within himself the virus of Italy's cultural demise, what Luperini memorably terms "the luxury of lightness." In his final testament of *Six Memos*, Calvino sadly assumes the position of a narcissistic censor proselytizing for his own belle-lettrist tastes. Precisely because he bemoans in this treatise the debilitating effects of consumer culture, his found antidote of a literature of style that celebrates its own removal from all social meaning remains in the end deeply unsatisfactory.[20] Certainly his choice of "lightness" as the defining signifier of his poetics, in its facile generality of reference and, thanks to Milan Kundera, modishness at the time, exemplifies the complicity of high culture with the bourgeois mentality of Berlusconism. Indeed, lightness arguably becomes as a result the favorite buzzword of Italy's spectacularized culture, encompassing and reinforcing the narrower valences of several other key terms: "weakness," which Vattimo deploys interchangeably with lightness; "softness," with which Bonito Oliva evokes the charm of a mollifying formalism; and, as Zygmunt Bauman points out, a whole vocabulary of "liquidity."[21] Above and beyond its meaning with respect to specific stylistic choices, "lightness" in other words enacts the principle of equivalence intrinsic to the operations of exchange value, thus encapsulating the logic of the market at its purest.[22]

The shortcomings of Calvino's poetics become manifest in his weirdly optimistic reading of Kafka's short story, "The Bucket Rider." Kafka's narrative concludes with the image of the protagonist floating in a levitating bucket past a nearby range of "ice mountains" because his neighbors have refused to fill his bucket with coal. Calvino reads this harrowing ending as a celebration of the magical power of flight. He thus ignores Kafka's insistence on the social exclusion and banishment of the protagonist, an emphasis that moved Walter Benjamin to remark, "There is no more hopeless vista than that of 'the regions of the ice mountain' in which the bucket rider drops out of sight forever." By fixating on the fantastic dimensions of Kafka's writing, Calvino upholds in *Six Memos* the conservative notion of literature as a "purely" aesthetic phenomenon. Consequently, he fails to acknowledge what Jacques Rancière has called the politics *of* aesthetics, the logical consequence that, as a distribution of the sensible, aesthetics necessarily entails politics, albeit while assuming a relation to the political that may very well be oblique or complex. Invoking the values of lightness, exactitude, and visibility, Calvino reanimates a dead concept of beauty and retreats from the ideal of the sublime associated with an experimental modernism. He promotes a postmodernism that, to borrow a phrase from Frederic Jameson's *Valences of the Dialectic*, "gives the illusion of substance in its absence."

Calvino is in this respect an illustrative figure. After the Liberation, he moved and worked in the ambit of leftist intellectuals such as Cesare Pavese, Alberto Moravia, Pasolini, Luchino Visconti, etc., who tended to affiliate themselves with the PCI. Over the years, he trained an increasingly Voltairean skepticism on traditional communist dogma and gained international fame as the preeminent Italian novelist of his generation, while adhering to the view that literature is a game thoroughly divorced from social and political considerations.[23] Before formalizing this divorce in *Six Memos*, however, Calvino lived briefly in Paris and met regularly with Giorgio Agamben during the period when Calvino had begun to reflect on lightness and Agamben on the questions that led to his own theory of bare life. From 1974 to 1976, Calvino, Agamben, and Claudio Rugafiori undertook together to identify the fundamental categories of thought and experience as part of an unrealized plan to begin publishing a new journal that they envisioned covering the most urgent critical issues of their day. Rugafiori started his share of the exercise with *architecture* and *vagueness*, Calvino with *speed* and *lightness*, and Agamben with *tragedy* and *comedy*, *biography* and *fable*, and, most importantly, *law* and *creature*.[24] The last pair of categories inaugurates the understanding that it is precisely when stripped of our rights under the law that we arrive at degree zero of the "human creature," which is to say the point of "bare life."[25] This intuition in turn is the kernel of the genealogical and biopolitical reflections that twenty years later Agamben brings together in his landmark *Homo sacer*.

For Italy, the collective endeavor of Rugafiori, Calvino, and Agamben thus amounts to a strategic crossroads from which one of the culture's seminal figures sets forth on a path of aestheticized belle-lettrism, while another pursues the course of a reenergized, if problematic, relationship to the political. Notwithstanding his triumphs as an author of fiction, the politics of Calvino's aesthetics is often troubling and never more so than in *Six Memos for the Next Millennium*, where his ambivalence toward mass culture is channeled not into a productive and critical dialectic but rather into articulation of a poetics that too readily affirms the procedures of contemporary capitalism and its values of lightness, multiplicity, and speed.

In the third chapter, "Weakness," I assess the reception of poststructuralism in Italy by considering Gianni Vattimo's philosophy of "weak thought" (*pensiero debole*). His work makes clear the acritical and antipolitical bias of hegemonic thought in Italy relative to French philosophy as exemplified by Derrida, Deleuze, and Foucault. Although critics often deride pensiero debole as merely a symptom of "the long 1980s," no one has offered a clear account of how the claims of this theoretical school to increase freedom and reduce violence compare to the critical impact of Derridean deconstruction. Like the French poststructuralists, Vattimo may take Nietzsche and Heidegger as sources of inspiration, but by its author's own admission the strategy of weak thought fundamentally consists in exalting exchange value. Criticism indeed has no place in Vattimo's methodology (including criticism of Heidegger's politics, for example), as he aims to replace critical thinking with a conservative revival of the hermeneutic tradition. If Vattimo's official goal is to undermine epistemological certainty, his unconscious one is to produce the kind of nihilism favorable to unbridled capitalism, notwithstanding the politics supposedly evinced by his election in 1999 to the European Parliament as a member of the Democratici di Sinistra and his late conversion to Marxism in 2004. Of course, it may be true that we criticize the society of exchange value only at our own peril insofar as envisioning an alternative state of things nowadays often seems impossible. Yet it is hard to see how reducing the world to exchange value has resulted in anything more than increased suffering. If we really wish to redeem capitalism, as Bernard Stiegler suggests, a radical new ecology of values, media, and mass culture is needed. This is the challenge for leftist thought today, a challenge that Italian intellectuals mostly have preferred to evade in order to look "more modern than all the moderns," if we may cite Pasolini's turn of phrase with the appropriate dash of irony.

Hostile readers who wish to assign to poststructuralism the responsibility for an ever-lengthening list of present-day ills, from cultural relativism to the death of the subject, are by now overly familiar voices. Richard Wolin echoes the general tone of outrage: "As intellectual solvents, deconstruction and Foucauldian genealogy are too effective for their own good. By the time they are through working their magic and casting their spells, all trace of substantiality has been eliminated."[26] *Pace* Wolin, I contend throughout *After La Dolce Vita*, and especially in the chapter on Vattimo's ideology of weak thought, that French poststructuralism as exemplified chiefly by Derrida, Foucault, and Deleuze maintains a sense of critical purpose by persisting at all times in questioning the operations of power, including the corporate power of capitalism.[27] On this score, French philosophy ought to be distinguished from its Italian counterpart, which on the whole has worked to validate the status quo of contemporary mass society.

Over the course of numerous books, including *Weak Thought*, *The End of Modernity*, and *The Transparent Society*, Vattimo espouses a nihilist theory of postmodernism. More specifically, he calls on his readers to withdraw from foundationalist strategies and welcome the drift of endless interpretation in the wake of Nietzsche's announcements of the death of God in *The Gay Science* and of the transformation of the true world into a fable in *The Twilight of the Idols*. At the same time, he insists on total dissolution of history as a consequence of Jean-François Lyotard's definition of postmodernity as the end of historical metanarratives. The most crucial reference for Vattimo, however, is Heidegger's philosophy of Being, whose terminology and logic he accepts in all their metaphysical splendor. In addition, he rereads Foucault's promising notion of an "ontology of actuality" in a shallow, pseudo-Heideggerian direction.

Unlike, say, Derrida, Vattimo does not feel the need to criticize notions such as Spirit or Being, preferring to cite or "correspond" with Heidegger's notions regarding the end of metaphysics and the *Ereignis* of technology rather than to scrutinize their meaning. Vattimo likewise never questions Heidegger's political beliefs. Far from representing a less phallogocentric way of thinking, weak thought in this light seems to epitomize the wish for a totalizing system of logic. Whereas deconstruction revolves around philosophical and performative strategies of problematization, around posing difficult questions, nothing of this sort is at stake for weak thought. Derrida declared his refusal to embrace Lyotard's definition of postmodernity in *Échographies*. Moreover, he decisively redefined the philosophical and political stakes of deconstruction through concepts such as "democracy to come" and "justice in particular" in his later works, beginning with *Specters of Marx*. It is no accident, then, that unlike Vattimo Derrida reflects on technology and the role of the media with care, starting with a questioning of names and concepts that refuses to accept neutral-sounding or conventional terms such as "means of communication" and that deliberately invents idiosyncratic terms such as "teletechnology" to call attention to the strangeness of the technological per se.

If Derrida does not adopt an apocalyptic tone when it comes to this domain, nevertheless he makes clear his awareness of the autoimmune threat of teletechnology (the possibility that it might become what Deleuze, at the end of his life, called the society of control. Vattimo by contrast looks at contemporary technology as a magical gateway to greater freedom and tolerance. Whereas deconstruction aims to suggest the possibility of the impossible, weak thought may be said to conform to the possibility of the possible, relentlessly apologizing for what already is. The chapter ends with an examination of Vattimo's recent confession, *Ecce comu* (2007), in which he reneges to a degree on the pledges of his earlier writings and explains his eleventh-hour return to communist politics in terms of a rediscovery of religious faith.

In the epilogue, "Softness," I analyze the rhetoric of Achille Bonito Oliva's writings on Transavanguardia, a movement that encompasses well-established painters such as Francesco Clemente, Sandro Chia, Enzo Cucchi, and Mimmo Paladino. Bonito Oliva has helped to market this movement internationally as a recuperation of the softness of sentimental, figurative subject matter. Not to leave any doubt about the implications of his position, he states in one of his most important essays, "The Achieved Nihilist," that "softness here signals an eclectic identity with no need for strong presence in the social." He makes copious use of the philosophy of Gilles Deleuze and Félix Guattari, interpreting their ideas in an exaggeratedly "vitalist" register in order to dissolve the resistant political project embedded in their thought. This rhetorical gambit exemplifies a central strategy of the establishment of hegemonic Italian intellectuals, which is to adopt the anti-essentialist vocabulary of poststructuralism while divesting it of critical and political meaning. The key signifiers that constitute the subject of my book thus often seem interchangeable in their cultural deployment. For example, Vattimo recurrently defines weak thought as a "lightening" of the metaphysical structures of Being, whereas Bonito Oliva characterizes Transavanguardia in his own words as "a sweet project," promoting the comforts of rediscovered lightness in contrast to the ponderousness of critical difficulty and complication. Vattimo and Bonito Oliva cite ad libitum exactly the same, narrow repertory of passages from Nietzsche.

Not surprisingly, Vattimo makes Adorno and the thinkers of the Frankfurt School into favorite targets of his polemic. He repeats throughout his writings that Adorno's apocalyptic prophecies regarding the media-driven culture of sameness have not come to fruition in a world dominated by subcultures, thanks precisely to the ubiquity of the media. However, in the light of Berlusconi's advance from a fortune in real estate to control of the nation's presses and broadcast outlets and ultimately to abuse of political power to exempt himself from the law, Italy seems as though it may be exactly the wrong setting in which to complain about the limits of Adorno's critique of the culture industry. Moreover, after thirty years of Italy's cultural and political decadence, there has been no real effort at self-criticism by those who helped to usher in the new era.[28] Although Vattimo published *Ecce comu* in a bid to draw attention to his triumphal return to leftist engagement, he astoundingly tries to position this return in philosophical continuity with the principles of weak thought, as I show in my analysis of his argument. As for Bonito Oliva, he seems happy to continue polishing his reputation for aesthetic eclecticism, as Mastrantonio and Bonami have remarked, by maintaining the pretense that culture is in a state of perennial transavanguardism.[29]

Although a somewhat bleak picture of the landscape may emerge from these pages, my desire is not at all to suggest that in Italy we have had no critical minds who might be counted on to elaborate an alternative cultural vision. Pasolini might almost suffice on his own to equalize the field of battle. Anderson is quick to recognize Antonio Negri and Giovanni Arrighi for their trail-blazing critiques of globalization in Negri's *Empire*, authored with Michael Hardt, and Arrighi's *Chaos*.[30] Giorgio Agamben and Roberto Esposito have been exploring important questions in the field of biopolitics with a critical, and in Agamben's case perhaps even apocalyptic, sense of urgency. Working in Negri's and Agamben's wake, Paolo Virno has diagnosed incisively our current forms of life and struggles with the "affects" of capitalism from cynicism to skepticism. In a pamphlet entitled "The Italian Difference," Negri himself identifies three of the most crucial contributors to Italian political thought, in Gramsci, the theorist of workerism Mario Tronti, and the feminist philosopher Luisa Muraro, who calls for a new "thinking of difference."[31] Negri finds particularly inspiring the ability of each of these thinkers to conjugate theory and praxis while placing emphasis on praxis.

However, the constellation of cultural productions that I examine in *After* La Dolce Vita clearly has come to provide in recent decades the hegemonic image of Italian culture both for Italy and for other nations. Even if it were true that figures such as Negri and Agamben have achieved wider recognition in the United States than in Italy, these thinkers have never been welcomed among either nation's readership with the same warmth as Vattimo or Calvino, who increasingly seem to exemplify a type of contemporary Italian culture that is beloved by Italian and foreign admirers chiefly for the qualities of being salutary, accommodating, and soft.[32] The plea for nonjudgmental forms of criticism in this context strikes me as a luxury that historical realities honestly do not permit. In writing this book, I have often pondered Foucault's expressed wish in "The Masked Philosopher" to dream of a criticism that would not judge but rather bring a book, a sentence, an idea to life. Although the limits of critical analysis may be all too clear, it nevertheless seems to me possible to keep meaningful ideas alive while judging well the questions that demand a cogent response.

1

Sweetness

The Italian Metamorphosis from *La dolce vita* to *Ginger and Fred*

In his *Prison Notebooks*, Antonio Gramsci argued that Italian intellectuals historically have preferred the cosmopolitan, universal, and aristocratic self-image derived from the mythic and rhetorical traditions of the Roman Empire and the Catholic Church. It may be argued that contemporary conditions in Italy have aggravated the tendency of the cultural elite to see itself as part of a utopian community superior to the claims of national affiliation. As a result, this group has felt free to ignore the nation's historically specific political and cultural dilemmas. From the painterly movement of Transavanguardia to the philosophical school of weak thought, from the novels of Italo Calvino to the semiotics of Umberto Eco, the apparent intention is to free Italy from the shadow of provincialism and to fulfill the promise of universal importance.[1]

Indeed, no efforts have been made to link Italy's present-day cultural mainstream to its late capitalist logic, as already has been done with respect to the United States in the writings of Fredric Jameson and David Harvey.[2] Eco, for example, in his "Postface to *The Name of the Rose*," makes clear that for him the aesthetic positions that he associates with the concept of postmodernism constitute an ahistorical category that can be extended back to Saint Augustine. An apocalyptic, critical approach to contemporary mass culture and mediation such as the one epitomized in France by Jean Baudrillard is also glaringly absent from the Italian milieu. What has prevailed instead is a formalist aesthetics that welcomes the dissolution of historical metanarratives as the prelude to an expanded freedom of irony, reappropriation, and ludic play. I maintain that Federico Fellini constitutes a distinguished exception to this intellectual panorama, not only because he refused through the end of his career to become a "cosmopolitan," universalist filmmaker in the Hollywood mold but also because his last films register the crisis point in which Italian ultraconsumerism culminates.

In what follows, I will analyze the strategic positions occupied in this culture by two of the director's films: *La dolce vita* and *Ginger and Fred*. Like quotation marks, the films bracket a period in Italian history during which the economic miracle of the 1950s and 1960s paved the way for the full-blown principle of spectacularism that emerges in the 1980s. In this sense, the itinerary from *La dolce vita* to *Ginger and Fred* encompasses the very genealogy of social and cultural change in Italy during those decades. I will contend that in Italy contemporary social conditions are premised to a unique degree on the complicity of mass culture with corporate capitalism, a phenomenon epitomized by the transmutation of the staggering success of Berlusconi-style commercial television into actual political power. It is this phenomenon that clearly prompts Guy Debord in the late 1980s to identify Italy as the chief example of what he calls the society of "integrated spectacle."[3] Reinforcing Debord's insistence on defining spectacle as "not a collection of images, but a social relationship among people, mediated by images," Giorgio Agamben concludes in *The Coming Community* that such a mediation of relationships ultimately results in expropriation and alienation of human sociality itself.[4] He makes us aware, in other words, of the violence intrinsic to the society of spectacle. We may well contrast the Italian state of things to the situation of the United States. Although undeniably driven in many respects by the logic of late capitalism, to invoke Jameson's phrase once more, contemporary American popular discourse frequently has involved critical reflection on gender roles, on race, and on national identities. In Italy, however, such considerations have entered into the public sphere of discussion only in the most superficial ways and subject to the resistance of a dismissive parochialism.

If *La dolce vita* dramatizes the conversion of Italy's newfound wealth into popular spectacle, *Ginger and Fred* satirizes the perverse consequences of this conversion of capital into image as manifested by Italian culture under the domination of Silvio Berlusconi's corporate empire. After the demise of Fascism, neorealism in the 1940s contributed to a new sense of national identity through an aesthetics informed by ethical and political engagement. By the 1980s, Fellini bears witness to the sustained metamorphosis of the always-problematic concept of Italian national identity into a mere consumerist drive associated with the "Italian Style." This phenomenon operated chiefly though fashion, design, and advertising to establish Italy itself as a brand, as its own cultural capital.[5]

Fellini's career may be divided into three discrete phases. In the first, he achieves two international critical successes, *La strada* (1954) and *The Nights of Cabiria* (1957), which both starred Giulietta Masina, won Academy Awards for Best Foreign Film, and contributed, according to the critic André Bazin, to the invention of a new mode of film realism that is phenomenological and poetic.[6] In the second phase, the director sublimely reformulates the language of modernism in cinematic terms in his masterpieces *La dolce vita* (1959) and *8½* (1963), both of which star Marcello Mastroianni. In particular, the French theorists Christian Metz and Gilles Deleuze have made clear the modernist affinities of this second phase.[7] Deleuze argues for continuity between the neorealism of the 1940s and the experimental Italian cinema of the 1960s (the latter of which is typified by Fellini's second phase) insofar as neorealism and the later experimentalism constitute a new mode of cinema through their invention of what the philosopher calls the "time image."[8] The film that is the key to an assessment of the relationship proposed by Fellini between film modernism and the Italian cultural dilemma is *La dolce vita*. Although formally constructed according to a "Cubist" ideal of fragmentation, *La dolce vita* exposes the vanishing point of modernist culture in Italy in the course of observing the emergence of the society of integrated spectacle that ensues from the so-called economic miracle.

The third and last phase includes films such as *Orchestra Rehearsal* (1979), *And the Ship Sails On* (1983), *Ginger and Fred* (1986), and *The Voice of the Moon* (1990), productions that reflect the filmmaker's controversial, and as I will argue generally misunderstood, turn toward social critique. *The Voice of the Moon*, his last feature-length motion picture, was not even distributed in the United States, and very few critical studies take seriously the political ambitions of his late films.[9] Of these features, *Ginger and Fred*, which stars both Masina and Mastroianni and thus may be said to conjoin metacinematically the first and second phases of the director's career, is the most important.[10] Even though casting both stars at first glance suggests a perfect synthesis of Fellini's early and middle styles, neither the phenomenological realism of *La strada* nor the explosive modernist poetic of *La dolce vita* is ultimately at issue in *Ginger and Fred*. More than either *And the Ship Sails On* or *Orchestra Rehearsal*, which both rely on the mediation of allegory, *Ginger and Fred* exemplifies the director's bitter attitude toward contemporary culture in Italy during the final phase of his career. With this film, he clearly abandons his comfortable role as the poetic chronicler of Italian social customs and embraces the antagonistic role of cultural critic.[11] In what follows, I maintain that Fellini must be recognized as one of the very few Italian intellectuals to confront the consumerist transformation of Italian society in the aftermath of the economic miracle. Unlike most members of the Italian cultural establishment (one thinks of Eco or Calvino) who quickly assented to the dominance of the culture industry, Fellini refused to be a mere spectator of his own spectacle.

Ginger and Fred exposes the dominance of private television in the Italy of the 1980s, a nation enthralled by the profiteering of Berlusconi and by the spread of consumerism accelerated in those years by the origination and popularization of the Italian Style in fashion and design. In Italy, as I contend throughout this book, the emergence of contemporary techniques of mediation has coincided not with a blurring of boundaries between the disciplines of knowledge or with a rewriting of the rigid social and political agenda of modernism, but instead with the unadulterated hegemony of consumer culture. In this respect, the importance of marketing, design, and fashion in defining a "new," but weak and amorphous, national identity, better known since the 1980s as the Italian Style, cannot be overestimated. Reflecting on the consolidation of this identity, *Ginger and Fred* might be said to extend and deepen the investigation of mass culture initiated in *La dolce vita*, albeit from a more melancholic perspective. When Marcello, the protagonist of *La dolce vita*, resigns his aspirations of becoming a modernist writer and of observing, like his friend Steiner, the funeral rites of high-cultural aesthetics, he prefigures the pathos of Pippo, the male half of the retired dance team whose story is chronicled in *Ginger and Fred* and whose routine consists of a staged simulation of Hollywood spectacle. That Fellini cast the youthful and the aged Mastroianni in both roles accentuates the genealogical connection between the journalist of *La dolce vita* and the tap dancer of *Ginger and Fred*.

Fellini may be said to have contributed, if involuntarily, to the phenomenon of the marketing of Italian culture in the 1960s inasmuch as the worldwide success of *La dolce vita* itself appeared to signal the sweet potential of a cosmopolitan consumerism. By the time of his last productions, however, Fellini was determined not to remain an accomplice in the metamorphosis of Italian culture. *Ginger and Fred* thus bitterly protests the oppressive banality of the full-blown society of integrated spectacle in Italy. This culture combines a halfhearted reaffirmation of the aesthetics of modernism with a fervent embrace of capitalism and political conservatism. Italy thus achieves what might be thought of as a perverse pastiche of the Gramscian ideal of national-popular culture. In the economy of such a culture, Berlusconi represents a new personification of the Machiavellian prince: a media tycoon and self-made politico who has established by corporate means the sort of national cultural hegemony that Gramsci hoped would one day belong to the political left.

Gramsci, of course, contended in his *Prison Notebooks* that Italy lacked a national-popular culture, meaning by this term the sort of intellectual and artistic works that might renovate the collective consciousness of society. In Gramsci's eyes, the national-popular is a nearly utopian principle that regulates the well-being of the national community. It is only with the triumph of commercial television in the 1980s, however, that a perverse version of national-popular, or more properly "national-populist," culture takes root in Italy. Although the cinematic neorealism of the 1940s did provide a myth of cultural unification, its productions can hardly be called popular. With the exception of a handful of films, most notably *Rome, Open City*, *The Bicycle Thief*, and *Paisà*, neorealism was not a grand success at the box office. Relative to the elitist aesthetics and intellectual challenges of neorealist film, commercial television succeeded in thoroughly penetrating Italian society of the 1980s. As Paul Ginsborg has pointed out, television has been the greatest constitutive element of mass culture in contemporary Italy, where for a general populace that does not like to read books and newspapers watching TV increasingly has become the ultimate—and only—cultural activity.[12]

For Gramsci, the national-popular need not imply a divide between low and high culture, since even Shakespeare exemplifies the category. For the society presided over by Berlusconi, television instead affirms only the crudest and most narrow-minded notion of the popular. The nation, which in Gramsci's argument does not represent the metaphysical foundation of a systematic nationalism but rather the social context of an open-ended search for collective ideals, in the current context designates the imagined community of an Italy based on the consensus of consumption. If the cinema in Italy offered an opportunity for oppositional cultural politics until the end of the 1960s, the rise of privatized television in the 1980s affirms the ideal of passive spectatorship of the operations of capitalism.[13] Fellini unflinchingly registers, and toward the end of his life assails, this drastic social transformation, joining the ranks of the very few intellectuals who have spoken out against the relentless commercialization of Italian culture.

In this chapter, I focus first on *La dolce vita*'s depiction of the agonized dialectic between a waning modernist aesthetics and an emerging spectacularism in Italy. I then consider how, twenty years after *La dolce vita*, *Ginger and Fred* looks back on the birth of this exhilarating culture of paparazzi, fashion models, celebrity impersonators, and globalized commerce with the bitterness of an unrelieved melancholy. Far from quixotically picking a quarrel with the television medium, *Ginger and Fred* delivers an accurate, poignant, and damning critique of the hegemonic commercial and intellectual culture of Italy in the 1980s. Fellini, who did not live to see Berlusconi become the nation's prime minister in 1994, fully understood that the mogul's spectacular brand of capitalism was eroding the contours of national identity and with them any political hope for the future.

The Spleen of Rome: Fellini's *La dolce vita*

In the 1960s, Fellini's first tactic of resistance to the power of the media was to attempt a cinematic reinvigoration of the aesthetics and critical claims of modernism. As we will see, however, the director ultimately stages, in the course of this reinvigoration, a dialectical, agonistic drama between the modernist form of his film and his mass cultural subject matter, a struggle that is always on the verge of spilling out of control and derailing his critical enterprise. Much later in his career, when he makes *Ginger and Fred*, he finds a way to successfully bring to light the complexities and contradictions of Italian mass culture by subjecting his own signature visual devices to radical deformation. In *La dolce vita*, Fellini limits his directorial intervention to an almost unconscious chronicling of the materialization of the Italian society of spectacle, the taking root of a transnational community in Rome, the symbolic capital of the postmodern empire.

This empire is signified throughout the film by the perpetual recurrence of popular songs (the 1960s hit "Patricia"), fashion models (the iconic Nico in the castle of Bassano di Sutri), international movie starlets (Anita Ekberg playing the temptress Sylvia), and absurd or meaningless occurrences that explode into media circuses (the newscast of the provincial "miracle"). Fellini even incorporates an Italian Elvis impersonator, played by Adriano Celentano, in a scene of inebriated dancing to rock and roll at Caracalla that foreshadows his persistent use of celebrity look-alikes in *Ginger and Fred*.[14] The inescapability in *La dolce vita* of that hallmark of the postmodern, the simulacrum, bears witness not only to the ascendancy of spectacularized mass culture in Italy but to the contemporary decline of modernist aesthetics with its emphasis on high art, abstraction, purity, and fragmentation. The film's interest, in other words, resides in its ambivalent depiction of modernism's decadence, a depiction that manages to criticize and surrender to postmodernity at the same time.

Fellini described in strikingly contrary terms his attempt in *La dolce vita* to reconfigure plot or narrative construction as a work of both deconstruction and recomposition: "We have to make a statue, break it, and recompose the pieces. Or better yet, try a decomposition in the manner of Picasso. The cinema is narrative in the nineteenth-century sense: now let's try to do something different."[15] That Fellini undertook to make a Cubist film in *La dolce vita* by cultivating a disjointed, highly original, paratactic narrative style (and by indulging a taste for caricature and grotesquerie not unfamiliar to his Spanish precursor) at odds with the linear plots favored in classic Hollywood movies ought to reopen the question of the modernist status of Fellini's masterpiece.

T. J. Clark has recently proposed that one of the most important manifestations of modernism indeed was the Italian cinema from the period of neorealism through the 1960s.[16] Moreover, critics such as John Orr and Frederic Jameson have generally identified the period from the late 1950s through the 1960s as the heyday of the modernist or "neomodernist" sensibility in sound film.[17] In their view, Fellini's classic works *La dolce vita* and *8½* should qualify as exemplars of this sensibility, if only by virtue of the films' production and release dates. Yet Fellini's very appropriation of the art-historical qualifier Cubist ought to alert us to the paradoxical nature of his aspiration. For if the critical periodization is correct, the development of a viable modernist vocabulary in sound film coincides historically with the abandonment of modernist aesthetics in other fields. Because modernism emerges belatedly in sound films, the director-auteur must struggle with the contradiction inherent in attempting to renew the modernist language game at a moment when its basic figures and tropes have been eviscerated or exhausted by literature and the visual arts. Fellini's keen awareness of this dilemma helps to explain the melancholic pathos of *La dolce vita*.

In this section, I approach the film as both an exposition and an instance of the exhausted modernist aesthetic prevalent in Italy at the moment of the economic boom. It is my contention that in the film Fellini revisits the canonical *topoi* of modernism precisely with the purpose of staging allegorical scenes of adieux or farewell to such topics. Accordingly, a significant part of my discussion focuses on unrealized episodes from the screenplay that I believe reflect Fellini's originally quite explicit fixation with the figure of the modernist intellectual. In addition, I hope to suggest how in *La dolce vita* the idea of modernism exemplified by the film itself compares to those of other artistic media, from painting to music to architecture. We might want to observe, for example, that Nino Rota's celebrated theme music for the feature is in fact a near-plagiarism of Kurt Weill's "The Ballad of Mack the Knife."[18] By comparison, the modernist commitment of an *auteur* such as Antonioni might seem more evident at first glance, given his celebrated cinematic appropriation of the visual techniques of abstract painting and the narrative techniques of the *nouveau roman*. However, Fellini's *oeuvre*, it might be argued, became in the 1960s more self-reflexive, ironic, and fragmentary in style, after the luminous phenomenological explorations of *La strada*, *Il bidone*, and *The Nights of Cabiria* in the 1950s. And at the same time that his films of the 1960s turned away from a realist cinematic vocabulary, they sponsored a powerful mythologizing of modern urban life, a mythologizing that does not rule out dramatic awareness of the obsolescence of the modern mentality.

A reflection on *La dolce vita* thus involves simultaneously examining a constellation of controversial notions such as modernism, neomodernism, and postmodernism, notions whose ambiguity increases when applied to cinema.[19] Studies of the relationship between cinema and modernism customarily begin with examination of the masterpieces of the silent cinema directed by F. W. Murnau, Fritz Lang, and Sergei Eisenstein. The silent era is regarded as a golden age insofar as the early cinema emerges as a modernist idiom in synchronicity with other arts, an idiom that, it is often noticed, would influence development of new literary techniques during the 1920s and 1930s in the work of writers such as James Joyce, T. S. Eliot, and John Dos Passos. According to Orr, the relationship between cinema and modernity is paradoxical: "In the cinema the modern is already history. But it has never been replaced."[20] He argues that "one can really speak of two 'modern' cinemas," meaning the silent films of the first decades of the twentieth century and the sound films of the 1960s and early 1970s, both of which in his opinion exemplify "a cinema of the reflexive will-to-power" as they "constantly speculate upon the power of the camera itself."[21]

Summarizing Raymond Williams's views on the place of mass culture and the arts in the twentieth century, Tony Pinkney sketches a similar historiographical model:

Film then occupies a paradoxical position within cultural modernity, dealing it a deathblow in the very instant that it brings its most intimate aesthetic potentialities to birth. For though as a medium it is founded upon Modernist "shock" experience within the metropolis, it leaps almost at once both behind and beyond Modernism, allowing only the briefest moment for the classic silent directors to actualize its "inherent" experimental potentialities. . . . But in another sense, as it moves into its own new technological phases of sound and colour, film takes a backward somersault behind Modernism, reinventing the latter's own realist past so thoroughly in the Hollywood domination of the medium that after the Second World War a new brand of auteur Modernism has to seek all over again to return film "to itself," to drag it back into that twentieth century whose very epitome it once was.[22]

Offering itself as the ultimate modernist signifier, cinema revives modernism at the very moment of its exhaustion. *La dolce vita*, we might say, represents a magisterial attempt on Fellini's part to reinvent the modernist cultural sensibility in the terms of 1960s European cinema. And yet Fellini's phenomenology of spectacularization and media hysteria provides as well one of the first holistic readings of the symptoms of modernism's demise in contemporary culture. Frank Burke aptly characterizes the film's spirit when he remarks that *La dolce vita* already presaged postmodernity "not because of any authorial intent but because the film was exploring a contemporary world verging on postmodernity."[23]

Not only does the film seem lacking in any "authorial intent" to celebrate the postmodern, as Burke rightly remarks, but it suggests an attitude that I would say already exemplifies a certain weariness and suspicion toward postmodern mass culture. The film begins with fascination for the celebrity culture epitomized by Sylvia and the paparazzi, but it ends by mourning the death of Marcello's intellectual ambitions as symbolized by his change of vocation from journalist to press agent. Fellini, it may be said, discovers in Marcello's distressing fate a prophetic image for the sort of extreme trivializing and commercializing of culture that seizes Italy in the 1970s and 1980s. This is not to say that *La dolce vita* offers an overt political program for resistance to corporate power. However, the film's visualization of the progress of Italian culture from elation to melancholic, disenchanted weariness is one of this culture's most powerful condemnations of the nihilism of the economic miracle. Fellini desperately attempts to defend against this nihilism through his searching, cinematic reinterpretation of modernism. There is no doubt, then, that even though the film criticizes the rigidity of an ossified modernism in the figure of Steiner, it also pursues through its own, original, Cubist methods an aesthetic alternative to the banalizing influence of commodity culture.

The very phrase *La dolce vita* indeed alludes, first of all, to the relative prosperity of the economic miracle during the 1960s, an affluence that seemed to inaugurate a new historical epoch after the ravages of World War Two. We might ask, Is *La dolce vita* meant merely to connote an innocuous stereotype about the Italian lifestyle during the years of the boom? Or does the phrase carry as well an ironic, critical significance, slyly propounding a logical equivalence between "sweetness" and decadence? We should not forget that the working title first proposed by Fellini for the film was *Babylon, Two Thousand Years After Christ*.[24] "Babylon" perhaps might be felt to suggest the hedonism of an international social order within which globalization is strictly a function of the expansion of capital markets. The final draft of the film's title, however, is no less evocative or suggestive than the rather overdetermined symbolism of the first. We might construe the adjective *dolce* as connoting, for instance, a sort of Kunderian unbearable lightness of being or a Calvinian postmodern comic lightness. The term might even be felt to anticipate the later ascendancy of weak thought, Gianni Vattimo's sweet mode of postmetaphysical philosophy, which affirms the principle that, as Nietzsche would have said approvingly, there are neither facts nor truths, only interpretations. More pointedly, however, the adjective seems a posteriori to controvert the sublime character ascribed by critics such as Lyotard and Jameson to most modernist and avant-garde art. In this sense, the title phrase might be said to signal a waning of the modernist outlook: its consumerist domestication, its populist familiarization.[25]

Written in a collaboration among Fellini, Tullio Pinelli, and Ennio Flaiano, *La dolce vita* remains one of the most incisive analyses of the vulgarity and corruption of the Italian political economy of the 1960s. The film's configuration in the form of a prologue, eight extended episodes, and two interludes allows Fellini to stage a drama of digression and eventual withdrawal from an increasingly distant modernist world.[26] We might say that if, as Cesare Zavattini asserts, neorealism developed as the art of the encounter, an art that places emphasis on the element of chance inherent in any random *rencontre*, Fellini by way of contrast perfects in *La dolce vita* a cinematic art of love at last sight. And he maintains this mode of perception throughout the film.

One of the first episodes revolves around Marcello and Maddalena's impromptu "pick-up" of a Roman prostitute and use of her apartment bedroom for almost farcically perfunctory lovemaking, while she sits in her kitchen smoking cigarettes and drinking coffee. The sequence, it should be noted, starts in a Roman nightclub where a Javanese dance troupe entertains a wealthy and star-studded crowd, before Fellini's camera follows Marcello and Maddalena on their nocturnal escapade. Combining the visual motifs of primitivist art, haute couture, the decadence of the aristocracy, and prostitution, the iconography of the sequence evidently rehabilitates a favorite theme of French Impressionist painting. When the couple leaves the prostitute behind at dawn like an abandoned cliché, the camera performs the first of many allegorical adieux that punctuate the narrative. The same valedictory gaze will be bestowed on Steiner, the film's modernist intellectual figurehead; on Marcello's father; and in the end on Paola, the pseudo-epiphanic girl on the beach.

The paratactic narrative structure of *La dolce vita* thus transforms every segment into a memorial tableau, the representative value of which is enhanced by the looseness of the plot connections, as if the disjunction between episodes threw each one into higher symbolic relief.[27] This shoring of fragments recalls the archetypal plot structure of modernist fictions from Eliot's *The Waste Land* to Joyce's *Ulysses*. Arguing for a connection between this sense of "decomposition" and the repertory of Christian images in the film, Robert Richardson finds a resemblance between *La dolce vita* and *The Waste Land* based not only on their common episodic structure but also on a common ethical attitude: "Both the film and the poem are twentieth-century versions of *Ecclesiastes*, visions of the hollowness of contemporary life. . . . Both *The Waste Land* and *La dolce vita* tell a modern story, or better, they reveal modern conditions against an older and supposedly richer background."[28]

A more pertinent model for Fellini, however, than Eliot's poetry seems to me Baudelaire's. A crucial working hypothesis in this essay is that, just as Baudelaire's work is positioned on the border between romanticism and modernity, Fellini's magnum opus defines the imaginary limit between modernity and postmodernity. The comparison with Baudelaire finds a strong root in the two artists' shared inclination toward "decadence." Of course, as Pier Paolo Pasolini rightly observes, Fellini's case is rather one of a "neodecadent" achievement, a cinematic revival of an earlier, fin de siècle mentality: "For my part, I declare to the four winds that Fellini's work signals and formalizes the vigorous return of a taste and of a stylistic ideology which have characterized the European literature of decadence." Pasolini is quick to recognize, however, that Fellini's neodecadent stylistic signature develops, like that of the great Italian modernist author, Carlo Emilio Gadda, in the direction of sheer pastiche, of an altogether "subjective, grotesque, violent, visceral, and distorting" experimentalism.[29]

La dolce vita might well be retitled the "Spleen" of Rome, and Marcello, the film's brooding protagonist, evidently represents in some sense the last of the urban *flâneurs*.[30] As if to achieve the photovisual equivalent of Baudelaire's description of Parisian street life during the Haussmann era, Fellini portrays Marcello as a kind of voyeuristic flâneur who takes "an immense joy to set up house in the heart of the multitude, amid the ebb and flow of movement, in the midst of the fugitive and the infinite."[31] The Italian director shares with the French poet a strong urge to allegorize the social conditions of the modern city. In both cases, the result is a transformation of the immediate moment into a "mémoire du présent," to use Paul de Man's formulation. (As an example of this effect, we might think of the scene of Marcello and Sylvia's wading in the Fontana di Trevi.) Such a memory ought "to extract from fashion whatever element it may contain of poetry within history, to distil the eternal from the transitory."[32] Of course, Baudelaire's aspiration to the melodramatic sublime is replaced in Fellini's films of the 1960s with a more satirical vision of the sweetness of fulfilled capitalism. No doubt Baudelaire's modernism signifies his alienation from mass culture as well and, as Benjamin has suggested, represents a critique of empty, bourgeois acquisitiveness and conformism.[33] From a later historical vantage, Fellini in contrast seems perpetually to be asking whether modernism in its decadent stage has retained any of its oppositional and critical value. The *dolce* of his film's title insinuates that modernism may have lost its capacity to shock and thus its critical pointedness, ultimately affirming nothing more than the mere spectacle of its own exhaustion. That *La dolce vita* itself nonetheless exudes a certain vitality has to do with the film's discovery of a cinematically original language with which to renew and relinquish the modernist ritual. However, Baudelaire and Fellini certainly have in common important affinities such as, for example, their sensitivity to boredom and delight in fashion, the latter enthusiasm given greater urgency by their alertness to the transience of certain cultural paradigms.[34]

Accordingly, I would like to pay particular attention in what follows to the feature's *air de famille* with the modern and the modernist imagination, downplaying the relevance of certain traditional references such as Dante. Critics as diverse as P. Adams Sitney, Barbara Lewalski, and Anne Paolucci repeatedly have advanced readings of the film as an allegorical pastiche that chiefly alludes to Dante's *Commedia*. According to this perspective, the film's inaugural image of a statue of Christ being flown across Rome by helicopter encodes a dire, Catholic warning. No less ominously, the enigmatic fish that appears on the beach at the conclusion substitutes symbolically for Dante's Satan.[35] The figure of Steiner is interpreted as a kind of parodic analogue of Virgil, and the mysterious girl at the beach either as Beatrice (Lewalski) or as Matelda, the iconic figure of sexual innocence encountered by the pilgrim at the summit of Purgatory (Sitney, Paolucci).[36] It might be said, however, that such readings of *La dolce vita* as a kind of Dantesque roman à clef run directly counter to the testimony of Fellini himself, who often repeated after the film opened that it was not his intention to provide a moralistic depiction of Italian society. As the director put it during a talk at the Centro Sperimentale di Cinematografia, his aim was to film a trial as seen not by a judge but by an accomplice.[37] Indeed, I would venture that the morally fluid and antimetaphysical attitude of *La dolce vita* is not consistent with the theologically and teleologically definite order of the *Commedia*.

Remarkably few, if any, critics have recognized the greater relevance of modernist sources to Fellini's undertaking in the film. The celebrated prologue, in which Marcello and his journalistic sidekick Paparazzo ride in a helicopter convoy that is air-lifting a statue of Christ to the Vatican, is exemplary on this score.[38] The exuberant aerial tracking shots of the lead helicopter hauling its freight through the sky over Rome suggest, if anything, the ascendancy of human technology over the religious, rather than any portentous return of the spiritual. And in its absurdist, celebratory interpretation of science as a new religion, the film seems to position itself as the latest addition to a cultural genealogy that includes poems such as Marinetti's "The Pope's Monoplane" and Apollinaire's "Zone," the latter of which refers to "le Christ qui monte au ciel mieux que les aviateurs" (Christ who ascends to heaven better than aviators).[39] We might say that Fellini quotes the avant-garde gesture of contaminating religion with science in order to lay claim to the title of a late-modernist auteur, the Picasso of cinema, and in order to set the film's historically irreverent tone with the proper *sprezzatura* or "appearance of bravery."[40]

At the same time, the prologue establishes as a theme the complicity of modern technology with consumerist mass media. The early modernist enthusiasm for technology thus is tempered by a more critical view of the symbiosis between telecommunications and journalism, a linkage that may be read as one symptom of a culture already on its way toward the crisis point of late capitalism. The film's insistence on the interdependence of photography and the cult of celebrity, and its final revelation of Marcello's professional fate as the public-relations agent of a second-rate actor, also contribute to the impression that we are watching the modernist ideal nearing a cul-de-sac. The disturbing outcome of Marcello's *Bildung* at the end of *La dolce vita* may be understood in this sense to allegorically prefigure the turn toward the apocalyptic spectacularism of the 1980s that Fellini will anatomize in *Ginger and Fred*. Notwithstanding its loose formal structure, its renunciation of a synthetic point of view and indulgence of an apparently aimless visual reverie, *La dolce vita* does provide a logical center. To dramatize the plight of the high modernist sensibility, Fellini needs a representative of the stern modern intellectual to play the foil to the film's population of metaphysically "weak" journalists and photographers. He assigns this function to the character of Steiner, Marcello's friend, mentor, and modernist role model. The Steiner segment represents the blind spot of the film's oblique narrative, or as Lacan would put it, the "point de capiton" of the imaginary and symbolic threads of *La dolce vita*.

The Still Life of the Modernist Intellectual: Steiner

Fellini's ideas for *La dolce vita* evolved from an abandoned, earlier project, *Moraldo in città*. The latter was conceived as a continuation of *I Vitelloni*, the director's portrait of a group of idle, provincial men of the 1950s. *Moraldo in città* would have recounted the story of one of these men as he moved to Rome to establish himself in the capital. Fellini eventually decided, however, that it would be more interesting to encounter Moraldo-Marcello at a later stage in life, years after his original resettlement, and to dramatize his confrontation of an altogether different series of existential events. Given this important reconceptualization of the project, it is interesting to note that one crucial element of the screenplay of *Moraldo in città* that Fellini retains in *La dolce vita* is the figure of Steiner.

The film's producer, Dino De Laurentiis, begged the director to no avail to eliminate the grim story of Steiner's murder of his children and suicide. Another producer, Angelo Rizzoli, was unhappy as well with this segment, a mean "divertissement" that he believed to be authored by Flaiano, the caustic Italian writer who was coauthor of the screenplay for *La dolce vita*.[41] However, as Kezich argues (and as Fellini's insistence on retaining the character affirms), Steiner, the figure of high-mindedness, is the logical pole of the film.[42] If, as I will argue, the character of Steiner epitomizes the fate of the modernist intellectual in a society increasingly suspicious of difficulty and purity, it is hardly surprising that his first appearance in the film occurs in a church where he has gone to pursue his research.

While shadowing a beautiful woman, Marcello enters a church that (incongruously for Rome) is designed in a high-modernist architectural style. Once inside, he happens to meet Steiner, who engages him in amiably didactic small talk. In search of a Sanskrit grammar, Steiner indicates his happiness at encountering Marcello, who appears in turn eager to be instructed by his older and more serious friend. Marcello sheepishly pretends to be gathering some material for an upcoming book, while Steiner unconvincingly feigns enthusiasm for the banal columns that Marcello has been publishing in the tabloids. Yet Steiner himself exhibits from the outset all the daring of a sterile imagination. Asked to play the organ, or as he pompously puts it, to elicit the "mysterious voices coming from the earth," he settles for the most well-known, not to say hackneyed, of Bach's fugues (the D minor), after a joking, momentary flirtation with jazz. Marcello's devotion to his friend seems misplaced in its blindness to Steiner's disturbingly alienated state. Indeed, the older man's dramatic function seems far closer to that of a Pirandellian author sought after by his lost characters than as a Virgil guiding Marcello's Dante, some critics have suggested. The Pirandellian strains of Fellini's *8½* have been acknowledged most often, but as Manuela Gieri further contends, their presence can be felt throughout his entire oeuvre.[43]

Remarkably, throughout the development of the Steiner subplot, it never becomes clear precisely what his calling and profession is. Is he a writer, a critic, perhaps an editor? His generically cerebral character supplies nothing more than a token of the high modernist intellectual as such. Paradoxically, as the narrative advances this token accumulates a more allegorical valence on account, rather than in spite, of its generality. It must be noted that Fellini wanted to cast the great Italian writer, Elio Vittorini, in the role of Steiner, but Vittorini declined.[44] As a representative of a stereotypically cryptic, "high" modernism, a kind of secular priest of the intellect (who is perhaps most at home in high-modernist churches), Steiner is hopelessly out of step with society.

This point is made in a subsequent scene during a soirée set in Steiner's apartment. Steiner hosts a gathering of his cosmopolitan, artistically inclined friends, a party to which he has invited Marcello and his unhappy girlfriend, Emma. Several speakers by turns deliver epigrammatic pronouncements on various subjects, but the overall impression is one of tiresome cliché. (Interestingly, Fellini took pains to cast real intellectuals and artists as members of Steiner's coterie, among others the writer Leonida Rapaci, the painter Anna Salvatore, Letizia Spadini, and the poets Iris Tree and Desmond O'Grady.) A few moments later, Marcello notices a painting on the wall by that exemplary Italian modernist painter Giorgio Morandi, and expresses his admiration to Steiner, who replies that Morandi is the artist he loves most on account of the painter's clarity and precision: "Such power, precision and rigor. You could say art has left nothing to chance." Immersed in a metaphysical luminosity, Morandi's bottles come to stand for the ultimate modernist objects: difficult and yet pure and auratic at the same time.

Fellini's choice of subject for his commentary on the decline of modernist culture was not arbitrary. Morandi's career might be said to recapitulate that of high modernism in painting generally. From an initial devotion to Cézanne and Cubism, the Italian painter developed his own, original variant of de Chirico's *pittura metafisica* by insisting on an abstract figurativeness that was akin in spirit to minimalism and conceptual art. Gaining recognition after World War Two, he was praised for demythologizing de Chirico's metaphysical vocabulary in favor of objects that reveal a metaphorical value through the conditions of light, time, and space.[45] We could say that in this sense Morandi is the painter par excellence of aura. The picture in Steiner's apartment represents the type of art that for a night even Marcello can embrace without qualms. In his words, it is an art that is clear, neat, without rhetoric or lies, that does not flatter ("non adulatrice").

We should note that, contemporary to Fellini, another important Italian filmmaker had inserted an homage to Morandi in his first major work. In *Accatone*, Pasolini shoots the character of Stella washing a series of bottles overtly reminiscent of the glassware in a Morandi painting, when the protagonist, Accatone, arrives to pay her a visit. Rather than photographing an actual painting and interpreting it through a character's sententious commentary, Pasolini achieves a much subtler and more poetic evocation of Morandi's art. Bringing the bottles to cinematic life, Pasolini asserts their deeply felt emotional presence and the poetic significance of Morandi's still life. The achievement of the camera indeed is to defeat the stillness of the still life (or the deathliness of what the French and Italians would call *nature morte*) in a feat of almost evangelical transumption, as if to resuscitate the bottles like so many miniature Lazaruses. The more conventional, prosaic, affectless quotation of Morandi in Fellini's film indicates the director's deep skepticism toward the possibility of renewing the authority of a drained modernism.

We might conclude that this cultural and intellectual society ought to fall subject to a hermeneutic of suspicion even before the turning point in the film of Steiner's suicide. Marcello, after all, is a spiritual flâneur, floating with ease and charm through his encounters with different people and ideas. Despite all the levity that he and some of the other guests contribute to the occasion, however, the soirée itself is disfigured by the recurring appearance of an ominous sign. A distracting beam of light repeatedly flashes and expires through the living-room window. It is difficult not to feel that the insistent, mechanical reappearance of this spotlight threateningly signals from the outside that the sheltered world within is coming to an end.

The discomfort is increased by Steiner's idle entertainment of his friends with a tape recorder. When an American woman poet describes Steiner as being as tall as a Gothic steeple, another amused guest records her words and repeatedly plays back the sentence on tape. The repetition quickly drains the conceit of any charm, revealing it as clumsy bombast, despite Steiner's humble and polite protests against what he apparently regards as undeserved praise.

Poet: Primitive as a Gothic steeple, so high up you can't hear the voices below.
Steiner: If you could see my real stature, you would see I am really no higher than this. (He makes a gesture with his index finger and thumb.)

The descriptive simile likening Steiner to a Gothic steeple is powerfully resonant, since for one of the chief figures of modernism, namely Proust, a Gothic cathedral was the most apt metaphor for the construction of an inspiring novel.[46] Here, the Gothic no longer stands for the ambitious, spiritual arrogance of the heroic modernist enterprise; instead, it has become a banality.

Then the tape continues, revealing Steiner's recording of a series of natural noises, from thunder to the whistling of wind to birdsong. The artificial amplification and isolation of the sounds suggests an experience of nature not as a benign or harmonious referential system but as a simulacrum divorced from any context. Following Marcello's and Steiner's discussion of Morandi's painting, the inclusion of the tape recorder in the scene appears to enact a kind of Benjaminian pessimism regarding the hieratic value of the artwork in an age of mechanical reproduction.

When Steiner thereafter enters his children's bedroom in order to examine the youngsters in their sleep, his paternal scrutiny seems cold and *unheimlich*—as clinical as his mechanical recording of the natural world. Another modernist "fauve" painting in the form of a portrait of Christ by Georges Rouault hangs on the wall in the background. Given this ominous tableau, it becomes difficult to take at face value Marcello's claim that he wishes to visit the Steiner household more often, as it provides refuge. Rather than living "in the harmony of the successful work of art" as Steiner had encouraged him to do, Marcello will succumb to his usual ambivalence before ever setting out on a new path. In the aftermath of Steiner's killing of his children and suicide, Marcello's existential indecision will come to seem an insurmountable psychological impasse.

If modernism must be viewed, as Walter Benjamin declares, under the sign of suicide, *La dolce vita* offers in the character of Steiner an image of the ultimate, allegorical suicide.[47] When Marcello arrives at the grisly scene and discovers what has happened, he seems for once genuinely stricken and distraught. Reaching his friend's apartment in the EUR section of Rome, he looks at Steiner's corpse seated in an armchair and at the children who lie dead in their beds. "I do not know anything, I really do not know anything," Marcello numbly repeats to the investigators. On the wrenching evidence of this moment, we might conclude that Marcello is formulating a negative "phenomenology of the spirit" insofar as his rational self-awareness seems to diminish as he nears the unconscious mentality of the film's climactic orgy, a virtual mise-en-scène of the death of the subject.[48] Frederic Jameson in fact has even proposed that, in contrast to the films of Antonioni and Bergman, *La dolce vita* might be regarded as on its way to postmodernity by virtue of its deconstructed subject.[49] When Steiner's wife arrives at the apartment building, a mob of photojournalists await her on the street so as to snap her picture at the moment she learns of her husband's act. "Do you think I am an actress?" she asks in puzzled amusement, before the reason for her sudden celebrity has been explained to her. The private nature of her trauma will be exploited for public consumption as the flashbulbs of the photographers pursue her without pity or remorse.

In a genuine sense, then, Fellini visualizes Steiner's suicide as an event that sets spectacularized, contemporary celebrity culture in motion. The character's acts of infanticide and self-annihilation enact on an allegorical level not only the terminus of modernism's aesthetic possibilities but also the psychological encounter with the Real, the moment of awakening to the antisymbolic, oppressive materiality of the culture that is to come. The reiteration of key visual elements from the party sequence in the discovery of the dead bodies—the image of Steiner seated in the living room, the children lying in their beds—sheds a withering retrospective light on the existential course imagined for Marcello by Emma, when she remarks in the earlier party scene that they too will one day live in a house like Steiner's. Underscoring the point through Emma's suggestion, the film raises the possibility that Steiner in some sense commits suicide in Marcello's place. The modernist temptation to the heroic act of self-annihilation is dismissed through elimination of a secondary character, as it will be through sheer parody in *8½*. When Guido Anselmi crawls under a table to shoot himself during a press conference gone awry, Fellini performs a mock gesture that constitutes a necessary prelude to the achievement of the ecumenical, happy ending of *8½*.

Editing *La dolce vita*:
From Ivory Tower to the Tower of Babel

After much struggling, Fellini never wound up shooting two episodes included in the original script of *La dolce vita*. At least one of these omissions is particularly telling. A few days after the accidental death of another friend, Marcello visits a writer, Dolores, who lives in a tower by the sea (and in whose role Fellini wanted to cast the actress Louise Rainer). He discovers with Delores what he feels is a new capacity for sympathy and understanding in an unusual relationship for him, to which he repeatedly returns despite various interruptions. However, when Dolores at last fully enunciates her opinion of Marcello, both as a writer and a man, the judgment comes off as harsh and narrow-minded:

> Dear, what you have written is exactly as you are . . . almost everything. Easy, dispersed . . . in fact, you like your lifestyle, that is the truth. . . . You like it and you recognize yourself in it . . . and, therefore, it is only natural that when you write you write like this. . . . Yes, you are able to express puzzlement, emotions, contempt, but I am afraid that it's all very superficial. You should know well, my dear, that authentic experiences are interior. Adventures in the outside world, curiosities . . . all you enjoy so much . . . is just a waste . . . a convenient excuse to do whatever you like. . . . I am afraid you are becoming an endearing buffoon, my dear. . . . Watch out.[50]

Again growing restless, Marcello turns suspicious of the rhetorical pathos that domestic isolation seems to enforce, and disdaining Dolores's earnestness he flees the tower and his last possibility of achieving some form of grace.[51] That this episode was not included in the finished film might be explained in various ways, but the chief suggestion I wish to make is that it is redundant. We have already observed Steiner's function in the narrative as a kind of substitute for Marcello's potential suicide. A more analytic or nuanced representation of the defeat of his residual intellectual ambition would have been superfluous, particularly given the film's interest in mapping the new cultural and intellectual territory that lies beyond modernism.

The ivory tower, that most cliché icon of high modernism, had already crumbled. Fellini leaves the viewer of the finished film instead with the tower of Babel. In the final cut of *La dolce vita*, the episode involving Dolores is replaced by a briefer, more playful interlude that almost casually prepares the viewer for the film's stunningly bleak conclusion. Alone at the beach, in search of inspiration for his book, Marcello immediately is distracted by the appearance of a young girl, whose graceful persona reminds him of a painted fresco of an "Umbrian angel." She is listening to "Patricia," a popular hit song, at high volume. After momentary irritation at the intrusion, Marcello gives up and lets her turn the music up full blast. The loud, mindless pop tune and his rapid acquiescence to its assault dramatize his lack of commitment to the demanding vocation of art.

Modernist Architecture and Its Discontents

According to John Orr, one of the chief legacies that high modernism leaves to the late or "neo"-modern is modernist architecture.[52] In a sense, the star of *La dolce vita* is Rome itself in all its "stupendous fragmentariness," to borrow George Eliot's apt characterization of the city.[53] Of the Eternal City's multitudinous strata of construction, it is the modernist layer that is assigned the most threatening role in the film. A useful contrast may be drawn between Fellini's use of architecture and painting in the film. The camera approaches Morandi's bottles, as it were, with an implicitly competitive attitude and a sure faith that cinema will have the last word. By contrast, architecture exposes more fully than painting does the terminally formulaic condition of modernism in the 1960s and presents itself as the symbolic tombstone of the ideology. This is because, in the Italian sociohistorical context, modernist architecture not only reveals a strong link to Fascism but, during the period of the economic boom, embodies a pathological, manic drive to financial speculation. No less starkly than in an Antonioni film, modernist architecture in *La dolce vita* furnishes the setting of every threatened or actual death scene—from Emma's attempted suicide, to the heart attack suffered by Marcello's father, to Steiner's murder-suicide.

Fellini first establishes a strong visual association between modernism and death when Marcello drives Emma to the hospital after her attempt to kill herself. The director shoots the interior of the hospital with an emphasis on the abstract, ascetic, modernist qualities of the building, an edifice that, like Steiner's residence, is located in the EUR. Languid tracking shots frame Marcello and direct our attention to the cold, empty spaces of the hallways and rooms. The cinematography is awash in white light, lending itself to an effect that is strikingly distinct from the visual style of the rest of the film. The hallucinatory sequence in the hospital almost seems to belong to another work entirely, such as Antonioni's *The Eclipse* or Orson Welles's *The Trial* or Bernardo Bertolucci's *The Conformist*. We should note as well that Marcello's and Emma's barren-looking apartment, a nightmarish version of a Corbusian "machine" for habitation that Fellini presents as colorless, sterile, and almost empty of furniture but for a bed, also belongs to the EUR. It is in this district, which was to have been the centerpiece of Mussolini's planned urban renewal of Rome, that we find the severe modernist church in which Marcello first meets Steiner and Steiner's elegant flat where the film's most brutal acts of violence take place.

La dolce vita implies some degree of political awareness insofar as it observes both Rome's problematic status as a model for the modern city and the historical origin of this problem under Fascism. At a congress on urban development in 1937, the Fascists anointed Rome the modern capital not only of the Italian nation and Catholic Christendom but of the entire world. The Esposizione Universale in 1942 that gave the precinct its acronym was supposed to establish Rome as the exemplar of the ideal modern city. Numerous Italian architects took part in an architectural contest during the years 1937–38 to develop the district that came to be referred to as the EUR and was then known as "E42." The contest was held under the supervision of the architect Marcello Piacentini, who proposed to uphold the crucially nebulous values of the rational, the modern, the Mediterranean, and the classic. Unsurprisingly, the different projects were gradually modified in the direction of the classical through insistence on certain materials such as marble and granite, on elements such as the column and the arch, and on Pythagorean proportions and mirrored symmetries. On this score, we might view the Palazzo della Civiltà Italiana—otherwise known as the "squared coliseum"—by Giovanni Guerrini, Ernesto La Padula, and Mario Romano as representative.[54] The building is distinguished by its forbidding, decorative arches; perhaps on account of this eerie mixture of luxury and menace, it appears in a number of Fellini's films, from *The Nights of Cabiria* to *Ginger and Fred*.

What Brunello Rondi has labeled the "science fiction" style of architecture that prevails in the EUR fascinated Fellini.[55] It should be further noted, however, that this fascination coexists with an anxious sense of alienation, a deeply Baudelairean melancholy that arises from witnessing the rapidly changing physiognomy of the modern city:

Paris change! mais rien dans ma mélancolie
N'a bougé! palais neufs, échafaudages, blocs,
Vieux faubourgs, tout pour moi devient allégorie,
Et mes chers souvenirs sont plus lourds que des rocs.

[Paris changes . . . but in sadness like mine
nothing stirs—new buildings, old
neighborhoods turn to allegory,
and memories weigh more than stone.][56]

Like Baudelaire, Fellini reads allegorical significance into the historical transformation of his surroundings in order to counteract the *horror vacui* of modernist urban planning. The very existence of the EUR elicits a feeling of cultural and spatial dislocation from which, the film implies, Marcello will prove incapable of recovering. Without a Haussmann-like visionary to reorganize the city plan, Rome bears only sporadic traces of modernity's influence. If sites such as the Via Veneto, the Caracalla baths, the Fontana di Trevi, and the sixteenth-century Odescalchi castle at Bassano di Sutri give the film a complement of opulent, one-of-a-kind, theatrical settings for sustained visual reveries, the modern suburbs of Rome represent the "wake-up call" of a mass-produced reality where life cannot be sweet. The episode involving Marcello's night on the town with his father dramatically encapsulates the film's sobering historical outlook. After a boisterous evening of dancing and drinking at the Kit-Kat club, Marcello's father accompanies the dancer Fanny to her apartment in the EUR. Once arrived at the city's modern, dehumanized periphery, he suffers a heart attack that cuts short the festivities and forces him to exchange hasty and fumbling goodbyes with Marcello.

The architectural settings of the film's scenes appear to alternate between two styles: that of a benign, dreamlike *ancienneté* associated with the pleasure principle and that of a grim, functionalist modernity associated with the reality principle. Fellini's oscillation between these modes brackets the older type like a quotation, a suspended fragment of the past that achieves by virtue of its rootedness in human history and memory a mythic, archetypal resonance. Assuming what appears at first glance to be a contrary stance in his essay "The Return of the Flâneur," Walter Benjamin expresses perplexity that the modernist imagination has seized on Paris rather than Rome as the city par excellence of *flânerie*:

> The *flâneur* is the creation of Paris. The wonder is that it was not Rome. But perhaps in Rome even dreaming is forced to move along streets that are too well paved. And isn't the city too full of temples, enclosed squares, and national shrines to be able to enter undivided into the dreams of the passer-by along with every paving stone, every shop sign, every flight of steps, and every gateway.[57]

Yet it is precisely Rome's historical overdeterminacy, so eloquently captured by Benjamin, that in Fellini's mind gives the city its undeniable allegorical value. By looking at the symbolically saturated, "unconscious" strata of Roman antiquity from the conscious, realist standpoint of modernism, the director finds a consoling alternative to the brutal, hypertechnologized capitalism of the later twentieth century. In certain respects, Fellini may be said to recapitulate Freud's view of Rome in *Civilization and Its Discontents*, where the psychoanalytic theorist treats the Eternal City and its buried ruins as a psychical entity with a long and copious past, a material representation of the various layers of mental life.[58] Like Freud, Fellini in *La dolce vita* appears to privilege the past when he contrasts the archaic, baroque regions of Rome, where the circulation of the streets replicates the exhilarating freedom of a primary process of the unconscious, to the palpable discontent of modern civilization, where the secondary mechanisms of conscious thought are denied the relief of condensation and displacement. If modernism finds in Paris its paradigmatic city, perhaps it encounters in Fellini's Rome its nemesis and corrective, a prelude to the double coding of postmodern aesthetics. As we will see, Fellini's reimagination of Rome's urban topography twenty years later in *Ginger and Fred* almost completely eradicates all traces of the city's Renaissance and classical history, displacing its ancient historical glories from the camera's eye with the contemporary, mass-produced banality of its suburbs.

The Death of the Epiphany

After the extreme shock delivered by Steiner's suicide, Marcello seems on the verge of a momentous decision, perhaps even of a conversion to *La dolce vita* of the title and a renunciation of his previous ambitions. We see him in the film's final episode presiding over an increasingly debauched party in Fregene as a sort of impromptu master of ceremonies. The orgy sequence achieves with satiric brio what Jean Baudrillard would call the transformation of the "scene" into the obscene. Bauman helpfully elucidates this dichotomy: "The world is no longer a 'scene' (a plane where the play is staged which, as we have the right to suspect, will be directed towards some concrete ending, even if we do not know in advance what it is); instead it is obscene: a lot of noise and bustle without plot, scenario, director, and direction."[59] The party appears to celebrate simultaneously the annulment of a friend's marriage and Marcello's new job as a publicity agent for movie actors. Accordingly, he reminds the guests with revealing lack of specificity that the party marks the annulment of "everything."

The ensuing revelry represents a transvaluation of all values initiated by a couple of transvestites dancing to the music of "Jingle Bells." As the party grows progressively duller following a striptease that only momentarily assuages the participants' restlessness, Marcello, the nominal "intellectual" of the group, promises to produce thousands of ideas for further performance, but in fact he is too pathetically drunk to articulate any. As he formulates his *raccourci* of late capitalist logic with respect to publicity, excess, and celebrity, the meaningless chatter and sexual titillation escalate toward a tired finale, during which Marcello sadistically humiliates a young girl from the provinces by riding and whipping her like a mule. This final sequence is crucial to an understanding of the film as allegorized cultural analysis. Baudrillard imagines the historical arrival of modernity as an "orgy," a moment of explosive liberation after which the "current state" of postmodernity looks like an experience of enervation or disappointment.[60] Taking our cue from the French theorist, we might view Marcello's participation in the antics at Fregene as the final discharge of modernist energy within the film.

An important point to note with regard to this scene is that it is the character of the transvestite, Mariuccio, to whom Fellini assigns the one line in the original screenplay that in any way elucidates the title. Observing the quickly degenerating atmosphere, he tells Marcello, "I love life . . . the very sweetest life. And you?"[61] Mariuccio evidently possesses the kind of innocence and melancholy reserved for an individual who has embraced without denial the chaotic but poetic nature of his own desires. Yet it is notable that Fellini does not keep Mariuccio's line in his final work. Seen through the eyes of the more embittered and fatalistic Marcello, the notion of *La dolce vita* might achieve congruence with the kind of *douceur* that, according to Baudrillard, is characteristic finally of the contemporary condition: "One asks what might come after the orgy—the work of mourning or of melancholy? Neither one nor the other . . . rather than fleeing into the future we prefer the retrospective apocalypse and revisionism in all things—all our societies have become revisionist; they rethink everything with a sweet calm [en douceur]."[62]

In the morning (the last of the numerous dawnings that punctuate the film), the guests file out of the villa like actors exiting the stage with theatrical flourishes and farewells. Walking through a wood of pine trees at the border of the seaside, the group seems melancholic and anxious. The only possible source of the *Lichtung* they hope to find is the vast and empty sea itself.[63] Yet the only event of interest results from the discovery of an enormous fish on the beach that, one bystander observes, has been dead for three days. Some critics have proposed to interpret this event as a Christic metaphor, relying on the traditional association between fish and Jesus and the reference to the three days. It seems to me instead that Fellini's camera performs a powerful subversion of a potentially auratic spectacle here, discovering in the fish the sign of a grotesque and hostile cosmos. Through a remarkable medium shot of the fish's dead eye returning the gaze of a disquieted Marcello, Fellini suggests a confrontation that is primarily aesthetic and epistemological in its contours. If Benjamin is correct that the model of the auratic experience is the investment of an object with the ability to return the gaze, then the fish in *La dolce vita* represents the ultimate travesty of such experience.[64] What is certain is that here, at the finale, Fellini avoids any suggestion of resurrection or deliverance for his characters and hence any hint of a redemptive religious message.

Marcello begins to walk along the shore of the beach, when Paola, the girl whose personal pop-music soundtrack diverted him from his book, appears in the distance, waving to catch his attention and gesticulating to remind him of their previous encounter. His reunion with the young siren indeed promises to enlarge on the charged significance of their first meeting. As Frank Burke writes, "When Marcello encounters her earlier, . . . he is able to relate to her only as an icon . . . purely as simulation. . . . One could also argue that the film itself does precisely to Paola in the final scene what Marcello did earlier . . . 'reproducing' her as an icon of spirituality."[65]

Fellini toys with our expectation of a fleeting "moment of being" or epiphany that will enlighten the anxious hero, an expectation in keeping with the classic narratives of modernism. Marcello, however, appears to miss his opportunity for inspiration, unable as he is to hear Paola's shouted attempts at communication over the noise of the ocean. Resigned to his condition, he walks away to join a woman from the previous night's group of partygoers.[66] The piercing last shot of the film lingers on the sweet, benevolent smile of the young girl. Marcello is absent from the picture, the epiphany has not happened, and the riddle of modernity has not been solved. Foucault perhaps best captures the hermeneutic elusiveness of such a moment, when a few years later he envisions the very concept of man inviting its own annihilation "like a face drawn in sand at the edge of the sea."[67] It is of crucial significance that Fellini chooses for the final drama of failed consciousness one of the favorite loci of high modernism: the seaside encounter with a young girl.

Not only can we think of the narrator's crucial encounter in *La recherche* with Albertine, *la jeune fille en fleur*, but also of Stephen Dedalus's sublime moment of self-discovery in *A Portrait of the Artist as a Young Man*. In Joyce's *Bildungsroman*, Stephen walks along the seashore as he ruminates on his newfound ambition to "create proudly out of the freedom and power of his soul, as the great artificer whose name he bore, a living thing, new and soaring and beautiful, impalpable, imperishable."[68] A few moments later he spies a girl by the water and undergoes an overwhelming epiphanic realization:

A girl stood before him in midstream, alone and still, gazing out to sea. She seemed like one whom magic had changed into the likeness of a strange and beautiful seabird. . . . She was alone and still gazing out to sea; and when she felt his presence and the worship of his eyes her eyes turned to him in quiet sufferance of his gaze and then quietly withdrew her eyes from his and bent them towards the stream, gently stirring the water with her foot hither and thither. . . . Heavenly God! cried Stephen's soul, in an outburst of profane joy. . . . A wild angel had appeared to him, the angel of mortal youth and beauty, an envoy from the fair courts of life, to throw open before him in an instant of ecstasy the gates of all the ways of horror and glory.[69]

Clearly, Stephen's vision of the young girl represents a conversion experience of sorts in the *Portrait*, a conversion away from organized religion and toward artistic self-determination that in some sense represents the antithesis of Marcello's capitulation to the pressures of a spectacularized capitalism in the wake of Steiner's suicide. In considering Fellini's opinion of the "classic" modernist conversion myth, we ought to keep in mind that, as originally scripted, *La dolce vita* was to have ended on a different and somewhat more hopeful note with respect to a possible epiphany.

In its iconography and overall outlines, the final scene had a more Proustian than Joycean quality. Marcello in fact meets not with a single "angel," but with a group of young girls, "sweet feminine figures, . . . calm, safe, and joyful as girls are when in company," arriving at the beach.[70] He recognizes Paola, and their brief conversation leaves them both with a feeling of happiness. When he tries to interest her in the dead fish, however, her attention wanders, and after a few minutes she runs away. Fellini describes Marcello as he watches her withdraw in the company of her friends: "He is gripped by a profound, inexplicable emotion; he does not really know if it is sorrow or joy, desperation or hope. . . . Marcello's turmoil is agonizing. He looks far off; in the luminous and still sea, the little girls run wild with joy, mysterious messengers of a new life."[71]

Yet in the finished film, it is Marcello who walks away from Paola, as he perhaps bows to an advancing sense of reality. We cannot fail to notice the emotional implications of his decision—we may expect Marcello's abandonment of the girl to occasion no artistic inspiration, merely an elegiac pang of regret. If the myth of epiphanic self-realization is both deconstructed and lamented by *La dolce vita*, quoted as the residue of a past from which we have to distance ourselves, it will be translated into a kind of absurdist afterlife in *8½*. Whereas Fellini in *La dolce vita* aims to survive the apocalypse of modernity by presenting his images as the last, viable modernist signifiers, he no longer cultivates any illusions about the efficacy of his own art in *8½*, a film whose title evokes the cryptic labeling of abstract expressionist paintings of the 1940s and 1950s. After an archetypally modernist convalescence at a pseudo-Thomas-Mann-style sanitarium, the protagonist Guido Anselmi embarks on a search for enlightenment via an encounter with a beautiful girl in white whom he has glimpsed at the spa.[72] Unlike *La dolce vita*, though, *8½* uses its familiar quest narrative in an evidently parodic mode and concedes without reservation the untimeliness of Guido's dream of purity.

The latter film concludes with the justly famous image of the cast of characters holding hands and dancing in a circle. Guido directs everyone to their position and then finally joins the circle to the strains of Nino Rota's haunting theme music. At the time of the feature's release, most critics and viewers found this denouement puzzling in its transmogrification of life and art into sheer spectacle. It is strangely fitting that the closing scene of *8½* was originally shot as the promotional trailer for the film's theatrical release. Not satisfied with the narrative crescendo of the original ending and conscious of the surreal energy that the scene exuded, Fellini revised his plan so as to incorporate the trailer's visually metonymic, allusive summation of the larger film. The redemption of the film medium from all that is not spectacular and cinematographic is now accomplished; no longer is film, as in Kracauer's theory, supposed to redeem physical reality. Eco neatly puts in perspective Fellini's mature achievement of having "lived to redeem the cinema from what is external to itself."[73] Yet over the years the director himself was unable to sustain the illusion of having reconciled modernist aesthetics and postmodern exhilaration. Increasingly, he came to abandon the more optimistic stance of his earlier works. By the time of *Ginger and Fred*, Fellini adopts the pessimistic outlook of a prophet unheeded and unwelcome in his own nation. Ironically, the director finds himself at the end of his career fighting the assimilation of his own youthful designs to Silvio Berlusconi's campaign to redeem television from what is external to commerce.

La dolce vita Twenty Years Later: *Ginger and Fred*

[*On TV, a commercial spot: a beautiful woman holds a large slice of mortadella close to her face.*]
Woman: No, my dear, I am not jealous. Please go ahead and feel free to choose *her*. It is Mortadella Lombardoni!

—*Ginger and Fred*

In the years intervening between *La dolce vita* (1960) and *Ginger and Fred* (1985), Italian cinema underwent a systemic crisis. This crisis took place simultaneously with the triumph of commercial television in Italy and its transformation of state-controlled broadcasting into an entirely advertising-based business. Indeed, the late 1970s saw a dramatic decline of more than 50 percent in the number of tickets sold at cinema box offices in Italy, a decline that coincided with the return of the American movie industry to absolute dominance at the box office.[74] As Stephen Gundle has observed, it was TV rather than the film medium that was responsible for the development and promotion of consumer culture in Italy during this period, since, like its neorealist predecessor, the modernist cinema of the 1960s from Fellini's *La dolce vita* to Visconti's *Rocco and His Brothers* maintained a wary stance regarding industrial society.[75] Italian film of the 1960s took a generally pessimistic view of the social transformations occurring from 1958 to 1963. Another factor contributing to the conflict between cinema and television in Italy was the historical hegemony of the political left over film production and the equally firm power of the Democrazia Cristiana and the Catholic right over broadcasting. Only toward the end of the 1970s, after conspicuous electoral gains by the left, was there a *lottizzazione* that divided control of the three state channels—RAI 1, 2, and 3—between the Democrazia Cristiana, the Socialists, and the Communists. By that time, however, the success of privatized television had compelled the state channels to change their priorities. The left thus never really had an opportunity to shape the cultural agenda of Italian TV in any meaningful sense.

In the years following World War Two, film played a decisive role in providing a poor, socially divided Italy with a new political identity. After deregulation of broadcasting, Italy proved more receptive than other European nations to TV programs imported from the United States, suggesting the absence of a strong national cultural identity.[76] Although far from being total successes, the neorealist film movement of the 1940s and early 1950s and the modernist cinema of the 1960s largely attempted to call national attention to the social and political problems of modern-day Italy. That appeal through the nation's movie theaters quickly was drowned out by the flood of commercials through its televisions. The construction of national identity during the 1960s entailed dealing with fundamental reservations, especially among intellectuals, about the processes of modernization and industrialization. These reservations manifest themselves in a variety of forms, from the anti-elegiac poetics of anxiety elaborated by directors such as Michelangelo Antonioni to more widespread expressions of anti-industrialist, nostalgic pathos.[77] In the 1980s, however, the nation appears to overcome its ambivalence, to welcome the practices and effects of contemporary capitalism. If, as Silvana Patriarca suggests, Italy's national identity has vacillated since the *Risorgimento* between feelings of inferiority and manic overcompensation, the latter mood evidently dominates the 1980s.[78]

We may speak of an Italian national identity in the 1980s insofar as we recognize such a notion as a function of consumerism, as coinciding with the cultural logic of slogans such as "Italian Style" and "Made in Italy." It is no accident that fashion designers such as Giorgio Armani and Gianni Versace achieved preeminence in the 1980s partly through affirmation of Italy itself as a brand, a guarantee of quality and good taste to the consumer. The search for an Italian national identity thus finds Pyrrhic consolation in ceaseless acquisition and consumption of Italian products, a process that suggests a vicious circle.[79] In this connection, it is worth noting the prominent role that Guy Debord assigns to Italy in his analysis of mass culture. He identifies Italy in *Comments on the Society of the Spectacle* (1988) as a prime example of "integrated spectacle," which he clearly distinguishes from other types of spectacle such as the "diffuse" form associated with the United States and the "concentrated" form manifest in Germany and Russia.[80] By integrated, he seems specifically to mean the uncanny synergy of politics, culture, and business in Italy.

Even more tellingly, Debord ascribes to an Italian politician the symbolic responsibility for articulating the credo of the new epoch: "The most profound summing up of the period which the whole world entered shortly after Italy and the United States, can be found in the words of a senior Italian statesman, a member simultaneously, of both the official government and the parallel government, P2, Potere Due: 'Once there were scandals, but not any more.'"[81] Adopting a position that harkens back at least to Giacomo Leopardi's argument in *Discourse on the Present State of the Customs of the Italians* (1824), Debord emphasizes the overwhelming, negative role of spectacle in the economy of Italian society.[82] A central preoccupation of many of Fellini's films is to explore the modern-day manifestations of spectacle in Italy, from the circus to the variety show, celebrity-chasing tabloid journalism, and commercial television. In the films he directed in the 1980s at the end of his career, however, Fellini renounces the innocence of a mere observer and adopts a riskier position of openness to being scandalized. My focus here is the significance of this turning point in the director's career. What distinguishes *Ginger and Fred* from his other films, it seems to me, is his determination in this late-career masterpiece to stage an encounter with the Real of Italian culture, which is to say the society's obscene, materialized fulfillment and incarnation in Italian television. Uncharacteristically for one of Fellini's narratives, *Ginger and Fred* offers its protagonists no hint of redemption or transcendence at the end, as is the case in such classic productions as *La strada*, *The Nights of Cabiria*, and

La dolce vita. At the end of Fellini's career, it becomes impossible for him to produce spectacular fantasies and visual epiphanies and imperative to expose television as the core of Italy's cultural trauma.

To understand this condition at the time of *Ginger and Fred*, it is useful to review the history of privatized television in Italy. The government monopoly on broadcasting lasted from 1954 to 1975, when the industry was deregulated and private channels were allowed to proliferate. Berlusconi seized the opportunity to establish a private monopoly and, due to a legislative vacuum, became a mogul in a few short years. Under the corporate umbrella of Fininvest, he built a media empire that included the private channels Canale 5, Italia 1, and Rete 4. In February 1985, a law was passed that finally addressed the growth of private stations, but limiting itself largely to recognition of the duopoly of the state-controlled system known as Radio Televisione Italiana (RAI) and Berlusconi's Fininvest. A new law, popularly referred to as *Legge Mammì*, went into effect in 1990 that codified the market shares of the RAI and Fininvest, for all practical purposes stabilizing and formalizing the duopoly. However, an amendment sponsored by Walter Veltroni and supported by Fellini, Marcello Mastroianni, and Alberto Moravia, among others, managed to limit the quantity of advertising breaks during broadcasts of films. Richard Dienst has noted that, whereas other countries, particularly in Europe, managed to reach some sort of compromise between official state television and private broadcasting, Italy experienced "an especially strong swing" from one to the other.[83] Contemporary Italian TV exemplifies the most extreme tendencies of commercial broadcasting, according to Paul Ginsborg, who notes that in 1984, the year before Fellini began production of *Ginger and Fred*, the industry was responsible for assaulting the public with fifteen hundred ads per day, a figure that represents more than the total of all other European nations combined.[84]

The influence of privatized broadcasting in the 1980s dramatically changed the relationship between culture and consumerism in Italy. Over the course of the decade, even the RAI gradually abandoned educational programming and social and political analysis in order to compete against the private sector on its own terms of ratings and market share: "Taking public and private together, Italian television presented a sorry picture. A massive number of imports from the USA dominated the programmers' weekly fare. All this demonstrated that Italian television was deeply lazy. It was also self-referential, a pathology which Umberto Eco described as 'neo-television.'"⁸⁵ Eco indeed established the opposing concepts of "paleo-television" and "neo-television" to describe the differences between programming before and after deregulation. Whereas paleo-television stands for the kind of TV produced by the state monopoly "for an ideal public, both meek and Catholic," neo-television corresponds to a kind of TV that "talks less and less about the external world" and increasingly "about itself and about the contact that it establishes with its own public."⁸⁶ As an especially egregious symptom of neo-television, Eco singled out the "hold-all" variety show that contains different programs and indiscriminately mixes styles.⁸⁷ As we shall see, Fellini lampoons this genre in *Ginger and Fred* by means of the mock program "We Are Proud to Present."

It might be argued that the explosion of commercial television in the 1980s succeeded in bringing to the fore what had already been an implicit dynamic of the culture for a significant period of time. In an essay written in 1974, Pasolini contends that, beyond any overt allegiance to conservative and religious ideologies, television works in synchronization with the dictates of consumerism and what he mysteriously refers to as the "new power."⁸⁸ Resolving this mystery, the advent of Berlusconi's empire of consolidated media, business, and political properties clearly exemplifies the new power in practice. We might say, adopting a Hegelian point of view, it is at this moment that television becomes for-itself what was in-itself. In this sense, the self-referentiality of neo-television that Eco points out should not be regarded as an innocuous characteristic of the new medium, but rather as a symptom of the medium's achieved, cynical self-consciousness.

Late in his career, Fellini began to manifest overt hostility toward television. A memoir he published in 1980 entitled *Fare un film* clearly voices the attitude. After admitting to some fascination with the potential of television and comparing its mode of perception to the eye of an extraterrestrial creature, he declares in the book his utter disappointment at the medium's banal reality.⁸⁹ A few pages later he declares: "A verdict on my experience in television? In sum, it seems to me disappointing and singularly mediocre."⁹⁰ Having just completed *Block Notes* and *I clowns* for TV, Fellini insists that, though broadcasting may appear to promise a more intimate relationship between director and audience, it finally precludes meaningful communication through its obliteration of the image's religious or sacred aspect.[91] Whereas Fellini regards theater and film as ritualistic forms of art, he evidently condemns television to a permanent lack of aura.

From a technical standpoint, Fellini complains that TV makes no allowance for proper editing and obliges a director to seize the attention of a diffident spectator, to immediately entertain. He protests against the so-called hold-all variety shows that eventually supply the model of the mindless program-within-the-film "We Are Proud to Present" in *Ginger and Fred* and that became ubiquitous in Italy with the privatizing of television:

> Have you ever spent an entire Sunday afternoon in front of the television? Throughout the different shows circulates a willful atmosphere of Sunday relaxation, a petulant, righteous festiveness. . . . Well, all this seems to underline the lugubrious, depressing, hypnotic character typical of a consistent swath of televisual experience. . . . the informative parts alternate, but it would be better to say they transform themselves inadvertently into fashion reviews, variety numbers, the arbitrary appearances of celebrity guests, but above all games of every kind. . . . The visitor sinks into a Sunday afternoon as animated, noisy, and unreal as certain recreational ambiances in mental asylums, hospitals, hospices, places in other worlds where life is interrupted, alienated, decayed, absent.[92]

If Fellini was always something of a "captor of epochs," as Michel Chion has described him, he assumed late in life the riskier role of an outspoken cultural critic.[93] His very project in *Ginger and Fred* of criticizing television, the ubiquitous medium of everyday life, underscores the point. His protests against the television industry generally respond to the specific, and in many ways anomalous, situation of contemporary Italy and avoid any trace of conservative nostalgia for the glories of art cinema. Fellini links the commercial excesses of TV to the hysterical, exhibitionist tendencies of Italian society, thus articulating the question of proper use of the medium in terms of national identity. Behind the glitziness of Italian television shows, he claims to perceive the mental laziness, vulgarity, ignorance, wiliness, and infantilism of a nation that is incapable of growing up politically and that takes an interest only in "funeral rites" masked as entertainment.[94] He discerns the nihilism and exhaustion of a medium that in Italy has become thoroughly implicated in the culture industry. The perception is all the more stirring because some detractors alleged that Fellini's own work belonged to the "symptomatology of Italian hysteria," as Calvino put it.[95] Certainly the director's analysis of Italian culture could not be accused of political or ideological bias. Not only was he never a member of the leftist establishment, but he counted among his intimates the center-right leader and recurrent prime minister, Giulio Andreotti.[96] That Fellini did not belong to the Socialist or Communist Party, however, makes his scathing indictment of Italy's vulgarism all the more startling and persuasive.

As Jacqueline Risset points out, Fellini identified popular engrossment in commercial television programming with obliteration of basic forms of community in Italy.[97] It should come as no surprise, then, that on a professional level his relation to the industry and its increasingly corporate establishment was contentious. Even if Fellini did not like to discuss politics thanks to his reserved temperament, he grew increasingly alarmed at the hegemony of the spectacular in Italy, a phenomenon inextricably entwined with a name Risset claims "he would never forget": Berlusconi.[98] Throughout the 1980s, Fellini waged an often difficult legal and cultural campaign against Berlusconi and summed up his opinion of the magnate's brand of entertainment in an editorial published in the magazine *L'Europeo* on December 7, 1985: "Such TV does not deserve to survive."[99] Precisely because of its direct treatment of the problem of television's role in contemporary culture, *Ginger and Fred* rather than *Amarcord* or *Orchestra Rehearsal* ought to be recognized as Fellini's most political film.[100]

In an interview originally published to accompany the broadcasting of *Ginger and Fred* on the RAI, Fellini comments on the three lawsuits he brought against Berlusconi to thwart the broadcasting of Fellini's films on private television. The director was appalled most of all by the commercial breaks constantly interrupting his work. He concedes in the interview that, despite the victory of the amendment to the Legge Mammì, the loss of the three lawsuits brought under Fellini's own name ultimately resulted in a verdict "sanctifying" Berlusconi's right to hack apart other filmmakers' work according to the imperatives of advertising.[101] In the same interview, Fellini describes a motion picture as something "alive" that ought not to be fragmented by the arbitrary insertion of commercials. Although in this pronouncement he espouses a passé view of the organic nature of art, the director's legal campaign against Berlusconi represents one of the few contemporary examples of an artist or intellectual publicly resisting the principles of the Italian culture industry.

The director in fact represents one of the few thinkers who call attention to the dangers involved in Italy's plunge into spectacular consumerism and nihilism. As unlikely as it might sound at first, Fellini thus may be said in his last film productions to build on the dissident legacy of his famously militant fellow director, Pasolini. Perhaps not coincidentally, Fellini's professed hostility toward the anthropological mutation gripping Italy intensifies after Pasolini's death in 1975. Accordingly, Fellini develops in his later films and writings an increasingly overt critique of Italian mass culture and mediation. He was so successful in the role of provocateur that, at the end of his career, he could not obtain funding for the numerous films he was still planning. Absurdly, he was left with no other choice but to shoot ads for broadcast in order to make money. Fellini's last work behind the cameras was to direct three commercials for the Banco di Roma in 1991.[102]

In an interview with Vincenzo Mollica, the director explains that he had not waged his crusade against ads as such, but against their indiscriminate flooding of the airwaves without any thought for their placement. In fact, he expresses some fascination with the creative possibilities of the form, with its requirement of telling a story in less than a minute. It is interesting to recall in this connection the director's appropriation of what was meant to be the trailer for *8½* as the very conclusion of the film itself. Yet if Fellini may have been interested in the creative possibilities intrinsic to the rapidity and compression of advertisements, he ultimately was suspicious of their fetishized role in the economy of Italian culture. As we have seen, his one legal victory was obtained in working with Veltroni, Moravia, and Mastroianni to amend the Legge Mammí in 1990 so as to limit commercial interruptions of films.[103]

In spite of this victory, however, the director lost the larger war. As he admits in the interview, Berlusconi over the years had become the owner of most of Fellini's cinematic oeuvre. By purchasing the publishing house Rizzoli, Berlusconi acquired the rights to many of the director's most famous films, including *La dolce vita*, *8½*, *I Vitelloni*, and *Juliet of the Spirits*, which was originally produced by Rizzoli. Berlusconi also snapped up the titles of Fellini's own production house, Cineriz, after the company, which the director created in the wake of *La dolce vita*'s success, went bankrupt a number of years later. In a telling verbal slip, Fellini grudgingly concludes in the interview that all his works were in the hands of Berlusconi's holding company Fininvest, which he erroneously calls "Filminvest."[104] The director's symbolic impotence might be considered absolute as he undertook the making of his final and most polemical film, *The Voice of the Moon*, which was produced by Mario and Vittorio Cecchi Gori, but funded by Berlusconi. However, Fellini at least was able, as Burke reports, to get a clause in his contract that prohibited Berlusconi from broadcasting the film on his networks and to insert in the film's poster a caricature of the tycoon.[105]

In a preface to the *Ginger and Fred* screenplay entitled, "Fellini Gets Angry," the director describes the effects of television advertising on the public and the work of art:

The arrogance, the aggression, the massacre of television advertising inserted into a film! It is like violence against a human being: it beats it, wounds it, steals from it.... Whoever performs this violence, in my opinion, ought to be condemned as a highwayman, a thief, a cutthroat. He has committed a horrible, infamous misdeed.... And I do not understand how, before this crime, there arises the indifference not only of the judicial system, but also, in general, of the consumers who witness the damage to their right to watch a film in peace as it has been conceived by its author. Perhaps what is taking place is a sort of habitualization to television advertising, a habitualization consisting of approximation, a lack of attention and of concentration.[106]

Noteworthy in the essay is Fellini's adoption of a key concept from Pasolini, when Fellini charges the publicity machine of mass culture with having precipitated an "anthropological mutation" in the viewer: "The public has changed, has adapted to an anthropological mutation; it does not judge. The inundation of images poured through our homes at every hour of the day has probably given rise to a new spectator: impatient, distracted, capricious, violent."[107] Pasolini originated the phrase "anthropological mutation" in the 1970s to describe the negative linguistic, behavioral, and ethical effects of Italy's so-called economic miracle. In an article first published in *Il Corriere della Sera* on June 10, 1974, under the title "Gli Italiani non sono più quelli" and then collected in the volume *Scritti corsari* under the title "Studio della rivoluzione antropologica in Italia," Pasolini stressed how the values of the middle class had radically and "anthropologically" shifted in the direction of consumerist "ideology" and a modernist "tolerance" of the American type.[108] Ten years after the initial publication of this essay, Fellini in *Ginger and Fred* confronts the fully achieved consolidation of the consumerist ideology first decried by Pasolini. As Tullio Kezich has observed, *Ginger and Fred* can be viewed in a genuine sense as a sustained exploration of the Pasolinian domain of "post-history."[109]

It is highly significant that in the Italy of the 1980s Fellini found in Pasolini's radical criticism the words with which to define the cultural conditions that he faced in his last works. At the end of his career, Fellini shares with Pasolini the heretical conviction that the economic miracle of corporate enterprise, the press, and television has converged in Italy to create arguably the most decadent and baleful configuration of the culture industry in Europe.

Reading Fellini with Lacan

Ginger and Fred recounts the story of two tap dancers, Amelia Bonetti (Giulietta Masina) and Pippo Botticella (Marcello Mastroianni), who are reunited in the 1980s after a hiatus of some twenty years. A television variety show entitled "We Are Proud to Present" has invited the duo to perform their act, which imitates the dancing of Fred Astaire and Ginger Rogers. Fellini caustically and ironically defined *Ginger and Fred* in an interview as "*La dolce vita* twenty years later."[110] What, we may ask, are the real points of comparison between the two films? As in *La dolce vita*, the setting is contemporary Rome and the narrative themes revolve around celebrity culture and the triumph of the simulacrum. As in *La dolce vita*, Mastroianni is the leading man. Here, however, the apparent similarities between the two films come to an end. Whereas the characters of the earlier film seem anxious yet vital in their search for an apt response to the end of an epoch, the protagonists of the later film appear resigned to a spectral afterlife in the postapocalyptic culture of hype and excess that afflicts Italy in the 1980s. Fellini once defined his aim in *La dolce vita* as capturing the decadence of the Roman belle époque in the manner of an accomplice, rather than a judge. *Ginger and Fred* ought to be recognized as the director's unequivocal indictment of contemporary mass culture.

Italy in the 1960s reached a historical conjunction at which its rich, multilayered cultural tradition collided headfirst with the mutated rhythms and spaces of everyday life and the inequitable development of society ensuing from the economic miracle. As Angelo Restivo has observed, the Italian productions of the 1960s make up the national cinema that has been most "visible" in confronting the triumph of late capitalism.[111] Fellini's *Ginger and Fred* may be regarded as the ultimate assessment of the consequences of this triumph. The reunion of the film's main characters, Amelia and Pippo, twenty-odd years after their separation in the 1960s allows the director to register the changes in the national identity over the same period of time.

The film's analysis of capitalism in contemporary Italy centers on two focal points: the peculiar structure of commercial television and the degradation of the urban and suburban space of Rome. In pursuing this argument, Fellini appears to concede that the enlargement of everyday life into a spectacle to which his films famously have contributed may have found its parodic apotheosis in the procedures of commercial TV. Calvino has described Fellini's cinematic oeuvre as one in which the sort of depiction that we usually associate with caricature becomes visionary.[112] In *Ginger and Fred*, however, the director refuses to offer the hoped-for consolation of such a transformation, leaving us to contemplate the bathos of a culture that has become a self-caricature.

Although the film vividly uncovers the hypocrisies of Italian culture, it cannot truly be classified as a satire, if we mean by the term something like what the poet W. H. Auden observed when he declared: "Satire is angry and optimistic; it believes that once people's attention is drawn to some evil, they will mend their ways."[113] *Ginger and Fred* shows no sign of such optimism. To the contrary, it is, along with *The Voice of the Moon*, the most despondent in tone of all of Fellini's works. The director must have known these films would have difficulty finding a receptive audience; his awareness perhaps adds to the air of pathos that pervades the last two productions of his corpus. The film's categorization as satire finds a rationale only in an extremely restrictive sense, if we consider the derivation of the genre's classical Latin name *satura* from the adjective *satur*, which means "full" or "replete" and provides the etymological root for the word "saturate."[114] *Ginger and Fred* certainly can be said to bring to light the conditions of saturation—of ideological distortion and exaggeration—of the contemporary society of spectacle.

Giorgio Agamben has argued that spectacle today represents the extreme form of the expropriation of the common, of the possibility to communicate, and finally of language itself.[115] In his opinion, this is why everything today can be called into question except spectacle.[116] As a work of cinematic art, *Ginger and Fred* demonstrates an arresting readiness to expose, and be exposed to, the brutality of spectacle in the peculiar historical context of contemporary Italy. In his production notes, Fellini indicates an initial plan to include a sequence of iconic images from films such as Chaplin's *City Lights*, Eisenstein's *Potemkin*, and his own *La dolce vita* (specifically, a shot from the Fontana di Trevi scene), which through digital processing he would decompose, disintegrate, and pulverize. His aim was to enact the violence of the society of spectacle, a society that ends up destroying its own masterpieces. Even without this sequence, the film preserves something of the intent.

We may observe how the film elaborates its poetics of exposure to the conditions of late capitalist Italy in Fellini's emphasis on the vulnerability of the aging protagonists, who are forced to "follow the fleet" of spectacle in performing for the variety hour, "We Are Proud to Present." The show's Italian title, "Ed ecco a voi," which literally means "this is for you," encapsulates the passive exposure of the viewer (and, of course, of Amelia and Pippo) to the inanity of commercial television. This poetics can also be discerned in the director's insistence on unveiling "the stupid enjoyment" of advertising, to use a Lacanian phrase. Precisely for this reason, critics who stress the satirical edge of the ersatz television ads in *Ginger and Fred* strike me as misguided. The ads are hardly interesting as examples of Fellini's gift for comic mannerism; instead, they tend to reiterate a simpleminded association of food and sexuality in dully predictable terms.[117] Fellini's point, it seems to me, is to show how, beyond a certain degree of saturation, advertising ceases to be capable of provoking desire and simply reasserts ad nauseam the logic of mindless gratification, of stupid enjoyment.

Moreover, the bogus commercials are not very funny, unless one allows oneself a sardonic smile at, for example, the promotional spot for the fictitious brand of pasta called "Scolamangi," which claims to cause you to lose weight as you're eating it. Such a smile would respond not to the creativity of the mock advertisement's formal presentation, which is not especially remarkable, but rather to the critical point that the ad's outrageous, impossible claim exposes the stupid core of the contemporary Italian publicity machine. In an attempt to discount Fellini's devastating depiction of advertising in *Ginger and Fred*, critics sometimes cite the fact that he himself directed a few commercials toward the end of his career, notably broadcast spots for Barilla, Campari, and Banco di Roma. It is true the director may have taken an interest not only in the narrative and visual possibilities of such a short form, but also, frankly speaking, in the money, since at the time he was having difficulty finding other work. Yet he clearly also was not amused by the sight of Italian society's saturation in advertising, as we know from his own published opinions and his legal battles with Berlusconi. With respect to Fellini's critical outlook, as Peter Bondanella points out, some of the most telling scenes in *Ginger and Fred* take place at the Termini railway station in Rome, where the camera reveals a giant effigy of a *zampone* or pig's trotter filling the entire visible space. In these scenes, which are strategically placed at the beginning and ending of the film, the director starkly shows us that commerce has come to literally, physically saturate the social space of Italy.[118]

Ginger and Fred elaborates its poetics of exposure through the invention of what might be called "neo-Realist" methods of cinematic visualization. On meeting with the conditions of contemporary Italian culture, Fellini's affinity for the spectacular results in a sort of paradoxical, ironic return of neo-Realism. In this instance, however, "the Real" of Felliniesque neo-Realism does not stand for the ideal of a demystifying approach to the social and political realities of postwar Italy, but rather, following Lacan, for the encounter with the domain that resists symbolic meaning.

The screenwriter and theorist Cesare Zavattini defined Italian cinematic neorealism in its classic sense as the "stalking" (pedinamento) of reality that proceeds not as a work of mimesis but as simultaneous exploration and construction of reality.[119] French critics from Bazin to Deleuze insist on the unique ontological project of neorealism as its defining stylistic trait.[120] Indeed, it may well be said that the entire realist aesthetic of cinema established by Bazin is predicated on his thinking about neorealism. For Bazin, the uninterrupted, long take that he identifies as one of neorealism's signal achievements, with particular reference to De Sica's *Umberto D.* (and that is also important, one might add, for Rossellini's *Paisà* and for Visconti's *The Earth Trembles*), guarantees a genuine openness to reality insofar as the interpretive manipulation of the editing process is kept in check. Thus we can say that the political promise of neorealism rests firmly on its ontological openness and fluidity. In the 1940s and early 1950s, neorealism promoted a new, social image and identity in Italy, a nation with a cultural history extending back to classical antiquity, but with a young and uncertain sense of itself as a unified political body that the Risorgimento had done little to strengthen. Appropriating Benedict Anderson's well-known concept, Restivo describes neorealism in terms of its intent to create an emancipatory "imagined community" that would displace the Fascist culture of conformity and aggression.[121]

The movement from neorealism in its classic sense to the neo-Realism exemplified by *Ginger and Fred* indicates Italian cinema's emerging value in the present day as a means of exposing the Real, rather than as a means of presenting an encounter with reality. To speak of the Real, of course, is to refer to one of the three orders of psychic life defined by Jacques Lacan in his psychoanalytic theory, the other two orders being the Imaginary and the Symbolic. According to Malcolm Bowie, the Symbolic, the Imaginary, and the Real are not mental drives but "orders each of which serves to position the individual within a force-field that traverses him."[122] The development of this three-part taxonomy has followed an interesting itinerary, first in the French theorist's own work and then in that of his critical readers. In Lacan's earlier writings, the Symbolic order at first appears to take priority on account of its status as the domain of language, of the unconscious, of the unconscious structured like a language, and of the rules of intersubjectivity. In this phase, the Imaginary seems to fulfill a negative function as the realm of illusionary, frozen, narcissistic identifications. After his structuralist period, Lacan reorganized his theory and assigned to the Real an increasingly important role to play. The Lacanian Real is radically different from the Freudian notion of reality as the locus of external limitations on the workings of the pleasure principle.

It is necessary to keep in mind several definitions of the Real in order to grasp the significance of the concept. First of all, the Real in Lacanian theory is what cannot be symbolized. What this statement means is that, more than comprising the domain of the ineffable, the Real imposes the opaque material presence of an indigestible object or a traumatic encounter on the psyche. As Lacan declares, "The Real is that which always comes back to the same place."[123] In its opposition to psychic representation and imaginative reproduction, the Real may be said to constitute a sort of constant hallucinatory state beyond the grip of interpretation. Another of Lacan's formulations suggestively characterizes the Real as a relentless, ambient noise that is "ready to submerge" the subject in traumatic "outbursts": "For the Real does not wait, and specifically not for the subject, since it expects nothing from the word. But it is there, identical to its existence, a noise in which everything can be heard and ready to submerge in its outbursts what the 'reality principle' constructs within it under the name of the external world."[124] The ambient noise that Lacan describes might remind us of the immanent, inescapable clamor of the society of integrated spectacle, which in Italy's case is epitomized by Berlusconi's brand of advertising-saturated television. Cinema thus may provide the privileged site of a traumatic encounter with the Real. Contemporary viewers expect the medium to perform the task of dynamic imaginative representation, rather than to stage the emergence of a static, inert, opaque presence. In the latter case, film, in its working as a sort of analog for the immanent process of life (to adopt Deleuze's position), mimics the psychic effect of an encounter with the Real, which, first and foremost, is unexpected.

In the context of Fellini's oeuvre, this overturning of expectations is doubly effective. His work represents the cinema par excellence of phenomenologically crystalline encounters with life, encounters that achieve closure through the recurrent ending of his films with the arrival of dawn (e.g., *La strada, The Nights of Cabiria, La dolce vita*), which, after the dream of the film, gently reinserts the viewer into the course of life. He is the director of the most baroquely exuberant cinematic tableaux, staging the Fontana di Trevi sequence of *La dolce vita* in a way that makes the image immediately mythical, memorialized through its very occurrence. To recognize, in addition to all this and at the end of all this, that he is the director who most uncompromisingly confronts the Real of contemporary Italian culture is all the more painful.

The neo-Realist effects that Fellini achieves in *Ginger and Fred* expose the ideology of market-oriented television and the nation's acquiescence to a merely consumerist identity. To understand his critique of mass culture, it is necessary to consider Fellini's sarcastic depiction of Berlusconi in the film. The director repeatedly derides the tycoon's aggressive salesmanship in the person of Fulvio Lombardoni, the fictive media magnate whose name resonates throughout the faux TV advertisements that punctuate the narrative. Of course, Berlusconi's real-life ascent to the position of prime minister has transformed Italy into a nation in which the mass media, and television most of all, play an exceptionally direct role in constructing national identity and political power. Fellini brings to light the consequences of this ideological mutation by examining its reflection in the changed urban and suburban space of Rome. Whereas in *La dolce vita* he presented the dichotomy between Rome's glorious, antique center and its squalid periphery, in *Ginger and Fred* he reduces the "eternal city" to its barren outskirts. It has become a familiar observation that a critical consequence of late capitalism is the eradication of urban topography in favor of a suburban sprawl distinguished only by the venues and signposts of consumerism. Nowhere is this process more vividly exemplified than in the Roman vistas of *Ginger and Fred*.

Ginger and Fred has been defined—accurately, in both cases—as the most and the least Felliniesque of the director's works.[125] It is the most Felliniesque because it represents the culmination of his ability to capture the spectacularism of life. It is the least Felliniesque because it strikes an angry note that clashes with the bittersweet wistfulness of his other features. The director attacks privatized television in *Ginger and Fred* through mocking emphasis on the vulgarism of commercials and the inanity of the hold-all variety program "We Are Proud to Present." Fellini makes repeated use of one figure in particular to highlight the emptiness of the medium, namely the celebrity impersonator or look-alike. Throughout the film, we are presented with a seemingly infinite series of impersonators aping historical personalities such as Clark Gable, the Italian pop singer Celentano, Franz Kafka, Ronald Reagan, and Queen Elizabeth, all of whom have been hired to participate in "We Are Proud to Present." The figure of the look-alike is fascinating to Fellini because it emblemizes the television industry's inability to create: "And this is the question of the impersonators: someone who looks like another, as TV would like to bear a resemblance to the cinema, to the chronicle, to reality."[126] On this score, the director diagnoses the industry's methods of domination as symptoms of what Dienst has called the "programmatic parasitism of television."[127] It should be remembered, however, that Fellini disclaimed any intention of demonizing the medium itself, as he considered television per se to be merely the "mirror" or "reflex" of the collapse of the larger cultural and social system in Italy.[128]

Of course, the director's care to distinguish between the medium and its manipulation by big business did not soften his pessimism regarding the effects of such control. Whereas for a film theorist such as Siegfried Kracauer cinema redeems physical reality by disclosing its uncanniness, corporate television for Fellini seems to work in order to expose the most abject, "Real" underpinnings of so-called reality.[129] According to Lacan, reality achieves consistency when the subject recognizes that the Real, the domain of experience that resists symbolization, coincides with the lack or a priori absence of the object. It is imperative to Lacan's theory that a clear distinction between reality and the Real be always maintained in order to avoid the possibility of an "overflowing" of the Real, of its occupying the imagination with its inert, stupid, material presence.[130] Television in *Ginger and Fred* becomes the ultimate incarnation and presentation of Italian culture as an obscene object of enjoyment. Whereas cinema as a medium still holds the promise of a nonsaturated fantasy space, indeed of a screen for the projection of desires, Italy's advertising-saturated television obstructs any possibility of fantasy through the relentless representation of desire as being already fulfilled.[131]

The *fegatelli*, or snippets of fake advertising scattered throughout the film, repeatedly display sexualized images of food at the moment of its ingestion. These images present the viewer not with a mise-en-scène of desire, but with the obstructing prospect of its perpetual consumption. The polarity that structures *Ginger and Fred*, in other words, is not the dichotomy between cinema as the medium of referentiality and television as that of simulation. It is rather the antagonism between cinema as the locus of fantasy and television as the vehicle for suppressing fantasy by presenting objects of obscene enjoyment. In keeping with a view of television advertising as the traumatic core of mass culture, Fellini repudiates the idea of commercials as benign solicitations of an endless chain of desire. He emphasizes instead their function as illustrations of *realized* desire, a function that hinders or preempts the subject's fantasy life. In contrast, the director's renovation of the cinematic medium in *Ginger and Fred*, which works to maintain the boundary between the Real and reality, seems still to make possible the reproduction of desire as such instead of its "realization" or obliteration.

Fellini's three lawsuits against Berlusconi to prevent the intrusion of commercials into the director's films thus may be seen to affirm a deep-rooted aesthetic and ethical hostility to the techniques of publicity in effect under the postmodern Italian regime. What was at stake for Fellini in the lawsuits may have been more than simply his legal rights as an artist. At stake perhaps was the fact that the fantasy life evoked by Fellini's cinema found itself jeopardized by Italy's increasing conformity to the logic of integrated spectacle. The pertinence of the dialectic between cinema and television in Italy, I have been arguing, has to do not with the ontological distinction between degrees of referentiality, but rather with the place of desire in present-day capitalist society. Whereas cinema, as Fellini presents it, seems potentially to be on the side of fantasy, television is on the side of the Real, which makes up for its lack of symbolic consistency by asserting the inert presence or return of a meaningless object. Even the name *fegatelli*, which translates as "little livers" or "innards," conveys something of the obscenity of the object of publicity. The word hints at the sort of uncomfortable and even disgusting enjoyment generally associated with devouring an animal's entrails.[132]

Fellini argues in *Ginger and Fred* that the rise of Italian commercial TV promotes an unself-conscious culture of narcissism, a space that is all image and no interiority and that corresponds to a mode of desire at once subjectless and lackless. The cinema, even in the form of Hollywood productions such as, say, the musicals of Fred Astaire and Ginger Rogers, encourages a positive desire that originates in loss and lack; television, according to Fellini's view, represents a realm saturated by advertising and the ambient noise of mass culture, a lackless universe in which the subject does not desire so much as renounce any principle of identity per se in a crescendo of nihilism. It is precisely in their acts of nihilistic renunciation that Fellini's "Ginger" and "Fred" resemble two Beckettian clowns lost in a postapocalyptic void to which they barely can respond. That the most flamboyant and visionary Italian filmmaker reaches at the end of his career much the same outlook as Beckett is a sad comment on the mutation of Italian culture from the 1960s to the 1980s.

The narrative of *Ginger and Fred* can be divided into two parts. The first part starts with Amelia's arrival at Rome's Termini train station, recounts her reunion with Pippo, and culminates in their rehearsal for the show. The second part revolves around the live broadcast of the two protagonists' dance act, which is interrupted by a power failure or blackout bringing the show to a temporary standstill, and concludes with their parting at Termini once again. The first section is more caustic and sardonic. The second, as it chronicles the delicate renewal of Amelia's and Pippo's sense of mutual solidarity, is more lyrical. In what follows, I concentrate on two metaphors that are particularly crucial to understanding the relation between the narrative segments: the tap dance and the blackout.

At first glance, we might surmise that Fellini means to highlight the derivative character of Amelia's and Pippo's craft by emphasizing their use of "Ginger" and "Fred" as stage names, their own former celebrity, and their age. On such a view, it might seem that he presents their act as a fetishistic imitation of the extravagant musical numbers in Hollywood movies of the 1930s and 1940s. Yet he rapidly undermines any suggestion that his main characters entertain a fascination with the stardom or cult value of their namesakes. In an early scene at the Hotel Manager, Amelia explains to the assistant director of "We Are Proud to Present" the virtuosic eclecticism of her routine with Pippo, which progresses through a series of diverse styles from tap to flamenco. And in one of Pippo's first demonstrations of his talent, he poetically evokes with his feet the noise of a typewriter and of a train. It is not devotion to the cult of celebrity, then, that moves Amelia and Pippo to imitate the legendary American dance partners, but rather a passion for their art. Unlike the celebrity impersonators whose identity is entirely consumed by their act, Pippo and Amelia preserve a sense of personality distinct from their stage personae. Indeed, Fellini arrestingly employs the motif of tap dance to suggest the conditions not of the spectacular but rather of a painful and political historicity.

The crucial speech concerning tap dance occurs midway through the film and belongs to Pippo. Asked by a journalist to explain the meaning of tap, he initially gropes for something to say and, echoing the lame tagline of an ad for "the *porchetta* Lombardoni," can only mumble that tap dancing is "something more." Yet in the next breath he gains inspiration, enthralling Amelia and the reporter with an impassioned account of the origins of tap dancing:

Tap dancing . . . was the Morse code of the black slaves. A kind of wireless telegraph . . . in the cotton plantations. . . . The black slaves could not talk among themselves, because if they spoke instead of working, the overseer whipped their skin off. . . . So what does the black slave do? He communicates with the comrade of his plight in this way [Mastroianni mimics the dance steps with his fingers]: "Watch out, there is the guard!" . . . "I have a knife." Or rather, "I love you." . . . "And I too."[133]

Tap dance in fact did have its beginnings in the resistance of the slaves to the oppressive censorship of colonial property owners, after the Slave Act of 1740 prohibited drumming.[134] The oppositional value of the art form is what elicits Pippo's admiration and soon does the same for Amelia, who is surprised to discover for the first time the historical significance of tap: "We were tapping together for fifteen years and you never told me anything! But look, Pippo, this is something very important, most beautiful. I have goose bumps, look."[135] It is the one moment in the film when Pippo, who we learn spent a period in a hospital psychiatric ward after the dissolution of his partnership with Amelia, shows something more than a ludicrous, unfocused peevishness toward the world.[136]

Notwithstanding Pippo's erratic manner at other points, it is telling that Fellini positions this quasi-didactic speech at the exact center of his film. The director implies a contrast between contemporary mass entertainment and the almost forgotten idea of an art that is referentially grounded in a particular form of life (slavery) and a specific political project (liberation). He underscores this dichotomy, it seems to me, by calling attention to the belatedness of Pippo's articulation of the meaning of tap dance. That Amelia had no prior hint of the dance's social and cultural importance from her partner despite their fifteen years of performing together indicates that it is only now, as the duo prepare to perform on TV and thus to take center stage in the present-day society of spectacle, that Pippo feels a need to recall publicly the foundation of tap dance as a secret, coded means of communication between slaves. It is another moment at which the film posits a historical caesura, calling our attention to a definite change in the cultural climate. Many critics from Peter Bondanella to Millicent Marcus have stressed the metacinematic nature of *Ginger and Fred*, a film whose two main actors, Masina and Mastroianni, inevitably remind us of the director's past masterpieces such as *La strada* and *8½*. Although Mastroianni sports Fellini's signature porkpie hat in several scenes, the film gives little indication that his character ought to be understood in terms of a directorial identification. Pippo is neither a media careerist who dreams of being an artist as in *La dolce vita* nor a fretful cinematic auteur as in *8½*, but merely an erratic, buffoonish, has-been dancer. Nevertheless, when he delivers his speech about tap dance, Pippo momentarily seems to become Fellini's mouthpiece with respect to his understanding of the social value of art. As his many broadsides against television demonstrate in *Ginger and Fred*, Fellini evidently shares with Pippo a sense that something has gone wrong in the culture at large, necessitating a reminder of art's proper vocation as a work of resistance to the status quo.

Pippo's elucidation of tap dance is important for another reason as well. Many critics, as Marcus points out, have puzzled over the lack of continuity in the film between the scathing denunciation of the mass media and the sentimental story of the two dancers.[137] However, in the discussion of the history of tap the two motifs neatly coincide. The progression of Pippo's examples of tap-encoded statements from threats of violence to declarations of love slyly intimates that during their partnership he was expressing his devotion to Amelia through dance itself. Introduced on his first appearance in the film as a roguish prankster who leaves Amelia in tears by pretending at their reunion not to have recognized her, Pippo succeeds by means of his narrative of slave resistance in acknowledging his feelings for Amelia, in making a "referential" turn toward communication. His speech thus gives the film its center of gravity, a center identified with the act of storytelling. If we grant that Fellini's argument raises a potential analogy between the referentiality of tap dance and that of cinema, we may conclude that he regards the storytelling of the film medium along Benjaminian lines as a way of exchanging wisdom and of confronting real life and thus as opposed to the inane entertainment of commercial television.[138]

Fellini's cinematic enactment of his own oppositional theory, as it is conveyed by the logic of Pippo's speech, occurs through the figure of the blackout. Fellini uses the device as a sort of Brechtian alienation effect that allows both the characters and the spectators to achieve a critical distance before resumption of the narrative action. On the surface, the thought of a filmmaker whose reputation is based on his baroque, mannerist sensibility pursuing such a visually minimalistic and disruptive strategy might seem odd. This change of approach is precisely why *Ginger and Fred* marks a transition point in his career and is important from a symbolic perspective. Fellini appears to propose that the blackout might facilitate the emergence of an auratic space in which reveries, dreams, and fantasies have free reign. Even more importantly, as we will see, the blackouts in the film ultimately enable a critical recognition of mass-produced spectacle as the Real of contemporary social conditions in Italy. The blackouts serve, in other words, the didactic aim of defamiliarizing consumer culture's ubiquitous, inescapable acts of mystification.

The first instance of a blackout takes place in an early scene at the Hotel Manager, while Amelia is conversing with the assistant director of "We Are Proud to Present." In the dim light of candles hurriedly lit by the hotel's staff to remedy a power failure, Amelia proudly shows the distracted assistant director old snapshots of herself and Pippo when they were touring the stages of Italy at the height of their professional success. Here the interruption appears to frame the incongruity of Amelia's emotionally charged reminiscence with the assistant director's worries about production-related practicalities. The second, more important instance arises shortly after the start of the climactic performance on TV of Amelia's and Pippo's dance routine to the strains of "Let's Face the Music and Dance." Fellini enforces the alienation effect of the blackout by cutting to an exterior shot of the now-inert broadcast antenna that rises atop the city's Centro Spaziale Televisivo. This crosscutting between the darkened soundstage and the dead antenna conveys the sense of a spreading apocalypse, a catastrophe not limited to the interior spaces of the television studio, but symbolically extended outward to the cosmos. The most crucial effect of this cataclysmic disruption of the spectacular is to reveal the persistence of the delicate bond that still unites Amelia and Pippo and moves them to resolve, at least momentarily, on running away together. Pippo melodramatically declares that the light has been extinguished forever and, after imagining the blackout as the result of a terrorist attack, comforts himself and Amelia with the thought of the newspaper headlines sensationally celebrating their demise after the event. Even more comforting for Pippo is the illusion that the blackout has restored his capacity for dreaming: "But you know that I do not at all feel bad here? It's like in dreams, far from everything. A place where you don't know where you are, nor how you got there."[139]

It is noteworthy that Fellini, a filmmaker whose main accomplishment may be identified with his ability to evoke the poetic principles of dreams, feels compelled in *Ginger and Fred* to remind us of their necessity. Beguiling use of low-light visuals punctuates many of his works, including *La dolce vita*, where the procession of the Roman aristocrats through the gloomy castle of Bassano di Sutri is one of the most poignant sequences of the film. Whereas in such earlier productions darkness seems to correspond to the phenomenological quest for a dream space, in *Ginger and Fred* it refers to a quest that has become symbolic and polemical in character. The blackout represents an epistemological break that does not arrive at the natural resolution of dawn, as in *La dolce vita*, but rather at the traumatic resumption of the show that must inevitably go on.

The director further accentuates the alienation effect of the blackout by dwelling on his protagonists' ghostly condition. Earlier in the airing of "We Are Proud to Present," a show participant, who claimed to be able to record the voices of the dead, played back an audiotape of a voice allegedly belonging to a deceased spirit. The name of the phantom speaker, we are told, is Pippo. The episode supports the impression that the personages of Pippo and Amelia are more "Real" than "realistic," more like lifeless presences who cannot be assimilated in any way to the prevailing cultural order than vital figures capable of effecting a critical or historical intervention in this order. In fact, not even a sentimental resolution is in the offing for the pair. Although the blackout restores the two main characters' affection for each other, it fails to bring about their romantic rapprochement. Pippo tells Amelia of his time in a psychiatric ward, leading her to assure him that she would have tried to help him if she had known. Yet in the end his laconic summation of their situation remains for both of them the last word on their existential possibilities: "Only these crazy people could have remembered us. We are ghosts that come from darkness and return into darkness."[140]

Fellini's avoidance of a sentimental happy ending has surprised many critics. Throughout the film, the couple's dealings with the TV show producers are punctuated amusingly by the producers' repeated comment that it would be better for the show if the pair were married. That they are not, and will not be, is more than a merely aesthetic act of rebellion on Fellini's part against the conventions of narrative pulp dictated by the marketing of Hollywood and commercial television. Amelia and Pippo are ghostly remnants of an earlier time who, given their historically, culturally, and politically alienated state, cannot afford the luxury of a symbolic resolution.

Here again, I wish to note, it becomes clear to what degree *Ginger and Fred* ought to be regarded as a departure from Fellini's earlier oeuvre. Beginning at least with *La strada*, the director concludes a number of his major works with moments that, if not "happy endings," at least represent a glimmering of epistemological clarity. In the memorable final shot of *The Nights of Cabiria*, Masina's character Cabiria looks hopefully into the camera after having spotted a joyful procession of people in the woods. In *La dolce vita*, Marcello momentarily glimpses a horizon of meaning in the smile of Paola, the young girl at the beach, even if he must finally turn away from her. In *8½*, the visionary, circular dance of the film's characters at the end celebrates the coincidence between the Imaginary and Symbolic orders of creation. In *Ginger and Fred*, however, this moment of "appearance" has become impossible, signaling a radical change in the conditions of twentieth-century Italian culture.

Ginger and Fred thus constitutes an astute artistic meditation on the disappearance, in our world of simulacra, of the very possibility of "appearance itself." Slavoj Žižek explicates this condition: "To put it in Lacanian terms: simulacrum is imaginary [illusion], while appearance is symbolic [fiction]; when the specific dimension of symbolic appearance starts to disintegrate, the Imaginary and the Real become more and more indistinguishable."[141] The concluding shot of Pippo drifting into the nighttime crowd at Termini after having confided to Amelia his deluded ambition of becoming a TV variety show host, while the voiceover of a television ad playing in the train station blares over the soundtrack, beautifully illustrates the conflation in contemporary life of the Imaginary, the space of narcissistic configurations, with the Real, the order that resists symbolization. The disembodied voice of the TV ad with its numbing materialist message promoting Fulvio Lombardoni's products is the film's ultimate moral and heralds the final victory of a Real that no longer functions properly as a whole supporting the symbolic order but has overrun reality to become an all-encompassing negative domain.[142] As I have already mentioned, Fellini's production notes indicate his original plan to apply digital processing to the Fontana di Trevi scene from *La dolce vita* in order to obliterate the image.[143] A central aim of *Ginger and Fred*, in other words, is to explore destruction of the Imaginary, nullification of Symbolic meaning, and the triumph of the Real. Whereas the director sets out in *La dolce vita* to decompose and recompose the image à la Picasso, he clearly shows in *Ginger and Fred* that the project of contemporary cinema contains no *pars construens*. Deconstruction of the visual is no longer a prelude to analytic or synthetic recomposition of the visionary, but the last gasp of a culture drifting toward the blindness of consumerist nihilism.

Undertaking a filmic revision of modernist aesthetics ends for Fellini not with an embrace of a postmodern language, as Burke suggests, but with a new critical mode that, as I have been arguing, ought to be defined as neo-Realist in the sense of establishing a new reality principle for the society of integrated spectacle. That is, the director reexamines the spectacle of contemporary culture no longer from the perspective of creative, imaginative potential but rather with an eye to the paralytic emptiness of commercial mass society in Italy. For an auteur such as Fellini who over the years was accused of having betrayed the mission of neorealism, it must have been an ironic and bitter fate, in the last years of his life, to have assumed the role of the neo-Realist filmmaker of postmodern Italy.

One of his most effective methods in *Ginger and Fred* of calling to our attention the negative effects of the Italian metamorphosis is to visualize Rome no longer as the mythic, symbolic realm of decadence and desire that we know from *La dolce vita*, *Roma*, and *Satyricon* but as a hermeneutically impoverished city that precludes any conception or expression of desire, because it has been saturated by the ideology of the Italian Style, its cliché imagery, and its products. Shot like all the rest of the director's films in Studio 5 of the Cinecittà complex, *Ginger and Fred* boasts only a small number of external scenes, as its story of course revolves around the production of a TV show. When Amelia arrives at Termini station at the beginning of the film, however, and proceeds by bus to the suburban Hotel Manager, Fellini's camera reveals extraordinary vistas of urban dilapidation and debasement. The bus ride itself requires passengers to fight the distraction of the bus's portable TV, which harangues them with commercials and interferes with the reverie of sightseeing. When the passengers do manage to turn their attention to the city, they encounter not the beauty of Rome's antique monuments, but the juxtaposition of garbage on the sidewalk with a streetside poster advertising "Clean Rome."[144] While the bus is on its way to pick up one of the show's guests, Admiral Aulenti, on the Avenue Cristoforo Colombo, Fellini edits together several tracking shots that linger on posters hawking a bizarre panoply of products: grotesquely oversized sandwiches, a pair of shoes whose heels surreally metamorphose into legs, toothpaste squeezed out onto exaggeratedly long tongues. At one point, Amelia's observation of a group of athletes exercising amid garbage and fumes cuts to a close-up of a poster that bears the legend, emblazoned in an enormous typeface, "Elegant Perfume. Italian Style."[145] The streets of Rome are populated in *Ginger and Fred* by vagrants, the homeless, and immigrants all trying to sell the humblest goods, from flowers to cheap cigarette lighters. Amid this scene of poverty and suffering, a transvestite who has accompanied Amelia on the bus gently buys her a bouquet.

With the arrival of the bus at the Hotel Manager, Fellini situates us in the city's nondescript outskirts, the sort of locale he associates in *La dolce vita* with the indignities of the reality principle. He thus makes clear through erasure of Rome's historic urban center from the visual topography of *Ginger and Fred* that the "eternal city" of antiquity and the Renaissance has no place in a capitalist culture reliant on the prefabricated spaces of the suburbs to extend and strengthen the grasp of consumerism. The director's penetrating critique of suburban experience involves a disquieting episode that takes place early in the narrative in an empty lot just outside the Hotel Manager and facing the discotheque Satelit. This genre of deserted, lunar landscape is familiar from a number of Fellini's films such as the barren vistas of *8½* that supply the ideal backdrop and stage set for the director's dreamlike style but makes its appearance in *Ginger and Fred* with a subtle difference. In *8½*, it is just such a space (in which the protagonist, Guido Anselmi, is supposed to begin shooting his latest movie production) that provides the setting for the climactic dance of the film's characters; the empty lot in *Ginger and Fred* near the Centro Spaziale Televisivo instead hints at a certain possibility of violence hidden in the suburban environment.

While the celebrity impersonators drunkenly stumble and sway in the direction of the ramshackle Satelit, a motorcycle gang appears on the scene and ominously circles Amelia, while a drug addict sidles up to her on foot and asks for money. The initial shots in the sequence are filmed in a hallucinatory manner, complete with steam and bluish colors, and might be considered the most classically Felliniesque passage of the entire film. The visuals seem to hover on the brink of the sort of phenomenological transfiguration for which Fellini is famous, a description of life bordering on sweet awareness. Yet Amelia's enchantment at the scene (she herself starts to dance as she watches the impersonators) is suddenly broken by the threat of violence and the traumatic intrusion of the Real of consumer society. In a sense, the sequence represents Fellini's deconstruction of his own penchant for phenomenological reveries. As T. J. Clark has shown, steam offers the modernist tradition with one of its recurrent tropes for the surface of life that is coming into being and so for the freedom of the imagination.[146] Steam thus relates crucially to the possibility of appearance and to modernist epiphanies. The steam that envelops the lunar landscape outside the Satelit, however, is menacing precisely because it is not the prelude to any epiphanic revelation, but merely a kind of index of saturation, a warning that signification itself, the very disclosure of the imaginary, has evaporated, a hint that desire is in the air, but only as the referent of a consumerism that is at once overdetermined and nebulous, mystifying, obscure.

The interior spaces of this suburban culture are not much better than the exterior ones. Fellini's Centro Spaziale Televisivo is a labyrinth of noisy corridors and hallways that culminate in a kitschy round stage with an entrance door composed of multifaceted mirrors and an orchestra in the shape of a musical ideogram. Dante Ferretti's beautiful set designs and Danilo Donati's costumes are glittering, but lugubrious. Even Termini station, the site where the film begins and ends, is revealed by Fellini in a newly bleak light. The old nucleus of the train station dates back to 1864, but the station's modern expansion was initiated in 1925 under the architect Angiolo Mazzoni. Unfinished because of World War Two, Termini's modernization was resumed in 1947, eventually to be completed in 1950 after the Resistenza had infused Italian architecture with new, "neorealist" ideals.[147] In *Ginger and Fred*, Fellini shows us the latest stage in the station's development by detailing the transfiguration of the central piazza through the endless distortions and vandalisms of advertising. At the end of the film, an enormous replica of a pig's trotter grotesquely occupies the center of the station, serving as a Real reminder of the triumph of corporations over society and its public, communal spaces.

Far from encouraging the satisfactions of the pleasure principle, the strategies of advertising in Fellini's film deplete the collective unconscious of all energy, transforming the most "unconscious" city of all, Rome—with its complex architectural layers and architectural condensations—into a Lacanian "Real Space." Although the unconscious, which is structured as a language, may be symbolically efficient and still may have a story to tell, the Real, once it is confused with the imaginary as is increasingly the case in the contemporary culture of simulacra, represents a complete loss of meaning. The bloated pig's trotter inhabiting the Termini station is a token of the Real that, through its opacity and stolid presence, obstructs the restless and suggestive circulation of the imagination, the comings and goings that constitute the genius loci and pleasure principle of a railway station. It is for this reason that Fellini's commencement and conclusion of his film in Termini is so painfully effective. In place of the imaginative promises of train travel, the film shockingly substitutes the symbolic failure of our culture of the Real.

Sweet Criticism

One fact quickly becomes apparent from examining the reception of Fellini's campaign against Berlusconi during the 1980s, a struggle the director waged not only legally but also artistically in both *Ginger and Fred* and *The Voice of the Moon*. Surprisingly few critics are prepared to acknowledge the depth of Fellini's commitment to a melancholic project of revolt against Berlusconi and the cult of Italian consumerism. Only the French critics were ready, when *Ginger and Fred* was first screened at the Palais de Chaillot in Paris, to recognize the film as a polemic against Berlusconi's business practices, which have been almost exclusively responsible for the spectacularizing of contemporary life in Italy. Jean-Paul Aron, for example, perceptively argued in *Il Corriere della Sera* that if Fellini's target in the film is not television, this is not because his real interest resides with the sentimental story of his two protagonists but because in fact he aims at exploring an even more widespread loss of meaning in contemporary culture.[148] By contrast, American and Italian critics have seemed generally embarrassed to admit the political and critical aims of Fellini's last films.

These commentators tend to invoke the reassuring image of the director as an apolitical creative genius who only occasionally indulges a taste for mockery and surely would never be so naïve as to engage, like a contemporary Don Quixote, in a battle against commercial TV or contemporary mass culture. In bringing this chapter to a close, I examine two particular essays on his last films that are symptomatic in their discomfort at the thought of Fellini's hostility toward Berlusconi and in their attempts to downplay that hostility. Tullio Kezich's assessment of the film is exemplary in this regard: "The question of what the film is 'against' is taken up particularly in France, where *Ginger and Fred* is released at the very moment *le Cinq*, the private broadcasting channel of Italian origin that is authorized by the Socialist government and will have a troubled and ephemeral existence, makes its appearance on the scene. But the most intimate substance of the enterprise is elsewhere."[149] Pursuing this line of argument, Kezich insists that the French critics' understanding of the film as an exposé of the "cultural genocide" committed by privatized television was simply motivated by their anxieties about le Cinq and not a genuine response to Fellini's supposedly "obvious" social satire.[150] The Italian critic is also careful to protect Fellini, the creative genius, from any charge of indulging in nostalgia for the golden age of his youth.

Kezich's final suggestion that the film is ultimately a retelling of an elaborate joke, a bet mutually entered into and won by both Pippo and Amelia to survive and even further investigate the world of television, is a mystificatory misreading. In support of his claim, the critic incorrectly cites the "last" scene of the film in which, according to him, "When the time comes to say goodbye, they [the two protagonists] have the pride to have made it and to accept requests for autographs."[151] Kezich conveniently forgets that in fact Fellini's last shot is of a television commercial loudly publicizing the merits of "Mr. Lombardoni's" products to the travelers passing through Termini. Far from being uplifting, the ending of the film is profoundly dispiriting. If in the end the restored mutual trust of the two protagonists is presented in a positive light, any sign that such feelings might lead to practical action is restricted to Amelia, who gives some money to Pippo and invites him to visit. He, on the other hand, pathetically expresses his hunger for pig's trotter as soon as he sees the giant simulacrum in the atrium of Termini and, even more disturbingly, confesses a desire to become a TV show host. Far from being a celebratory moment, the request of passersby for autographs to which Kezich refers only serves to underline ironically the misguidedness of Pippo's professed ambition. A victim of the machine of commercial television, Pippo drifts away at the end into the darkness of Termini in search of a last drink. In his aimlessness and imaginative weakness, he fulfills the image that, as I already have noted, the film proposes of him as a ghost whose voice has been captured by the tape recorder that magically preserves the utterances of the dead.[152]

When *Ginger and Fred* was released in Italy, Umberto Eco was perhaps the only critic to complain about its supposedly unfair portrayal of Italian television. In an article for the weekly *L'Espresso*, he laments the fact that Fellini's image of television has been designed not by Daumier, nor even by Grosz, but by Hieronymus Bosch: "Never mind, television in *Ginger and Fred* is a beautiful piece of grotesque, but goes beyond the satire of customs—and it reaches the point that all the targets of Fellini's discourse will have an easy time to say 'Yes, but we are not really like this.'"[153] That Eco, a key theorist of the postmodern in Italy, did not like the film's attack on Berlusconi-style TV perhaps should not strike us as surprising. He seems to impute to Fellini the sin of taking an "apocalyptic" attitude toward contemporary mass media, rather than being "integrated" in a sophisticated way. It is interesting to notice that, in espousing a balanced view of the postmodern, Eco uses the same adjective—"integrated"—that Debord employs to name an unconstrained form of the society of spectacle. Eco clearly cannot bring himself to admit what, for example, the critic Gualtiero de Santi says of Fellini's film: "Felliniesque irony . . . has eruptions of sulfurous corrosiveness, but hardly reaches the base, horrible level of television programs."[154] What to Eco looks like hyperbole, an "apocalyptic" appraisal of television, looks to another critic like an understatement. Eco's outrage, in other words, may badly miss the mark. Why, we might wonder, does he find it problematic that Fellini's criticism of television in *Ginger and Fred* ventures beyond a simple "satire of customs?" Eco's strange assumption is that a director known for his visionary poetic powers, whose talent for the "grotesque" the critic himself acknowledges, ought to become a sort of comic social realist when it comes to television. Eco thus denies Fellini the authority to criticize the society of spectacle by metaphorical or allegorical means.

Yet the critic's accusation warns us that, applied to the topic of the TV industry, Fellini's stylistic exuberance might be mistaken for a concession to the rhetoric of the televisual. Such an assumption may explain—from a psychological, if not a logical, view—Eco's reproach of the filmmaker, at another point in the review, for having been "excessive." I have suggested already how Fellini's stunning defamiliarization in *Ginger and Fred* of the visual devices through which he depicts in earlier films the historical and epistemological uncertainties of contemporary life—the darkness of the blackout, the steam-shrouded vacancy of the lot outside the Satelit—in fact advances a sharp indictment of Italian mass culture. What I have been calling the film's neo-Realist methods serve to unveil the sleaziness of Berlusconi-style TV and the mystifications of the Italian culture industry in the 1980s. Consequently, one of the most asinine and malignant figures to appear in *Ginger and Fred* is the celebrity *literateur* whom Pippo and Amelia encounter in the Centro Spaziale Televisivo, a parasitic windbag who brags of his political connections, leeringly hits on young women, and ridicules Pippo for his juvenile attempts at rhyme. Fellini takes aim at television in *Ginger and Fred*, but also at a literature and culture whose most public representatives are sycophants. In this sense, Giovanni Grazzini is right to maintain that "*Ginger and Fred* is the best film made so far on the unreality in which we live, as codified by television."[155]

Why is it that, despite the evidence of his lawsuits and films, the critical consensus has refused to admit that Fellini was capable of political criticism and cultural resistance? What is the logic behind repeated denials of the director's final efforts to unmask (albeit in a melancholic register) the hypocrisies of contemporary Italian society? Perhaps one answer may have to do with a certain stereotype of Italy that often extends to its representative artists such as Fellini, namely a simplistic view of the culture as responsive to no principle other than the hedonist philosophy of carpe diem. This cliché probably has been encouraged by the nation's political instability and weak historical identity, to say nothing of a cultural establishment that in recent years has proven one of the most submissive in Europe to the graspings of big business.

An even more important reason might be found in Fellini's function in the economy of Italian culture as the modern-day avatar of the romantic genius. At one level, Fellini has always been characterized as an auteur, a category that in French criticism from the Nouvelle Vague onward connotes the aesthetic, ethical, and political deliberateness of the most serious directors. Fellini, however, would seem to fulfill his function as an auteur only in a curious sense. As Carla Benedetti has argued compellingly, a crucial characteristic of modernity is the obsolescence of the concept of genius and the rise instead of the idea of an author engaged in acts of reflective and conceptual mediation, busy constructing a poetics of conscious, theoretically nuanced choices.[156] Benedetti rightly observes, however, that there remains a need to identify viable spaces for art with an element of unreflective or semiconscious spontaneity.[157] Although in Benedetti's eyes the modernist myth of the death of the author in certain cases clears just such a space, the example of Fellini's critical reputation vividly suggests that, in the Italian context, the idea of "the author" is still compatible with that of unreflective creative genius.

A prominent example of such a view of Fellini is presented by Peter Bondanella, when he asserts, on the topic of the director's attitude toward the advertising business, that "as he was a genius, Fellini perhaps had understood toward the end of his life that a commercial could also be a work of art."[158] What is remarkable about Bondanella's reasoning here is his assumption that the idea of an artistically valid advertisement is so difficult—so profound—as to require the imaginative capacity of a genius and also an entire lifetime's effort of reflection. At any rate, genius for Bondanella manifests itself in embracing the commercial's artistic possibilities without second thoughts, as his insistence on the conclusiveness of Fellini's supposed epiphany makes clear. From such a standpoint, the role of the genius is evidently at odds with that of the critic.

Unlike an auteur of the Nouvelle Vague such as Jean-Luc Godard, Fellini was never regarded as a theoretically systematic artist, but rather as a genius who succeeded in accessing the unconscious mythical types of Italian culture. Fellini's adoration of Carl Jung's theory is well known and an important point to remember, as Jung (unlike Freud) confronts us with the petrified landscape of the archetypal unconscious. In films such as *8½* and *Juliet of the Spirits*, Fellini certainly contributed to the idea of the director as a medium for the unconscious. In *8½*, for example, the character of a medium is the ultimate alter ego for the director himself in the famous Asa-Nisi-Masa sequence, which revolves around an encoded name that clearly points toward the Jungian anima. Once Fellini's outlook grows overtly critical, deliberate, and reflective, it is ignored or denied by the majority of critics. When the director challenges his audience's expectation that he perform as the unconscious chronicler of Italy's late capitalist prosperity, he meets with reactions ranging from irritation to critical deafness and blindness. Yet the fact remains that his late films abandon the project of visual flânerie in favor of bearing witness to their cultural moment.[159]

The angry indictment of Italian society in *Ginger and Fred*, I have been arguing, startlingly yet movingly aligns the film with the Pasolinian ideal of uncompromising cultural criticism. Fellini's late-career masterpiece clearly thematizes the near-impossibility of one's "waking up" in the society of integrated spectacle. The blackout sequence in the film offers the protagonists and the audience a problematic opportunity to step out of the dream and noise of the show. In fact, it may be said that the protagonists do manage momentarily to awaken from the horror of the dream, allowing themselves the painful trauma of an encounter with the Real. In the end, however, the show must go on according to the ruling logic of spectacle, and the lights as a result come back up to restore order. The film's inversion of the metaphorical value conventionally attributed to light and darkness is a measure of Fellini's awareness that daydreaming today has nothing to do with the seductive activities of fantasy and everything to do with a compulsive, hypnotized state of engrossment in the flow of capital.

In its inimitably Felliniesque way, *Ginger and Fred* ultimately enacts what Žižek defines as the fundamental fantasy of mass culture: the return of the living dead.[160] Pippo's description of himself and Amelia as "ghosts" underlines this point. Unable to find their proper place in the text of tradition, Amelia and Pippo hover in that space identified by Lacan in his seminar on *Antigone* as between two deaths: the symbolic and the actual.[161] Symbolically dead, the film's two protagonists can only "follow the fleet" of the spectacular society's desireless drive, albeit succeeding through their spectral reunion in alerting us to a traumatic eruption of the Real out of this very drive. The decisive alienation effect of Fellini's film thus takes place not in the moments of blackout but in the uncovering of the meaningless brutality of experience lived through by the two protagonists. Because "Ginger" and "Fred" are granted neither distance nor refuge from the milieu of their culture, their estrangement paradoxically becomes permanent in its immediacy, their awakening impossible.

2

Lightness

A Lion's Marrow

At the time of his death in 1985, Italo Calvino was rightly regarded as one of the greatest literary figures of his day in Italy. An author and editor with a long record of accomplishments in realist and experimental fiction, journalism, and literary criticism, he received numerous awards during his lifetime, notably the Legion d'onore in 1981. Yet in spite of his well-established curriculum vitae, a peculiar misconception has colored the reception of his writings ever since. For some time, particularly in the United States, Calvino's achievement has been identified almost exclusively with the fabulist narratives he produced over roughly the last two decades of his life, beginning with *Cosmicomics* (1965), works that solidified his fame internationally.[1] Throughout this period, Calvino's fiction propounds an idea of literature as a delightful spectacle elaborated by means of stylistic variation, from the serial travel narratives of *Invisible Cities* to the phenomenological descriptions of *Mr. Palomar*. His critical statements during these years reflect his commitment to defining the boundaries of Italian culture in formalist terms and his uneasiness with the idea of a literature whose aesthetic and political implications are entangled with one another. Responding to this view of the relation between literature and culture, the novelist and critic John Barth identified the symbolic character of Calvino's work as a crucial example of what Barth called the "literature of replenishment," which is to say the postmodern solution to the exhaustion of modernism.[2]

Calvino assumes in his mature essays the manner of what his Italian editor Mario Barenghi describes as a "tourist of culture," authoring numerous diaristic accounts of his travels in Russia, the United States, Japan, Iran, and other nations, writings in which the reader encounters a quasi-semiotic sampling of lifestyles.[3] Calvino similarly manifests his restlessness with respect to contemporary thought by incorporating terms and concepts from whatever disciplines seem to have captured the intellectual spotlight of the moment, whether anthropology, ethnology, or computer science. He describes the intellectual in his essay "Cybernetics and Phantasms" (1967), for example, as a programmer involved in a computational process (*Saggi* I: 204–25).

His last book, *Six Memos for the Next Millennium*, brings together a series of lectures he was preparing to deliver at Harvard but was unable to complete (he died abruptly in September 1985). Each of the five lectures expounds on an artistic virtue that he held to be fundamental: lightness, quickness, exactitude, visibility, multiplicity. A sixth lecture on consistency was planned but never written. The general method of these lectures or "memos" is to oscillate between each assigned ideal and its opposite. Justifying contemporary literature by appeal to this principle of equivocation as well as an impromptu mix of aesthetic, existential, anthropological, and quasi-scientific notions, he winds up advocating a theoretically heterogeneous revision of the principles of modernist art. In the lecture "Lightness," the first value discussed in the book, he exalts literature by likening its function to that of the software that runs computer hardware. Instead of bringing to light the critical value of writing, however, the simile presents literary activity as no more than a faint reflection of "the second industrial revolution," which Calvino observes has reshaped the social order into "a flow of information traveling along circuits in the form of electronic impulses."[4]

Along much the same lines, when extolling the anthropological importance of literature he takes pains to avoid ascribing any subversive potential to mythic or folkloristic forms. His emphasis on the anthropological cannot be aligned with a view of popular culture as a potential means of critique and action, an outlook famously taken by the Marxist philosopher Antonio Gramsci, for instance. After resigning from the PCI, Calvino appeared suspicious of the thought that literary art might address ethical or political considerations. He remained resolute in his vision of the poetic imagination engaged in a quest for a higher epistemological purpose that is identified variously with anthropological or scientific disciplines.

Such a vision, however, begs the question of what is gained by remaking poetry in the image of a more technocratic discipline. What idea of culture, that is to say, does Calvino embrace in his late career? What positive significance do the values espoused in *Six Memos* finally possess?[5] The vast majority of critics have hailed the later Calvino as a writer who avoided ideological prescriptions and resisted the trap of dogmatism, because he understood the impossibility of reconciling a positive political agenda with the artistic demands of fiction.[6] On this view, his tone of intellectual enlightenment—of knowingness—bespeaks a refreshing irreverence toward what he himself at one point dubs "the categorical imperative" of historicist seriousness.[7] (Barth's praise of Calvino as an exemplar of "replenishment" is telling in this regard.) It may be argued instead that Calvino's idea of contemporary culture does not entail any significant break with the legacy of modernism. On this view, he merely repackages certain features of the modernist creed, most notably insistence on the autonomy of the work of high art and allegiance to a cultural canon entirely made up of such works, by identifying these features with popular signifiers such as lightness. This gambit, however, cannot be played in the name of modernism's ideology of the new and avant-garde experimentalism. Calvino's project thus must operate through continuous denial of its nihilist lack of convictions. What he fails to acknowledge is the need for art of the present day to reexamine modernism and its aesthetics with a critical eye.

To understand properly Calvino's mature project, we should keep in mind that his literary career as a whole actually consisted of two distinct phases. The succession of these phases represents a shift from a stance of critical engagement with Italian society during the years immediately following World War Two to an attitude of acceptance during and after the so-called economic miracle of the late 1950s and early 1960s. The first phase of Calvino's professional output runs from 1945 to 1957. Over this interval, he embraces a wide variety of fictive modes ranging from realism to fantasy, in works such as *The Path to the Spiders' Nests* (1947), *The Crow Comes Last* (1949), *The Cloven Viscount* (1951), *Entering the War* (1954), *Italian Folktales* (1956), and *The Baron in the Trees* (1957).[8] At the same time, he publishes an extensive body of essays and articles in the leftist journals *L'Unità*, *Rinascita*, and *Il Contemporaneo*. These early essays read like revolutionary manifestos, declarations of the author's longing for a purposeful social role and eagerness to demystify the workings of history from a politically engaged perspective. In "The Marrow of the Lion" (1955), Calvino fiercely reappropriates as his own credo Gramsci's doctrine of the pessimism of the intelligence and the optimism of the will, concluding that "in every real poetry there exists a lion's marrow, a nutriment for a rigorous morality, for a command of history" (*Saggi* 1: 23–25). In such youthful efforts, Calvino writes in the first-person plural, in the name of a community that, after the experience of World War Two, recognizes the necessity of resistance to intellectual hegemony in Italy.

After the War, the center-right won the political battle and controlled the state apparatus, while the left occupied itself with influencing civil society and cultural issues.[9] Gradually, however, Calvino abandons the first-person plural voice and adopts the first-person singular in his critical prose. Such a change may be understood to signal his withdrawal from the idea of writing as a response to social and ethical questions and his turn to a more solipsistic conception of literary activity.[10] With awareness of the changing Italian cultural and political climate, Calvino in the 1950s and 1960s at first betrays nostalgia for that moment following the end of the War when the nation seemed vigorous and full of hope. In the lecture "Three Currents in Italian Novels of Today," which he read successively at Columbia, Harvard, and Yale in 1959 and 1960, Calvino defends (albeit in a regretful tone) his choice of the fantastic genre as a response to the increasing impossibility of realist fiction in a society of depleted energy: "My first novellas and my first novel dealt with the partisan war: it was a colorful, adventurous world, where tragedy and cheerfulness were blended. The reality around me has never given me again images so full of that energy I like to express . . . and thus I feel the need in my narrative efforts to alternate realistic and fantastic stories" (*Saggi* 1: 73–74). Responding to a questionnaire on the nature of the novel for the journal *Nuovi Argomenti* in 1959, he describes his time as the age of a world without "drive" (spinta), a world in which it is impossible to read in another's story a narrative of general interest, leaving the writer with the option of repeating only what he knows about himself (*Saggi* 1: 1527).

Calvino, however, seems eventually to find consolation in the age he defined as an "unexpected *belle époque*." Although troubled by Italy's consumerist excesses during the economic miracle, he soon comes to renounce the ideal of a literature engaged with current events, which he fears might affirm an anachronistic commitment to dialectical historicism.[11] In "*La belle époque* inaspettata" (1961), Calvino welcomes the possibility of regarding life not as an experience "tense and embattled and thorny," not as an anguished choice between good and evil, but as a spectacle that is "predictable and reassuring" and reveals its every feature for the gratification of the spectator (*Saggi* 1: 91). In an essay composed in 1965 titled "I Will Not Give Breath to My Trumpet Again," Calvino concluded that an age of conviction had ended, precluding the possibility of writing literary works with the intent of changing historical reality or advocating new values (*Saggi* 1: 144). Some ten years later in 1976, Calvino laconically decreed that the idea of man as the subject of history was finished (*Saggi* 1: 352).

As the final articulation of his literary principles, *Six Memos for the Next Millennium* elucidates its author's ambitions in significant ways. We may begin to assess the place of *Six Memos* in both Calvino's oeuvre and the terrain of contemporary Italian culture by contemplating the implications of the book's very title. In 1988, the executors of his estate published the text of the Charles Eliot Norton Lectures in Poetry that Harvard had invited him to deliver in the fall of 1985. Calvino was still completing the lectures at the time of his death on September 19. A prefatory note to the American edition by his widow remarks that he "was delighted by the word 'memos'" and assures the reader that in English the book bears his chosen title. Yet the English term that so enthralled him confronted his executors with a linguistic dilemma regarding the Italian edition. The Devoto-Oli dictionary does not include any cognate whatsoever of the English "memo," admitting no shortened form of the Latin *memorandum* into Italian. Calvino's estate in fact rejected the closest Italian rendering: *Sei promemoria per il prossimo millennio*. An editorial note reveals that the eventual official title, *Lezioni americane. Sei proposte per il prossimo millennio*, reflects Pietro Citati's decision rather than Calvino's own choice.[12] Barenghi explains that Calvino usually referred to his lectures in Italian as *proposte* or proposals (*Saggi* 2: 2965). Barenghi furthermore remarks that Calvino preferred "Six Memos for the Next Millennium" over alternatives such as "Six Literary Values for the Next Millennium" or "Six Legacies for the Next Millennium," because the word *memos* suggested simplicity and "stylistic lowering" (*Saggi* 2: 2965). By bringing to mind the disposable communications involved in mundane corporate and bureaucratic settings, Calvino's favored word choice undercuts the title's ambitious claim to historical importance. The title signals the text's minimalist character, embeddedness in mass society, and unwillingness to assign too much weight to its own message.

According to the *Oxford English Dictionary*, "memo," a shortening of the gerund derived from *memorare*, means "a note of something that is to be remembered, or the record (for future reference) of something that has been done." Calvino's memos indeed dwell between past and future in the sense that they propound his five central values (lightness, quickness, exactitude, visibility, and multiplicity) by drawing examples from the literary canon and urging the reader to follow the lead of these imaginative models.[13] Yet the utterly contemporary term "memo" also conveys the sense of "a record of a commercial transaction," to cite the *OED* again, as well as the particular legal meaning of "a document in which the terms of a transaction or contract are embodied."

Why did Calvino choose for his contribution to the renowned Norton Lectures a title so implicated in the language of commerce and bureaucracy? Charles Stillman, a Harvard alumnus, established the series in honor of the university's first professor of the history of art with the stipulation that the talks celebrate poetic expression, an aim that the bequest states was to be "interpreted broadly" across the fields of literature, music, painting, architecture, etc. Calvino apparently pays homage to this spirit in an early draft of the opening of one of the memos by expressing pride in Italy's tradition of ecumenism with respect to the arts (*Saggi* 2: 2958). Even more tellingly, he writes to instruct himself in the margins of this draft: "In all [the lectures] a reminder of the irreplaceable nature of literature and writing, in a world which will not want to read any longer" (*Saggi* 2: 2961). Evidently, what is at stake in Calvino's memorialization of cultural precedents is nothing less than the survival of literature as such.

It is all the more striking, then, that he identifies his project with a word as unpoetic as memo, a word that pares away the imperative claim of the Latin gerund (*memorandum*: what must be remembered), leaving a signifier that, like a receipt, registers nothing more than the impersonal transactions of market society. The title that Calvino gave the book in this sense emblemizes the disjunction between the commodified language of late capitalism and a humanist mode of thought and speech. If, to an imagination that thrives on qualities such as lightness and quickness, the term *memo* promises the exhilaration of a rapid, efficient communiqué, it also interprets such expression as a function of consumer culture.

Notwithstanding the dire view of the future signaled by his anxious thought of a world that has lost the urge to read, Calvino seems to greet with enthusiasm the challenge of devising a new aesthetics in *Six Memos*. In a brief exordium to the lectures, he declares his intention to avoid speculating on the fate of the written word "in the so-called postindustrial era of technology" and to concentrate instead on his vision of a "future of literature [that] consists in the knowledge that there are things that only literature can give us" (*SM* 1). This insistence on the purity of literature, on its isolation from problematic sociological and political concerns, begs comparison, I think, not only to the Gramscian aspirations of the younger Calvino but to the aims behind Gramsci's own critical undertaking as well. Although he may not have solved the question of the relationship among art, history, and society in Italy, Gramsci clearly established the terms of the inquiry. He frames this investigation most convincingly in his celebrated *Prison Notebooks*, where he places special emphasis on the correspondence between literary culture and national identity. It is particularly noteworthy that in the eighth notebook he underscores both the historicist and the proleptic purposes of his own criticism when he refers to his observations as "*pro-memoria.*"[14]

While carrying out his exploration of the nature and limits of artistic practice, Gramsci eschews any hint of the pedagogical or didactic in order to discern more clearly what the work of art contributes to our inner life. He steers clear of both the narrowness of a stringent Marxist realism à la Lukács and the emptiness of an abstract, aesthetic formalism: "Given the principle that one should look only to the artistic character of the work of art, this does not in the least prevent one from investigating the mass of feelings and the attitude toward life presented in the work of art itself."[15] In a sense, he works to inscribe art and culture in a moral or ideological circle. Observing that it is absurd to speak in a strict sense of fighting for a new art, he states: "One must speak of a struggle for a new culture, that is for a new moral life that cannot but be intimately connected to a new intuition of life."[16] By contrast, Calvino in *Six Memos* never considers the possibility that our changed perceptions of life, which he acknowledges through allusions to technological innovations and mass media, might bring about a changed definition of culture.

Six Memos of course is predicated on a modernist conception of art that regards the artwork as singular, autonomous, and aesthetically self-sufficient. According to this view, there is no need to discuss art's ethical utility, as the lack of connection between politics and aesthetics is a given, a priori rule. Yet even though Calvino may be right to eye with suspicion naïve attempts to equate art and politics, particularly in a literary culture that has witnessed the decline of social realism, he unduly simplifies the author's creative task, altogether neglecting the concerns of ethics, politics, and the politics of aesthetics that together make up the immanent field of forces to which critics respond when speaking of the novel as an inherently democratic genre, for example by virtue of its polyphonic, dialogical structure. Pretending that literature or art does not at any rate uphold its own politics, or to borrow the French critic Jacques Rancière's term metapolitics, Calvino avoids the questions that are most urgent for understanding the role of the work of art in contemporary society.[17] For example, in the memo "Quickness" his endorsement of literary short forms leaves the impression that he is surreptitiously advocating not only what he deems to be the classical measure of the Italian tradition but also his own signature method. In so doing, he fails to give any consideration to the political dimensions and limitations of short fiction, as I will observe later. Indeed, his attempt to establish a hierarchy of forms for our times might itself seem anachronistic and misguided.

Six Memos portrays its five fundamental ideals as eminently literary, while claiming for them an indefinite or hidden existential significance. In his first lecture, Calvino in fact depicts literature "as an existential function, the search for lightness as a reaction to the weight of living" (*SM* 26). However, his existentialism, distanced as it is from historical exigencies, seems curiously abstract. Particularly in the first three memos, "Lightness," "Quickness," and "Exactitude," Calvino defines each quality in relation to its conceptual antithesis (weightiness, slowness, or vagueness), oscillating between extremes without ever arriving at a synthesis.[18] He devises his rhetoric in these lectures to enforce an oxymoronic or paradoxical outlook, according to Alberto Asor Rosa.[19] Embracing simultaneously an exemplary virtue and its dialectical opposite—say, exactitude *and* vagueness—he settles the impasse in every case by defending the advantage of his preferred term on the ground of personal taste.

Of course, one might ascribe his wavering between extremes to a refusal to reduce the complexity of reality to metaphysical absolutes. His approach then might be perceived as a deconstruction of each theoretical value by reading it through its opposite. However, close attention to the memos suggests less a skeptical overturning of ideals than accommodation of incommensurables. On this score, his critical method belongs to a well-established Italian intellectual tradition. According to Massimiliano Biscuso and Franco Gallo, a guiding tenet of Italian culture is the necessity of equilibrium, of mediation between extremes.[20] In keeping with this spirit, Calvino shows less interest in exploring the complex logic of the oxymoron than in achieving a dialectical "happy ending" that harmonizes contraries, as may be observed from his adoption of the Latin dictum *festina lente* ("make haste slowly") as his motto in the lecture on quickness (*SM* 48).

Calvino thus updates for the postmodern epoch what Giulio Bollati has dubbed "the Italian Ideology."[21] According to Bollati, the distinguishing Italian attitude, which can be traced back to the Risorgimento, is the aspiration to make modernity compatible with the values of a backward, agricultural society.[22] This ethos encourages an instinct for compromise, which Cesare Luporini deems responsible for the distorted reception in Italy of Leopardi's anarchic, extremist thought.[23] In the first memo, "Lightness," Calvino's appeal on behalf of an indirect approach to reality may be read as a continuation by other means of precisely this ideology. Indeed, if one were forced to identify a metavalue in *Six Memos*, one might well name the ideal of "balance"; it can hardly be accidental that Calvino positions the memo "Exactitude" at the center of his series of lectures, reinforcing on an architectonic level a sense of logical equanimity.[24]

Following Rancière again, we might say that the fact that we can point to no criteria to establish a correspondence between aesthetic and political values does not therefore mean that art and politics have nothing to do with each other. The horizons in any case meet because every politics has its aesthetics and vice versa. For Rancière, there may be no formula that ensures the result, but there are certainly always choices.[25] For Calvino, by contrast, the moment of choice is perpetually deferred, blurred, ambiguous. Reinforcing the Italian ideology of *medietas* (literally, "middleness" or "moderation") so astutely delineated by Biscuso and Gallo, his memos enforce through their counterbalancing of clashing principles a Manichean understanding of the relation between literature and extraliterary reality, an overly schematic binarism of terms.

Over the course of Calvino's career as a whole, then, a fundamental shift takes place in his reflections on the relationship between literature and politics. In essays from the 1960s such as "Whom Do We Write For?" and "Right and Wrong Political Uses of Literature," though resisting the idea of the natural harmony of the literary and the political he nevertheless still persists in proposing more complex or more oblique correlations between the two domains. He maintains that literature should never voice a truth already possessed by politics, but also that writing cannot limit itself to affirming a mere "assortment of eternal human values."[26] If in his earlier work he assigns literature the pivotal task of giving a voice to "whatever is without a voice," however, he seems to have largely forgotten this task by the time of *Six Memos*.[27]

As Asor Rosa argues, Calvino aims in *Six Memos* to preserve or conserve, rather than question, the past.[28] Reading his ars poetica, we encounter references to more than ninety artists, a roll call that is almost exclusively European and, with the exceptions only of Emily Dickinson and Marianne Moore, entirely male. These figures represent Calvino's ideal of a cosmopolitan intellectual community, from whose accomplishments he aims to extrapolate a *mathesis universalis* for the literature of the next millennium. The principle of cosmopolitanism in fact is a longstanding theme of his critical writing. In an essay published in *Il Contemporaneo* in 1956, he attacks the supposed anticosmopolitanism behind Gramsci's idea of the "nazional-popolare." Maintaining that the "reactionary habit of peasant self-indulgence" (*Saggi* 2: 2186) needs no encouragement in Italy, Calvino reaches an alarming conclusion: "It will be a matter of a few years, but we must bet on a panorama of Italian culture in which the North is going to count more, in which the internationalist *forma mentis* will arrive to dominate all our actions and thoughts" (*Saggi* 2: 2187). Although he wrote these words in 1956, his antipathy toward the notion of the national-popular seems to resonate in the image of literary culture set forth in *Six Memos*. For the most part, the exemplars of literary achievement that he names in his final treatise belong to earlier generations and evince his attachment to an idea of the canon that largely overlooks women and allows consideration of non-Western cultures only in the aestheticized mode popularized by Roland Barthes in *Empire of Signs*.[29] Calvino only briefly praises Dickinson for her lightness of tone (*SM* 16) and Moore for her exactitude in describing animals (*SM* 75). Whereas Beckett, Borges, Gadda,

Joyce, Leopardi, Montale, Musil, Proust, and various other men constitute the general artistic paradigm, Dickinson and Moore function as decorative exceptions.

As expressed in *Six Memos*, Calvino's interest in women's cultural roles is limited to the anthropological importance of the figure of the witch. In "Lightness," he writes:

> In order to move onto existential ground, I have to think of literature as extended to anthropology and ethnology and mythology. Faced with the precarious existence of tribal life—drought, sickness, evil influences—the shaman responded by . . . flying to . . . another level of perception, where he could find the strength to change the face of reality. In centuries and civilizations closer to us, in villages where the women bore most of the weight of a constricted life, witches flew by night on broomsticks or even on lighter vehicles such as ears of wheat or pieces of straw. . . . I find it a steady feature in anthropology, this link between the levitation desired and the privation actually suffered [*SM* 27].

Despite his admission that in the recent past women "bore most of the weight of a constricted life," he fails to consider how women artists and thinkers have responded to the burdens that patriarchal society has imposed on them specifically *as* women. He instead takes the heretical female figure of the witch as a sign of a generalized anthropological impulse to counteract the suffering of material "privation." When it comes to non-Western cultures, Calvino unapologetically affirms in the exordium that "the millennium about to end has seen the birth and development of the modern languages of the West, and of the literatures that have explored the expressive, cognitive, and imaginative possibilities of these languages" (*SM* 1). By repeated appeals to universal anthropological criteria and the formal complexity of Western literature, he consistently dodges the most pressing ethical questions concerning contemporary art and culture, particularly with regard to the status of women and non-Western communities.

In his final lecture, Calvino declares that this end-of-millennium reality revolves around the phenomenon of multiplicity: "Knowledge as multiplicity is the thread that binds together the major works both of what is called modernism and of what goes by the name of the *postmodern*, a thread—over and above all the labels attached to it—that I hope will continue in the next millennium" (*SM* 116). What exactly, we might ask, does this condition signify to Calvino? He declares his intent "to show that in our own times literature is attempting to realize . . . [an] ancient desire to represent the multiplicity of relationships" (*SM* 112) and seemingly aligns this task with the larger goal in *Six Memos* of highlighting literature's existential and anthropological dimensions. The relationships that seize his imagination, however, are formal or material rather than social or political relations; he sharply sympathizes, for example, with Perec's "passion for catalogues, for the enumeration of objects . . . a passion extending to menus, concert programs, diet charts, bibliographies real or imaginary" (*SM* 122). Moreover, his insistence on the "ancient" nature of his fascination reveals a need to legitimate his own "postmodern" poetics by directly tracing its heredity back to a classical point of origin (he thus concludes the book by invoking Ovid and Lucretius). Clearly, multiplicity has nothing to do with the thoughts and histories of those who stand outside the patriarchal Western tradition or who fail to abide by its decorum. To the contrary, Calvino equates the ideal with an archival or encyclopedic reification of this tradition: "Each life is an encyclopedia, a library, an inventory of objects, a series of styles, and everything that can be constantly shuffled and reordered in every way conceivable" (*SM* 124). The reduction of life to "an inventory of objects," the flattening of subjective experience into an encyclopedia's documentary information, and the dissolution of justice and injustice into "a series of styles" dismayingly suggest the terms under which contemporary consumerism operates.

It might be said that Calvino's concept of postmodernity is "inhuman," although not in Lyotard's sense of the sublime challenge confronted by the artist when reason cannot contain the imaginative drive. It is inhuman in the sense that it represents Calvino's strategy for evading the demands of ethics and emotion.[30] *Six Memos for the Next Millennium*, it seems to me, is Calvino's most important and most tragic book not because it is his last, but because his theoretical attempt to outline the future of literature advances in the direction of a weak, nihilistic, and conservative formalism. Such a position, in Carla Benedetti's opinion, is specific to the Italian intellectual milieu. In *Pasolini contro Calvino*, Benedetti contrasts the American strain of literary postmodernism to its Italian counterpart, which she ironically labels "il postmoderno nazionale."[31] According to Benedetti's typology, Calvino furnishes a prime example of a "weakened" postmodernism inasmuch as he focuses narrowly on the stylistic qualities of the artwork and forgoes critical engagement with social realities. By contrast, American writers such as Thomas Pynchon and Donald

Barthelme create metropolitan fictions that, unlike the works of their Italian peers, are able to confront directly the "semiotic disorder" of changing urban populations and historical catastrophes:

Postmodern literature in Italy has not had the same capacity to relate to contemporary life in its most alienating negative effects. For us what seems more established is the other soul of postmodernity, which is ironic-necrophiliac, revolving around the self-reflexive mechanisms of writing, capable of constructing fictional or metafictional spaces, but enclosed in an intertextual labyrinth, in a space sometimes melancholic, sometimes euphoric, but at any rate reassuring of an entirely literary world.[32]

It is noteworthy that in an article of 1962, "I beatniks e il sistema," Calvino proudly applauds Italy's repudiation of beatnik culture and acceptance of corporate industry, circumstances that translate into a literature that is "poor in rebels" (povera di ribelli; *Saggi* 1: 99–100). Calvino offers in this essay an interpretive key to understanding the genealogy of Italy's toothless, conformist brand of mass culture, a mentality that decades later will find in *Six Memos* one of its most acute expressions.

Antonio Moresco has rightly characterized *Six Memos for the Next Millennium* as a sort of postmodern rewriting of Giovanni Della Casa's sixteenth-century primer on manners, *Galateo* (1558).[33] As I have noted already, Calvino proclaims from the outset his reluctance to address questions regarding the fate of literature under the spectacularized conditions of late capitalism. Like the privileged Della Casa, Calvino instead devotes his attention to issues of artistic propriety or etiquette. In place of the ideals of traditional, neo-Platonic aesthetics such as beauty, integrity, harmony, and purity, he devises a list of contemporary virtues that appear calculated to give an impression of virtually mediated exhilaration. Yet the question remains whether such exhilaration, as he conceives it, has any positive ethical meaning, whether his privileged signifiers possess any urgency. Certainly, his postmodernism runs deeper than infatuation with the literary methods of pastiche, stylistic contamination and amalgamation, and mock-historical commentary that inform his most popular works, from *Invisible Cities* to *If on a Winter's Night a Traveler*. As evinced by his final book, Calvino's affinity for the spectacularism of mass mediation manifests itself in the form of what Moresco has dubbed the author's "publicist imagination."[34] In the memo "Visibility," for example, he proposes a new way of reading based on his "favorite [childhood] occupation of daydreaming *within* the pictures [of comic strips]" without paying attention to the words, a habit that amounted to "a schooling in fablemaking, in stylization, in the composition of the image" (*SM* 94). This odd suggestion of a hermeneutics rooted in fantasy and unconcerned with meaning might well be said to consort with the basic assumptions and procedures of advertising.[35]

Working from the beginning of his career for the publisher Einaudi, Calvino reacted to growing historical and cultural disillusionment in Italy during the 1960s by embracing the mode of thinking of the culture industry. At the end of his life, he winds up in *Six Memos* composing an ostensibly general theory of literature that promotes his style of writing without always fully acknowledging such an aim. It is true that Calvino makes room among the numerous writers he evokes in the book for those who seem alien to his approach, such as Gadda and Musil. At strategic junctures, however, his most crucial examples are dutifully, as Moresco puts it, "calvinized."[36]

In this light, we can more fully comprehend Calvino's self-approving insistence on the superiority of short narrative forms, which in a fit of hyperbole he labels the "true vocation of Italian literature" (*SM* 49). Although the Italian tradition is doubtless crowded with lyric poets and writers of short stories and aphorisms, we might ask whether we ought to greet with approval the relative paucity of great novelists as Calvino does.[37] For one thing, his selective reading of this tradition ignores the novel's potential importance in rousing the political consciousness of the bourgeoisie. What he takes to be Italian literature's proper orientation arises from unfavorable historical conditions that since the early nineteenth century have kept Italy at the margins of the great bourgeois creative process. It is thus perhaps appropriate that the most egregious case in *Six Memos* of the calvinizing of another author takes place in the commentary on the work of the nineteenth-century poet and philosopher Giacomo Leopardi.

In his *Discourse on the Present State of the Customs of the Italians* (1824), Leopardi laments the absence in Italy of social discourses, moral habits, and a "truly modern national literature" of sufficient vitality to encourage a strong national character.[38] Contemplating the comparative modernity of various European nations, Leopardi puts Italy in last place and bitterly observes that "strolling, shows, and churches are the principal occasions of social interaction that Italians have."[39] Whereas in other European societies the novel becomes an established genre after the sixteenth century, a division occurs in Italy between intellectuals and the general populace that encumbers the development of what Gramsci will refer to as the "national-popular" genre, hence of the novel.[40] In his acute analysis of the absence of popular forms in Italy, Gramsci assigns a special value to novels (particularly to serial novels), which he regards as the main vehicles of literature's national-popular character. Unlike Calvino, he regards the predominance of short forms in Italian literature not as an indication of a poetic *telos*, but rather as the symptom of a fundamental separation in the society between writers and the public.[41]

In an essay titled "The Lost Fortune of the Italian Novel" (1953), Calvino nominates Leopardi as the father of the ideal Italian novel on account of the predilection he demonstrates in *Operette morali* for the stories of adventurers (as in the dialogues between Nature and an Icelander and between Christopher Columbus and Pedro Gutierrez), for his psychological finesse, and for his linguistic ability (*Saggi* 1: 1508). Significantly, Calvino omits any mention of the quality that would have made Leopardi the ideal moral artist: his relentless critical attention to social and ethical contradictions. As Camus has argued, the novel may be said to exude a spirit of rebellion, a spirit that it translates onto the level of aesthetics.[42] Unlike the mythic culture of classical antiquity, which produces a predominantly fantastic literature, modernity in Camus's eyes establishes an inherently critical narrative mode with the invention of the novel. Responding to a precise set of adverse historical, political, and sociological circumstances, Italian literature's investment in the short form betrays its fundamental acquiescence when it comes to the problematic struggles of modernity.

Calvino's attachment to the short story, it seems to me, cannot be treated along Benjaminian lines as a nostalgic homage to storytelling that responds to the extinguished possibility of transmitting wisdom or experience. Calvino (who does not quote Benjamin in the final version of *Six Memos*) originally reserved space for the German critic in the first draft of the first memo, a draft titled "Cominciare e finire" that since has been published as an appendix to the book. In this early version, Calvino stresses Benjamin's ideas with respect to the role of the commercial classes in diffusing and consolidating the art of storytelling.[43] Yet we ought to remember that from this observation Benjamin himself makes a further point regarding the social value of storytelling: "An orientation toward practical interests is characteristic of many born storytellers. . . . [Every real story] contains, openly or covertly, something useful. In one case, the usefulness may lie in a moral; in another, in some practical advice; in a third, in a proverb or maxim. In every case the storyteller is a man who has counsel for his readers."[44] Whereas Benjamin wishes to point out the potential benefits of storytelling as moral argument, Calvino reframes the topic with an exclusive eye to the anthropological and sociological place of the merchant and trade classes. (Benjamin ultimately places the emphasis in his analysis on exchange of experiences between "much-traveled" men, rather than on merchants per se.[45]) Calvino proceeds in the draft memo to describe the "narrative community" in Boccaccio's *Decameron* as "a perfect market in which everybody gains some profit" (*Saggi* 1: 745). What is used for capital and what regulates a transaction in this "perfect market," however, remains obscure. Whereas Benjamin describes the utility of storytelling as unveiling the "epic side of truth, [which is] wisdom," Calvino's "profit" is a blurred image.[46] He nonetheless persists in using financial metaphors to elaborate his poetics in this initial draft, at one point presenting storytelling as a process of "bargaining" (mercanteggiare).

One of the most difficult things to do when it comes to *Six Memos* is to describe the tone of the lectures. Are they optimistic, pessimistic, or a complex mélange in the Gramscian tradition of pessimism and optimism? Although the cheerful associations surrounding Calvino's values at first glance might seem to betoken a stance of historical optimism, a dire undercurrent runs beneath the rhetorical surface of the memos and insinuates an ominous sense of disproportion between the goodness of the values and the badness of the world. Calvino voices this anxiety most vividly in the memo "Exactitude":

It sometimes seems to me that a pestilence has struck the human race in its most distinctive faculty—that is, the use of words. It is a plague afflicting language, revealing itself as a loss of cognition and immediacy, an automatism that tends to level out all expression into the most generic, anonymous, and abstract formulas, to dilute meanings, to blunt the edge of expressiveness, extinguishing the spark that shoots out from the collision of words and new circumstances [*SM* 56].

Astonishingly, in the next sentence he announces that "I don't wish to dwell on the possible sources of this epidemic" in politics, mass media, education, or any other domain. Instead, he simply asserts the conviction that "literature, and perhaps literature alone, can create the antibodies to fight this plague in language" (*SM* 56). Yet, to sustain the figure, one might well demand how Calvino can prescribe a remedy for such a menace without any diagnosis of the condition. His perplexing refusal to confront the reasons of the present crisis in language gives an impression of thorough, if unacknowledged, nihilism.

Calvino's weak postmodernism is indeed often indistinguishable from nihilism. It is no accident that, in one of the manuscript drafts of *Six Memos*, he inscribed as a marginal addendum to a list of the lecture topics, next to exactitude and visibility, the question, "And nothingness?" (*Saggi* II: 2964).[47] To ascribe to Calvino a nihilistic outlook might bolster the comparison to Leopardi, who is often hailed as the archetypal Italian nihilist owing to his philosophical materialism and sensism, his distrust of religion, and his poetic tendency to metaphysical vagueness as exemplified by his most famous lyric, "The Infinite." On a closer look, however, the two writers' strains of nihilism betoken dissimilar, even antithetical, perspectives. Whereas Leopardi's despondency results in biting analysis of the failings of Italian culture, Calvino's ensues in facile, anxious, and reactionary dismissal of such failings ("I don't wish to dwell on the possible sources of this epidemic"). An extended comparison of the *Operette morali* and *Six Memos for the Next Millennium* will help us bring to light the nature and scope of Calvino's project.

Operette and Memos

Calvino declares in a letter written in 1984 that Leopardi's *Operette morali* is the book from which he derives everything he writes (*Saggi* I: xlviii).[48] Asor Rosa has identified Leopardi more particularly as the central figure behind *Six Memos*, a work that he labels the "*Operette morali* of the twentieth century."[49] Yet Leopardi's importance for Calvino is more evident as a function of what the later writer rejects from his predecessor's example than of what he absorbs. The most basic distinction between the two authors is that, unlike Calvino, Leopardi represents a central figure in the Italian moralist tradition. He was a literary artist who strove to bring about the coincidence of poetry and moral philosophy. Luporini has described Leopardi as the sort of thinker who, rather than identifying philosophy's primary task with methodological developments within metaphysics, science, or epistemology after the Renaissance, sees this task as articulating an optimistic or pessimistic vision of the world in relation to specific human experiences.[50]

Written from 1824 to 1832, the *Operette morali* consist of essays and dialogues in the mode of "satiric prose shorts," as Leopardi put it in a letter to his friend Pietro Giordani, and are devised to exact revenge on the world.[51] In these texts, the poet highlights the themes of human unhappiness, the decadence of civilization, the nihilistic effects of fashion and fashionable ways of thinking, and the disparity between man and nature. Throughout the *Operette*, Leopardi is relentlessly aggressive and sarcastic, intent on showing an admiration for the Enlightenment compatible with an attitude other than reflexive optimism. As their title and Leopardi's comment to Giordani suggest, the *Operette* reside in a space of ethical travails, of discomfort, hence of satire. Not only does the formulation ironically intimate through the diminutive form a certain chagrin regarding the utility of such literary works, but through the plural it also subtly implies the disunity of moral codes that they uphold. In a passage of the *Zibaldone* written on July 27, 1821, Leopardi explains the importance of his effort to sustain a satirical tone in his writing: "In my dialogues, I'll try to bring comedy to what until now belonged to tragedy . . . and I believe that the weapons of ridicule, which are greatest in this very ridiculous and cold century, and also for their natural strength, may be more useful than those of passion, of affection, of the imagination, of eloquence."[52] By labeling his works *operette*, Leopardi underscores their scandalousness in affirming the virtues of materialism, atheism, and antimythologism in the Italian context. On this score, the distance between Leopardi's *operette* and Calvino's memos may be seen to summarize all the difference between their respective notions of "lightness."

Whereas Calvino fetishizes lightness as a source of aesthetic and existential delight, Leopardi treats the imagery of lightness as a means of representing human absurdity or foolishness. It is precisely by means of such imagery that one of the first of the *prosette* ridicules the self-congratulatory notion of historical progress and repudiates a heroic view of modernity. In the "Dialogue Between Hercules and Atlas," Atlas is ordered by Jove to hold up the earth, but this load turns out to be so inconsequential that Hercules proposes to toy with it as if it were a balloon. Yet instead of providing an occasion for pleasure, the lightness of the burden gives reason for alarm insofar as it signals a decline from the prior substantiality of human labor and existence. For this reason, Hercules fears that while playing with the world he will "crack it like an egg since its shell feels so light that it must have become quite thin."[53]

According to Novella Celli Bellucci, a curiously ideological use of Leopardi has been a defining characteristic of modern Italian criticism.[54] The tendency from Francesco De Sanctis to Benedetto Croce and numerous other contemporary commentators has been to repress the challenging aspects of Leopardi's thought, his materialism and atheism, in order to foster his reputation as a lyric poet of interiority.[55] While praising him as a lyricist, for example, Croce condemns him as a philosopher on account of his pessimism, which supposedly arises from unreliable passion rather than from trustworthy reflection.[56] In the period since the end of World War Two, however, there are some signs of dissent from the prevailing reading of Leopardi. Critics such as Luporini and Walter Binni have reacted against Croce's dismissal of Leopardi's philosophical achievements.[57] These later readers emphasize a more comprehensive view of Leopardi as an exemplary civic poet and thinker not just for Italy but for all of Europe. More recently still, Luporini's and Binni's deviations from the critical consensus have been importantly extended and revised by Antonio Negri in *Lenta ginestra* and Massimiliano Biscuso and Franco Gallo in *Leopardi antitaliano*. Negri, for example, downplays the "progressive" side of Leopardi's work on which Luporini dwells, because the description implies a dialectical movement, a sublation, that is incompatible with Leopardi's fundamentally anti-idealist, antihistoricist position.[58] Rather than read Leopardi's works in a Heideggerian vein as Antonio Prete has done in *Il pensiero poetante*, Negri and Biscuso and Gallo, although adopting altogether different tones, have focused on the ethical, civic, and—in Negri's eyes, at least—revolutionary meaning of the poet's thinking.

One might say casually that Calvino shares with Leopardi a basic affinity for the achievements of the Enlightenment.[59] Yet they remain fundamentally at odds regarding the continuing significance of such achievements. Leopardi is a direct descendent of eighteenth-century rationalists and sensists, and as well a follower of such seventeenth-century moralists as La Rochefoucauld. His primary interest in the Enlightenment in fact focuses on the example of the moralists, on reviving their effort to ascertain the best conditions for the common good. He has less sympathy for the sort of Enlightenment metaphysics professed by Leibniz that idealizes an abstract notion of cosmic harmony and more for the kind of social and skeptical critique performed by Voltaire. Like Voltaire, Leopardi devotes his attention to the vicissitudes of history and human suffering. Calvino, it should be noted, was well aware of Leopardi's position in this regard. He mentions in one of the drafts of "Lightness" his intent to compare Candide to Leopardi's "Icelander" as figures who are both spectators to and victims of the endless catastrophe of nature and human history (*Saggi* 2: 2971). The celebrated "Dialogue Between Nature and an Icelander" in the *Operette morali* recounts the death of a courageous Icelandic explorer at the hands of a hostile and infinitely resourceful nature that, by burying the explorer in a fierce desert sandstorm, transforms him into a mummy (*OM* 199).

Although fascinated by the Enlightenment, Leopardi never accepts its faith in progress, which he notably derides in his poem "The Broom" as "that magnificent, progressive destiny of humankind." Far from enforcing a trust in reason as such, Leopardi's historical perspective presupposes the courage to criticize failed or bad attempts to rationalize society, as befits an artist and critical thinker looking back on the aftermath of the French Revolution. His detachment from any perfectionist or optimist rhetoric stems from a wariness regarding the problem of revolution.[60] Moreover, his interest in the Enlightenment is dominated, as Luporini suggests, by an inclination to interpret all political questions in terms of public interest, or to be more precise, in terms of equality.[61]

One of the merits of critics such as Luporini who take Leopardi seriously as a thinker is to have recognized the continuing importance of his polemic against the instrumentality of reason, an argument that may be said to anticipate in crucial respects the analysis of culture developed by members of the Frankfurt School, particularly Adorno and Max Horkheimer in *Dialectic of Enlightenment*.[62] On this score, Guido Guglielmi has also shed light on the cogency and depth of Leopardi's criticism of modernity. Leopardi, according to Guglielmi, sees the aporia of modernity but does not try to furnish a dialectical resolution.[63] Guglielmi keenly observes the significance of Leopardi's distrust of speed and quickness, as expressed in the *Zibaldone* or in the "Dialogue Between Fashion and Death" in *Operette morali*.[64] Construing the speed that has come to be characteristic of modernity as the accelerating rhythm of an impetus toward death, Leopardi, in contrast to Baudelaire in the nineteenth century and Calvino in the twentieth, consistently exposes the "lack of poetry in the modern world" that is the poet's great historical intuition.[65] Fittingly, Guglielmi characterizes Leopardi as a "poet of protest, not of self-limitation."[66]

By contrast, Calvino's attachment to the Enlightenment ideal is stylistic and aesthetic in concern rather than moral and political. Reversing Guglielmi's formula, we might perceive Calvino in this light as a poet of self-limitation, not of protest. Evoking such neoclassical principles as "geometry" and "lucidity" from the start of his career, he repudiates the visceral tendencies of avant-garde art (such as what Pollock or Pasolini exemplifies), opposing these impulses in an essay titled "Challenge to the Labyrinth" to the rationalist, abstract inclinations of contemporary artistic experimentation with which he feels more comfortable (*Saggi* 1: 116). For him, the Enlightenment affords the order and optimism that permit him to negotiate the chaotic labyrinth of culture and repudiate the pessimism of those artists and intellectuals whom he defines in 1962 as "the 'Lent keepers' of mass culture" (*Saggi* 1: 106). He never acknowledges the contortions and disappointments of historical reason as Leopardi does; consequently, his allegiance to the past is in this specific sense less compromised, more innocent. It is telling that in a pair of interviews of 1968 collected under the title "Two Interviews on Science and Literature," Calvino takes pains to distance himself from Adorno's and Horkheimer's *Dialectic of Enlightenment*, which he criticizes for being in his opinion too simplistic (*Saggi* 1: 235).

Calvino's readings of Leopardi tend to avoid the myth of the grave, pessimistic poet. He refashions Leopardi instead in the image of an "idyllic" thinker whose principal accomplishment was to perfect a lighthearted and accurate style of writing. Like most mainstream Italian critics from De Sanctis onward, he thus represses Leopardi's significant and incisive work as a cultural critic and moral philosopher. We may begin to gauge the degree to which Calvino refuses to recognize this side of his predecessor if we return to *Six Memos*, where he discusses the poet's work prominently in the first three lectures. In "Lightness," for example, he praises Leopardi's poetry for its verbal poise and agility, for, as he puts it, removing the weight from language "to the point that it resembles moonlight" (*SM* 24). Even when Leopardi articulates "the unbearable weight of living," Calvino alleges, he does so through buoyant images of "the happiness he thinks we can never attain" (*SM* 24).

This contrary reading of the poet culminates in "Exactitude," where Calvino concludes that his argument in favor of clarity and precision is ultimately supported by Leopardi, after originally having invoked him, on the basis of a passage in the *Zibaldone*, as a proponent of such antithetical, sublime qualities as vagueness, obscurity, and profundity:

So this is what Leopardi asks of us, that we may savor the beauty of the vague and indefinite! What he requires is a highly exact and meticulous attention to the composition of each image, to the minute definition of details, to the choice of objects, to the lighting and atmosphere, all in order to attain the desired degree of vagueness. Therefore Leopardi, whom I had chosen as the ideal opponent of my argument in favor of exactitude, turns out to be a decisive witness in its favor. . . . The poet of vagueness can only be the poet of exactitude [*SM* 60].

Calvino thus transforms the poet whose most celebrated lyric bears the title "The Infinite" into the poet of "the indefinite," an ideal that supposedly spurs Leopardi to "observation of all that is multiple, teeming, composed of countless particles" (*SM* 60). Ignoring the possible ethical and religious connotations of the concept of infinity, Calvino projects onto Leopardi his own preference for an "extensive" or objective indefinite, for an idea of literature aimed at reproducing the minutiae of "sensations as they mingle together and create an impression of infinite space, illusory but pleasurable all the same" (*SM* 63).[67] Yet an attentive reading of "The Infinite" quickly casts doubt on such an approach to the poet. The very last lines, "In that immensity my thought is drowned / And sweet to me is the foundering of that sea" (Così tra questa immensità s'annega il pensier mio: / e il naufragar m'è dolce in questo mare), hinge on the verbs "foundering" (naufragare) and "drowned" (s'annegare), indicating the poet's self-abandonment to what ultimately has the look of an "intensive" or subjective reverie rather than an extensive event.[68]

Taken together, the *Operette morali* and the *Discourse on the Present State of the Customs of the Italians* in fact give the impression of a stubbornly subjective, idiosyncratic voice, one that finds itself in perpetual discord with those of Leopardi's contemporaries. A self-conscious independence thus galvanizes the poet's thinking and writing, enabling him to resist the dominant Italian ideology in Biscuso's and Gallo's sense of the imperative to maintain a decorous equilibrium aloof from ethical and political considerations.[69] This tension between the individual and the mass declares itself most emphatically when Leopardi discusses fashion. He examines at length the pernicious effects of fashion and its relentless pressure to conform in one of the most well known of the *Operette morali*, the "Dialogue Between Fashion and Death." Rejecting the suggestion that fashion constitutes one of the privileged symbolic systems of modernity, he stresses rather its kinship to oblivion: death and fashion are "sisters" insofar as both are daughters of "caducity" (*caducità*; *OM* 75–78). The dialogue allegorizes the nihilistic workings of fashion, which it portrays as directing destructive influences against memory and the achievements of civilization and thus inaugurating "the century of death" (*OM* 77). Shunning a Baudelairean view of fashion as one of the crucial elements of modernity, Leopardi underscores the historical shortsightedness of the ideology of the new. Yet it is noteworthy that even a reader as sympathetic to Baudelaire as Walter Benjamin appreciated the urgency of Leopardi's polemic against fashion. Benjamin used a sentence from the dialogue as an epigraph for several entries of his own writings on the Parisian arcades.[70]

Calvino's deeply ambiguous attitude toward fashion may be discerned chiefly in his precarious balancing between cultural conservatism and intellectual faddishness. Although his invocations of the literary canon and classical mythology evince his loyalty to tradition, his abandonment of an expressly humanist concept of knowledge in favor of a modish farrago of ideas derived from structuralist, poststructuralist, and scientific thought clearly betrays his susceptibility to the appeals of fashion. His writing may be judged as fashionable insofar as it aims to dissolve ethics into aesthetics and to establish a "lifestyle" brand of literature, a mode of representation that comfortably reappropriates the available signifiers of contemporary culture without rigorous critical examination. Calvino thus avoids philosophical and moral pomp at the price of ideological coyness. Although, as I have noted, he announces in the exordium his distaste for speculation regarding literature's historical circumstances and fate, he crams *Six Memos* with references to the triumphant phenomena of the moment: from software and computer science to anthropology, ethnology, postmodernism, and lightness, a term that Milan Kundera made the *mot du jour* with the publication of his novel *The Unbearable Lightness of Being* in 1984. Indeed, Calvino generally does not champion the new in *Six Memos* so much as he alludes knowingly to it, striking a peculiar note of exhaustion or nihilism that might be said to resonate with Leopardi's description of fashion as a sort of death instinct. It is no accident that in the two memos on what arguably are his most fashionable principles, "Lightness" and "Quickness," Calvino winds up dwelling on figures of melancholy and ultimately confessing his own melancholic temperament.[71]

In the last of the *Operette*, "Dialogue Between Tristan and a Friend," Leopardi elaborates his polemical stance against the nineteenth century through the figure of Tristan, a melancholic yet strong-minded philosopher who is determined to expose unpleasant truths in the name of integrity and morality (*OM* 227-234). Here as elsewhere in the *Operette*, Leopardi posits an ideal of moral judgment grounded in the individual's judgment rather than in the law of the state or the popular will. As I already have remarked, the plurality of the title accordingly may be said to indicate a horizon of disparate ethical codes. The effectiveness of the final dialogue is a measure of the directness with which Leopardi confronts the *doxa* of his times, not through dialectical argument but rather through sustained sarcasm. At one point, Tristan pretends to embrace the "profound philosophy of newspapers," a philosophy that, by stifling any unpleasant or critical reflection, gives rise to the "masters and light of the present age" (*OM* 231). After having noticed that in his times it takes longer to read a book than to write it, Tristan tells his friends, "Personally, I think that the next century will nicely cross the immense bibliography of the nineteenth century off its list" (*OM* 231). From a position on the outskirts of the social order, Leopardi performs a biting critique of modern Italian culture, a critique that gives rise to some hope for renewal in spite, or perhaps in virtue, of its aggressive iconoclasm. "But long live statistics!" fumes Tristan acerbically, "Long live the economic, moral, and political sciences, the portable encyclopedias, the manuals, and the many beautiful creations of our century! And may the nineteenth century live forever! Maybe very poor in things, but extremely rich and generous in words, which has always been an excellent sign, as you know" (*OM* 232). On this score, it is telling that Calvino names the encyclopedic impulse so derided by Tristan as the source of the rhetoric of multiplicity that he codifies in the final lecture of *Six Memos*. Such rhetoric, he states, corresponds to an idea of "the contemporary novel as an encyclopedia, as a method of knowledge, and above all as a network of connections between the events, the people, and the things of the world" (*SM* 105).

As Tristan's sardonic tone makes clear, Leopardi's ultimate aim in the *Operette* is provocation or satire. One of the most striking differences between Leopardi and Calvino in fact is in their opinions of satire as a literary form. In an essay titled "Definitions of Territories: Comedy," Calvino confesses that he prefers the comic to the satiric mode of literature, because satire implies a "moralistic" attitude characteristic of those who perceive themselves as being superior to others (*Saggi* 1: 197). Calvino's definition of the genre as a supercilious and exclusionist mind-set does not take into account the aim of satire to criticize by communicating, its complicated and ironic ways of addressing the other, its capacity of trusting the addressee to be a possible accomplice. He ignores the possibility that satire may reveal the ethical and political dimensions of culture since the Enlightenment, apparently equating any attention to such factors with moralism. One might wonder how Calvino could even claim to adore the *Operette morali*, given his evident abhorrence of the book's *modus operandi*.[72] On this account, we should recall that Leopardi defined the *Operette* in a letter to Pietro Giordani of September 4, 1820, as "prosette satiriche."[73] And in a letter to Antonio Fortunato Stella of December 6, 1826, Leopardi voices the wish that the actual complexity of the *Operette* will be recognized, as the impression of their "lightness" should be merely "superficial."[74]

In light of their divergent aesthetics, the discrepancy between Calvino's and Leopardi's uses of classical mythology is revealing. Calvino, on the one hand, admires Vulcan's "concentration and craftsmanship," Mercury's "swiftness and mobility," or Arachne's virtuosic dexterity as if no historical distance separated such characters from the reader (*SM* 54, 10). Without a trace of self-consciousness, he nominates these figures as exemplars of his "postmodern" precepts. Leopardi, on the other hand, reinscribes the mythic archetypes in satiric scenarios that connote the degradation of modern, industrial society. *Operette* such as "The History of the Human Race," the "Dialogue Between Hercules and Atlas," or "The Wager of Prometheus" present the gods not as images of the heroic but as exaggerations of human vanity. "The Wager of Prometheus," for example, recounts a competition among the gods for the best creation, a contest that results in Prometheus' humiliation when his entry, a human being, exhibits its wretchedness and barbarism. In the same essay, Vulcan—who, as we have remarked, represents for Calvino an archetype of craft—is ludicrously depicted by Leopardi as the inventor of an economically efficient pot that cooks entire meals in no time (*OM* 98).

Leopardi does not, in other words, regard the revival of archaic myth and ensuing reaffirmation of the canon as a raison d'être of literature. In the *Operette morali*, he reformulates that mythology in skeptical, absurdist accents in order to mount a sustained philosophical critique of tradition per se. Calvino, as we have seen, invokes the ancient myths precisely for their canonical prestige, in order to legitimate the technocratic, antimoralist terms of his argument and to deflect scrutiny from the dehumanizing vision of culture that such terms uphold. It hardly should be surprising, then, that figures of self-defense, concealment, and withdrawal pervade the rhetoric of *Six Memos*. In "Lightness," for example, he devotes special attention to the fable of Perseus and Medusa, because it celebrates the hero's ingenuity in using his mirrorlike shield to view the monstrous, thus suggesting that "Perseus's strength always lies in a refusal to look directly" (*SM* 5). Similarly, the one moment in the lectures when Calvino renders a summary judgment of his personality for the reader requires him, according to his own figure, to put on an allegorical mask. In "Quickness," he confesses:

Certainly my own character corresponds to the traditional features of the guild to which I belong. I too have always been saturnine, whatever other masks I have attempted to wear. My cult of Mercury is perhaps merely an aspiration, what I would like to be. I am a Saturn who dreams of being a Mercury, and everything I write reflects these two impulses [*SM* 52].

In typically equivocal fashion, he presents his writings as the effects of a tension in his mind between an ostensibly mercurian fantasy and an underlying saturnine reality, a reality that immediately reveals itself to be one more fantastic disguise among others. It is no wonder that in "Exactitude" he imagines language itself as a void, as a *mise-en-abîme* that does not even mark any sort of critical or philosophical end limit but that merely invites blind persistence: "The word connects the visible trace with the invisible thing, the absent thing, the thing that is desired or feared, like a frail emergency bridge flung over the abyss" [*SM* 77].

Ultimately, according to Biscuso and Gallo, the *Operette morali* point up the ethical necessity of philosophically self-conscious thinking. This is the lesson Leopardi leaves for the twentieth century, a lesson that encourages deliberate pursuit of solidarity.[75] Whereas Leopardi manages, as Guglielmi has observed, to avoid the extreme consequences of his nihilist sympathies thanks to his "communicative intention," Calvino shows little sign of such an inclusive or sociable impulse, even in *Six Memos*. His interest seems to float in a strictly aesthetic space, without ever touching the ground of ethical involvement or responsibility. The never-completed sixth memo on consistency, we will find, was the lecture in which he was planning to take on the topic of intersubjectivity in literature with emphasis on the relation between "the 'I' and others." This fact is notable for two reasons. First, as the successive drafts of *Six Memos* show, Calvino was struggling fiercely with this self-appointed task and seemed unable to come to grips with it. Second, that questions of human relations are largely left out of the completed memos suggests the depth of his discomfort in confronting such issues, his need to bracket ethical or political matters for special treatment. We might remark accordingly that in *Six Memos* the ultimate referent or horizon of the text is never the human bond, as it is in the *Operette morali*. The dialogical structure at work throughout the *Operette* makes the author's "communicative intention" evident even in the most nihilistic and cosmically catastrophic pieces.[76] It is worthwhile recalling in this connection the "Dialogue Between Plotinus and Porphyry," in which Plotinus persuades Porphyry to refrain from committing suicide not for a love of life in itself but rather for the comfort of his friends. The question of the other instead brings to mind for Calvino the image of none other than Melville's Bartleby, a character who is impervious to any persuasive or friendly appeal, who leaves the impression of a solipsist basking in the endless narcissism of his "potentiality not to be."[77] Perhaps it should not surprise us that after his desertion of the PCI, Calvino championed a literature rigorously isolated from moral concerns. "Moral problems," he writes in 1967, "arise not in the field of literature but in the field of practical behavior" (*Saggi* 1: 236). In an essay of 1974, he expresses unhappiness with readers who place demands on the political intelligence of authors and their works: "I have always had reservations regarding the negative connotations that the word evasion has in the language of historical-literary criticism" (*Saggi* 1: 110).

If Leopardi's assessment of the potential of literature may strike later readers as gloomy, it should not be deemed nihilistic from a moral standpoint, as he strongly implies that writing possesses a distinct ethical significance. In a well-known passage in the *Zibaldone* of April 13, 1827, for example, he raises the idea of an essay in the form of a letter to a young poet of the twentieth century that would have affirmed at length the need for human solidarity in the face of a hostile nature. We might also recall "Parini's Discourse on Glory" from the *Operette* in which Leopardi pronounces Giuseppe Parini to be a great artist, because Parini's writing, like Alfieri's, incites the reader to action (*OM* 123–49). As Walter Binni explains, Leopardi perceived literature as an energetic intensification of the desire to act.[78] Calvino, in stark contrast, conceives of literature as a play of surfaces and disguises that through its gamelike contrivances confronts the reader with a truly nihilistic emptiness.

We might propose, then, that the sort of lightness Calvino espouses in his final book reveals the specific pedagogical aims of the postmodern genre of the memo: a levity that rules out intimacy a priori, rendering the addressee anonymous and the responsibility of writing altogether less imposing. If instead we open the classic of epistolary modernist pedagogy, Rainer Maria Rilke's *Letters to a Young Poet*, we find Rilke emphatically warning us against the danger of trivializing our relation to the world, or in other words against the threat of lightness: "If only human beings could more humbly receive their mystery—which the world is filled with, even in its smallest Things—could bear it, endure it more solemnly, feel how terribly heavy it is, instead of taking it lightly."[79] The prêt a porter pedagogy of *Six Memos* instead aims at neither the sense of heavy moral obligation evoked by Rilke nor the feeling of confessional intimacy achieved for example by Pasolini in *Lutheran Letters*, but rather at the élan of utterly minimal expectations.

The Lightness of Nihilism

The first and longest of the memos, "Lightness," thus frames Calvino's nihilism in a crucial way. At the beginning of the lecture, he announces: "I have come to consider lightness as a value rather than a defect" (*SM* 3). The defensive formulation is revealing, since, with greater force than the English "lightness," the Italian word *leggerezza* conveys the negative moral connotation of a "lack of control in behavior because of scant seriousness and frivolous negligence," according to Devoto-Oli. Throughout *Six Memos*, Calvino determinedly ignores the figurative association of the word and concentrates on the literal. In this sense, the text may be said to illustrate his self-proclaimed method of writing by means of "subtraction of weight" (*SM* 3). As in the other memos, Calvino immediately makes clear that his reasons for preferring the value of lightness over weight have little justification. He announces that he finds the merits of weight "not less compelling" (*SM* 3). This logical oscillation, however, does not seem to result in any innovative or synthetic outcome. The binarism of the values persists until the very end, since Calvino is more interested in reasserting the equanimity of the Italian cultural ideology—an interest he admits is grounded in an abhorrence of the "noisy, aggressive" quality of contemporary life [*SM* 12]—than in a deconstructive dialectic.

If "Lightness" is the most important of the memos, it is so because it strategically occupies the introductory position in the sequence, and also because it is where Calvino's rejection of any ethical or political outlook is most evident. Although he proclaims his eagerness to "situate this value [of lightness] in the present and . . . project it into the future" (*SM* 3), he names only the circumstances of his past as a reason for championing such a virtue. In one of the rare autobiographical confessions of the lectures, he describes what the literary milieu was like when he began writing professionally: "When I began my career, the categorical imperative of every young writer was to represent his own time" (*SM* 3). Clearly, we are in for a morality tale in which an older, wiser Calvino will recount how he came to recognize the naiveté of his youthful political hopes and involvement in the PCI.

Full of good intentions, I tried to identify myself with the ruthless energies propelling the events of our century, both collective and individual. I tried to find some harmony between the adventurous, picaresque inner rhythm that prompted me to write and the frantic spectacle of the world, sometimes dramatic and sometimes grotesque. Soon I became aware that between the facts of life that should have been my raw materials and the quick light touch that I wanted for my writing, there was a gulf that was costing me increasing effort to cross. Maybe I was only then becoming aware of the weight, the inertia, the opacity of the world—qualities that stick to writing from the start, unless one finds some way of evading them [*SM* 4].

His mockery of "the categorical imperative" of historicism, his evident equation of the "good intentions" of political engagement with "the ruthless energies . . . of our century," and his patent distaste for "the frantic spectacle of the world" suggest an uncaring cynicism with respect to contemporary Italian society and culture. When he avows his goal of "evading" (sfuggire) the weight of the world, he may be said to admit to a kind of cowardice, an inability or unwillingness to cope with "the facts of life."

The very compositional history of *Six Memos* gives the impression of a retreat from problematic ethical questions. Surveying the draft materials published by Barenghi, it becomes obvious that what Calvino cut from the final version of the memos is any overt treatment of the relationship between the subject and others. This concern actually supplied working titles for several of the lectures through several months of early drafts before being ruled out. On February 23, 1985, we find this list of lecture topics: "to begin and to end," "the encyclopedia and nothingness," "your fellow man—interdependence," "singularity and universality—precision and vagueness," "velocity—short forms; in the epoch of the image and of lack of time," and "lightness—atoms and the alphabet" (*Saggi* 2: 2961). All of the final values are in some manner already contained or alluded to in this early draft, but what is striking is the unexpected presence of the category "your fellow man—interdependence." On March 12, we find in Calvino's notes the proposed theme of "the individual and the other; *Amerika* (*Candide*? Man in the vastness of the world)" (*Saggi* 2: 2961). In another note from the same day, next to the values that he will include in the final version of the memos, he lists one that will not: "plural subjectivity (Kafka's *Amerika*, the 'I')" (*Saggi* 2: 2961). Yet despite undergoing numerous revisions into slogans, such as on April 6, "reciprocity, people, intersubjectivity, and solipsism" and, written in English on April 19, "sense of connection," the question of the subject's social or ethical obligations fails to make it into the final, published text. Apropos of the final memo on consistency that Calvino was still writing at the time of his death, Barenghi states: "We can only guess that some ideas relative to the relationship between the 'I' and others would have been recuperated" (*Saggi* 2: 2964). Calvino himself acknowledges that this particular question is troublesome for him, writing next to the heading "others vs. the 'I'" in some notes composed on June 23 the comment "my problem" (*Saggi* 2: 2965).

His inability to come to terms with this question, it would seem, explains his fixation with the notion of literature as mythic ritual or pseudo-epistemological game rather than as engagement, intervention, historical witnessing, or critical reflection. At the least, such an anxiety is evident in his reappropriation of the myth of Perseus and Medusa to justify his fantastical, fabulist style of narrative. As we have already learned, Calvino idolizes Perseus, because his killing of Medusa while fixing on her reflection in his shield symbolizes the poet's ability to perceive "what can be revealed only by indirect vision" and thus to avoid the "slow petrification" of the world by history and politics (*SM* 4). Of course, the *proton pseudos* or false premise of this argument is that such forces are like Medusa's terrifying prospect, a grim assumption at the threshold of the new millennium. In the end, the simile begs the question what exactly is so unnerving about the Medusa and invites another look at Calvino's argument.

At the most fundamental level, the myth he uses to describe the petrification of the world also famously allegorizes the evasion of sexual difference. If we in fact credit Freud's classic explanation, the myth of Medusa may be understood from a psychoanalytic perspective to express the fear of castration in the form of a defensive fantasy. In his celebrated short essay of 1922, Freud explains that to the male imagination the horrific Medusa's head stands for the female genitalia, which by means of its snakelike hair and magical power of hardening encodes the promise of an eventual reinvigoration of the penis.[80] Given Calvino's unqualified enthusiasm for the narrative of Perseus and Medusa, it is amusing to notice as well that when he praises Cyrano de Bergerac's lightness in describing the natural world, he approvingly fastens on a passage in which Cyrano "proclaim[s] the brotherhood of men and cabbages" at the moment of envisioning the outcry of a cabbage about to be beheaded: "Man . . . I offer you my children as seed; and as a reward for my courtesy you have my head cut off!" (*SM* 21-22). This sympathy for a vegetable that Calvino deems a great poetic intuition, an attitude that disallows any form of "anthropological parochialism" (*SM* 22), clearly involves once again an elaborate thematizing of the dread of castration. The final effect is less a poetic evocation of the cabbage's experience than an anthropomorphic projection onto the natural world of masculine anxiety with respect to the sexual other. As I already have noted, Calvino pays scant attention to women writers in *Six Memos*. The literary ideal that he promotes for the next millennium evidently will perpetuate a familiar, decorous blindness when it comes to the feminine imagination.

I observed earlier that the only women whom the memos truly celebrate are witches. Calvino situates the discussion of witches at an important strategic juncture in the argument of "Lightness." Whereas in the initial part of the lecture he is content to illustrate the idea of lightness through citation and exposition of a variety of literary models, in the final part he seeks to translate the notion into a general theory of literature. At the point of transition between the two tasks, he asks the rhetorical question, "Have a great number of threads been interwoven in this lecture?" only to conclude, "There remains one thread . . . that of literature as an existential function, the search for literature as a reaction to the weight of living" (*SM* 26). Of course, when Calvino speaks of an existential function, we are not supposed to think of the type of engagée literature and thought practiced by Sartre. Calvino, we know, seeks instead an existentialism congruent with the principles of "anthropology and ethnology and mythology" (*SM* 26–27). It is here that he invokes the image of witches flying on their broomsticks as evidence of an "anthropological" impulse to compensate for suffering through imaginative escape. Having subtracted all moral or political meaning from writing, he now attempts a halfhearted reenchantment of literature by linking it to more fashionable structuralist disciplines. Yet in the second lecture, "Exactitude," Calvino weakens even this concession to ethical criticism when he discusses the ethnological dimensions of literary culture. Reflecting on the use of folklore and fairy tales in his own fiction, he contradicts his earlier claim to an interest in ethnology by confessing that this method did not result from attachment "to an ethnic tradition," since his roots "are planted in an entirely modern and cosmopolitan Italy," but rather stemmed from an attention to "style and structure" (*SM* 35). Calvino, then, invokes anthropology and ethnology in *Six Memos* to reassure himself that literature still responds to some set of human needs, while refusing to think about the moral and political implications of such needs. Witches, for example, may represent women's need for freedom from "a constricted life" (*SM* 27), but only insofar as such a need is understood to confirm the overriding "anthropological" necessity of literary illusionism and thus to deny its own specificity and fundamental otherness.

His disconnection from the Italian ethnic tradition exposes the bad faith of his situating literature's existential meaning in the domains of anthropology, ethnology, and mythology.[81] For if to be rooted "in an entirely modern and cosmopolitan Italy" is to be cut off from the country's "ethnic tradition," the appeal to ethnology can have no existential pathos for contemporary Italians. With respect to anthropology, his position is similarly inconsistent. Though ostensibly exalting the anthropological function of literature, his approval of Cyrano de Bergerac's "brotherhood of men and cabbages" prompts him, as we saw, to express disdain for any "anthropocentric parochialism" (*SM* 22).[82] On the last page of the final lecture, "Multiplicity," Calvino divulges his true hope for literature. What he dreams of achieving is a form of writing entirely divested of the personal or the subjective: "Think what it would be to have a work conceived from outside the self, a work that would let us escape the limited perspective of the individual ego, not only to enter into selves like our own but to give speech to that which has no language, to the bird perching on the edge of the gutter, to the tree in spring and the tree in fall, to stone, to cement, to plastic" (*SM* 124). His ultimate ambition, in other words, is not a literature that responds to any anthropological need but rather one that enables us to evade such a need and to embrace a cosmic, inhuman perspective. The idea of a lightness that uplifts the imagination against the ponderousness of historical reality thus metamorphoses into a multiplicity that permits "escape" from the human altogether, an escape that amounts to a nihilistic dispersal of the self among all the animate and inanimate objects of the universe.

In this connection, we ought to pay close attention to Calvino's reading of Kafka's short story "Der Kübelreiter," a title that Calvino translates as "The Knight of the Bucket" in the lecture on lightness. His calculatedly cheerful interpretation of the tale demonstrates in what ways the very doctrine of lightness, as he gives it, masks an underlying nihilism. Written in 1917, the story allegorizes a widespread condition of the time in Austria, namely lack of coal, which Calvino feels compelled to remind us was "a real situation in that winter of warfare" (*SM* 28). Kafka's narrator ventures outdoors with a bucket to buy some coal. The bucket magically bears him on his way through the air, but when he reaches the coal merchant's underground shop, the bucket has risen too high off the ground. Although the merchant seems to want to help the narrator, the merchant's wife intervenes, turning the narrator away without one shovelful of coal. Being at this point too light, the bucket drifts off until it has carried the narrator away beyond the ice mountains.

Calvino characterizes Kafka's parable as mysterious, opening "the road to endless reflection" (*SM* 28). Unlike the shaman who represents "privation that is transformed into lightness" or witches, the hero of this narrative does not appear to be endowed with any supernatural powers of his own (he relies on the bucket for his aerial transportation) and seems unlikely to find anything to warm himself in the regions where he is headed (*SM* 28–29). Yet Calvino oddly avoids any further speculation on the hero's plight such as the conclusion of the story itself invites. Instead, his observations lead him to a tautological celebration of flight for flight's sake that belies its upbeat rhetoric with the circularity of its reasoning: "In fact, the fuller it [the bucket] is, the less it will be able to fly. Thus, astride our bucket, we shall face the new millennium, without hoping to find anything more in it than what we ourselves are able to bring to it. Lightness, for example, whose virtues I have tried to illustrate here" (*SM* 29). This reading of Kafka's story is puzzling at best. Calvino evidently wishes to find a moral of redemption in the image of lightness that is clearly not Kafka's point and that ignores the evidence Calvino himself brings to our attention regarding the hero's probable fate. The last sentence of the story, which Calvino does not quote, is decisive: "And with that I ascend into the regions of the ice mountains and am lost forever" (und damit steige ich in die Regionen der Eisgebirge und verliere mich auf Nimmerwiedersehen).[83] The ending makes clear that the ability to fly offers no consolation to the narrator, implying in fact an equivalence between flying and dying. The German formulation "und verliere mich auf Nimmerwiedersehen" is more forceful in conveying the ineluctability of the narrator's passage than the English translation, which might be rendered more literally as "and lose myself never to be seen again." The ice mountains thus delimit the one-way border between life and death, a border that the narrator will have to cross "numb" and with "frozen tears" dimming his eyes.[84] When the coal merchant's wife finally shoos away the narrator with her apron (because his bucket is too light), it is difficult to see how one could take her gesture, as Calvino does, to delineate a horizon of redemption. The narrator's destiny is very similar to that of Gregor Samsa in "The Metamorphosis," who in the end is shooed away with a broom by a charwoman.[85]

Calvino constructs an escapist fantasy to explain the story, interpreting the narrator as a sort of modern-day incarnation of a medieval "knight errant": "It may be that Kafka only wanted to tell us that going out to look for a bit of coal on a cold wartime night changes the mere swinging of the bucket into the quest of a knight errant or the desert crossing of a caravan or a flight on a magic carpet" (*SM* 28). This attempted reading of "Der Kübelreiter" along the lines of chivalric or epic romance depends entirely on Calvino's rendering of the German word *Reiter* in the English manuscript of the lecture as "knight," which is the only textual rationale he offers for his interpretation. In English, however, the correct translation of *der Reiter* is "the rider" (in the Schocken Books edition of Kafka's short fiction, the translators Willa and Edna Muir indeed give the title as "The Bucket Rider"); the German for "knight" in Calvino's sense is *der Ritter*.[86] The disparity between the correct and incorrect renditions of the title corresponds to divergent understandings of the narrator's role in the story. The unromanticized but not nihilistic character of "the bucket rider" aligns with an image of the protagonist as a sufferer of human callousness. The romanticized but nihilistic spirit of "the knight of the bucket" consorts with an impression of the hero as a solipsist who has been elevated "above the level where one finds both the help and the egoism of others" (*SM* 28) and who simply takes the cruelty of other human beings as an excuse for his flights of fancy. The first is a skeptical reading of the figure of flying; the second is a cynical one. Calvino's misreading of Kafka's tale thus may be said to mark the difference between modernism and a nihilist postmodernism. Whereas Kafka focuses on the ethical and existential pathos of the title character's situation, Calvino strips the plot of its existential premise and anguished conclusion, thereby reducing the figure of flying to an ornamental motif.

This escapist interpretation might appear all the more incongruous if we consider it in the light of how other eminent critics have understood Kafka's story. Walter Benjamin, for example, observes: "Accursed is the rider who is chained to his nag because he has set himself a goal for the future, even though it is as close as the coal cellar. . . . There is no more hopeless vista than that of 'the regions of the ice mountain' in which the bucket rider drops out of sight forever."[87] Underlining the hopelessness of the last line, Benjamin highlights Kafka's larger aim of deconstructing the comic logic of the conventional fairy tale. Calvino's pretense that there is something inherently noble about flying into "the ice mountains" of the next millennium instead tries to reimpose a happy ending on the narrative. Such a gesture misses the point of Kafka's project in general. In a letter to Gershom Scholem written in 1938, Benjamin remarked that to do justice to Kafka's peculiar achievement one ought to realize that he sought always to capture the purity and beauty of failure: "One is tempted to say: once he was certain of eventual failure, everything worked out for him en route as in a dream. There is nothing more memorable than the fervor with which Kafka emphasized his failure."[88] Calvino's misreading of the story thus suggests an incapability of recognizing the urgency of failure in Kafka's fiction, its "fervor" precisely in Benjamin's sense.

His denial of the tragic weight of Kafka's story moreover may be regarded as indicative of the memo's overall approach to its title topic. Surfing the Zeitgeist, Calvino embraces the signifier "lightness" that Milan Kundera made popular and inescapable only a year before *Six Memos* was written with publication of *The Unbearable Lightness of Being*. Calvino, however, eschews all of the philosophical meanings that Kundera assigns to the term.[89] In his novel, Kundera introduces the question of lightness in response to the Nietzschean idea of eternal return: "Putting it negatively, the myth of the eternal return states that a life which disappears once and for all, which does not return, is like a shadow, without weight, dead in advance."[90] The most important ethical consequence of a world without return, Kundera suggests, is that everything is cynically permitted, even reconciliation with Hitler.[91] In a passage that we ought to align with "The Bucket Rider," Kundera relates lightness to insignificance and weight to truthfulness, using kafkaesque imagery:

The heavier the burden, the closer our lives come to earth, the more real and truthful they become.
    Conversely, the absolute absence of burden causes man to be lighter than air, to soar into the heights, take leave of the earth and his earthly being, and become only half real, his movements as free as they are insignificant. What then shall we choose, Weight or Lightness?[92]

For all of the lip service he pays to the opposite value of weight, Calvino does not revive Kundera's existential and philosophical dilemma. Instead, as his reading of Kafka's short story appears to confirm, Calvino celebrates what is merely in the air, lightness in the sense of a flight into nihilism or solipsism, without indulging in unnecessary pathos or thought.

The Consistency of Lightness

Sadly, Calvino died before being able to compose the one memo that his editor believes might have complicated his argument regarding "the egoism of others." At the time of his departure for the United States, he had completed five lectures and, as Barenghi informs us, was planning a sixth. This final lecture, "Consistency," was to revolve around a discussion of Melville's "Bartleby, the Scrivener" and would have been written at Harvard (*Saggi* 2: 2957). The topic of consistency emerges in Calvino's draft notes starting on June 23, 1985. What was the significance for him of this theme? We have already remarked on Barenghi's conclusion that the missing memo would have recovered the question of the subject's relationship to others. He furthermore proposes that exploration of the dialectic between solipsism and intersubjectivity would have permitted Calvino to write in a more autobiographical manner. We ought to recall here Calvino's confessional inscription of the phrase "my problem" next to the heading "others vs. the 'I'" in these notes, a heading that links references to Goldsmith's *The Vicar of Wakefield*, Kafka's *Amerika*, and Melville's "Bartleby" (*Saggi* 2: 2964–2965).[93] This invisible problem exerts a curious influence on the published text of the lectures, a book that in its title promises six memos but delivers only five. The enigma of an unwritten concluding lecture that survives solely in the form of fragmentary notes tantalizingly suggests a last testament left by Calvino for future reflection.

The *OED* defines "consistency" as "constantly adhering to the same principles of thought or action." Rereading crucial passages of *Six Memos* in the light of some of Calvino's other writings and Melville's "Bartleby," we may begin to approach the question of what consistency meant to Calvino. In his own work, it hardly seems as though he aimed at "constantly adhering to the same principles." His fiction by turns embraced neorealism (*The Path to the Nest of Spiders*, which revises the mode as much as illustrating it), fantasy and science fiction (*Trilogy*, *Cosmicomics*), structural experimentalism and metafiction (*If on a Winter's Night a Traveler*), and phenomenological description (*Mr. Palomar*). Why was Calvino increasingly drawn to consistency over, for instance, the term "openness," which appears in earlier drafts? We know from his editor that, in the concluding memo, he intended to discuss the social relations of the individual. We might infer from this that, broadening the scope of *Six Memos* beyond strictly formal or stylistic matters, "Consistency" would have dealt head-on with what Calvino frequently has designated by means of the euphemism the "unwritten world" and that he opposes to the "written world" in the title and argument of a 1983 lecture delivered at New York University.[94]

The problem that becomes evident in this talk is that he sees no possible point of contact between the two worlds. As he himself puts it, "I have started with the irreconcilable opposition between the written and the unwritten world; if their two languages merge, my reasoning collapses" (*Saggi* 2: 1872). Although we cannot expect language magically to repair reality, his radical partitioning of existence into the written and the unwritten with all truth value assigned to the latter reduces literature to mere replication of material conditions. Because Calvino does not qualify the unwritten world in any other way than as *non scritto*, this domain suggests inert materiality untouched by religion, sexuality, politics, or ethics and thus seems of little interest from a human perspective. As he conceives it,

118 *Lightness*

literature is doomed to mirror the surface of the unwritten, but never to imagine alternatives or ask what lies beneath the surface. Such is the task Calvino reserved for himself in the last years of his life, when his emphasis on the phenomenological in *Mr. Palomar* inaugurates a new narrative poetics. Benedetti has suggested that Calvino's adherence in his later work to a mimetic or descriptive poetics represents his way of reenchanting literature, at a moment when writing seems to have lost its cultural prestige. Yet, as Benedetti herself asks, why should literature be limited to description, when it may witness, elicit confessions, or incite resistance?[95] The consistency of Calvino's written world thus resides in its continuous effort to reproduce the objective appearances of things while avoiding any question of their subjective, moral meanings.

Whenever he acknowledges in *Six Memos* the cultural shallowness and conformism of what he labels in the exordium "the so-called post-industrial era of technology," he retreats from any thought of literature as a potential means of criticizing this dilemma to assertions of the abstract, formal purity of language. Perhaps the most glaring such abdication of his own logic occurs in "Exactitude," when he condemns the hallucinatory and dehistoricizing influence of the mass media:

> We live in an unending rainfall of images. The most powerful media transform the world into images and multiply it by means of the phantasmagoric play of mirrors. These are images stripped of the inner inevitability that ought to mark every image as form and as meaning, as a claim on the attention and as a source of possible meanings. . . . This plague strikes also the lives of people and the history of nations. It makes all histories formless, random, confused, with neither beginning nor end. My discomfort arises from the loss of form that I notice in life, which I try to oppose with the only weapon I can think of—an idea of literature [*SM* 57].

Missing from this statement of purpose is any sense of *how* literature counteracts the pestilence of mass-produced spectacle, unless simply by restoring a principle of form whose "loss" gives rise to Calvino's "discomfort." Yet even by his line of reasoning, such a solution is inadequate. As he puts it, the "phantasmagoric" operations of the media devour "every image as form and as meaning, as a claim on the attention and as a source of possible meanings." This oscillation between form and meaning corresponds to the dialectic between the visible and the hidden, the linguistic and the ineffable, the *mondo scritto* and *non scritto* that we have seen was a crucial preoccupation and that he never quite settled. Here, however, the dialectic simply collapses. By the final sentence, "meaning" has been forgotten, and it is only "the loss of form that I notice in life." The cited passage is the most critical assessment of contemporary culture in *Six Memos*, but the pestilence of which it speaks cannot be opposed strictly in the name of formalist aesthetics. If history has fragmented into "random, confused" histories, only a literature that can envision new moral choices and modes of life will be able to escape a merely decorative function. Calvino's blindness to ethical and political horizons is particularly damning in this context.

Regarding television's transformation of memory into "a rubbish dump" of images, he similarly maintains in "Visibility" that the proper response is not imaginative confrontation of this quandary, but celebration of the figurative or "icastic" essence of writing, which manifests itself in the achievement of "a well-defined, memorable, and self-sufficient form" (*SM* 92). Although apparently picturing himself in opposition to the Zeitgeist, Calvino chooses an unsettling metaphor to describe the way of thinking most conducive to such an achievement: "The imagination is a kind of electronic machine that takes account of all possible combinations and chooses the ones that are appropriate to a particular purpose, or are simply the most interesting, pleasing or amusing" (*SM* 91). To conflate the imagination with an "electronic machine" aimed at maximizing gratification hardly seems like a gesture of defiance toward the culture of mass mediation. Moreover, the idea of pleasure as a sort of calculus or algorithm to be computed in an automatic manner betrays a mentality that allows no occasion for the unexpected, the unthinkable, the sublime, or the challenging—in which no space exists for the imagination. We should not be surprised that at this point, during the one moment in *Six Memos* in which he overtly explicates his view of present-day conditions, he proposes a weak, conciliatory response to "the growing inflation of prefabricated images" typical of contemporary life (*SM* 95). Faced with this inflation, he contends, there are only two possibilities: either start from scratch like Beckett, whose fictional experiments take place in a world after the end of the world, or pursue a postmodernism of ironic quotation. "We could recycle used images," he writes, "in a new context that changes their meaning. Postmodernism may be seen as the tendency to make ironic use of the stock images of the mass media, or to inject the taste for the marvelous inherited from literary tradition into narrative mechanisms that accentuate its alienation" (*SM* 95).[96]

Calvino's alternatives of Beckett or postmodern pastiche as models for the next millennium cannot be said to constitute a real choice, since it is hard to imagine a continuation of Beckett's narrative endgames and even harder to imagine trying to outdo them. In the unused draft memo titled "Cominciare e finire" that Barenghi claims would have supplied some of the material for "Consistency," Calvino in fact describes Beckett as the first author to capture the exhaustion of all stories.[97] So we are left with a postmodernism chiefly defined by the procedures of estrangement and irony. Far from challenging accepted conventions in such a way as to grant the reader a sense of analytic distance, however, such methods affirm an all-too-conventional rhetorical ideal. In the case of "estrangement," Calvino uses the word not with an eye toward its Brechtian suggestions of demystification and critique, but rather toward the hypnotic effects of the "marvelous." The emphasis is in keeping with his tendency, since at least 1957, to praise Brecht not for being politically committed but for adopting as "his first, marvelous principle that the goal of theater is to divert" (*Saggi* 1: 1514).

When it comes to "irony," Calvino appears to restrict the concept to a recycling of the "used" or "stock" images that have become the vulgata of popular culture.[98] Can such a cannibalizing of mass media images, however, serve as a cure for the "plague" of the contemporary society of spectacle? Whereas the Romantic notion of irony that Schlegel introduced in his *Lyceum* fragments thrived on the ceaseless interaction of metaphysical contrasts, postmodern irony as Calvino defines it refuses "ontological" oppositions. On the latter view, however, irony is more representative of an acceptance of received habits of thought than an iconoclastic confrontation of such habits. Calvino's position may come into sharper focus if we consider it in relation to Umberto Eco's general definition of postmodernity. Eco likens the postmodern condition to the predicament of a man who wishes to declare his love to a knowing and sophisticated woman, but who knows that the expression "I love you" is a shopworn cliché. The man solves his problem through the technique of saying, "As Barbara Cartland would put it, 'I love you,'" thus articulating his feelings and commenting ironically on tradition at the same time.[99] As the postmodern does for Eco, irony for Calvino benignly functions as a winking style of citation. Postmodern irony according to his conception does not permit the destabilizing of old habits of thought so much as their coy reinforcement, a revival achieved by bracketing them with quotation marks.

What did Calvino see in "Bartleby, the Scrivener" that corresponds to such a view of present-day culture? What was the point of spotlighting Melville's enigmatic tale at the end of *Six Memos*? Reflection on the reasons behind Calvino's choice is not, I think, irrelevant. The narrative of "Bartleby" radically problematizes the questions of otherness and moral obligation in capitalist society, whose suppression I have been arguing is the hallmark of Calvino's nihilism. Indeed, he was fascinated by a story in which the main character, when asked to perform his job, invariably repeats, "I would prefer not to." It is significant in this respect that the character of Bartleby, a legal copyist, is defined by his refusal to write memos. Melville tells the story of an indulgent Wall Street lawyer who becomes obsessed with Bartleby, ostensibly one of three clerks in the lawyer's offices, as a result of the scrivener's gradual refusal of all tasks. The lawyer, who is also the narrator of the story, describes himself after some initial surprise as "considerably reconciled" to Bartleby, because of his employee's steadiness, "unalterable demeanor," and quality of being "always there" (*GSW* 53). More than once the narrator insinuates the possibility that Bartleby is indeed his "melancholic" double: "A fraternal melancholy! For both I and Bartleby were sons of Adam" (*GSW* 55). As if to confirm the kinship, the narrator at a later point amusingly admits to getting into the involuntary habit of using the word "prefer" on "all sorts of not exactly suitable occasions" (*GSW* 58).

Melville thus gives the reader the impression that Bartleby stands for the reverse or obverse of life under capitalism, its nihilistic core.[100] It is not by chance that, before living in New York, Bartleby lived in Washington and so has ties to both the financial and political capitals of the United States. When the narrator depicts Bartleby, who he eventually discovers is living in the law offices, surveying the emptiness of Wall Street after working hours, both the scrivener and the city's financial district take on enlarged, allegorical dimensions: "Of a Sunday, Wall Street is deserted as Petra, and every night of every day it is an emptiness. . . . And here Bartleby makes his home, sole spectator of solitude which he has seen all populous—a sort of innocent and transformed Marius brooding among the ruins of Carthage" (*GSW* 55). The necessities of business and the "constant friction of illiberal minds" on Wall Street eventually drive the lawyer to get rid, albeit reluctantly, of his uncooperative employee (*GSW* 65). Imprisoned on the charge of vagrancy in the Halls of Justice, which the narrator refers to as The Tombs, Bartleby refuses to eat and, after a last encounter at which he tells his employer "I know you, and I want nothing to say to you," he dies (*GSW* 71). Whereupon the narrator learns that Bartleby had been a clerk in the Dead Letter Office in Washington, where he was partly responsible for the burning of undeliverable mail (*GSW* 73). The lawyer imagines these letters filled with "pardon for those who died despairing; hope for those who died unhoping" and concludes, "On errands of life, these letters speed to death" (*GSW* 74). Like the perplexed and apparently remorseful narrator, the reader will never know what may have been the circumstances in Washington that explain Bartleby's behavior.

Giorgio Agamben recently has interpreted the scrivener's perpetual negativity as the effort to articulate a "pure, absolute potentiality."[101] In Agamben's eyes, this attempt should be read in contrast to the Western tradition of ethics, which he feels reduces the ambiguity of potentiality too frequently to a matter of will.[102] Bartleby's suspension of will between yes and no in the utterance "I would prefer not to" thus amounts to a refusal to negotiate the passage to actuality and a clinging to creative potential. Of course, to reach such a conclusion, Agamben has to disregard entirely Melville's emphasis on the historical and social circumstances of his characters. The Italian commentator thus ignores the Wall Street setting and dismisses as a trivial distraction the narrator's final words regarding Bartleby's position relative to the suffering of others.

Perhaps Calvino, like Agamben, was enthralled by the consistency of Melville's protagonist in the sense not of his refusal to act but rather of his delicate indecision between yes and no, acceptance and refusal. Calvino similarly may have regarded Bartleby's ambivalence between being and nothingness as a foundation for equivalence and as well for potentiality.[103] In "Cominciare e finire," he maintains that his ideal of a book that could contain the universe coincides in fact with the "perfect representation of nothingness" (*Saggi* 1: 752). We ought to recall as well that he was so enchanted by the category of the possible as to dedicate an entire novel, *If on a Winter's Night a Traveler*, to serial rehearsal of the openings of ten hypothetical novels all bearing the same title. In "Visibility," Calvino moreover defines the imagination in terms of potential: "Still there is another definition in which I recognize myself fully, and that is the imagination as a repertory of what is potential, what is hypothetical, of what does not exist and has never existed, and perhaps will never exist but might have existed" (*SM* 91). Given such signs, we might surmise that Calvino would have been sympathetic to the strain of contemporary Italian thought that encourages ironic detachment. This mentality is epitomized by Agamben's contempt for ethical concerns in his reading of "Bartleby" and, to a lesser degree, may be associated with some of the positions adopted by the school of so-called weak thought.[104] For all such thinkers, Bartleby's constant avoidance of action may serve as a curious emblem.

By insisting on a metaphysical reading of Melville's story, Agamben erases the social, moral, and political questions explicitly raised by Bartleby's refusal to work and Melville's presentation of the character's refusal. Antonio Negri and Michael Hardt make this point clear in *Empire* when they propose a compelling alternative reading of "Bartleby" in line with the "long tradition of refusal to work."[105] In Negri's and Hardt's view, Bartleby stands for "the refusal of work and authority, or really the refusal of voluntary servitude, [that] is the beginning of liberatory politics."[106] Yet even though the two critics appreciate the pathos of such a position, they do not fail to observe as well that such a stance is *only* a beginning, one premised on Bartleby's absolute passivity, the emptiness of a beautiful soul "continuously . . . on the verge of suicide."[107] Pursuing some of the implications of Negri's and Hardt's interpretation, I wish to propose that Bartleby occupied a central place in Calvino's literary and political imagination not only because "consistency" in Melville's story coincides with potentiality or virtuality but because this potentiality represents nothing more than the empty rebellion of nihilism, the gesture of a suicidal soul rather than a prelude to action. My suspicion is that Calvino may have been drawn to Bartleby precisely because the character of the scrivener does not represent a straightforward example of political or emotional commitment and hence cannot be lionized as a hero of nonviolent resistance. The potentiality not to be, which Agamben explicates so well, freezes Bartleby in a moment of nonchoice that Calvino seems to hold particularly dear.

When his first novel, *The Path to the Spiders' Nests*, which was originally published in 1947 and recounts the story of the *Resistenza* in the mode of a fairy tale, was reissued in 1964, Calvino wrote in a new preface that the finished work could not console him for what he had lost in writing it. He claims that, although barely sufficient to the composition of his first book, his experience properly preserved would have helped him to write his last book. This paradoxical assertion may be said to align its author with Bartleby in the sense that Calvino would have preferred not to have written his first book. In the preface to the reissue of *The Path to the Spiders' Nests*, then, he performs a signature gesture of refusal. Although at the end of his life he acts in a manner atypical of Bartleby, insofar as he leaves behind the record of *Six Memos*, Calvino again seems to have assumed the scrivener's disinterested air when challenged to rethink the relation between "the 'I' and others" or to consider the link between art and politics. In his last book, as in his first, he celebrates the meaninglessness of the virtual or potential. Many readers and critics seem mesmerized by the image of Calvino isolated like Bartleby in the tombs of contemporary culture, silenced in the act of sending out memos that, on errands of life, sped to death.

3

Weakness

The Parable of Weak Thought: The End of Leftist Hegemony

Gianni Vattimo and Pier Aldo Rovatti edited a collection of philosophical essays that was published by Feltrinelli in 1983 under the title *Weak Thought* (Il pensiero debole). The book seemed to spell out the agenda of a new movement, and Vattimo, who originally coined the term "weak thought" in 1979, quickly became its best-known and most successful proponent.[1] The main purpose of weak thought is to propose a reading of Heidegger's philosophy not as the narrative of an anxious search for the poetic recovery of Being, but rather as the process of its weakening and "lightening." This reading is made possible by interpreting Heidegger through Nietzsche, explaining the former's insistence on the end of metaphysics through the latter's notion of nihilism, which Vattimo interprets as the weakening of formerly accepted moral and religious values.[2]

Vattimo's more phenomenologically oriented collaborators in the volume also celebrate the weakening of reality by literature.[3] Rovatti advocates the superiority of fiction and *récit* or narration over any philosophical mode that is oriented toward critical activity.[4] With his fabulist energy, Calvino becomes the paradigm of the new way of thinking: "In the moment in which philosophy has to respond to its own need of opening up to narration, the narration of an experience of thought—as is the case with *Palomar* by Italo Calvino—can be a symptom and a happy encounter."[5] Far from cultivating any "pathos of truth," Calvino produces in the character of Palomar the only plausible image for Rovatti of the contemporary hero: a comic and even slightly "stupid" protagonist who is concerned only with his own trivial misadventures.[6] Palomar's floating subjectivity, which neither adheres to the generic functions of a stock character nor quite fits into a conventional story with a well-ordered plot, is nevertheless a role model for the philosopher himself.[7]

Like Umberto Eco's semiotics, Calvino's aesthetics played a fundamental role at the time in establishing a cultural climate that eschewed criticism of mass culture. Calvino's *Six Memos for the Next Millennium* provides a good example of the "appropriation" of the five physical properties of lightness, rapidity, exactitude, visibility, and multiplicity in a manner that, according to Mario Perniola, results in an effect similar to that of mass communications, which he regards as "the opposite of knowledge." The achievement of the book in Perniola's eyes is to upend the meaning of the terms by redeploying them in discussions of literature and aesthetics.[8] For Perniola, Calvino thus offers the perfect response to the conflict between communication and literature by eschewing any logical or ethical argument in favor of a clever "meta-aesthetics."[9] It might be added, however, that Calvino's cunning meta-aesthetics and Vattimo's equally cunning metaphilosophy largely avoid critical approaches that would require them to confront the most difficult questions and disputes of their time.

In the overall economy of Italian culture, for example, Vattimo represents the apotheosis of an acritical trend that Eco initiated in the 1960s with studies in semiotics such as *Opera aperta* (1962), *Apocalittici e integrati* (1964), and *La struttura assente* (1968). Eco's writings became fashionable for disdaining the hierarchical order of traditional, genre-based aesthetic theory and for considering topics that included comic strips such as *Steve Canyon* and *Peanuts* and comic book characters such as Superman. He thus inaugurates a criticism that used high culture to comment on and legitimize popular culture and the media. Eco's message, which Vattimo helps to reinforce, is that the society of technologically advanced communication ought to be neither feared nor criticized, but rather merely studied with regard to its evolving epistemological modes. It is not at all surprising therefore to find that Eco contributed an essay to Vattimo and Rovatti's *Weak Thought* that celebrated the pleasures of unlimited semiosis and of the encyclopaedia as a form of labyrinth.[10] In the context of Italian theoretical debates, as Viano has observed, such a view of language and culture in terms of unlimited semiosis typically heralds a return to recognition of the spiritual character of the world.[11]

Whereas for Gramsci early twentieth-century conditions raised the hope that the forces of hegemony might be overthrown through intellectual confrontation of civil society, for Italy's educated classes the numbing aesthetic conformism of the 1980s, the years of the so-called second Italian miracle, seemed more or less to represent an acceptable, or at any rate inevitable, effect of mass culture. Perry Anderson has remarked acutely that the traditional leftist intelligentsia of the PCI was caught "quite unprepared" for the rise of "a fully commercialised mass culture" in Italy.[12] It is important to notice that before the nation's collective embrace of the media, one group of Italian philosophers undertook a project of critical and political resistance to what they regarded as the "crisis of reason" of the 1970s. Published in 1979 under the editorship of Aldo Giorgio Gargani, the anthology *Crisis of Reason* assailed the limiting order imposed by the canonical ideal of reason.[13] The book addresses the increasing untenability of classical epistemology and invokes Einstein, Mach, and Feyerabend for their constructivism and relativism in establishing nonprescriptive procedures and methodologies within the scientific field.[14] Following a line of reasoning that could be defined as Foucauldian in its analysis of the political regime of truth, contributors to the volume, ranging from Carlo Ginzburg to Francesco Orlando and Nicola Badaloni, highlight from different vantage points the correlation between the claims of reason as they traditionally have been defined and authoritarian social practices. Many of the authors, including among others Franco Rella, Vittorio Strada, and Badaloni, acknowledge the predicament of Marxism in the present day, while refusing to contend with it from a reactionary position such as Vattimo adopts in *The End of Modernity* (1985) and *The Transparent Society* (1989) when he hails the triumph of exchange value over use value.

In his essay "Interpreting and Transforming," Strada specifically proposes that the most important task for contemporary critical thought is to renounce not the emancipatory narrative of Marxism but rather its most doctrinaire manifestations such as totalitarian régimes or Marx's criticism of religion (*CR*, 179–97). One of Italy's most important Marxist philosophers, Badaloni calls for a repudiation of determinist economic and social theories through renewal of Gramsci's search for hegemony beyond the strictures of ideology (*CR*, 241–79). More particularly, Badaloni stresses the necessity of "moving toward Gramsci" by relinquishing structuralism in order to stress the strategic importance of social relationships (*CR*, 273). In the last essay of *Crisis of Reason*, Carlo Augusto Viano investigates the continuity between a criticism of reason and a criticism of capitalism, while bearing in mind the importance that Max Weber assigned to the linkage between capitalism and rationality. Viano suggests that ascribing historical finality to reason makes dialectic more powerful than scientific method, although he observes that from the formulation of this "strong" theory of reason ensues the possibility of a "weak" theory that assumes rationality as a self-regulating analytic logic (*CR*, 347). His somewhat negative use of the latter adjective in passing may be seen as the gauntlet thrown down that Vattimo eventually takes up as the central theme of his own work. Most of the philosophers in the book are clearly indebted to Nietzsche's insight that meaning in the world is a human production, yet none of them pursue a reading of the German philosopher revolving around nihilism. Indeed, the rhetoric of the anthology tends more to a vitalist terminology of energy and force than a language of weakness, particularly in the case of Gargani's profession of hope for a new order of truth that might lead to a new "muscular tension" and an "accumulation of energy" (*CR*, 44–46).

Proposing a genealogy for contemporary philosophy that proceeds from the structuralism of the 1960s to the quandary of Marxism and what they derisively label the "negative thought" of the 1970s, Vattimo and Rovatti rebuke the contributors to *Crisis of Reason* for maintaining theoretical assumptions that supposedly affirm conventional claims to "power, capacity to control, implication, totalization" (*PD*, 8). What becomes immediately apparent as a fundamental premise of their undertaking is its desertion of the Marxist legacy on every level.[15] Never mentioning Gramsci, Vattimo and Rovatti refer to Marx only in passing in a convoluted explanation of the political implications of Heidegger's thought, including his sympathy for Nazism:

> The *Introduction to Metaphysics* grasps the very root of the constitution of our civilization's conceptual language; in this respect it represents that very "complement" which has been called for to fill the lacunae of Marx's *Capital*. This might allow a rereading of the political writings and speeches from Heidegger's rectorship period, in which his admittedly equivocal approach to Nazism as "destiny" may simply bear witness to his recognition of the *necessary* predominance of socio-political structures over individual ones in human experience [*AD*, 53].

One characteristic trait of Vattimo's thought in general has been its insistence on continuous equivalences among disparate concepts, as if in a kind of theoretical performance of exchange value, which as a concept looms large in his definition of postmodernity. Even so, to construe some sort of equivalence between Nazism and Marxism on the grounds that both are concerned with the sociopolitical must rank as one of Vattimo's most intellectually careless suggestions.

To be sure, Vattimo does not refrain in *The Adventure of Difference* from stigmatizing the French poststructuralists, in particular Althusser, for their allegedly merely rhetorical expressions of leftist sympathy: "Much of present-day French philosophy and criticism is given up to the old exercises in rhetoric, gaily pursued as the true path to revolution" (*AD*, 39). In the introduction of *Weak Thought*, he and his coeditor assert more prescriptively that Nietzsche's discovery of the nexus of metaphysics and relations of domination—which was an insight, they allege, that Marx perhaps shared—ought not to lead us to pursue simplistically a philosophy of emancipation as "demystification" (*PD*, 9). The surreptitiously defensive tone of this credo quickly leads to avowal of the hope that their undertaking in the book might not be interpreted as "abdication" or "apology" for the existing order (*PD*, 10). Rovatti and Vattimo conclude the introduction with a turn in what they feel will be a new and uplifting direction: "For now, we can attempt some little movement, a lightening" (*PD*, 11).

In "Dialectic, Difference, Weak Thought," his seminal contribution to the anthology, Vattimo proposes that the dismantling of dialectic through Adorno's negative method and Benjamin's micrological pathos leaves philosophical thought with Heidegger's ontological difference and new conception of being as the only basis of meaning: "What is most radical in Heidegger is that the discovery of the linguistic character of the event of Being reverberates on the very conception of Being itself, which results in the stripping off of the strong traits attributed to it by the metaphysical tradition" (*PD*, 20). What is most important to Vattimo is that Heidegger's dissolution of metaphysics occurs weakly, which is to say without reappropriation, or in Hegelian terms without a slave who becomes master (*PD*, 21). Vattimo wishes to liquidate not only the most famous figure of Hegel's phenomenology but with it all modes of dialectical thinking, especially Marxism, in favor of a new focus on *pietas*, *Verwindung*, and *Andenken*, which he names as the three coordinates of a weak ontology. He emphasizes pietas or piety as a sign of attention to transience and mortality in addition to the more clearly Heideggerian notions of Verwindung, which he associates with "resignation" and "distortion," and Andenken, which literally means "thinking toward" but is usually rendered as "remembrance" or "recollection." As a weak alternative to *Überwindung* or overcoming, however, Verwindung is a concept that, as Vattimo himself reminds us, differs from Andenken insofar as it occurs only three times in Heidegger's texts: in *Holzwege*, *Vorträge und Aufsätze*, and *Identität und Differenz*.[16] It thus is fair to say that Vattimo's decision to highlight this concept is itself something of an original choice.

By attributing a strategic role to the notion of Verwindung, he in fact aims to position himself polemically against any charge of harboring an ambition to "overcome," which is to say, to criticize. He instead affirms the attitude of resignation or distortion that welcomes the progressive unfolding of what Heidegger would have called *Dasein*, meaning the primordial condition of human being in relation to the world. This unfolding for Vattimo coincides with the end of claims to metaphysical certainty, which uphold traditional forms of knowledge: "*Aufklärung* is still the one connotation of metaphysical Being in modernity, because it defines the latter as an era of overcoming, of criticism" (*EOM*, 168). In defense of weak thought's insistence on resignation or distortion, he thus perpetually argues against the sin of critical ambition. He condemns Adorno's aesthetic theory, for example, for having maintained faith in "the critical power of the work with respect to existing reality."[17] In spite of the example that Heidegger sets by assigning to poetry a strategic role in the return to Being, Vattimo defines contemporary aesthetics in terms of its "lightening of being" or "ornamental character," taking the stance that beauty ought not to be regarded as the sign of a manifestation of truth (*TS*, 71–72). In his writings of the late 1980s, he seems to equate art with the Transavanguardia movement in painting that originated in Italy and reached the height of its influence at precisely the same time. According to the movement's main publicist, the art historian Achille Bonito Oliva, Transavanguardia's primary aim was to recuperate the lightness of decorative images and dreams, as we shall see in the next chapter.

Vattimo at first acknowledges in "Dialectic, Difference, Weak Thought" that his hermeneutic approach to ontology, which allows for the occurrence of being only through historical transmission of interpretations and the symbolic, memorial function of art conceived as a monument or residue, may lead to a damaging "inability to be critical" (*PD*, 27). As his argument proceeds, however, he presents this trait of weak thought as an advantage rather than a limit (*PD*, 27). By the time of *The End of Modernity* (1985), which sets out to define postmodernity in terms of Nietzschean and Heideggerian philosophy, he argues that "the 'post-' in the term 'postmodern' indicates in fact a taking leave of modernity. In its search to free itself from the logic of development inherent in modernity—namely the idea of a critical 'overcoming' directed toward a new foundation—postmodernity seeks exactly what Nietzsche and Heidegger seek in their own peculiar 'critical' relation to western thought" (*EOM*, 3). From the overdetermined typographical hedging of this passage, we may see how problematic for Vattimo is the very idea of an interpretive "overcoming." He indeed flags this term with quotation marks to convey an admonishing skepticism toward the suggestion that critical, hence dialectical, progress might require projects of reappropriation including "not only theoretical developments, such as for example the Lacanian elaboration of Freudianism, but also (and perhaps more fundamentally) the political developments of Marxism, revolutions and socialism" (*EOM*, 24).

He casts additional doubt on the notion of serious or meaningful works of thought when he refers to Nietzsche's and Heidegger's "peculiar 'critical' relation" to the Western tradition in a formula that both qualifies the activity of critical engagement as "peculiar" and denies or suspends its value through repetition of scare quotes (*EOM*, 3). A few pages later, he concludes:

> The ideas of Nietzsche and Heidegger, more than any others, offer us the chance to pass from a purely critical and negative description of the post-modern condition, typical of early twentieth-century *Kulturkritik* and its more recent offshoots, to an approach that treats it as a positive possibility and opportunity. Nietzsche mentions all of this—although not altogether clearly—in his theory of a possibly active, or positive, nihilism. Heidegger alludes to the same thing with his idea of a *Verwindung* of metaphysics which is not a critical overcoming in the "modern" sense of the term. . . . In both Nietzsche and Heidegger, what I have elsewhere called the "weakening" of Being allows thought to situate itself in a constructive manner within the post-modern condition [*EOM*, 11].

This passage may be considered the programmatic manifesto of weak thought. It voices a position that eschews criticism, a mode that from

Kant to Marx, Adorno, and beyond has been the most prized aspect of reason. Vattimo sets Nietzsche and Heidegger in opposition to this genealogy, arguing that they "allude" to or gesture toward his notion of weakness through their reflections on nihilism and Verwindung, but he does not substantiate this claim by examining the two philosophers' writings in depth or by any other means of assessing their specific views. He seems content merely to assert a vague, spiritual correspondence with the German thinkers, a gambit that also helps Vattimo justify his otherwise evidently self-regarding effort to establish a positive, conciliatory outlook toward postmodernity. It is important to notice the overall evolution of his rhetoric from self-doubt regarding the apologetic orientation of weak thought to pride in its renunciation of the aims of criticism and of overcoming, and ultimately to gratification in its affinity with nihilism.

Nihilism indeed supplies Vattimo with the topic of his boldest proposition, which is that we may equate the exhaustion of values intrinsic to nihilism with the consumption of use value resulting from the present triumph of exchange value: "In order to understand adequately Heidegger's definition of nihilism and to see in it an affinity with Nietzsche's, we must attribute to the term 'value'—which reduces Being to itself—the rigorous sense of 'exchange-value.' Nihilism is thus the reduction of Being to exchange value" (*EOM*, 21). Here he bases his interpretation on two short definitions of nihilism, provided by Nietzsche in a note to the 1906 edition of *The Will to Power* and by Heidegger in the prodigious study of his philosophical predecessor titled simply *Nietzsche*. For Nietzsche, "nihilism" means the situation that follows the death of God and devaluation of the highest values, a condition that in the note to *The Will to Power* he summarizes thus: "Since Copernicus, man has been rolling from the center toward X."[18] By describing this state as a perpetual, ongoing Copernican revolution, Nietzsche suggests the impossibility of the foundation of Being, according to Vattimo (*EOM*, 118). To the extent that Heidegger perceives nihilism so conceived as a process that ends when "there is nothing left" of Being and that entails not only dissolution of Being as foundation but the forgetting of Being altogether, he should in fact be understood to oppose the Nietzschean view, as Vattimo himself openly admits: "It would appear that Heidegger's mode of thought is the opposite of nihilism" (*EOM*, 118).[19] Yet the Italian philosopher nevertheless insists on the continuity of the two thinkers, even as he has to concede the forced, distorted character of this depiction: "For Heidegger, Being is annihilated in so far as it is transformed completely into value [as it is in Nietzsche's thought].... Heidegger himself—from a more Nietzschean than Heideggerian point of view—is also a part of the history of the accomplishment of nihilism" (*EOM*, 20).

He thus paradoxically claims that Heidegger's concern with death and mortality marks him as a nihilist. More than advancing an argument, the claim seems to affirm the triumph of exchange value in modern-day culture (*EOM*, 20–22). By the 1980s the cachet of Marxist economic categories had certainly diminished, yet Vattimo accomplishes his own "transvaluation" by reversing the original relation between the terms of use value and exchange value in the direction of what can only be called a celebration of consumerism. The novelty of weak thought consists in this nondialectical reversal, which is predicated on the supposed superfluity of use value under the conditions of postmodernity. By belittling the "moralistic terms" of Marx's critique of exchange value and the Frankfurt School's "nostalgia for reappropriation" of use value (*EOM*, 25–26), Vattimo travesties an important philosophical and political legacy in order to promote his own pastiche of nihilism. In so doing, he hopes to realize the advantages of "the new possibilities of the symbolic that have been opened up by technology, by secularization, and by the 'weakening' of reality that are typical of late-modern society," transforming the reality of experience into fiction in the name of a "freedom" that sponsors the "performative" operations of "the mass culture and mass media" (*EOM*, 28–29).

At the apex of the postmodern era, weak thought thus assigns to the aesthetic the strategic role of "de-realization" (*ST*, 117).[20] In Vattimo's eyes, it is in the 1970s that the domain of the mass media reveals itself to be not demonic but rather democratic in the manner of Babel (*ST*, 103). It is tempting to say in retrospect that, had he waited for a few more years before making this pronouncement and thus witnessed the cultural and political effects of Berlusconi's consolidated media power, Vattimo might have refrained from pronouncing so blithely what he himself characterized as his "mediatic optimism" (*ST*, 104). If the mentality of the Italian Left can be summed up by Gramsci's famous call for "pessimism of the intellect, optimism of the will," we should ask what politics is possible in a world where both pessimism and critical agency are abandoned in response to the demands of mediatic optimism to be "faithful" to its agenda (*ST*, 109).

134   *Weakness*

After reading René Girard, Vattimo found his way back to religion in the 1990s through the concept of secularization.²¹ Writing as a novice theologian, he advocated a lighter, "postmodern" version of Christianity that might be free of the weight of dogma and in perfect harmony with capitalism. During a world congress of philosophy in Istanbul in 2004, he tells us in his autobiography, he came to the understanding that the typically hermeneutic concept of the event or appropriation of Ereignis should in fact be conceived not à la Heidegger in poetic but rather in political terms.²² Vattimo, who served as a senator for the European Parliament from 1999 to 2004 as a member of the Democratici di Sinistra, recently has recanted some of the most extreme implications of weak thought in the pamphlet *Ecce comu*, which to an extent offers a belated political and philosophical mea culpa by proclaiming the newfound relevance of socialism.²³ In *Ecce comu*, he reaffirms the importance of the Marxist legacy as the sole dignified complement of the Christian message in contemporary society, inaugurating his new appraisal of the relationship between philosophy and politics with the declaration "Yes, I have changed my mind" (*EC*, 40) and even praising Venezuela's leader Hugo Chavez (*EC*, 98). He suddenly appears to recognize the advanced symptoms of the dissolution of democracy that is taking place in Italy as a result of the spirit of passive resignation stifling the country (*EC*, 63). He rightly does not shy away from judging the current Berlusconi régime to be significantly worse than the preceding administration of the Democrazia Cristiana and possibly to represent a new form of Fascism (*EC*, 61).

It would be hard for Vattimo to deny that the new millennium has not delivered the progressive decrease in violence and real need that he so enthusiastically predicted and advertised to his readership in the bulk of his writings. I use the latter verb deliberately, since Vattimo's renunciation of critical thinking has meant, among other things, adoption of a pollyannaish, placating rhetoric that has led to what he himself describes proudly as his "popular" standing. This rhetoric consists in constant reiteration of an extremely narrow repertory of quotations from Nietzsche's and Heidegger's texts that turns these citations into jingles of postmodernity, thus achieving an overall effect comparable to that of an advertising campaign. In the remainder of this chapter, I analyze Vattimo's positions vis-à-vis style, nihilism, difference, media, Nazism, the "ontology of actuality," and religion in order to explain the development of weak thought in its crucial dimensions.

Vattimo's Postmodern Success

As Pierre Bourdieu has shown, it is crucial to understand the intellectual and cultural meaning of a certain movement or historical moment in terms of prestige and success. How did Vattimo manage to acquire recognition and philosophical capital on a worldwide scale unmatched by other Italian philosophers? How do his ideas operate in order to solicit sympathy and approval? I intend to address these issues not from a strictly sociological point of view but rather with an eye to the more broadly cultural and political implications of his positions, focusing especially on how his use of a specific theoretical jargon in the 1980s made it possible for him even to acquire a kind of popular celebrity. Beyond the philosophical rationale for weak thought, it is certainly possible to read his ideology as contributing in complex and important ways to the politics of culture in Italy during the 1980s, as aiding the decisive retreat from the legacy of the PCI or Italian Communist Party and the constitution of a new cultural hegemony that is disciplined by the operations of the media. Moreover, by examining the place of weak thought in the larger context of Italian culture during this period, we may begin to discern a pattern of complicity between the dominant culture of the years of Berlusconi's ascendancy to power and the postmodernist theories of some very influential, allegedly "progressive" thinkers.[24]

In his autobiography, Vattimo boasts of his international prestige, and also of his presence in the media and general popularity: "I can speak of being the only truly popular Italian philosopher."[25] We should note that to some extent his claim was ratified, albeit with a stronger dose of sarcasm, by a television comedy sketch program entitled "Quelli della Notte" that aired nightly on Rai 2 in 1985. Each episode started with one of the hosts announcing the advent of "weak thought, Reaganite debilism" (*NBG*, 92). "Lightness" (a favorite word of advertisers) becomes the ideal of a new aesthetic *koiné*, which was adopted by the likes of Vattimo, Calvino, Eco, and to a certain extent Achille Bonito Oliva.[26] Vattimo gave pride of place in his vocabulary to "weakness," yet it remains an open question whether in the end the word adds anything of meaning to the discussion that is not already covered under the concept of lightness.[27] Both values bespeak a positive view of relinquishing critical activity in keeping with the aestheticized, "go with the flow" mind-set of contemporary culture. Of course, as Adorno demonstrated, aesthetics does not have to be politically reactionary and indeed can be radically meaningful without reducing art to the sum of its political messages. However, even if the correlation between aesthetics and politics is never easy or direct, as Rancière suggests, every aesthetic has a politics, "a distribution of the sensible."[28] In the case of the constellation of authors we are exploring, their common antirealist orientation, fabulist approach to various disciplines, and relentless repetition of leitmotifs as if to mount advertising campaigns all suggest a shared commitment to the aesthetic as an ideological apology for the operations of mass culture.

In recounting the sources of inspiration for weak thought, Vattimo writes: "Technology is relieving social relations of their weight, making them lighter, less heavy. The idea behind weak thought was to turn that to an advantage, to the point of realizing a form of liberation. Emancipation through inflation: if you receive just one television channel, whatever it tells you seems like gospel truth; if you have twenty, you take it or leave it" (*NBG*, 87). He authors these reflections in 2006, when it has become sadly clear that Italy's "twenty television channels" and multiple presses and publishing houses, the majority of which are owned by Berlusconi, have enormously impoverished the quality of the nation's journalism, public discourse, democracy, and culture. Yet even as late as 2003, some five years into his term of service in the European Parliament and a full ten years after Berlusconi was first appointed to the office of premier, Vattimo is able to characterize the alliance between Berlusconi's "free market ideology" (*liberalismo*) and the conservative fundamentalism of the Lega Nord as most likely "a contingent phenomenon" due to the "peculiar personality" of Berlusconi as reflected in his ability to mediate divergent positions (*NE*, 91).

Weak thought has met with sharper criticism "from little provincial Italy," as Vattimo ruefully puts it, than from readers abroad (*NBG*, 88). Throughout the 1990s, he made efforts to clarify weak thought as a philosophical system, most notably in a series of lectures delivered at the University of Bologna at the invitation of Eco. In the United States he has been widely read and admired, earning in particular the approval of Richard Rorty.[29] Rorty's support was especially important to Vattimo, allowing him to feel he was not "just some little Italian" but rather someone "who cast a shadow internationally" (*NBG*, 98–99). Yet even in Italy his influence has been widely and deeply felt, outweighing the dissenting arguments raised against it.[30] The promise of a "nonaggressive ethics" and lightness of spirit mobilized against the "heaviness" of the leftist agenda has proven irresistible, in the process aligning neatly with a familiar touristic stereotype of what present-day Italian culture ought to look like: in essence, a fantasy of the hedonism that Fellini criticized in *La dolce vita*.[31]

In this sense, in the specific setting of poststructuralist philosophy, weak thought is in a category of its own. It is true that Habermas undertook a political critique of poststructuralism in *The Philosophical Discourse of Modernity* (1987) that gave special attention to Heidegger, Derrida, and Foucault. The mere fact of Habermas's opinion might lead some to think that weak thought joins the ranks of philosophies based on a "philosophy of subjectivity," as he puts it, and thus avoids the fight for social emancipation and justice.[32] Yet, unlike Vattimo, Derrida and Foucault neither claimed at any point to want to break with nor ever in fact abandoned the Enlightenment project. Indeed, it is more than possible to argue that, albeit in ways very different from each other, they managed to invigorate the very necessity of criticism for contemporary culture.[33] Derrida writes: "I therefore have no *thesis*, properly speaking, to propose. Only a belief, perhaps a naïve one: I would like to be able to carry out, modestly, the critical or deconstructive analysis of what does not work and 'isn't going well [*ne va pas*],' of what should *come* and remain to be thought, remain to be done."[34]

Weak thought, on the other hand, has forsaken by definition any effort to redefine the critical responsibilities of philosophy, resulting in a defense of postmodernity as a cultural and ideological brand. Unlike Derrida, who always resisted adopting the fashionable terminology du jour such as the language of "the postmodern," Vattimo professes his philosophical allegiance to the conceptual constellation of postmodernity even after initial enthusiasm for the discourse has faded. In *The Transparent Society*, he states that the postmodern is not a "fad" but rather a term whose meaning "is linked to the fact that the society in which we live is a society of generalized communication . . . of the mass media" (*TS*, 1). He persists in reminding us in 2003 that he is one of the "few remaining 'believers' in postmodernity" although he does not reflect on the reasons for his isolation (*NE*, 153). He, like Eco, studied at the University of Turin with Luigi Pareyson, a prominent Italian philosopher whose work focused on aesthetics and religion. After writing a dissertation on the concept of doing in Aristotle, he wished to study Adorno, but Pareyson directed him to Nietzsche as a fitter subject of study for the time.[35] Although his pupil Santiago Zabala speaks of Vattimo's "Maoist phase" in the 1960s, it must have been short-lived insofar as by 1968 we find him boasting of his "Heideggerianism," which he insinuates is more sophisticated than Hegelian Marxism, and being reassured in Pareyson's company that they both possess greater radicalism than the student protesters in Turin because "we are people absolutely outside the organicity of this situation" (*NBG*, 61).

What Vattimo seems to consider anticapitalist in Heidegger is his resistance to modernity, a trait the Italian philosopher thought Heidegger shared with Lukács, whom he nonetheless held to be less interesting for thinking in terms of power rather than being. Vattimo continues to claim that there is a left-wing Heideggerianism that calls not for a return of Being, which is the default right-wing position, but rather for an ethics of Verwindung or resignation to the epochal nihilist weakening of ontological foundations. Yet Heidegger's belief in overcoming metaphysics not through human action but rather through acquiescence to the vicissitudes of Being, through the acceptance of every worldly event from the Holocaust to the excesses of capitalism, can hardly be regarded as conducive to a "leftist" attitude.[36] Identifying a leftist stance with "resignation" is one of several snobbish paradoxes that punctuate Vattimo's writings. For example, he also does not hesitate to interpret Heidegger's archaic search for Being as something improbably à la mode: "The 'essential word' that Heidegger always sought, even in his unrelenting return to the dawning moments of European philosophy, is perhaps much closer to the daily chatter of the late-modern world than to the arcane silence of the mystic and the sacred experience."[37]

Over the years, Vattimo studiously avoids the language of power and resistance.[38] From the late 1960s through the 1980s, Deleuze and Foucault approached Nietzsche on a new footing by focusing on his ideas of force and power, while Derrida transformed Heidegger's notion of the destruction of metaphysics into the task of critical deconstruction.[39] Vattimo attacks Derrida's rejection of Heidegger's metaphysical vocabulary of Being on the grounds that modest thought must accommodate itself to ontology.[40] The Italian philosopher's hostility to deconstruction as an immodest intellectual project betrays a fundamental discomfort with the way, for example, Derrida problematizes what he calls "the task of reading" in *Of Grammatology*. Whereas the Derridean mode of investigation consistently raises questions of gender, racial, and cultural otherness, Vattimo's approach perhaps is best captured by the title of a philosophical yearbook that he edited for publication in 1992: *Lightening as Responsibility*. Throughout his oeuvre, he reinforces the stress of Italian postmodernism on "lightness" as a code word for a posture of deferential acceptance, as when he writes in his autobiography that "the only possible history of Being is the growing lighter, the losing weight of Being itself" (*NBG*, 24).

Systematically refusing to acknowledge any aspects of contemporary power, he proves indifferent as well to questions of biopolitics and to any consideration of Debord's analysis of the society of spectacle. He seems convinced, as Zabala puts it, that "the history of political power in the West is nothing but a weakening of strong structures of power: from absolute monarchy, to constitutional and democratic states."[41] Yet to cast doubt on this narrative of enlightened progress, we need only contemplate the record of genocide in the twentieth and twenty-first centuries and the example of the Holocaust, which Vattimo refuses to do most glaringly in relationship to Heidegger, given the importance of the German philosopher to his own thinking. Indeed, Marramao aptly observes that Vattimo seems to lead philosophical and political reflection back to metaphysical forms, instead of identifying "a new and more pervasive form of power in the operations (that are 'weak' only in appearance) of the conventionalization of order and the 'disciplinary' sectoring of labour-related functions and the divisions of knowledge."[42] By Vattimo's own accounting, the biographical seeds of his disdain for any intellectual concern with power and especially for the sin of "revolutionary moralism" were sown during the 1970s, the years of terrorism in Italy during which the Red Brigades were killing people and issuing death threats against others, including, at one point, Vattimo for not being sufficiently radical (*NBG*, 81–83).

He describes the primal scene of weak thought as one in which, while reading rhetorically violent letters from his Leninist students, he arrived at the insight that the Nietzschean superman could not be a revolutionary. Accordingly, he has an epiphany that what is necessary to liberate human being is not a critical solution of political problems but rather a call for "weakening as a way of eluding power" (*NBG*, 85), which as a principle clearly informs his agenda of encouraging a hermeneutical resignation derived from Heideggerian *Verwindung* and Nietzschean nihilism. "Weak thought came to life not out of fear of terrorism," writes Zabala, "but as a response to the terrorist interpretation of the Italian democratic Left during the 1970s, as a recognition of the unacceptability of the Red Brigades' violence."[43] It well might be replied, however, that, although terrorism was a soberingly painful problem in Italy during the 1970s, to attempt to reduce the contributions of leftist Italian philosophy to its most violent fringe would be a shortsighted mistake. Since the 1960s, new ways of discussing the role of the working class and the operations of biopolitics have been elaborated by figures such as Mario Tronti and Antonio Negri as part of Autonomia Operaia, a movement that remains philosophically productive and resonant today at the time of post-Fordism.[44]

Weak thought, by contrast, may be seen to have squandered the important legacy of leftist and critical thought in Italy from Gramsci to Negri. Its popular success as a doctrine at home and abroad has been based on confirming the cultural stereotype of a mild, sweet Italian style of life and thought.[45] Weak thought in other words appeals to readers by offering not only the example of philosophical renunciation of violence but also, in books such as *The End of Modernity* and *The Transparent Society*, justification of the phantasmatic and escapist dimensions of postmodernity that embraces the weakening of the principle of reality in the name of "mediatic optimism," to cite Vattimo's formulation from an essay added to the third edition of *The Transparent Society* (2000).[46] This essay in fact offers one of the clearest articulations of his postmodern theory, advocating complete rejection of the Frankfurt School's pessimism with respect to mass culture and a corresponding celebration of postmodernity as the triumph of aestheticization within the consumerist logic of the media.

Vattimo's Style: The Jargon of Postmodernity in Italy

Over the course of several decades of critical thinking, Antonio Negri has established himself as the most important ideologue of a constellation of political phenomena in Italy, including the student demonstrations associated with the "movement of 1977," the search by workerist groups for everyday forms of resistance to capitalism under the aegis of Autonomia Operaia, and most recently the critique of global capitalism mounted in a series of books beginning with *Empire* that he has coauthored with Michael Hardt. Negri regards weak thought as the nadir of Italian philosophical achievement in a country that has been disfigured by the lack of a real public space:

> If Italy does not have a center, Italian philosophy is not even provincial: it is only weak, and has been a weak philosophy forever in the face of politics and of the masters, the dictators, and the popes. Since the nineteenth-century decline of ideas and discussion, perhaps the vilest point has been reached when some authors, with a certain pride, proclaimed their thought and their definition of the philosophy of the present to be "weak." Others labelled it more appropriately "pensiero molle": soft thinking. It seemed that what was at stake was the attempt to find the right climate for the postmodern under the tepid Italian skies: in reality we were dealing with the attempt to crush the wealth of articulations and surfaces of reality, of *dispositifs*, and of assemblages of French poststructuralism against the horizon of Heideggerian ontology. More perversely, it was a question of denying the history of insurgencies and resistances that accompanied the first building-up-from-below of a public space in Italy, the first democratic building-up since fascism. . . . Weak thought has translated into Italian a Foucault and a Deleuze whom it has disguised as soubrettes.[47]

This harsh condemnation exposes a central operation of Vattimo's teaching. As Negri bluntly observes, weak thought premises its defense of postmodernity on the surreptitious "attempt to crush" the critical implications of French poststructuralism for Italian philosophy, a closed-mindedness that works hand in hand with the denial of "the history of insurgencies and resistances" of Italy in the 1970s.

The very etymology of the term *deconstruction* signals a critical function. Although Derrida's thought became more explicitly political in the 1990s with publication of *Specters of Marx* (1993), "Faith and Knowledge" (1996), and *Rogues* (2003), his preferred mode of investigation from early in his career was always to question privileged structures of meaning in order to reveal how they work to repress difference, for example pursuing this way of reading in relation to the Heideggerian conceptual apparatus in *Of Spirit: Heidegger and the Question* (1987).[48] Particularly in the books he coauthored with Félix Guattari, Deleuze created an entirely new conceptual vocabulary comprising ideas such as assemblages, becoming (minoritarian), deterritorialization, and nomadism that, Paul Patton suggests, emphasize processes of creative transformation or "lines of flight" whose meanings are inherently political.[49] For his part, Foucault redefined the critical task of thought as one of establishing the conditions of possibility in order to imagine ways of transgressing their limits.

In addition to failing to engage in any serious way with French poststructuralism, weak thought has also ignored the Frankfurt School's development of the critical inheritance of Hegelian dialectic. The group's members, particularly Adorno, were interested in the possibility of transforming the social order through a cultural and political praxis that avoids universalist ideology and rejects the Hegelian theory of the identity of subject and object. Staying at all times aware of the possibility of imagining a different order of things, the Frankfurt School thinkers insist on the dynamic complication of logical and institutional principles. In his analysis of the culture industry, Adorno refuses any artificial, final reconciliation of social contradictions in order to maintain a dialectic that is deprived of resolution yet never lapses into a state of resignation.

In the introduction to *Weak Thought*, Vattimo and Rovatti repudiate the efforts of French poststructuralists to respond to the philosophical tradition, particularly the work of Foucault and Deleuze, on the grounds that they remain too nostalgic for metaphysics and thus are not sufficiently sophisticated in their understanding of the "oblivion of Being" espoused by Nietzsche and Heidegger (*PD*, 9). According to the authors, the advantage of weak thought is its "weakness before the world and society" inasmuch as nowadays we not only must acknowledge the connection between metaphysics and relations of domination but also must avoid the trap of hoping for emancipation through dialectical procedures of unmasking and demystification. As they see it, the appropriate frame of mind limits itself to focusing solely on discursive procedures and "symbolic forms": "Weak thought is then a metaphor and in a certain way a paradox" (*PD*, 10). Yet its paradoxical welcoming of reduced philosophical scope does not preclude weak thought, in Vattimo and Rovatti's judgment, from consideration of the past through pietas, as well as of the present and even the future, despite the fact that it may appear to be "impeded" in trying to envision what is to come by its hermeneutic nostalgia for historically given situations or epochs (*PD*, 11). One of Vattimo's most philosophically and politically revealing acknowledgments of the consequences of accepting prevailing conditions without critical resistance occurs at the end of *The Transparent Society*, where, after toying with the idea that the market might counter the process of cultural derealization, he concludes: "On the other hand, even if this is a very difficult and complex field, the development of a financial economy in which what are bought and sold are increasingly less concrete goods and more 'titles,' names, and futures . . . seems to indicate an irresistible tendency of economics itself to transfer its activities onto the plane of the imagination, freeing itself from any realist link" (*ST*, 120).

Weakness, like the corresponding values of lightness, sweetness, and softness, in this sense may be said to reflect the ideology of a nation that throughout the 1980s identified itself with the uniquely spectacularized model of capitalism branded "Made in Italy." The elusive, multivalent resonances of these terms reinforce at the ideological level the increasingly abstract, "immaterial" forms of capitalism that are catalyzed by the speculative volatility of the financial markets and the spectral virtuality of the mass media. It is no wonder that under the conditions of capitalism, as Marx and Engels famously declared in *The Communist Manifesto*, "all that is solid melts into air." Indeed, the sociologist Zygmunt Bauman has observed that general discussion of the current stage of modernity is dominated by metaphors of "being light" and "being liquid."[50] As a response to the changing conditions of modernity, Vattimo's work avoids any attempt to renew the difficult task of criticism and instead settles for praising the joys of lightness, softness, and above all weakness as means of achieving postmodern freedom.

Some commentators, such as Carlo Augusto Viano, recognized the apologetic tendency of weak thought as soon as the doctrine was introduced.[51] Viano remarks that Italian philosophy often regards itself as the place where problematic philosophical questions raised elsewhere may find a solution.[52] As he points out, this attitude in no small measure confirms the general stereotype of Italian culture as "easygoing" (*VP*, viii). Something similar seems to happen in the case of weak thought vis-à-vis poststructuralism, if we consider Vattimo's frequent claims to have resolved the crisis of foundational thought while dismissing the contributions of Derrida, Deleuze, and Foucault as inadequate. Yet, as Viano tartly observes, the stance of "the weaklings" who espouse *il pensiero debole* in fact amounts to little more than a weakening or simplifying return to French structuralism.[53] In his eyes, weak thought merely perpetuates a customary spiritualist love of what is vague and indeterminate (*VP*, 17).

Where a critical reader well might diverge from Viano is over his conviction that, as a result of this affinity, weak thought aligns itself with the refusal of industrial culture (*VP*, 18). He believes that the so-called culture industry in Italy is liberal and secular and that spiritualism and its offshoots therefore oppose it by definition (*VP*, 20). When it comes to Vattimo, however, this generalization does not hold true. Writing before Vattimo elaborates his position on technology and mass media in *The Transparent Society*, Viano proposes that the key to understanding weak thought is its supposedly anti-industrial inclination. Yet the true achievement of weak thought in fact may have been to conjoin a new version of spiritualism with a triumphal celebration of Italy's role in the era of global capitalism. Such a well-tempered solution brings us back, as Viano initially observed, to the stereotype of Italian culture as the land of easy compromises. In this connection it is revealing that, as an ideal contemporary example of the activities of the Nietzschean superman, Vattimo names the figure of the tourist who exercises a form of attention that is more aesthetic than realistic in a specific institutional setting: the museum, which in his eyes offers the paradigm of the perfect coexistence of a plurality of styles and represents a school of aesthetic tolerance (*NE*, 55–58).[54] Vattimo seems to be unaware of the long genealogy of critique repudiating the potential operation of the museum as an instrument of cultural control, which dates back at least to Adorno's seminal essay "The Valéry Proust Museum." In this treatise, Adorno argues that the museum inherently enforces a conservative politics by decontextualizing the work of art and isolating it from the conditions of material production.[55] If Vattimo's praise of the museum implicitly places Italy in an ideal symbolic position in his postmodern philosophical pantheon, the recent controversy surrounding the *beni culturali* and their commercial exploitation by Berlusconi's government casts a decidedly harsher light on Vattimo's idealized site of aesthetic bliss.[56]

Of course, poststructuralism and its postfoundational ontology are characterized by a preponderance of categories, such as difference, pluralism, becoming, etc., that appear vulnerable to being co-opted by the mutational logic of capitalism. Yet we well may argue that an emphasis on "becoming" à la Deleuze or on "différance" à la Derrida risks confirming the power dynamic that is implicated in consumerism in order to turn the means of this dynamic to the ends of strategic resistance according to a relation best explained by Foucault.[57] By contrast, Italian intellectuals such as Calvino, Vattimo, and Eco have reinterpreted poststructuralism in a manner that privileges the purity of the aesthetic. This reading enforces an attitude of critical resignation and passivity. When Adorno analyzed the influence of German existentialism and Heideggerian philosophy in *Jargon of Authenticity* (1967), he exposed a culturally and historically peculiar argot as the predominant form of mystification in the Germany of his day.[58] As he famously put it, ideology at that time had shifted into language (*JA*, xxi).[59]

Following his example, we may discern the rise of a poststructuralist jargon in Italy, beginning in the 1960s and culminating in the 1980s and 1990s, that resembles its German predecessor to the extent that it operates chiefly by means of magical expression, idealization, self-congratulation, and a coercive positivity. In its Italian manifestation, this rhetorical repertory constitutes a demagogic veil for the growing contradictions of the "Made in Italy" society. Such a strategy realizes its potential, according to Adorno, when it pervades the entire social scale "reaching from sermon to advertisement" (*JA*, 43). On this score, it is significant that the language of weakness, lightness, sweetness, and softness preferred by contemporary Italy's most celebrated intellectual figures mimics the banality of advertising in repetitive use of idealized tautologies and expressionist gestures, as we have remarked at other points. Italy's current jargon thereby achieves what Adorno would describe as "arbitrary effect-connotations" (*JA*, 43). Its popularization appears to be driven by impulses related to the spread of stereotypes resulting from tourism and the global marketing of Italy's cultural capital. Since the Second World War, Italy increasingly has treated its monumental, architectural, and artistic inheritance as a means of promoting the nation's image as a place where visitors can escape into the unfettered play of consumerism, an image that both exploits and displaces an older depiction of Italy as the site of a culturally enlightening Grand Tour.[60]

Weakness, lightness, sweetness, and softness thus are words "covered with a luminous layer of insulation," to borrow a phrase from Adorno, meaning that precisely their imperviousness to critical questioning enables them to mediate the economy of mass culture (*JA*, 44). Of these words, the oldest pedigree and thus the most auratic status belong to sweetness, which may be regarded as supplying the Italian tradition with a guiding thread from the *Dolce Stil Novo* and Petrarch to Fellini and beyond. Lightness and softness operate in a more recent register that is familiar from the promotional cant used in commercials, although one could argue that lightness has also acquired a patina of high literary grandeur, thanks to the importance that both Calvino and Kundera have given the term.

At first glance, it seems by comparison as if weakness denotes a less intrinsically idealized condition than the other categories and in this sense offers less value as an instrument of publicity. Yet it may be observed that, in a more complex manner than with the other signifiers, weakness encodes a positive ideological gain at the price of a negative semantic charge. The notion of weakness, that is, more fully conforms to the ideological purposes of a language of obedience. The concept perfectly encapsulates the reasoning behind Vattimo's insistence on the philosophically crucial importance of Heidegger's Verwindung, for example.[61] Relative to the other categories whose meaning is explicit, weakness is at once a more ambivalent and a more revealing term. In the tactics of its wavering between the literal and the figurative, we may discern the advancing disintegration of the word's very semantic aura, its assimilation to the procedures of bad consciousness.[62] Consequently, weakness plays a pivotal role in the hegemonic jargon of contemporary Italy. In this respect Vattimo ought to be regarded as what Adorno would have called the "matador" of the cultural strategy that the jargon represents.[63] One of Vattimo's central rhetorical gambits is to present himself as a philosopher of good temperament who is averse to the despised "tragical attitudinizing" of his rivals (*NE*, xxvi).[64] He claims a merely "exhortative" ambition for his work because philosophy in his eyes no longer may pretend to demonstrate the truth or to increase knowledge (*VRF*, 64–65). For him, the true philosopher is not an engaged thinker who seeks a "critical 'overcoming'" of the contradictions of our time but rather a quietist who wishes only to hasten our "taking leave of modernity" (*EOM*, 3).

We may view the pedagogical goal of exhortation that Vattimo assigns to philosophy as a quaint remnant of a formal Catholic education, but such an ideal also consorts to an unsettling degree with the logic of advertising, which after all continuously aims to "exhort" the consumer.[65] It is useful on this score to recall Foucault's observation that the Western critical tradition arises in response to the Christian pastoral and thus originates in the act of questioning the Church's exhortation of its members to obedience as a route to religious salvation.[66] As we will see, Vattimo's complicated but fundamental allegiance to Catholicism plays an important role in the construction of his philosophy. The not-so-secret weapon in his strategy of exhortation is obsessive repetition. Vattimo's style—and, according to Adorno, Heidegger's style too—is characterized by formulaic citation of the same, few textual loci in all of his books. It is also characterized by a tautological circularity of reasoning that recalls the truisms of marketing campaign slogans, as when Vattimo defines modernity as "that era in which being modern becomes a value" (*EOM*, 99). Perhaps in an attempt to deflect such considerations by elaborating the religious implications of his exhortative method, and with evident desire to introduce a controversial note into the discussion, Vattimo complains in the preface to *Beyond Interpretation* (1994) that the concept of weak thought has been interpreted too literally by readers and claims that instead it was meant all along to suggest the scandal of nihilism in the arms of theology.[67] Certainly, it is within a theological horizon that the possibility of a more challenging and engaged reading of the idea of weakness begins to emerge. For example, we might recall Paul's paradoxical uses of the category in the Second Epistle when he declares, "My grace is sufficient for thee: for my strength is made perfect in weakness" (12:9), and asserts, "For when I am weak, then I am strong" (12:10).

Yet when applied to philosophy and not read in a strictly religious context, the adjective *weak* seems like a gesture of intellectual willfulness. By his own assertions, Vattimo himself has established that, as a natural outgrowth of the metaphysical tradition's legacy of nihilism, weak thought stands opposed to the modes of inquiry and thought typically associated with "criticism" or "the critical." Such a polemic, however, risks blinding itself to the importance of the questions raised by the approaches that it denounces. One key achievement of poststructuralism has been to renew the philosophical question of force, which largely has been ignored by structuralism, as Derrida pointed out in his seminal essay "Force and Signification" (1963). He maintained that new attention had to be dedicated to the relationship between force and history precisely because the teleological framework of history "belongs to the system of metaphysical oppositions" and therefore can begin to be called into question and engaged meaningfully "only through a *certain* organization, a certain *strategic* arrangement which, within the field of metaphysical opposition, uses the strength of the field to turns its own stratagems against it, producing a force of dislocation that spreads itself throughout the entire system, fissuring it in every direction and thoroughly *delimiting* it."[68]

Weak thought systematically fails to recognize the meaning of the strategic operations of force in the context of poststructuralism. Indeed, Vattimo maintains in *Beyond Interpretation* that we ought to regard what is at stake in the hermeneutic task as a conflict not of forces but rather of interpretations, in order to conceive of truth in terms other than those of the will to power (*BI*, 83). For him, the conditions of possibility of experience belong to a state of historical precomprehension. However, as Deleuze observes in his magisterial *Nietzsche and Philosophy*, Nietzsche's vital lesson was to find Kant's idea of critique wanting insofar as it represents "a force which should be brought to bear on all claims to knowledge and truth, but not on knowledge and truth themselves; a force which should be brought to bear on all claims to morality, but not on morality itself."[69] According to Deleuze, Nietzsche then discovered a stronger, more compelling version of critique by redirecting it toward criticism of values.[70] What is at the core of the Nietzschean genealogical venture, then, is not mere interpretation but active evaluation. Nietzsche himself declares, "Every will implies an evaluation," and Deleuze adds, "Genealogy does not only interpret, it also evaluates."[71] The crucial idea of criticism in post-Kantian philosophy no longer focuses on the limits, but rather on the creative possibilities, of transgression or transvaluation.

Among others who inscribe their work in a post-Nietzschean philosophical horizon, Deleuze, Derrida, and Foucault engage in evaluating the forces and strategies of power in order to discover new spaces of becoming, freedom, and transformation. (Foucault specifically follows Nietzsche's lead by evoking Kant in order to overcome him.[72]) Nothing of this sort of discovery is possible with Vattimo's conservative reading of Nietzsche, whom Vattimo deprives of any critical ability to challenge or problematize.[73] After years of accepting weak thought, Romano Luperini has observed, the Italian intellectual establishment seems to have lost the ability merely to muster a critical "attitude."[74] The task of criticism that Kant, Marx, and Adorno reaffirmed and reinterpreted over time was renounced by the proponents and supporters of weak thought, who prefer instead to adopt a strictly hermeneutic approach at a time when the rise of the society of spectacle and biopolitical methods of control have made questions of political and cultural power increasingly urgent.[75] In this sense, Vattimo's theory symptomatizes the overall complacency of Italy as a society from the 1980s to the present day. Ideologically, weak thought represents a way of thinking that has never resisted—and in fact has facilitated—Berlusconi's ascent to power by encouraging passive receptivity toward popular opinion.

The success of the doctrine in Italy and abroad has likely been reinforced by conventional stereotypes about Italy's Mediterranean character. Since at least Rousseau and Montesquieu, it has been all too typical of a certain strain of cultural analysis to explain social and historical developments in terms of the shaping of an essential national temperament by local factors such as geography and climate. Madame de Staël, for example, suggested the existence of two distinct European literary paradigms: a literature of the North and another of the Mediterranean. One of the most vociferous advocates of categorizing cultures on the basis of fundamental national differences was Nietzsche, who harshly criticized German culture, especially in its decadent, Wagnerian manifestations, and exalted the Italian Renaissance as a model of historical vigor.[76] By his time, however, Italy, which was still relatively young as a unified nation, had become mainly a site of tourism and convalescence for foreign visitors.[77] Luigi Barzini, the don among scholars of Italian stereotypes, speaks of visitors to the country getting "addicted to the amiable and mild ways of Italy."[78] He cites Stendhal's praise of Italians' bonhomie and helpfully attributes their general happiness to their accomplishment in the art of not thinking, naming Goethe's traveling companion as corroborating evidence for his argument.[79] Predictably, he concludes that in Italy "life is malleable, a soft, yielding matter which can be shaped by any form."[80]

By way of elaborating the wisdom of weak thought, Vattimo translates this sort of comforting, touristic image of Italy into a philosophical register. Although he avoids the overtly nationalistic sentiments of Gentile's and Heidegger's philosophies, Vattimo nevertheless affirms in his works many of the most cliché preconceptions about Italian identity. It is no surprise, then, that the ideal contemporary illustration of the Nietzschean superman in his eyes, as we noted earlier, is the figure of the tourist and that he constantly makes approving use of tourism as a metaphor for postmetaphysical thinking. An amenable, well-tempered personality, an attitude of pietas, reverential acceptance of tradition and conventional wisdom, aversion to criticism, and "active" nihilism are all attributes of the ideal weak thinker as well as of stereotypical, post-Renaissance Italians in general. From Vico to Croce, Italy's philosophers have long represented a reassuring escape from the most demanding implications and revisions of Enlightenment thought, and in this sense Vattimo belongs to an established Italian tradition. With the success of weak thought in the cultural marketplace, Italy becomes the global capital of Verwindung inasmuch as it offers a place for convalescence from the severity of Germanic metaphysics and criticism. Weak thought on this account may be viewed as the most sophisticated of strategies for marketing Italy to the hyper-knowing tourists of contemporary consumerism.

Nihilism: The Triumph of the Exchange Value

For Vattimo, postmodernity in the Lyotardian sense of an end of belief in metanarratives offers a rationale for nihilism, which he sees as the destiny of the Western world.[81] His nomination of nihilism as the postmodern value par excellence has nothing to do with such predictable explanations as a general pessimism about mass culture, or as in the Russian novel, the problem of evil.[82] Nihilism as he understands the concept instead encompasses the end of metaphysics, the end of modernity, and the triumph of exchange value over use value. This reading hinges on a presumption of Nietzsche's and Heidegger's philosophical proximity to each other as well as of a convergence of their thinking apropos of nihilism and the end of metaphysics that their writings hardly corroborate.[83] Vattimo explains this convergence in terms that simplify both thinkers' ideas to the point of caricature: "The History of Being is the history of how objective truth gradually dissolves; therefore, it is nihilism, the history of nihilism as sketched by Nietzsche" (*NBG*, 24).[84] He delivers one of the most concise statements of his view of nihilism in the preface to *Nihilism and Emancipation*, where he follows a Nietzschean lead in defining it as "the dissolution of any ultimate foundation, the understanding that, in the history of philosophy and of western culture in general, 'God is Dead' and the 'real world has become a fable'" (*NE*, xxv). His reasoning proceeds from the initial premise that Nietzsche wholly identifies nihilism with interpretation. Of crucial importance for Vattimo is the German philosopher's famous declaration in *Twilight of the Idols* that, because of the devaluation of supreme values, there are no facts but only interpretations (*BI*, 12).

Even more dubiously, Vattimo proposes that Heideggerian hermeneutics ought to be classified as nihilist. He maintains that this is the only proper conclusion for "the Heideggerian left," by which he means a Heideggerian who is not devoted to the task of a mystical recuperation of Being and who recognizes instead that the interminable weakening of Being is the only means to an overcoming of metaphysics that might not itself be metaphysical (*BI*, 13).[85] He pays no attention either to Heidegger's own overt criticism of nihilism, particularly in relation to Nietzsche's philosophy, or to the possibility that Nietzsche's own approach to nihilism may be more cautious and qualified than the Italian philosopher grants: "We may say that—in Nietzsche's and Heidegger's use of the term—nihilism is the consumption of use value in exchange value" (*EOM*, 22).

Vattimo's emphasis on ontological nihilism thus is inspired by Heidegger, although Heidegger would never have given nihilism a positive value. In *Nietzsche*, Heidegger confronts nihilistic dissolution of Being with extreme dismay, concluding that "the essence of nihilism is the history in which there is nothing to Being itself."[86] Although to reconstruct Heidegger's complex relation to Nietzsche would involve an overly lengthy digression, it will be enough for our purposes to note that Nietzsche's thought, particularly his notion of will to power, represented for Heidegger the fulfillment of metaphysics in the sense of a final, decisive forgetting of Being, not the new beginning of a process of lightening as Vattimo wishes us to believe.[87] From Heidegger's perspective, Nietzsche's will to power is not a psychological faculty but rather the "innermost essence of Being" (*essentia*). Nihilism as the "devaluation of the highest values" is the name of the unfortunate logic of the history of Being thus defined (*existentia*).[88]

According to Vattimo, however, Heidegger refuses to acknowledge his closeness to Nietzsche, because he refuses to recognize the nihilistic implications of his own conception of Being as neither foundation nor presence, but rather as the result of a remembering (An-denken) of Being's "historico-destinate apertures" or events.[89] As Vattimo sees it, the will to power and the eternal return are not descriptions of Being but only "modes" in which Being occurs at the end of metaphysics. To conclude otherwise means to lend credence to fascist interpretations of Nietzsche, a mistake that he thinks Foucault makes, for example: "An interpretation of Nietzsche that only sees his philosophy as an 'unveiling' of the fact that Being is will to power, and so endorses a morality of power, struggle, conflict, remains on this level of still metaphysical description. This is the 'fascist' way of reading Nietzsche, but there are also traces of a similar interpretation to be found in Foucault."[90]

During the 1980s, Vattimo glorifies the capitalist logic of postmodernism qua nihilism in *The End of Modernity* (1985) and *The Transparent Society* (1989). As we know, nihilism for him means not an affirmative, vitalistic force *à la* Deleuze but rather the decisive victory of exchange value over use value (*EOM*, 21). Being simply consumes itself, and there is no metaphysical use value to save. In a manner typical of his general rhetorical method, Vattimo resorts to a tautology to explain what has been gained with this victory when he observes that ultimately the market itself is responsible for demythologizing the concept of use value (*TS*, 70). He calls for unrelenting ideological exaltation of exchange value on the grounds that such a position consorts with what in his view is a philosophically sophisticated preference for "fable" over "reality": "Generalized reification, as the reduction of everything to exchange value, is precisely that world which has become a fable.... The consumption of Being in exchange-value, that is, the transformation of the real world into a fable, is nihilistic even in so far as it leads to a weakening of the cogent force of reality" (*EOM*, 26–27).[91] For a variety of reasons, we may wish to avoid the error of reacting to Vattimo by insisting on the absolute importance of use value and so preserving in inverse form the schematic logic of weak thought. Yet we surely ought to acknowledge that his polemical single-mindedness renders him oblivious to the evident strategic reality, often stressed by Adorno, that in the overall economy of the culture industry "exchange value depreciates qualitative differences."[92]

The rationale for Vattimo's acritical idealization of exchange value, as Franca D'Agostini articulates it, is that such a position exemplifies admirably coolheaded political moderation. On this reckoning, Deleuze and Foucault indulge in a cheap aestheticizing of political conflict that would have fanned the flames of terrorist violence in Italy, if their ideas had gained wider acceptance. Vattimo supposedly offers a way out of this bloody cul-de-sac through the simultaneously "radical" and "reasonable" response of weak thought (*VRF*, 12). One might well ask by way of reply just how politically responsible it is to attempt to link Deleuze and Foucault to the culturally specific history of Italian terrorism in the 1970s. At any rate, in the essays he wrote between 1972 and 1979, which are collected in *The Adventure of Difference*, Vattimo was already promoting the philosophical concept of difference as "the denial and destitution of presence" and thus as a needed defense against "every temptation to seek a dialectical harmonization . . . for example, in some political order passing as 'real socialism'" (*AD*,2 4–5).

The inadequacy of weak thought as a response to the ethical and political implications of Nietzschean philosophy has to do with the fact that Vattimo pays little attention to the contrast between active and passive nihilism, a contrast that is crucial for French poststructuralism. In a notebook entry of 1887, Nietzsche differentiates between active nihilism—which increases the power of spirit by pursuing new interpretations that result in the overthrow of obsolete values and creation of strong, adventurous forms of life—and passive nihilism, which settles for reactively acknowledging the disintegration of supreme values.[93] His distinction has a profound influence on Deleuze, who reminds us that "what Nietzsche calls self-destruction, active destruction, must not, above all, be confused with the passive extinction of the last man," yet ultimately the point is lost on Vattimo.[94] Invoking a passage of *The Will to Power* in which Nietzsche paradoxically claims that in their lack of need for articles of extreme faith it is philosophical moderates who will prove to be the strongest thinkers, Vattimo maintains that "at bottom, active nihilism is always passive and reactive too."[95] In keeping with his fundamental spiritualism, he cannot encourage active nihilism à la Deleuze or Foucault, because such a position would mean embracing vitalist notions of life, force, and will to power that would amount to a new metaphysics:

> If active nihilism wishes to avoid reversing its polarity and becoming a new metaphysics that puts life, force and will to power in the place of the Platonic *ontos on*, it will have to interpret itself in the end as a doctrine of the vanishing of Being—of vanishing, weakening, and so on as "the essential" character of Being itself. Nihilism is the process in the course of which, as Heidegger says in writing about Nietzsche, "There is nothing to Being itself."[96]

To imagine the overcoming of metaphysics as a deepening of nihilism is Vattimo's dialectical response to his genealogical predecessors: "This Being, which as Nietzsche writes in a passage cited by Heidegger 'evaporates,' is not just some false image of Being meant to be replaced by a solider, truer one."[97] His emphasis on this evaporation of Being reflects a distrust of epistemologically unifying grounds or rules, along with a conviction that to accept the fading of such principles itself positively represents a new way of thinking, a break with the past. So far, this position may seem familiar when compared with the general outlines of so-called Continental philosophy, especially, in ways that we briefly have considered, in its poststructuralist manifestations. Yet Vattimo reifies the Heideggerian notion of "a philosophy which sees what is constitutive of Being not as the fact of its prevailing, but as the fact of its disappearing" (*AD*, 5) to the point that it becomes an immobilizing gesture of self-complacency. For Heidegger, nihilism is not a viewpoint; rather it is "an event of long duration" that informs the history of the "decline" of Being, and thus a key movement in the modern history of Western civilization.[98]

Vattimo takes this view of nihilism as a privileged philosophical development a step further. He treats denial of traditional hierarchies and structures of meaning as a methodological breakthrough characteristic of the West in a manner that implies a kind of philosophical colonialism. More precisely, he identifies Western history with the advance of nihilism and secularization so as to grant the decline of metaphysics an importance that is ironically world-historical or evolutionary. The regressiveness of his position is particularly evident in a passage from *Nihilism and Emancipation* in which he declares that a philosophy of weakening and secularization disrupts the "widespread tendency . . . to react to Babel and postmodern pluralism" through identity politics and teaches us that "we all belong to the West and that westernization is a destiny that even the 'other' cultures that have freed themselves from colonial status and the label of primitive are unable to escape" (*NE*, 33). In the introduction to the same book, he coyly evades the question of the cultural specificity of hermeneutic nihilism: "Only in western thought and culture? This initial obstacle will not be discussed thematically in these pages" (*NE*, xxv).

In this context, his greatest challenge is to convince his readers that, by making possible our freedom from foundationalist discourses and unleashing the plurality of hermeneutic views, nihilism offers us a possibility of social emancipation. As with most neoliberal thinking, freedom turns out to be the supreme value in Vattimo's theory rather than, say, equality. Although at the end of his career he will reverse his position on this and other questions in an effort to recover his bona fides as a leftist in *Ecce comu*, it is important to realize that one of the most important characteristics of his "leftist nihilism" as he articulates it in the vast majority of his writings is its refusal to affirm the claims of equality. He suggests that advocating for equality in a society that worships competition is an ineffective strategy by comparison to the cause of reducing violence, which puts the left "in a much better position" (*NE*, 98). Yet he undermines his own argument that reducing violence is an inherently better response to the capitalist logic of development than demanding equality, when a few pages later he contends that in economics we should sacrifice strong protection for "greater freedom of initiative" (*NE*, 108). By way of reply, we might invoke Elena Ferrante's recent observation that the greatest social problem in contemporary Italy is the nation's "suspension of disbelief," which has turned its citizens into mere spectators of Berlusconi's media circus.[99]

In this sense, notwithstanding Vattimo's leftist sympathies, his teaching represents the most cogent prehistory of the cultural and political logic of Berlusconi's Italy, which has adopted with a vengeance the philosopher's call for a "weakening of the principle of reality."[100] Throughout the bulk of his career, Vattimo implicitly rationalizes his lack of attention to crucial cultural and historical questions in terms of his fidelity to the purity of ontological assumptions. Such a purist approach ought to be assessed in comparison to Derrida and Foucault, not Heidegger, in its political ramifications. In this context, the limits of weak thought are particularly clear when it comes to Vattimo's reading of the concept of difference. Whereas the French thinkers are intent on criticizing the "Oedipal" difference between Being and entity, Vattimo seems determined to avoid reducing the question of difference to the ontic level.

The Misadventure of Difference

In *The Adventure of Difference*, Vattimo blames French poststructuralism for its narrow conception of difference:

What I have called "the philosophy of difference," inspired by Heidegger and prevalent today in a certain sector of French culture, tends to obscure and forget the various ways in which difference can be problematized. It can in general be accused of failing to absorb the suggestion made in the last paragraph of *Being and Time*, both in its narrow literal sense (why is difference forgotten?) and its more general methodological sense (what about difference as such?). It tends instead to begin with the actual forgetting of difference, contrasting with that the type of thinking which strives rather to remember difference, rediscovering and presenting it in various ways, thereby aiming to position itself in some sense beyond "metaphysics" [*AD*, 64–65].

What he regrets is the unwillingness on the part of French poststructuralism to stay faithful to the letter of Heidegger's philosophy, to hold that only the difference between Being and entity counts. "Jacques Derrida's 1968 Paris lecture on *différance*," he writes, "may at the time have looked like a straight manifesto of the philosophy of difference, but today it looks more like a kind of epitaph or memorial for it" (*AD*, 137). Vattimo claims that Derrida's deconstruction of ontological difference reflects the French philosopher's preference for the performative play of deferring or differing, for indulging the impulse "to rewrite the text of metaphysics *parodistically*" (*AD*, 143). Parody, however, can only be achieved in the Italian philosopher's eyes from "a position of consciousness" and therefore is a device "of metaphyics and of presential thinking" (*AD*, 143). On this view, Derrida ends up thinking of difference as an absolute, an "archstructure [that] is not in history" but rather belongs to eternity, thus dissolving its philosophical potential (*AD*, 144).[101]

Vattimo also harshly criticizes Deleuze's vitalist emphasis on the endlessly varied differences of simulacra. In Deleuze's case, according to Vattimo, particularly in the works he coauthored with Guattari, difference becomes a matter of pure energy that through its distribution determines the inequalities that make life itself possible (*AD*, 145–46). Such a position in the eyes of the Italian thinker risks dangerous infidelity to philosophical origins: "There is a danger that we may get lost in the play of difference/repetition in which the 'philosophy of difference' has got lost" (*AD*, 155). With regard to this need to remain faithful to the philosophy of difference, we should note that Vattimo's choice of the word "adventure" in the title *The Adventure of Difference* is not meant to convey anything as lighthearted as the events of a heroic narrative. In fact, he invokes the term as it is used in Heidegger's thought, specifically in the *Letter on Humanism*, where it refers to nothing less than Being itself and its poetic deployments.[102] Judging the attempts of French philosophy to deconstruct ontological difference in an ontic direction to be a failure, Vattimo prefers the attempt to develop such difference in a hermeneutic domain that encompasses communication theory, information theory, and system theory (*AD*, 155). Philosophical worldliness in general never coincides for him with attention to sexual or cultural difference, but rather with a nearly obsessive "postmodern hermeneutical" fixation on communications and mass media. On this score, he follows the path of least resistance to embrace Italy's hegemonic contemporary culture.

The two anthologies *Il pensiero debole* and *Elogio del pudore*, which were edited respectively by Vattimo and Rovatti, feature male contributors exclusively, although what is at stake in both books almost might seem to suggest the outlines of a "philosophie feminine," if we care to recall that in Italy women commonly have been referred to as "the weak sex" and if we credit the stereotype of women as less assertive, less violent, and more bashful than men. Yet one is hard pressed to find in either volume any references whatsoever to feminism, women's issues, or even the ironic, critical language games of Derrida, who through such notions as différance, *hymène*, and *phallogocentrisme* deconstructed the entrenched, hierarchical privileging of male over female in Western culture. Derrida even occasionally made fun of Heidegger's resistance to any conceptualization of sexual difference.[103] Deconstruction certainly has drawn attention to, among other things, the importance of sexual difference as opposed to identity. In the process, Derridean philosophy has inspired and provoked feminist thinkers from Luce Irigaray to Judith Butler, albeit not without critical reservations on their part. In one of his later works, *Politics of Friendship*, Derrida renewed his thinking on sexual difference by examining the traditional exclusion of women from the polis, deconstructing a philosophical vocabulary that hinges on the ideals of male bonding and fraternity.

If we consider the example of Deleuze, it will suffice to remember that of all the modes of becoming that he envisions in *A Thousand Plateaus* the first and most strategic is "becoming woman," which he identifies as the "key" to all other becomings.[104] The notion of "weakness" articulated by weak thought in the "manic phase" of the 1980s never aligns itself in a political sense with Deleuzian "minoritarian becomings," as one might hope. Vattimo condemns any reappropriation of values per se as a form of reactive nihilism and a philosophical sin: "Examples are easily found to show that, in the face of devaluation of the highest values and the death of God, the usual reaction is one which makes a grandiose metaphysical appeal to other 'truer' values (for example, the values of subcultures, or popular cultures as opposed to dominant cultures, the rejection of literary and artistic canons, etc.)" (*EOM*, 25).

In his essay on difference in *Modern French Philosophy* (1980), Vincent Descombes has pointed out that the notion of difference that we encounter in both Derrida's and Deleuze's work is, first and foremost, not dialectical, not a basis for construction of identity.[105] Derrida's dynamic, performative interpretation of difference as différance (differentiating/differing) proceeds from Saussure's intuition that the meaning of a sign is not present or intrinsic in itself, but rather the result of the interplay between signs.[106] In Deleuze's case, he derives his understanding of the concept from Nietzsche's metaphysics of will to power as a philosophy averse to negation and contradiction, as a joyous affirmation of difference.[107] As Paul Patton observes, what is crucially at stake in Deleuze's view is the question of how different forces interact with each other: "Deleuze defines the will to power as the generic and differential element which produces the difference in quantity and subsequent difference in quality between forces. He draws on Nietzsche's description of the modes characteristic of master and slaves in order to distinguish between active and reactive forces, and to align the denial of difference with reactive forces and the affirmation of difference with active forces."[108]

Difference in Deleuze and Guattari's philosophical oeuvre thus manifests itself through a "minoritarian becoming" that reflects a qualitative rather than quantitative definition of what it means to belong to a minority (for example, women may outnumber men in a given culture, while nevertheless having less social standing and power). Moreover, Deleuze and Guattari insist on the centrality of difference in its political aspects by reminding us that all becomings can only be minoritarian. By contrast, Vattimo makes no attempt to translate the philosophical into cultural concerns and questions. Despite being gay and defending the expression of same-sex desire against the dogmatic attacks of the church, the Italian philosopher still can assert with pride that "I am not convinced that truth resides at the margins, that there is an ideal proletariat . . . that carries the authentic meaning of history, to which the alienated minority of homosexuals would belong" (B, 74). With this denunciation of the idea that "truth resides at the margins," Vattimo attacks the example set by Pier Paolo Pasolini, whose outspoken criticism of power in defense of diversity he regards as outdated on the grounds that in a secular society one cannot consider oneself emblematic of the rejected of the earth as the Italian poet did (B, 72–74).

The only justification for "minoritarian becomings" is not the search for justice, according to Vattimo, but rather attainment of a charitable attitude: "The recognition of 'new rights,' the attention given to all movements dedicated to rising awareness that lead to a reduction in objective violence against people are matters of charity" (B, 76). In an even more problematic passage in *Nihilism and Emancipation*, Vattimo pleads for forms of religious and cultural compromise, and even for coyness when it comes to being gay. Discussing the Italian literary tradition that dramatizes the plight of priests who struggle to maintain their vows of celibacy, Vattimo writes approvingly:

> The most recent book in this vein I have come across is the diary, still anonymous of course, of a homosexual Italian priest who recounts how he comes to terms with his own natural inclination. This he achieves by deciding, with the more or less explicit approval of his bishop, to remain in the priesthood and carry out his mission as best he can, while allowing himself a fling every once and a while in the world to which he feels he belongs and in which he finds a form of happiness.... What counts in this case is the fulfillment of a social duty ... more than the personal dilemma [*NE*, 63].

What is striking in this passage is Vattimo's praise of hypocrisy, as if it were a badge of merit on the priest's part to hide the "natural inclination" of his sexual preference in the name of a higher "mission" that he and his ecclesiastical superior are happy to forget when convenient.

Unsurprisingly, Vattimo, who often writes about religion, has never issued a word to criticize the Catholic Church's murky handling of cases of sexual abuse by Catholic priests. If we move from questions of gender and sexual preference to those of religious and cultural difference, Vattimo's disregard for such concerns becomes all the more glaring. In this respect, his response to the controversy in France over prohibition of the wearing of the chador and other religious symbols in public school is exemplary. He considers only banning the chador justified, because he considers the chador, unlike the crucifix, to be an "obtrusive" sign in European society (*AC*, 101). Whereas the French law banishes all religious icons, including the Christian, from public institutions, Vattimo claims a sort of transcendental role for Christianity vis-à-vis other religions in Europe, curiously reasoning that the Christian faith is ultimately a means to cultural secularization and thus an increase of tolerance.

In practice, weak thought stresses respect for the inheritance of the past and its fidelity of transmission at the expense of critical acuity.[109] Vattimo's failure to account for difference in large part ensues from the attitude of hermeneutic resignation with which he ascribes the conditions of possibility of experience to historical precomprehension (*BI*, 82–83). If truth can be found only in the historicity of our existence, as Gadamer defines it in *Truth and Method*, we will always be determined and constituted by our past, even by our prejudices, which for Gadamer have a positive value. Even if we think of the task of hermeneutics in terms of Heidegger's ontology rather than of Gadamer's historical approach, the movement beyond metaphysics toward a process of An-denken or recollection of Being easily may become another way of valorizing tradition. Of course, the insistence of hermeneutics on precomprehension, prejudice, tradition, and so on all are hallmarks of an enduring anti-Enlightenment perspective. This outlook makes it very unlikely to imagine an alternative to the norm, a transformation of the status quo. Vattimo indicates awareness of this shortcoming at the very moment of inception of weak thought as a movement:

A weak thought that is such first and foremost because of its ontological content, of its way of understanding being and truth, is also a thought that consequently has no more reason to vindicate the sovereignty claimed by metaphysical thought in relationship to praxis. Does this indicate a weakness in the sense of an acceptance of what exists and is given, and therefore a critical inability that is both theoretical and practical? In other words, does speaking of weakness of thought mean to theorize a diminished projective strength of thought itself? Let us not hide from ourselves that the problem exists [*PD*, 27].

The problem indeed exists at different levels. For one thing, weak thought as an operation of hermeneutic transmission tends to privilege the canonical over the exceptional, the well-established patrimony over "prophetic illuminations," as Vattimo himself admits (*PD*, 27). Such a way of thinking affirms a majoritarian view of literature and culture, the static and conservative reproduction of *idées reçues* in which margins and minorities cannot emerge. Weak thought thus deprives itself of the dynamic force for transformation that Deleuze and Guattari grant to minoritarian becomings. If philosophies of difference, as Paul Patton notes, have often been assimilated into politics of difference, such an integration cannot happen in Vattimo's case.[110]

In evaluating Vattimo's fidelity to the original, Heideggerian notion of ontological difference, it is useful to contrast his interpretation of Nietzsche's philosophy to the general outlines of the contemporary discussion of this body of thought in France. In French poststructuralism, Nietzsche's legacy generally has not been understood as the culmination of metaphysics à la Heidegger. Instead, the terms in which this oeuvre has been read are much more political, in the case of Deleuze and obviously in that of Foucault as well, with the latter providing a comprehensive assessment of the agonistic conflicts of interest that originate with the will to power. For Vattimo, by contrast, the fact that Nietzsche emphasizes (particularly in his essay "European Nihilism" of 1887) that every value is only the consequence of the struggle between forces and that therefore there are no eternal values can only validate nihilism as the ultimate philosophy (*AD*, 93). It is at this juncture that Vattimo's "autoimmune" theoretical tendency is at its clearest.[111] Even if the formula of weak thought, as Franca D'Agostini suggests, is in the first place more an associative logic than argumentative, she is right to observe that, by staying faithful to ontological difference, Vattimo also supports a hermeneutic that cannot be mixed with a philosophy of culture, thus presenting a philosophically "tough" side to the world (*VRF*, 18).

Reflecting on Technology from Heidegger to Vattimo

When discussing technology, Vattimo tends to radicalize Heidegger's thinking in an optimistic direction. The Italian philosopher treats technology as the promise of a postmodern utopia of information and communication, which through their dissemination and fluidity appear to exemplify the very virtues of weak thought. In his opinion, the reason Heidegger warns readers of the dangers of technology and the possibility that all might be consumed by the order of "disturbing things" is because he did not have full access to the virtual world of electronic communication and information technology.[112] Vattimo reassures us that we can now count on the "non-infernal" destiny of technology in contemporary society.[113] To draw such a conclusion, on the one hand he has to play down Heidegger's anxious, and at times defensive, position concerning technology, and on the other hand he must dismiss the reflections initiated by Adorno and Debord on the culture industry and the society of spectacle as the baseless, pessimistic tenets of thinkers who are still faithful to an obsolescent notion of use value.

If one had to recount Heidegger's views on technology, it would be fair to say that they change from initial pessimism in the 1930s, which is reflected in his opinion that Nazism could furnish an effective remedy for technological nihilism, to a more ambivalent position in his later career, which is articulated chiefly in "The Question Concerning Technology," *Identity and Difference*, and his final interview in *Der Spiegel*.[114] It is important to remember that, in "The Question Concerning Technology," his leitmotif is that the "essence of technology is by no means anything technological." In his eyes, this essence is rather an "enframing" (Gestell) or "destining" of the truth that "banishes man into that kind of revealing that is an ordering" and so, if not "demonic," represents something "mysterious" that fundamentally poses a danger to thought.[115] For the gendered subject that Heidegger calls "man," enframing as a way of revealing, bringing forth, or gathering the truth in other words raises "the possibility of pursuing and pushing forward nothing but what is revealed in ordering, and of deriving all his standards on this basis."[116] Technology in this sense threatens to confine the subject in a position from which it is impossible to achieve a deeper, more poetic, more primal relation to the "unconcealed" truth of the world: "Through this [enframing] the other possibility is blocked, that man might be admitted more and sooner and ever more primally to the essence of what is unconcealed and to its unconcealment."[117] In his reading of Heidegger's thinking, Vattimo minimizes the German philosopher's perplexity in order to affirm a much more optimistic, redemptive view of the technological domain, according to which metaphysics can be overcome only when our prevailing experience of technology ceases to be mechanical and becomes electronic (that is, digital).[118] Operating through a continuous process of recontextualization, "everything that we now include under the heading of the Internet" encourages the defamiliarization and ultimately the dissolution of reality and thus constitutes a prime model of a weak ontology (*NE*, 16).

Especially through his interpretation of the decisive epochal role played by science and technology, Vattimo attempts to cultivate the attitude of the "good-tempered man" described by Nietzsche, an attitude that he himself remarks on with some fascination:

> It is an attitude of this kind that Nietzsche describes in *Human, All Too Human* as the attitude of the "good-tempered man," who, having discovered that all metaphysical, moral, and religious "values" are only the result of the sublimation of impulses, interests and so on, does not simply reject these values but looks on them with an attitude of "limited" respect, which I think can be described by the Latin term of *pietas*.[119]

Contra Gadamer, Vattimo does not believe in the philosophical sustainability of the division of the *Wissenschaften* and sees the disseminative effects of the information age of technology as putting into practice the theoretical ideal of overcoming metaphysics, making possible our emancipation from the strictures of the subject-object relationship. If Heidegger or Adorno did not recognize the emancipatory potential of contemporary technology, according to Vattimo, this failing is due to the fact that in their time the dominant technical paradigm was still that of the motor, which they linked to an unsophisticated, center-periphery model of production and consumption of the technological (*NE*, 14). For Vattimo, Adorno's apocalyptic visions of mass culture were the consequence of his having missed a radical shift in our experience of technology. Yet it may be replied that what gives Adorno's thoughts on the topic continuing relevance today is his interest in the culture industry, not in motor-based technologies. Even if he lived before the age of the Internet, his very insistence on the term "culture industry" indicates his awareness that any distinction between structure and superstructure had become futile. When it comes to Heidegger, although he refers to power plants, turbines, jet aircraft, and radar in the seminal essay "The Question Concerning Technology," he also remarks (with evident scorn) on computational technology in *Identity and Difference*: "Today, the computer calculates thousands of relationships in one second. Despite their technical uses, they are inessential."[120] In other words, Heidegger responded to the alleged promise of the computer by issuing a warning against its "inessential" condition—a warning that Vattimo cheerfully ignores.[121]

Vattimo, for whom staying in tune with the postmodern Zeitgeist is of the utmost importance, drops the Heideggerian emphasis on terms such as "danger," "art," and "mystery" when discussing technology. He instead focuses on the "astounding" possibility that what Heidegger described as the "frenziedness" of technology might exemplify the supposedly liberating aspect of nihilism. In *Beyond Interpretation*, Vattimo in fact aims to strip the human sciences of any hermeneutic privilege and assign the position of chief importance to technoscience, the history of which he equates with that of Being (*BI*, 24). In his eyes, taking aesthetic experience as the exemplar of interpretive activity par excellence makes it impossible to grasp the nihilist task of contemporary hermeneutics, to arrive at the understanding that modern-day science has been "the principal agent" in a nihilist transformation of the meaning of Being (*BI*, 24). Remarkably, it never occurs to Vattimo to discuss or analyze technology in terms of strategic power relationships, as for example Foucault does when he interprets the panopticon as the triumph of visuality as a disciplinary instrument. Vattimo instead gives the impression that, once we have decided that technology makes manifest the meaning of metaphysics as will to power, the mundane vicissitudes of power in their political actuality may be regarded as forgettable epiphenomena of the larger *dénouement* of philosophy.

The crucial source of inspiration for Vattimo's equation of technology, postmodernity, and the overcoming of metaphysics is a declaration from Heidegger's essay "The Principle of Identity" in *Identity and Difference*: "The appropriation [Ereignis] appropriates man and Being to their essential togetherness. In the frame [Ge-stell] we glimpse a first *oppressing* flash of the appropriation. The frame constitutes the active nature of the modern world of technology."[122] Vattimo comments on this statement extensively in *Nihilism and Emancipation*, where he begins with the admission that it is a *hapax legomenon* ("once said") in Heidegger's corpus. Nowhere else does Heidegger suggest that the Gestell or enframing of technology, which is to say its position, imposition, composition, or disposition, makes visible the Ereignis that will help "man and Being reach each other in their nature, achieve their active nature by losing those qualities with which metaphysics has endowed them," and thus dissolve the subject-object opposition (*NE*, 14). In stressing this point, however, Vattimo conveniently drops Heidegger's explicit qualification of this "flash" of the "appropriation" as "oppressing" (bedrängendes).[123]

In fact, the German philosopher's overall argument in "The Principle of Identity" does not easily reconcile with Vattimo's reading of it. Although Heidegger makes clear that rejecting technology as "the devil's work" would be futile, he maintains that the technological world is not such that "it will absolutely prevent a spring out of it" in the sense of a leap that removes us from our current relation to that world.[124] He even suggests in an earlier passage that Ereignis might mean the transformation of Gestell, hence of the constellation of man, Being, and technology, in a manner that places the technological in a position of servitude to man rather than of dominance over him.[125] Far from affirming any emancipation through technology, he first and foremost calls for our freedom from technology in order to clear a path on which we may experience being in a more "originary way."[126] He seems especially contemptuous of the status quo of our understanding of technology, which is to say a view that Vattimo will celebrate as proper acceptance of the "ontology of actuality," but that the German philosopher derisively associates with the "chatter" of the times: "As long as reflection on the world of the atomic age, however earnestly and responsibly, strives for no more than a *peaceful* use of atomic energy, and also will not be content with any other goal, thinking stops halfway. Such halfwayness only secures the technological world all the more in its metaphysical predominance."[127] Ultimately, Heidegger rebukes the shortsightedness of those who refuse to grant the need for us to "spring out of" technology: "For this view is obsessed by the *latest news*, and regards them as the only thing that is *real*. This view is indeed fantastical."[128] Given Vattimo's contention that the *conditio sine qua non* of overcoming metaphysics is a historical reduction of violence and his insistence on the "ontology of actuality," it is difficult to avoid the conclusion that weak thought exemplifies precisely the "halfwayness" that Heidegger so clearly condemned.

At any rate, a certain rhetorical defensiveness epitomizes Vattimo's attempt to ventriloquize Heidegger's discourse on technology. He retreats from acknowledging the anomalous quality of the linkage between Gestell and Ereignis in "The Principle of Identity" when he claims that other late works by Heidegger corroborate this association (*NE*, 15).[129] Citing in particular the evidence of "The Age of the World Picture" (1938), Vattimo calls into question any reading of the essay that would characterize its position as skeptical or critical of modernity (*BI*, 24). Yet we well might ask whether a historical epoch can be embraced with unquestioning enthusiasm, as Vattimo proposes, in an interpretive context that claims to be true to the spirit of Heideggerian ontological reflection (*BI*, 6). At the very least, it is safe to say that Heidegger strikes a cautionary note with respect to the age of the world picture, an age in which the subject conceives of the world as an image, and Being consequently becomes an object of representation (*BI*, 25). Although Heidegger appears convinced in the end that our understanding will not advance by revolting against modernity, he also remains resolute throughout his argument in calling attention to the dangers of the modern worldview, such as the "possibility that the system might degenerate into empty exteriority" or the failure of comprehension that occurs when fulfillment of modern science's essence takes place so quickly as to be undetectable.

Whereas readers who take Heidegger seriously might conclude as a result that the age of the world picture poses important threats to philosophical or critical thought and, in this sense, might confirm Guy Debord's critique of the society of spectacle, Vattimo simply celebrates the current historical period for making possible a "dissolution of objectivity into pure abstraction" through the operations of technology. This dissolution means nothing less for the Italian philosopher than the dismantling of the metaphysical opposition between subject and object that has dominated the Western cultural tradition. That contemporary technology weakens what he calls "the principle of reality" is for him a sufficient guarantee of technology's status as a "good object," to borrow a term from Kleinian psychoanalysis.[130] The virtual reality of mass media, which represents the most sophisticated, pervasive, and hegemonic technology, constitutes in his eyes the most beautiful response to the crucial ontological questions that we face today.

Beautiful Media

In spite of his declared preference for philosophically "weak" methods, Vattimo may be said to present in his writings a decidedly "strong" interpretation of technology and media, which he equates *tout court* with postmodernity (*NE*, 3). Technology indeed plays a salvific role in his thought, fulfilling the need to overcome metaphysics and modernity (*NE*, 11). As he sees it, the newest technologies, in particular the Internet, have helped to dissolve the principle of reality or objectivity as the mediatization of our culture advances (*NE*, 16–17).[131] As a result, his theoretical exuberance at the worldwide spread of mass media apparently knows no limits. Such optimism regarding the function of the media in contemporary culture is at the root of weak thought's opposition to the Frankfurt School in general—and Adorno's aesthetic theory in particular, whom Vattimo accuses of being interested only in the purity of the avant-garde (*BI*, 72). Even when he himself raises the question whether his position entails a "too hasty apology" for mass culture, he dismisses the thought with the curious claim that, far from enforcing an artificial consensus of opinion, the media have changed our relation to reality positively by enhancing "the inconstancy and superficiality of experience" (*TS*, 58–59).

Throughout his reflections on technology, he never examines the supposedly neutral terms in which popular discussion of the phenomenology of mass media and electronic communication has taken place. He adopts a strategy, in other words, that begs comparison to those of other contemporary philosophers who give sustained consideration to technology, chief among whom, arguably, is Derrida. We do not find in Vattimo's handling of the topic the same degree of caution and care that Derrida demonstrates in his approach to technology, beginning with his use of terminology. In *Echographies of Television*, for example, Derrida rejects the accepted meanings that words such as "information" and "communication" have acquired in the technological domain because of their confusing, misleading implications.[132] He proposes to replace these terms respectively with "artifactuality" and "teletechnology" on the ground that both neologisms bespeak an actuality that is produced or edited rather than given. He thus performs the important philosophical task of exposing the biases of our received vocabulary when it comes to thinking about the current conditions of reality. As he puts it, actuality comes to us through a process of fictional fashioning because even transmission of a real, live event via a medium such as television requires technical and political choices that result in construction of what is actual: "'Artifactuality' signifies first of all that there is actuality . . . only in so far as a whole set of technical and political apparatuses come as it were to choose, from a non-finite mass of events, the 'facts' that are to constitute actuality: what are then called 'the facts' on which the 'news' or 'information' feeds."[133] Whatever negative or analytic purpose the mass media may have in weakening the claims of ontology thus must be understood in light of their positive or synthetic function in enforcing the claims of ideology. Neologisms such as artifactuality or "actuvirtuality" that defamiliarize our use of technology are important in helping us with the philosophical task of distinguishing the present from actuality, as untimely ideas often are those that enable us to reassess most fully the currency of prevailing conditions.[134]

Although Derrida perceives accelerated development of teletechnology in some respects as promising the equivalent of a "practical" deconstruction of obsolete concepts (such as, for example, those of the state and the citizen), he clearly maintains that, in spite of such a possibility, critical vigilance and education with regard to use of teletechnologies are needed to achieve a "counter-interpretation" of the media.[135] The deconstruction of actuality in his view ought not to lead to some sort of glorification of the simulacrum or denial of the singular event. To the contrary, such a line of inquiry by definition opposes "critical neoidealism."[136] Accordingly, we might conclude that Vattimo is too much of a "neoidealist" in relation to our historical circumstances to bother with questioning the constructed aspects of actuality. After all, his insistence on the fictive condition of the world, in emulation of Nietzsche's declaration in *Twilight of the Idols* that "the true world has become a fable" (*BI*, 7), presumes dropping all demands for truth or reality, hence for any basis of political engagement. For Derrida, however, the deconstruction of actuality that aims at a "counter-interpretation" of the media through a thoroughgoing process of critical examination ultimately helps to restore faith in the singularity of the event.[137] In the context of his reflections on artifactuality, he therefore reaffirms his belief in the messianicity of the event as the experience of "the coming other" and dismisses the idea of "the end of the great emancipatory discourses."[138]

In Vattimo's eyes, we should thank the media for enabling us to overcome our belief in the "unilinear" progress of history as more cultures and subcultures enter the stage of global public consciousness and as the rise of telematics wreaks nothing less than the dissolution of what Jean-François Lyotard called the "grand narratives" of metaphysics (*TS*, 2–6). The Italian thinker articulates his theory of the media most cogently in *The Transparent Society* (1989), which represents a philosophical response to Eco's earlier *Opera aperta* (1962). The title that Vattimo gives his treatise is misleading, however, because far from arguing for the value of transparency he acclaims the transformation of experience brought about by the mass media through the effects of oscillation and disorientation. To support this agenda, he elaborates his discussion of media and technology in a relentlessly cheerful rhetoric. Contesting Adorno's argument that the main achievement of the media has been to spread an oppressive sameness of opinion, for instance, Vattimo invokes as a counterexample the proliferation of worldviews and cultural voices that has accompanied diffusion of mass communications. With regard to the possible objection that having a voice does not amount to "true political emancipation," because merely possessing an independent opinion does nothing to redistribute the power of means that is held in the hands of capital, he coyly sidesteps the challenge: "This may be so: I won't pursue the issue here" (*TS*, 5–6). Questions of justice and power, in other words, hold little interest for him. He is much more concerned with the potentialities for creative shock value inherent in the mass media, which he feels have not been sufficiently explored by aesthetic theory (*TS*, 57). In *The End of Modernity*, he even intimates that mass culture makes possible the "death of art" that it once was hoped would result from "the revolutionary reintegration of existence" to the degree that the diffuse influence of the media brings about "a generalized aestheticization of life": "This can be said to occur because the mass media—who, to be sure, distribute information, culture, and entertainment, but according to the general criteria of the 'beautiful,' that is, the formal attractiveness of products—have assumed in the life of each individual an infinitely more important role than in any other era of the past" (*EOM*, 55).

With this suggestion, he positions himself in the wake of Walter Benjamin's "The Work of Art in the Age of Its Mechanical Reproduction" (1936), which in at least one version famously extols the possible merits of mass production for aesthetics. As is well known, Adorno criticized what he considered Benjamin's naïveté in accepting the decline of the auratic work of art as a historical *fait accompli*. Vattimo resolutely prefers Benjamin's narrative of the inevitable transition from the "cult value" of the work of art to its "exhibition value" to Adorno's hard opposition between use value and exchange value (*TS*, 48).[139] In this view, the notion of an artwork that enables social critique or political argument is a hopeless anachronism, a quaint reminder of an epoch in which it was still possible to believe à la Adorno in the necessity of use value (*EOM*, 62). Conscripting an unexpected spokesman into service for the triumph of the mass media, Vattimo contends that the idea of art as a "setting-into-work of truth," which Heidegger expounded at length in the "Origin of the Work of Art" (1936), betokens the German philosopher's preference for the exhibition value of the work (*EOM*, 62). Vattimo's attempted rehabilitation of the Heideggerian concept of art in the name of "exhibition" or "exchange" represents at best a questionable philosophical exercise, because it fails to acknowledge the well-known significance of Heidegger's efforts to recover through his readings of Hölderlin's poetry what can only be defined as art's original cult value.

The Italian Society of Spectacle
from *The Transparent Society* to *Ecce comu*

Placing his political belief in the weakening of the ontological "principle of reality" that he sees taking place through the mediatization of society, Vattimo writes about the issue of media ownership and the alleged "multiplication of interpretative agencies" with a tone of credulous optimism as recently as in 2003, more than two decades into Berlusconi's virtual monopoly of Italian information: "Stories about who is buying a controlling interest in a newspaper chain or television network are central elements in the news published by the very same newspaper and television networks" (*NE*, 17).[140] Although he sees the economic theory of the free market's self-regulating "invisible hand" as problematically metaphysical, he does not consider the obvious political danger of concentrated media ownership that has become especially problematic in Italy, where so far no legal remedy has been possible (*NE*, 36). Faced with the "persistent suspicion" raised by Habermas and Apel's theory of "unhindered social communication" that those in power might use the media as a means of social control, Vattimo maintains that, although such concern might be a good reason to regulate media companies, we ought not go too far in this way of thinking as we risk the sin of granting truth value to specific political positions: "But taken to the limit, it also posits a linkage between politics and truth and thus entails the risk of having to accept some form of mandarinate entrusted with making sure that the information transmitted by the media is uncontaminated" (*NE*, 85). In his opinion, the ultimate enemy that must be kept at bay appears by implication to be the specter of political totalitarianism, even if he will identify this threat in explicit terms only as an attitude of submission to metaphysical absolutes.

However understandable may be his reaction against the zealotry of the radical left or the extremes of "real" socialism, his hostility blinds him throughout most of his career to the (lately more urgent) manifestations of the media's political vulnerabilities that Guy Debord so prophetically assessed in their early state.[141] Debord's analysis of spectacle has proven to be an indispensable point of departure for contemporary cultural theorists from Giorgio Agamben, who traces the genealogy of spectacle through a theological route back to the phenomenon of glory, to Michael Hardt and Antonio Negri and to the Retort group, who affirm the relevance of Debord's critique to the operations of empire and the rationalization of so-called preemptive war.[142] Vattimo, however, requires no more than a sentence in *The Transparent Society* to dispose of the questions raised by Debord and to praise the spectacular for giving us a "softer" view of reality: "The society of spectacle spoken of by the situationists is not simply a society of appearance manipulated by power: it is also the society in which reality represents itself as softer and more fluid and in which experience can acquire the characteristics of oscillation, disorientation and play" (*TS*, 59). The rhetoric of this declaration upholds Vattimo's usual opposition between a sophisticated, postmodern perspectivism and a crudely realist metaphysics of truth. Yet it may be helpful to parse more carefully his insistence on dissolving "the principle of reality" and the "grand narratives" of emancipation via the aestheticizing of technology, in contrast to Debord's and Derrida's more sober responses to the disciplinary role of the media in mass culture. The Italian philosopher's viewpoint is particularly interesting when viewed in light of the development of Debord's thinking from the classic exposition of his theory in *The Society of Spectacle* (1967) to its subsequent refinement in *Comments on the Society of Spectacle* (1988), where he treats Italy as a decisive test case of his argument. In the earlier book, Debord points out that the hegemony of spectacle, which he deplores as "a visible negation of life," reinforces the logic of mutual alienation between spectacle and reality that eventually leads to the "empire of modern passivity."[143] Even more incisively than Adorno's criticism of the culture industry, his diagnosis of spectacle as a transmutation of capital into images may be said to prophesy the conditions of capitalist culture under the sign of postmodernity, despite the fact that he never refers to the postmodern as such.

Debord in fact names the period of "integrated spectacle" as the latest stage in the evolution of contemporary society, when cultural, economic, and governmental forms of domination converge. In *Comments*, he observes that spectacle has become an observable historical phenomenon and has also expanded its power over how people lead their lives since initial publication of *The Society of Spectacle*.[144] Most importantly, he distinguishes among three forms of spectacular power in modern history: concentrated spectacle, which promotes totalitarian ideology and arises in Stalinist Russia and Nazi Germany; diffuse spectacle, which represents a mystification of consumerism and originates in the United States; and integrated spectacle, which synthesizes the first two forms and emerges in Italy and France:

> The integrated spectacle shows itself to be simultaneously concentrated and diffuse, and . . . has learnt to employ both these qualities on a grander scale. . . . As regards concentration, the controlling centre has now become occult: never to be occupied by a known leader, or clear ideology. And on the diffuse side, the spectacle as never before puts its mark to such a degree on almost the full range of socially produced behaviour and objects. For the final sense of the integrated spectacle is this—that it has integrated itself into reality to the same extent as it was describ-

ing it. As a result, this reality no longer confronts the integrated spectacle as something alien. When the spectacle was concentrated, the greater part of surrounding society escaped it, when it was diffuse, a small part; today, no part. The spectacle has spread itself to the point where it now permeates reality."[145]

An important consequence of the new integrated spectacle is that it brings about the parodic (rather than revolutionary) end of the division of labor insofar as the "carnivalesque" explosion of publicity under the organizing principle of the spectacular coincides with total devaluation of "real ability" or knowledge.[146] In a society regulated by commodified public attention, "media status" becomes the only currency and is made so readily transferable that "a financier can be a singer" or "an actor can be president," because the cachet of stardom trumps the value of actual ability: "Most often these accelerated media particles pursue their own careers in the glow of statutorily guaranteed admiration."[147]

Although he never cites the example of Berlusconi, who was elected Italy's prime minister in 1994, the logic of Debord's argument perfectly fits the media mogul's career. After all, Berlusconi is someone who famously and improbably named his political party *Forza Italia* or "Let's go, Italy," after the slogan chanted by fans at the games of his soccer team, A.C. Milan, and who more recently has made a habit of appointing to political office the showgirls from his television shows. Unlike Vattimo, Debord is keen to criticize the "anaesthetic effect" of integrated spectacle on "self-proclaimed" democratic societies, observing that it ensures "*omertà*," or perfect censorship of everything in repudiation of the idea that criticism and transformation of society are possible: "The most profound summing-up of the period which the whole world entered shortly after Italy and the United States can be found in the words of a senior Italian statesman, a member, simultaneously, of both the official government and the parallel government, P2, *Potere Due*: 'Once there were scandals, but not any more.'"[148] Debord's reference to the cynical credo of a "senior Italian statesman" appears to be an allusion to the Christian Democrat Giulio Andreotti, who served as prime minister several times, was indicted in the 1990s for his association with the Mafia, and belonged to the membership of the Masonic lodge P2. It is exactly the widespread success of the Mafia that gives Debord his crucial example of the fundamental obscurantism of spectacular society, which we might add represents what can be understood only as the antithesis of Vattimo's benign paradigm of "transparency with oscillation."[149] Indeed, Debord grants Italy a special place of honor when it comes to what he calls "the modernisation of repression" in the guise of the governmental practice of using *pentiti* (penitents) or politically protected "informants" to dismantle, in particular, the progress of the extreme left.[150] In its cynical use of power, from state-sponsored repression to organized criminality, Italy exemplifies for Debord the avant-garde of spectacularized social "anaesthesis," an extreme of oppressive political conformism that leaves no room for resistance or reply.

In keeping with his conciliatory interpretation of Foucault's concept of the "ontology of actuality," which he first articulates in *Beyond Interpretation*, Vattimo maintains resolute silence throughout nearly the entirety of his oeuvre regarding the exceptional adventures of the Italian media and political establishment. Not until publication of *Ecce comu* in 2007, when he switches his focus from aesthetics to politics, does he begin to acknowledge the existence in Italy of a "mediatic bubble" (*EC*, 46). What is most startling about his assessment of this bubble is his adoption of a stance that is almost a mirror-image reversal of his earlier work. He invokes Adorno as a crucial point of reference, describes the new media as a "true *phármakon*" in the sense that it may act as a poison as well as a medicine, and accuses Italy's political parties of offering nothing more to voters than a spectacularized message, which has led to the result that "the problem of Italian democracy today . . . is that of not losing contact with the quotidian reality of society" (*EC*, 79, 50).[151] For readers familiar with his writings, Vattimo's valorization of "reality" and disapproval of "spectacularization" by way of a final counterinterpretation of the media must come as an entirely unexpected turn of events.

Heidegger and Nazism According to Vattimo

One of the most glaring instances of Vattimo's general aversion to philosophically problematic questions is his handling of Heidegger's involvement with Nazism. Notwithstanding publication in the late 1980s of Victor Farias's *Heidegger and Nazism*, which ignited an international debate on the topic, Vattimo has never deviated from the practice of rationalizing the German philosopher's politics.[152] By no means do I wish to suggest that the only ethical response to Heidegger's support for the Third Reich is to reject Heideggerian philosophy altogether; nor do I seek to impugn Vattimo's personal integrity or political convictions. On this score, the counterexamples of his contemporaries in French philosophy are instructive once again. In addressing the controversy, neither Lacoue-Labarthe nor Derrida gives any ground when it comes to assessing Heidegger's importance to philosophy in the twentieth century; yet both thinkers spare no effort in criticizing his espousal of Nazi ideas and policies. As we will see, Vattimo, unlike his French counterparts, does not take seriously the task of questioning Heidegger's ethical and political commitments.[153]

To better understand the significance of this avoidance on Vattimo's part, a brief review of the historical ledger is in order. Heidegger became the rector of the University of Freiburg in May 1933 with the delivery of his notorious inaugural address, "The Self-Assertion of the German University." In this speech, he affirmed without equivocation his allegiance to Nazi ideology, the primacy of the German nation, and the politics of *Gleichschaltung* or "realignment" that aimed to bring Germany's social institutions in line with the principles of the régime—in this case, by "purifying" the university itself through expulsion of Jewish faculty members. We know that Heidegger sent a telegram to Hitler to congratulate him on his vision of the university's role in German society and even came to regard himself as the *Führer* of the university's administration.[154] During the period of his rectorship, he gave several speeches stressing the importance of the spiritual mission of the *Volksgemeinschaft* or "people's community." In his last interview in *Der Spiegel*, Heidegger explained the ideological fascination of Nazism in terms of the achievement of a political system that could accommodate the modern, technological conditions of life.[155] It is remarkable that, as late as 1966, Heidegger is moved to state his skepticism regarding the idea that an alternative way of addressing such conditions may be found in democracy.

Although Heidegger resigned the rectorship after ten months, he persisted even after his resignation in commencing his lectures with the Nazi salute and wearing a swastika and did not renounce his party affiliation until 1945.[156] Whereas some fanatical critics of Heidegger, à la Farias, call for absolute repudiation of his ideas, more reflective readers may acknowledge the value of his historicization of being while censuring his practical and theoretical allegiance to Nazism, which they tend to discuss in order not only to judge Heidegger's individual culpability in life and work but also to confront further the catastrophe of the Shoah itself. A book such as Derrida's *Of Spirit*, for example, can be understood to belong to this category to the extent that it examines the complex consonance between Heidegger's changing vocabulary of *Geist* and the history of his relationship to the Nazi régime. Another, more crowded camp includes thinkers such as Lacoue-Labarthe and Hans Sluga, who, though rejecting definitive identification of Heidegger's thought with Nazi doctrine, nevertheless question Heidegger's surprising unwillingness to retract or to apologize for his former embrace of Nazism, even when asked to do so by figures such as Herbert Marcuse or Paul Celan.[157]

Vattimo appears to adopt much the same method in his approach to Heidegger that he used to minimize the more troubling political ramifications of Nietzsche's thought. In other words, he denies any suggestion of a relationship between the German philosophers' ideas and fascist culture by reading each thinker through a "defensible project," which he argues in Nietzsche's case means nihilistic reduction of metaphysical violence (*NE*, 53). Such a strategy, however, is much more apt for the nineteenth-century German philosopher than for his twentieth-century successor. For one thing, although Nazi propagandists and ideologues tried to reappropriate Nietzsche's ideas, he obviously had no direct, historical association with Nazism. Moreover, given Heidegger's concrete affirmations of the spiritual destiny of Western civilization in general and of Germany in particular, it is far more difficult to find a "defensible" reading of his agenda, no matter how Vattimo may welcome the challenge.[158] An exemplary gesture in this regard is his attempt in *The Adventure of Difference* to sanitize the record of Heidegger's compromises by reminding the reader in a footnote of the German philosopher's supposed good conduct after 1934:

As far as Heidegger's relations with Nazism are concerned, it is worth noting that after 1934 and his resignation from the rectorship, Heidegger took no further interest in politics and published virtually nothing more until the end of the War. Furthermore, it is highly significant that he devoted the years between 1935 and 1943 chiefly to working out an interpretation of Nietzsche in complete contradiction to the one offered by Nazi propaganda [*AD*, 59 n9].

Vattimo clearly aims to relegate the "factual" information of Heidegger's professed sympathy for Nazism to a footnote in order to reserve the main body of his argument for a purely philosophical reading of Heideggerian thought. Yet even his grudging concession to the facts glosses over the most urgent questions as he all too quickly concludes that Heidegger ceased to concern himself with politics after his resignation.

With this account, Vattimo dismisses the possibility that Heidegger's philosophy and politics might be interwoven, as instead Derrida and Lacoue-Labarthe convincingly have shown. Derrida, for example, has explored how the concept of spirit in Heidegger's work is always inscribed in highly charged and problematic political contexts.[159] Lacoue-Labarthe has observed as well that in its deepest meaning Heidegger's discourse of 1933 in fact endures to the end of his career. Indeed, the French philosopher suggests that the most convincing expression of Heidegger's politics may be his essays on technology.[160] Vattimo not only refuses to face the issue of the political in Heidegger's philosophy but also advances the dubious claim that Heidegger resisted Nazism through his reading of Nietzsche. We can assume that Vattimo probably is thinking here of Heidegger's refusal to recognize a biologism or philosophy of life in Nietzsche's thought, as Heidegger felt that the Nietzschean concept of the "vital" must be understood in terms of Being as Will to Power. It could be argued, however, that Heidegger's perception of Nietzschean philosophy as the culmination of metaphysics is not necessarily at odds with the Nazi ideology. The fact that Heidegger interprets Nietzsche's idea of race in metaphysical and not biological terms, Derrida reminds us, ought to prompt us to ask whether a metaphysics of race is more or less disturbing in its implications than a biologism of race.[161] As he put it in an interview, "Even if I owe a great deal to Heidegger, as do many others, he inspired me from the start with an intense political disquiet."[162]

Throughout his writings, by contrast, Vattimo gives the impression of being comfortable with Heidegger's affinity for Nazism and assumes an oddly manic air in defending the affiliation. He first proposes the image of Heidegger as a revolutionary figure in *The Adventure of Difference* and maintains this view through publication of *Addio alla verità* (Farewell to the Truth; 2009). Responding to Löwith's and Adorno's criticisms of Heidegger for abandoning the notion of subjectivity and exalting in its place the destiny of Being, Vattimo concedes that Heidegger renounces the "bourgeois-Christian" notion of the subject, but he improbably maintains that the German philosopher does so only to make a radical turn toward the "socio-political":

My approach does not deny the historical link between Heideggerian ontology and Nazism: it interprets it in a more radical fashion. Heidegger was not merely an apologist for Nazism; rather, it is simply that in the epoch of the formation of great "integrated" states (European Fascist societies, Stalinist Russia, the monopolistic United States, etc ...), he was acutely aware of the power that suprapersonal structures have over the individual, indeed more radically aware than anyone else, perhaps even more so than Marxist thinkers themselves. The *Introduction to Metaphysics* grasps the very root of the constitution of our civilization's conceptual language; in this respect it represents that very "complement" which has been called for to fill the lacunae of Marx's *Capital*. This might allow a rereading of the political speeches from Heidegger's rectorship period, in which his admittedly equivocal approach to Nazism as "destiny" may simply bear witness to his recognition of this necessary predominance of socio-political structures over individual ones in human experience [*AD*, 52–53].

According to Vattimo, Heidegger's greatest merit is not to have resisted these "suprapersonal 'forces'" in the name of the individual. Heidegger's insisting on language and thereby confirming our primal, constitutive belonging to a social-historical world, in Vattimo's eyes, succeeded in renouncing the clichéd individualism of the existentialists.

Vattimo tries to recast Heidegger's allegiance to Nazi politics and ideology as "the most positive and 'prophetic' dimension of his thinking" inasmuch as it affirms the unknown dimensions of experience that belong to the suprapersonal and thus by implication bears a superficial resemblance to the structuralist and poststructuralist criticism of subjectivity (*AD*, 53). In this sense, Vattimo achieves a Pyrrhic philosophical victory when he embraces Nazism as a reasonable price to pay in order to defeat the "metaphysical" violence of individualism. He does nothing to establish corroborating textual evidence in Heidegger's writings of such a purpose, aiming instead to "correspond" with or to paraphrase loosely the German philosopher's thought, as indeed Heidegger did with Hölderlin's poetry. This attempt at ventriloquism is not very convincing, particularly in light of Vattimo's refusal to analyze the significance of Heidegger's political positions either during his rectorship or in later years. In his often needlessly provocative book, Farias does succeed in evoking an important trait of Heidegger's influence on contemporary philosophy, which he calls "the effect of the obvious": "For numerous scholars, Heidegger's thinking has an effect of the obvious that no other philosophy has been able to achieve in France with the exception of Marxism."[163] Although he may not be right about the local cultural specificity of this effect, as is made evident by Derrida's vehement objection to his characterization of the French viewpoint, Farias's remark certainly offers an apt summation of Vattimo's acritical, credulous approach to Heidegger and points up more broadly the danger of a defensive, philosophically purist view of the German thinker.[164] Given Adorno's prior criticism of Heidegger's "obedient" tone of devotion to the unconcealment of Being (*JA*, 85), Vattimo's own obedience to this ideal seems to be an all the more willfully mystificatory attitude that results in a mise-en-abîme of the most questionable and disingenuous aspects of Heidegger's thought.

The attempt to recover a revolutionary Heideggerianism of the left, which as a general undertaking has been discredited by Derrida, is based in Vattimo's case on refusal to read Heidegger as advocating a return to Being, and also on the puzzling ascription of an implicitly progressive political message to his philosophy.[165] The reader's perplexity can only increase in light of the fact that Vattimo does not unequivocally condemn the German philosopher's Nazism, while also seeming intent on justifying his silence regarding the Holocaust in the years after the Second World War. Both Derrida and Lacoue-Labarthe have stated in no uncertain terms that, although they do not wish to reduce Heidegger's work to that of a Nazi ideologue, they must be unequivocal in condemning his politics, particularly when it comes to this appalling reticence. Lacoue-Labarthe is quite forceful in making the point that Heidegger did not just make an epistemological mistake; he "did wrong" in promulgating the notion of the historic destiny of the West.[166] The French philosopher finds Heidegger's taciturn reserve vis-à-vis extermination camps such as Auschwitz to be "unpardonable," especially in relation to Celan, who was hoping to hear from him some sort of expression of regret: "I can perhaps understand why he refused to say anything to those who, wielding their 'rights' as victors, were demanding explanations and accounts of his conduct. But I shall never understand why he said nothing to those survivors, such as Celan for example, who *looked to him* for some kind of statement."[167] So rigorously questioned, Heidegger's refusal to speak can be said to serve no other purpose than veiling or excusing Germany's crimes. Lacoue-Labarthe reminds us that the one public occasion on which the German thinker directly referred to the camps was in the course of a prosaic discussion of agriculture in one of four lectures delivered in Bremen in 1949 on the subject of technology. In this lecture, Heidegger writes: "Agriculture is now a motorized food industry, the same thing in its essence as the production of corpses in the gas chambers and the extermination camps, the same thing as blockades and the reduction of countries to famine, the same thing as the manufacture of hydrogen bombs."¹⁶⁸ Lacoue-Labarthe finds it intolerable that Heidegger does not name the Jews in his shockingly matter-of-fact conflation of agriculture with genocide and that he fails to recognize their mass murder as an "apocalypse," as a phenomenon deprived of any logic: "In the Auschwitz apocalypse, it was nothing less than the West, in its essence, that revealed itself—and it continues ever since to reveal itself. And it is thinking that event that Heidegger failed to do."¹⁶⁹

By contrast, Vattimo never calls Heidegger to task for his evasiveness regarding the Holocaust. Following his idolization of the "revolutionary" Heidegger in *The Adventure of Difference*, Vattimo remains quiet about Heidegger and Nazism in his main works of the 1980s: *The End of Modernity* (1985) and *The Transparent Society* (1989). At the time of publication of the latter, the "Heidegger affair," as it came to be known in the wake of Farias's book, was a full-blown scandal, but we find no trace of the controversy either in Vattimo's most relentlessly positive manifesto regarding postmodernity and the mass media or in the writings that immediately follow. In *Beyond Interpretation* (1994), for example, he makes no mention of the elephant in the room, instead depicting Heidegger in glowing terms as having initiated a revolt against the violence of metaphysics (*BI*, 29; *OI*, 38). Indeed, Vattimo adopts an exculpatory strategy in the book insofar as his comparison of the Heideggerian criticism of metaphysics to the Foucauldian investigation of the "ontology of actuality" may be understood to mitigate indirectly the dangerously teleological and prophetic character of Heidegger's notion of the epochality of Being.¹⁷⁰

In *Nihilism and Emancipation* (2003), the Italian thinker touches on the topic of Heidegger and Nazism in a perfunctory and parenthetical manner apropos of technology. To validate his own view of technology, Vattimo recollects Heidegger's uncharacteristically positive affirmation, in *Identity and Difference*, of the relation between technology and the Ereignis as the new event or appropriation of Being. Vattimo then recounts that Gadamer actually told him that the greatest regret of Heidegger's life was not his association with Nazism but rather the insufficiency of his attention to the correspondence between modern technology and the overcoming of metaphysics:

In the course of a recent conversation . . . Hans-Georg Gadamer confirmed to me that, when Heidegger presented his text for the first time as a lecture, he was very well aware, if indeed somewhat anxious about, the novelty of this affirmation with respect to the rest of his work. According to Gadamer, . . . it was not so much the wretched business of his involvement with (alas!) Nazism that Heidegger perceived as a failure of his thought but rather the insufficient elaboration of this intuited relation between the overcoming of metaphysics and modern science/technology [*NE*, 14].

In this passage, it is striking that Vattimo expresses his dissent from Heidegger's politics as an impulsive, cursory exclamation of distress that can be delimited by the parenthetic interjection rather than as a measured assessment of the German philosopher's stance that represents substantive opposition. Ultimately, Vattimo emphasizes Gadamer's attribution to Heidegger of a late belief in the emancipatory value of technology in order to reduce the troubling question of Heidegger's Nazi sympathies to an inconsequential matter that may be addressed in a passing rhetorical aside, thus preempting critical analysis.

Unlike Lacoue-Labarthe, Vattimo does not consider for a moment the possibility that Heidegger's final affirmation of technology may play a role in discharging or repressing his political bad conscience. Taking the German philosopher's statements on the topic at face value, Vattimo thus risks perpetuating a misleading equivocation. The final and most significant episode in his consideration of Heidegger and Nazism occurs in *Addio alla verità*, which enlarges on his previous positions. Vattimo seems to ascribe his own philosophical distrust for the metaphysical notion of truth as correspondence to the longstanding Italian tradition of Machiavellianism. In his eyes, Machiavelli's key intellectual error was to maintain that lying is justified only for the prince or archetypal political leader (*AV*, 25). On this reckoning, the advantage of abandoning a strong idea of truth supposedly consists in encouraging democracy and undermining fundamentalism. Yet as the primary historical example of a culture that rejects the ideal of truth, Vattimo paradoxically names the Baroque Age, which was characterized by both crushing social conformism as well as dissimulation.[171] Turning to a more recent case, he discusses the Italian political watershed of the 1990s, the *Mani pulite* ("Clean Hands") investigation of official corruption, not from the point of view of the prosecuting judges but rather from that of the government officials whose acceptance of bribes in his opinion represents putting into practice a right to lie in the name of the general interest (*AV*, 26). In what he optimistically defines as the age of democracy, we must recognize the true ground of politics as the ontology of actuality, once we have identified as such the totalizing, universalist claims of socialism, colonialism, and metaphysics (*AV*, 49).

Although he fleetingly admits that a politics without truth might open the door to despotism, his basic reading of Heidegger is at odds with such a position. On this account, the mistake that the German philosopher made in 1933, his "Hitlerian" choice, as Vattimo puts it, in fact resulted from a momentary, misguided belief in truth and foundations (*AV*, 112). Instead, the "revolutionary Heidegger" whom Vattimo wishes to recover is the thinker par excellence of the dissolution of metaphysics and thus an opponent of the violence of truth or the *datum*:

> It is here that we can say what becomes decisive for philosophy is a reflection on the sense of the error of the Nazist Heidegger. . . . Exactly moving from the premises from which Heidegger was moving, and which he misunderstood in adhering to Hitler's movement, one might begin anew to imagine a philosophy that might respond as well to Marx's request, that is to be able to modify the world through an historical initiative and not only by "observing" it. The sense of Nazi Heidegger's mistake has not been in the decision to choose his heroes, to become involved in a political adventure. But not even, and this is the essential point, the fact of having embraced an "objectively" false cause, instead of sticking to the "truth." Heidegger's critics have always reproached him for not having recognized his "mistake," once the war was over. . . . But could he really do it on the ground of a "discovery" of truth—theoretical, ethical etc.—as after all could have been done embracing what so increasingly appears to us as the "logic of Nuremberg"? [*AV*, 113].

Once again, the use of quotation marks is telling. In keeping with a stereotypically postmodern point of view, the very idea of the truth is made ironic by means of its suspension in scare quotes, as are the notions of observation, objectivity, discovery, and, last but not least, the truth value of the Nuremberg trials.[172] In this last instance, the effect is to cast into doubt the premise of the trial process itself, of the condemnation of Nazism in the name of universal human rights, albeit as enforced by the victors of the war. Vattimo is aware that he flirts with a dangerous revisionism here, but the theoretical triumph of not affirming the dubious universalist scope of human rights encourages him to justify Heidegger's silence:

> Heidegger cannot repeat the mistake to believe that now, finally, the real truth might have become evident. That is why he keeps his silence about his mistake-sin [errore-peccato], probably thinking that, in the new situation, what he can do without pretending to be truthful (like the judges in Nuremberg) is to stay silent

in order to continue his reflection on the way Being offers itself in our times . . . as the end of Nazism had not really occurred [*AV*, 114].

Ventriloquizing Heidegger with the transition to indirect discourse signaled by the interjection "probably thinking," Vattimo does not pursue an examination of accountability or "sin," to use his own term, so much as an exercise in sympathy.

Absolving the German philosopher for the sake of a truth that must be denied or disclaimed with quotation marks is a symptom of Vattimo's inability to recognize Nazism as a complex phenomenon that has to do with people, language, culture, art, and ideology rather than as some syllogistic consequence of the metaphysics of truth. Indeed, his habit of reasoning by equivalence is very much on display in the course of his argument, when he compares Heidegger's Nazism to Lukacs's or Bloch's Stalinism. The simile obscures the peculiar context of each of its terms and thus the historical difference between Nazism and Stalinism that can be conflated only on a theoretical level in the dark night of totalitarianism. As Lacoue-Labarthe has noted, one of the most striking traits of Nazism is that, unlike Stalinism, it lacks a specific, comprehensible ideology. This conceptual murkiness should have made a serious grappling with Heidegger's Nazism all the more urgent for Vattimo, instead of prompting him to settle for a troubling, unconvincing apologia.[173]

In Foucault's Wake: Vattimo's Ontology of Actuality

Without claiming that French poststructuralist thought represents a homogeneous and unified philosophy, we may observe some common concerns and points of departure in the efforts of Derrida, Deleuze, and Foucault to redefine the activity of criticism. In Foucault's case, we encounter the most direct and straightforward effort to reflect on such activity. In a series of essays written between 1978 and 1984 that include "What Is Critique?"; "What Is Revolution?"; his lecture to the Collège de France of January 5, 1983; and "What Is Enlightenment?" Foucault sets out to redefine criticism as a problematizing attitude and a form of resistance.[174] Unlike Adorno and Horkheimer, who sharply criticized the Enlightenment tradition in *Dialectic of the Enlightenment*, Foucault identifies a space for thinking in the wake of the Enlightenment that does not automatically reassert a consonance between rationality and domination.

Challenging the claim made by Habermas in *The Philosophical Discourse of Modernity* that French poststructuralism does not have adequate means to complete the Enlightenment project, Foucault reinterprets the project itself through the notion of "the ontology of actuality." As he puts it in "What Is Revolution?"

> It seems to me that the philosophical choice with which we are confronted at present is this: we can opt for a critical philosophy which will present itself as an analytic philosophy of truth in general, or we can opt for a form of critical thought which will be an ontology of ourselves, an ontology of actuality. It is this form of philosophy that, from Hegel to the Frankfurt School through Nietzsche and Max Weber, has founded the form of reflection within which I have attempted to work.[175]

In his use of the word *ontology*, Foucault seems to have in mind not the concept of Being as the history of metaphysics but rather an immanent field of action in which neither subject nor object is fully master of its own conditions. He imagines a scenario, in other words, where power and resistance operate reciprocally on each other.

Avoiding any suggestion of a grand, overarching philosophical narrative of Western philosophy, Foucault defines the ontology of actuality as the ground of our attention to the emergence of contingency: "Which is the present [actuel] field of our possible experiences? What is in question is not an analytic of truth, what is in question instead is an ontology of the present, an ontology of actuality, an ontology of modernity, an ontology of ourselves."[176] To escape being trapped by his or her specific historical tradition, the critic imagines ways to transgress whatever is presented as the necessary conditions of existence. Although criticism may be subordinate to science, philosophy, and politics, as Foucault observes in "What Is Critique?" it fulfills a purpose akin to that of virtue.[177] This virtue consists in confronting authority, in refusing to be governed completely, in honing the arts of "voluntary insubordination" and "reflective intractability": "I will say that critique is the movement by which the subject gives himself the right to question truth on its effects of power and question power on its discourses of truth."[178] In this sense, the importance of the Enlightenment resides not in offering us a paradigm for the legitimation of knowledge, but rather in problematizing power and suggesting its potential reversibility.

For Foucault, the Enlightenment is the age of critique in the sense that it rebels against the long period of the Christian Church's claim to absolute authority, which starts with dissemination of the Christian pastoral and is characterized by practices aiming at total obedience. This ecclesiastical mode of discipline, which calls on the individual to submit to being governed by the Church as the price of salvation, leads in turn to secular practices of governmentalization in the fifteenth century that include managing children, the poor, the family, and so forth.[179] Against the burden of historical tradition, critique, which is the attitude of modernity, aims at imagining the present otherwise than as it seems to be. The critic thus works to map the ontology of actuality by asking not what limits have been imposed on us, but rather what the possibility of transgressing them is.[180]

The thinker who in Foucault's eyes best understood the need for philosophy to question its own actuality is Kant. In his lecture before the Collège de France of January 5, 1983, Foucault observes that Kant's work has been foundational in two ways. First, he inaugurated the analytic of truth, investigation of the conditions of possibility for true cognition of ethical and aesthetic experience. Second, and more important for us, he made clear the necessity of an ontology of actuality in the sense of a critical understanding of the normative realities of his day in the essay, "What Is Enlightenment?" which responds to a query originally aired in the *Berlinische Monatsschrift*, as well as his studies of cosmopolitanism and race. In the context of this effort, the most relevant questions are neither strictly logical nor analytic in function, but rather temporal inasmuch as the main object of investigation is the field of possible experiences in the present. Whereas Kant was engaged chiefly in a negative attempt to judge the limits of his ontology, Foucault focuses in "What Is Enlightenment?" on the positive effort to transgress "the contemporary limits of the necessary": "The Point, in brief, is to transform the critique conducted in the form of necessary limitation into a practical critique that takes the form of a possible transgression" (franchissement).[181] Displacing the emphasis from critique as judgment to critique as resistance, Foucault calls for a way of thinking that is attuned more to contingent possibilities—and not simply to historicity per se—than to finitude in the Kantian sense.

Vattimo instead concludes that, after Kant and Hegel, philosophy no longer may consider itself to have a critical vocation (*VRF*, 52). For him, post-Hegelian thinking no longer regards the premise of "universal and stable reason" to be believable, and as a consequence philosophy cannot be granted the status of a "critical" science (una scienza di tipo "critico"; *VRF*, 51, 52). As usual, he sets apart the very word *critical* with quotation marks, presenting it as a concept that is doomed from now on to the limbo of cultural irrelevance. He never asks whether a different and updated role for criticism may be possible; in this respect, his reappropriation of the concept of the ontology of actuality deprives it of any critical purpose. In his later writings, beginning with *Beyond Interpretation* (1994) and continuing in *Vocation and Responsibility of the Philosopher* (2000) and *Nihilism and Emancipation* (2003), he elaborates the Foucauldian notion of the ontology of actuality as a dimension of weak thought, thus enlarging the scope of his approach beyond the insistence on nihilism characteristic of his earlier works.[182] To this shift of perspective he assigns such importance that, in the preface of *Beyond Interpretation*, he announces that a forthcoming philosophical summa, which apparently remains unfinished to this day, will be titled "Ontology of Actuality" (*BI*, ix). We may well ask, Why does he make such a concerted effort to incorporate this specific conceptual framework, given that he never previously demonstrates any affinity with Foucault?[183] If the ontology of actuality for Foucault ultimately aims at "reflective intractability," what can such a mode of inquiry have in common with weak thought, which exhibits the passive bias of the hermeneutic method toward interpretation, rather than interrogation, of textual and historical authority?[184] In this sense, the "attitude" of weak thought is acritical by definition because it presupposes the subject's ontological submission to the adventure of Being.

In the opening chapter of *Nihilism and Emancipation*, Vattimo offers the clearest explanation of what he means by the ontology of actuality:

The expression is meant to be taken in the most literal sense: it does not simply indicate, as Foucault thought, a philosophy oriented primarily toward the consideration of existence and its historicity rather than toward epistemology and logic— that is, toward what would be called, in Foucault's terminology, an "analytic of truth." Rather an "ontology of actuality" is used here to mean a discourse that attempts to clarify what Being signifies in the "present situation" [*NE*, 3–4].

He further qualifies this rather hazy notion of the "present situation" of Being as "the concrete historical situation of users of language" (*NE*, 4). This stress on the historicity of the relationship between Being and language begs the question whether Vattimo's interpretation of the ontology of actuality is not in fact merely a renaming of Heidegger's "epochality of

Being." By contrast, Foucault does not define the concept in metaphysical terms that attribute initiative and agency exclusively to Being. Criticism thus can be conceived of in his theory as a practice, an activity of resistance. Vattimo neutralizes the critical potential of Foucault's idea of ontology in order to align it with the view that interpretation of Being as event or appropriation, which is made possible by some of Heidegger's late statements, necessarily leads to the question of how Being makes itself manifest in its "actuality"—for example, through the triumph of technology in contemporary society. In the Italian philosopher's later writings, then, weak thought retreats from the morbidity of nihilism in order to recover a measure of worldliness in the eyes of today's spectacularized form of capitalism.

Whereas renunciation of the hegemonic narrative of Western metaphysics makes possible for Foucault our awareness of actuality and singularity, recognition of the actual meaning of existence for Vattimo presumes acceptance of this philosophical account. In his opinion, we may turn to actuality and discover the signs and traces of Being in the world only because metaphysics has fulfilled all of its possibilities at the end of history, and Being has revealed itself neither as presence, nor as object, but rather as event.[185] According to this reasoning, Heidegger's avowal of the epochal essence of Being as the sole "aperture" in which human beings and the world can interact authorizes the perspective of the ontology of actuality (*NE*, 6). Indeed, self-consciously imitating a typical Heideggerian gesture, Vattimo asserts that the ontology of actuality ought to be understood in relation to the two meanings of the genitive as the ontology that speaks of actuality while also belonging to it (*NE*, 8). That this style of philosophy might wind up as nothing more than an excuse for self-complacency is for Vattimo an acceptable risk in order to ensure overcoming metaphysics: "For philosophy, this entails the risk of becoming the apology of whatever is . . . but it is a risk that has to be run, otherwise the overcoming remains an empty word" (*NE*, 12). Moreover, his adherence to the tenets of hermeneutics necessitates a respectful frame of mind toward tradition, precedent, and the status quo. Now, as Foucault observes, the novelty of Kant's response to the question of what Enlightenment is consisted in isolating the specificity of the present by scrutinizing its difference from the past.[186] Such an interest in change as a conflictual process does not easily consort with the reverence of hermeneutics for accepted convention.

In a rhetorical gambit that seems at odds with his affirmation of Heidegger's concern for metaphysics and the unveiling of Being, Vattimo extols the notion of "actuality" as the key to a potential redefinition of philosophy as "intrinsically political thought" (*NE*, 86). Although he tries to link "the ongoing historical process" with a supposed "advent of democracy" at the end of metaphysics, he gives the impression that in the end we are merely spectators of the ontological unfolding of history (*NE*, 88, 89). The trouble with this argument is that it is difficult to see how our involvement in such a generalized occurrence might respond to any need for concrete practice, action, or criticism. At any rate, he proposes his reading of history in an uncharacteristically somber paragraph of the chapter "Philosophy, Metaphysics, Democracy" in *Nihilism and Emancipation*, in which he speaks of how difficult it is to "'represent' democratically the current sense of Being" and concludes:

[H]ence there remains an enormous distance between even this form of philosophy . . . and politics. But even if reflection on philosophy and politics does not take us (at least as I see it) very far down the road to reorganizing the relationship and the contribution of philosophy to politics, at least it may mean summoning philosophy back to a more radical awareness of the significance of the event, if that is what it is, of the end of metaphysics and the advent of democracy in philosophical thought [*NE*, 89].

As supporting evidence for his contention that democracy is an inherent consequence of Heidegger's historicizing of metaphysics, he cites a passage in "The Origin of the Work of Art" where the German philosopher declares that, among other ways, the original truth of Being makes itself manifest both through the "setting-itself-into-the-work" of art and "through the act which founds a state" of politics.[187] Vattimo's redefinition of the ontology of actuality thus suggests an urbanizing of the idea of the "epochality of Being" that delineates a space where Being can express itself in action.[188]

Yet we should note that Vattimo maintains studied silence about Heidegger's critique of actuality in the celebrated essay "Anaximander's Saying," which appears in *Off the Beaten Track* (Holzwege).[189] The German philosopher reflects in this essay on the "oldest saying of Western thinking" by developing his notion of the epoch of Being in terms of the belonging of the Stoic *epoché* to Being itself: "Out of the *epoché* of being comes the epochal essence of its destining in which authentic world-history lies. Each time that being keeps to itself in its destiny, suddenly and unexpectedly world happens."[190] Heidegger's definition of the epoch, then, is well ensconced in an ontological framework, leaving an epiphenomenal role to the happening of the world. That epochality has nothing in common with actuality becomes clear at the end of the essay when Heidegger defines *actuality* in relation to the advance of metaphysics in the epoch of Being as presence. The exact moment of this advance occurs with the translation of Aristotle's concept of *energeia*, which supplies the foundation of all philosophical thinking about Being, into Latin as *actualitas*: "*Actualitas* becomes reality. Reality becomes objectivity. . . . The decisive turn in the destiny of being as *energeia* is the transition to *actualitas*."[191] If for Heidegger the translation of Being into actualitas leads to metaphysical ordering of the world and eventually toward the brink of the abyss (*Abgrund*) that opens in the groundlessness of Being, for Vattimo it seems to signify an equivalence between history and ontology as Being qua event or appropriation that Heidegger himself would not have supported (*VRF*, 75).

Vattimo thus conveniently ignores Heidegger's association of actuality with reality and objectivity, in favor of his own equation of the term with the innocuously vague category of "the present situation," which certainly is more compatible with his call for dissolution of the principle of reality and the subject-object dichotomy on which it is premised. Although such a proposal may free ontology from its tragic destiny, it makes no sense from the perspective of the Heideggerian attempt to move beyond the metaphysics of presence. As we have seen, the German philosopher views actuality in terms of reality, objectivity, and presence. In *Addio alla verità*, Vattimo claims that Foucault resisted defining in a precise way the ontology of actuality but admits that the French thinker seemed to mean actuality to convey something like the historical, the particular data of history from which our present circumstances are constructed (*AV*, 37). Vattimo proposes instead to interpret the term more vaguely as the "common condition of our contemporary life" in accordance with the sense implied by words of Latinate derivation such as *actualidad, actualité, attualità* (*AV*, 37). Puzzlingly, the Italian philosopher settles in the end for equating the ontology of actuality with the hoary Hegelian idea of Zeitgeist, the "spirit of the age" (*AV*, 55). Whereas Foucault, then, uses the concept of actuality to move forward in a philosophical genealogy that includes Hegel among its previous exemplars, Vattimo moves backward by citing without any apparent theoretical reason Hegel's anachronistic notion of a spirit of historical determinism. The regressiveness of the gesture only undermines the point of Foucault's inquiry.

If the ontology of actuality appears in the economy of Vattimo's thought to be relegated to a mainly decorative role, this limitation has to do at least partly with his determination to link actuality to the postmodern. Explaining how the investigation of modernity may challenge the foundation of received assumptions about what he elsewhere calls, as we know, our "field of possible experiences," Foucault instead carefully brackets the idea of postmodernity and the evolutionary logic that it appears to uphold:

> I know that modernity is often spoken of as an epoch. . . . Situated on a calendar, it would be preceded by a more or less naïve or archaic premodernity, and followed by an enigmatic and troubling "postmodernity". . . . rather than seeking to distinguish the "modern era" from the "pre-modern" and "post-modern," I think it would be more useful to try to find out how the attitude of modernity, ever since its formation, has found itself struggling with a counter-modernity.[192]

Vattimo, however, maintains the stance he has held since publication of *The Transparent Society*: that postmodernity is not a fad but rather an apt description of our state of being in a "society of generalized communication" where "economic power is still held by capital" and consequently "the very logic of the information 'market' . . . demands that everything somehow become an object of communication" (*TS*, 1, 5–6).

In *Nihilism and Emancipation*, he thus argues that "postmodernity is specifically determined by technology" and represents "a transformation of (the notion of) Being as such" that can be thought through productively only by enlarging the Foucauldian interrogation of the present: "I believe that we can only speak intelligently about postmodernity, and about the significance that technology has in it, from a perspective that starts with Heidegger's teaching and goes to elaborate what might be called, using a term from Foucault's late period, an 'ontology of actuality'" (*NE*, 3). But the Italian thinker does not explain to us how it is possible to reconcile two viewpoints that are so starkly inimical to each other: the one concerned with the practices and power relations that determine our experience of the present (i.e., actuality in Foucault's sense), the other with a dissolution of historical direction that supposedly frees us from any need to master reality (i.e., postmodernity in Vattimo's own sense). In its original Foucauldian context, the ontology of actuality entails meticulous analysis of the situation of the present, the specificity of ourselves. What place would there be for this analysis in a postmodernity that usually is defined as the end of history in the form of either the demise of narratives of emancipation à la Lyotard or a "post-history" à la Ghelen? According to Foucault, the ontology of actuality represents a new beginning: a revolt against authoritarian constellations of power rather than the nihilistic celebration of "anything goes." We have seen that for Vattimo the postmodern continues to be a valuable reference because he identifies in postmodernity the end of metaphysics, the first flash of the Heideggerian Ereignis. Yet if, as he contends, this liberation of thought from first principles is achieved by surrendering to the pressures of an information market that merely perpetuates the economic power of capital, then Foucault's ontological project cannot survive. To invoke this project under the sign of such a postmodernity is to render it critically and politically meaningless.

Recently, Roberto Esposito has suggested that the best Italian philosophy in fact aims to articulate an ontology of actuality, if by this turn of phrase we mean interrogation of the present in a political register.[193] As examples of this effort, he names Machiavelli, Vico, Croce, and Gramsci. Yet the political register in Foucault's thought is not compatible with the ideological conservatism and veneration of power that correspond to what he calls "counter-modernity." We may well ask whether Machiavelli, Vico, and even Croce, notwithstanding his anti-Fascism, ought to be regarded as belonging to a "Foucauldian" genealogy insofar as their views are fundamentally authoritarian in Machiavelli's case and reactionary in the other two cases. Indeed, Foucault sets the Kantian idea of the Enlightenment or *Aufklärung* that inspires his own questioning of actuality in direct opposition to Vico's vision in the last chapter of *La scienza nuova* of the present of "today" as the herald of a "world era" that will bring about the providential order of "a complete humanity spread abroad through all nations."[194] *Pace* Esposito, then, it seems far more to the point to observe how Italy has been shaped by the Christian pastoral with its directives to obedience and respect for authority than to claim for Italian culture a strong affinity with the Enlightenment. On this score, Vattimo is no exception to the trend.[195] Unlike Derridian deconstruction, Foucauldian genealogy, or Deleuzian schizo-analysis, weak thought renounces the task of redefining the value of critical thinking for our times.

Christianity Lite: Secularization as Postmodern Religion

By the middle 1990s, Vattimo, like other poststructuralist philosophers such as Derrida and Nancy, embarked on a new examination of religion and its contemporary manifestations. In his thinking on this topic, the Italian philosopher assigns a central role to the category of the secular, the archetype of which he discovers in the doctrine of the incarnation.[196] Yet he also clearly frames his discussion of theological issues in the context of a renewal of his personal commitment to Catholicism, a commitment that dates back to his youth.[197] Voicing the argument of his book *Belief* (1999) in the first person, in fact he makes inescapable the autobiographical background of his return to religion. At the same time, he also names the constellation of worldly or epochal circumstances that have restored religious questions to relevance, such as the fall of the communist régimes in Eastern Europe, which Pope John Paul II famously helped to inspire; and the feeling of detachment from revolutionary politics that follows "the end of the struggle between the Good Empire and the 'Evil Empire' (as Reagan once called the USSR)" (*B*, 26–27).[198]

The primal scene of *Belief* takes place on "a hot afternoon" during which Vattimo places a telephone call from an ice cream shop in Milan to a figure whom he much admired and respected: the Thomistic philosopher Gustavo Bontadini (*B*, 69–70). The call, he tells us, concerns administration of an upcoming examination for a university chair. Yet Bontadini surprises Vattimo by asking him if he still believes in God, at which point he tells us, "I do not know whether my response was conditioned by the paradoxical situation in which the question arose: next to the telephone was a table of women, eating ice cream and drinking orange juice in the heat. So I answered that I believed that I believed" (*B*, 70). The formula "I believed that I believed" suggests a mise-en-abîme that drains the concept of faith of its idealist vitality and emblematically provides the Italian edition of the book, which inaugurates Vattimo's attempt to give a religious genealogy to weak thought, with the initial phrase of its title: *Credere di credere: É possibile essere cristiani nonostante la chiesa* (literally "To Believe in Believing: It's Possible to Be Christian Notwithstanding the Church").[199] In the English edition, the main title's regressive sequence of infinitive verbs (credere di credere) is shortened to a single, peremptory noun (belief) and the sarcastic subtitle is eliminated, giving the reader an impression of gravity or sublimity that is absent from the original. The convergence of the sacred and the mundane, solemnity and farce, in the juxtaposition of the epiphanic telephone exchange with the scene of women eating their ice cream soothingly domesticates the subject matter of Vattimo's reflections, as if tacitly to promise that his deliberation will be free of the austere labor of concentration associated with the not-so-hot climates of Königsberg or Denmark.[200]

In other words, the ironic equivocation "I believed that I believed" stands for more than mere postmetaphysical pragmatism.[201] Insofar as this statement represents a return to religion that disclaims any moral or messianic purpose, it encapsulates the modernized state of cynicism that Peter Sloterdijk describes as "enlightened false consciousness," as a "demoralized" mentality that "is afflicted with the compulsion to put up with preestablished relations that it finds dubious, to accommodate itself to them, and finally even to carry out their business."[202] Richard Rorty observes that Vattimo's most startling theological claim is that secularization is a result of the incarnation and thus represents both a constitutive trait of Christianity and its true destiny.[203] The Italian philosopher indeed argues that, in a manner similar to the Heideggerian *Verwindung* or weak "overcoming" of metaphysics, secularization paradoxically can bring us back to a lighter Christianity that is free from the weight of dogma. He appears to perceive the current state of Christianity as another dimension of the ontology of actuality, which is to say as a unique sign of the times.[204]

As Marramao points out, this rereading of the ontology of actuality in religious terms places Christianity itself in the position of "the event par excellence."[205] In *Belief*, Vattimo in fact proclaims that the "great event" of his spiritual life has been the "decisive discovery" that we ought to understand the "notion of weak ontology as a 'transcription' of the Christian message" (*B*, 40). From this personal conviction, he concludes that "the substantial link between the history of Christian revelation and the history of nihilism means nothing more and nothing less than a confirmation of the validity of Heidegger's discourse on the end of metaphysics" (*B*, 40). The congruence of Christian revelation with philosophical nihilism becomes unavoidable once we accept "a conception of secularization characteristic to modern western history as an event within Christianity [that is] linked positively to Jesus' message and to a conception of the history of modernity as a weakening and dissolution of (metaphysical) Being"

(*B*, 40–41). Carmelo Dotolo slyly describes Vattimo's argument as an itinerary that leads from the secularization of philosophy to a philosophy of secularization.[206]

Vattimo accounts for what might look like a happy coincidence between the implications of the doctrine of the incarnation for the history of Christian revelation and the implications of the Heideggerian Verwindung for the history of nihilism by positing a genealogy of ideas that encompasses Nietzsche, Heidegger, and René Girard. To think of Being no longer in metaphysical terms as a necessary structure but rather as an event in relation to which the individual subject stands as "an 'effect,' an heir, an addressee" amounts to a first step in acceptance of divine authority: "If, as I believe, religious experience consists in a feeling of dependence (as Schleiermacher rightly defined it), an awareness that my freedom is an initiative that has been initiated by someone else (as Pareyson put it), then the philosophical thought of Being as event is intrinsically oriented toward religion" (*B*, 92). The weakening of Being furthermore can be interpreted as the consequence of a process of secularization—"the process of drifting that removed modern lay civilization from its sacral origins"—which exemplifies the very essence of Christianity inasmuch as it represents "a positive effect of Jesus' teaching, and not a movement away from it" (*B*, 41). By affirming the centrality of the incarnation in terms of kenosis or the abasement and emptying of God as it is described in Philippians 2:7, Vattimo highlights the evidence in the New Testament for identifying the defining feature of Christianity as the denial of the transcendent features of divinity (taken as, say, a belief in resurrection that coincides with a belief in regained transcendence): "In this light, secularization—the progressive dissolution of the natural sacred—is the very essence of Christianity" (*B*, 50).[207]

In its stress on "emptying" the divinity of its transcendence, the theory of kenosis, which refers ultimately to Christ's self-sacrificial decision to empty himself of divinity and assume human form, bears a strong resemblance to the Italian thinker's interpretation of nihilism as a process of ontological weakening rather than as a philosophy of nothingness. Although it lies beyond the scope of my investigation here to discuss the merits of his thesis in Christological terms, it is worth noting that Vattimo fails to show any awareness of the long record of contestations of kenotic theology, criticisms that have been echoed by those theologians who take him to task for inadequate understanding of the alterity of revelation.[208] Significantly, he gives his contribution to a book coauthored with John D. Caputo the title "Toward a Nonreligious Christianity."[209] More broadly, he aims to demonstrate how a postmetaphysical way of thinking that is oriented toward persuasion and dissolution of violence and dogma in matters of faith may challenge more traditional religious views. Such a view is that of dialectical or crisis theology, which holds that secularization is rooted in awareness of the gulf between the human and the divine and thus leads to "an increasingly full illumination of the transcendence of God" (*B*, 48). Accordingly, his polemic targets both the conventional stigmatization of the secular as abandonment of religion and its modern reinterpretation as manifestation of the radical difference of God (cf. Barth, Bonhöffer, Levinas, etc.), contrasting both of these stances to his idea of secularization as fulfillment of Being's vocation (*AC*, 24, 36). Taking issue specifically with those thinkers who stress the modern view of God as wholly other, he contends that such a conception of divinity is unresponsive to the idea of the incarnate God and also presumes a philosophically untenable stability of Being (*AC*, 38–43).[210]

Of fundamental importance for Vattimo are Girard's texts of philosophical anthropology, *Violence and the Sacred* (1972) and *Things Hidden Since the Foundation of the World* (1978), which he read when the Italian editions became available in the early 1980s.[211] In these writings, Girard hypothesizes an original relation between the sacred and violence. Because the subject learns to desire the object mimetically, through imitating a model or mediator, our involvement in the social order inevitably leads to rivalries and conflicts that can be contained only by redirecting aggression at the symbolic figure of the scapegoat, whose slaughter restores harmony and therefore acquires a holy, ritual significance. As Vattimo sees it, Girard shows that the customary theological view of Jesus as a victim is wrong, that Jesus in fact came into the world to abolish the link between violence and the sacred precisely by suffering a death that was intolerable to "a humanity rooted in the violent tradition of sacrificial religions" (*B*, 37). Reading Heidegger in conjunction with Girard, then, would help us to imagine the progressive end of violence in as much as we may conceive simultaneously of the conclusion of the metaphysics of Being and the demise of sacrifice-based "natural religion."[212] That the problem of violence might be solved so neatly by the "'coming together' of the pieces of my personal religious-philosophical puzzle" prompts even Vattimo himself to wonder whether his train of thought is not too good to be true (*B*, 41).

No doubt, Girard's answer to this question would be affirmative. The French philosopher regards Vattimo's interpretation of his theory as a misunderstanding that arises from avoiding the idea of sacrifice to describe Christ's experience on the cross.[213] Girard does not hesitate to define Vattimo as a "café Catholic" who is all too ready to renounce the Catholic tradition in order to avoid any possibility of conflict.[214] Most importantly, Girard decries Vattimo's obsessive reliance on the Nietzschean dictum "there are no facts but only interpretations" and pointedly maintains that some facts are obvious, such as the persistence of the impulse toward scapegoating. Mimetic desire in this sense is an insurmountable limit. Indeed, the return to religion for Girard signals the exhaustion of philosophy and ideology in a world in which tragedy is resurfacing on every level: in politics, ecology, and society.[215] In Girard's eyes, Vattimo risks falling into the trap of believing that we may withdraw from the agonistic struggles of this world and thus gives credence to "a refusal of ethics" that is "one of the great clichés of modernity."[216]

What defines Christianity for Vattimo is not sacrifice but rather the ideal of selfless love, or to revert to the original Greek word, agape, which the Latin Vulgate renders as *caritas* and the King James Version as "charity." The locus classicus for this reading of the Christian religious character is of course 1 Corinthians 13:13, where Saint Paul declares that, of the three categories of faith, hope, and charity, the greatest is charity. With this precedent in mind, Vattimo asserts that charity ought to be regarded as the sole determining principle of a secularized Christianity. As such, charity stands opposed to justice, which requires use of concepts of the law and of natural rights that raise difficulties for the postmetaphysical agenda of secularization:

Besides all this, which could be another symptom of the return of Christianity, and the sentimental preference of love rather than justice, severity and the majesty of God, it is sufficiently clear that the New Testament orients us to recognize this [idea of charity] as the sole, supreme principle. . . . However, this "ultimate" meaning, precisely by virtue of its being *caritas*, is not really ultimate and does not possess the peremptoriness of the metaphysical principle [B, 64].

On this account, even the question of the Church's ethical stances in worldly affairs, which ensues from "the examples of a female priesthood and of the taboo of homosexuality" among others, is properly understood as a matter of charity rather than of justice (B, 76).[217] Vattimo's "sentimental" preference for charity or love condemns him to abandon the possibilities of critique and of practices that resist institutional forms of power, as these possibilities are compatible only with the search for justice. This is one of the several political consequences of his postmetaphysical return to Christianity.

If we compare Vattimo's theory of secularization to what Charles Taylor recently elaborates in *A Secular Age*, we encounter two approaches diverging at a crucial juncture. It is true that both thinkers discuss the secular in terms not of the relationship between church and state but rather of the problematic nature of belief today. Both similarly criticize "the subtraction theory," which holds that secularism consists in the loss of faith in the world as a response to modernity.[218] Vattimo, however, would hardly welcome Taylor's claim that secularization demands creation of new social practices and results in a more modern social imagination predicated on reinventing concepts such as those of agency and justice, on renewing the moral power of humanism's "immanent frame."[219] For Vattimo, salvation instead "has the features of lightness rather than justice" (*AC*, 55). He tends to discount the importance of the sociopolitical imagination in shaping the contemporary experience of secularization (*SA*, 572), preferring instead to regard it as the quasi-automatic consequence of God's historical incarnation or kenosis. Whereas Taylor's more anguished and engaged problematizing of the secular persistently confronts the question of justice, Vattimo's approach focuses on charity. As much as we may appreciate the possibility of a more lenient, less Augustinian reading of the moral dichotomy between the religious and the secular, Vattimo runs a specific risk in defining the aim of secularization as lightness. Hannah Arendt succinctly identifies this risk in *On Revolution* when she notes that the language of compassion often resists logical argument on the pretense of giving voice to suffering itself and in the process shuns the aim of restitution through either law or politics.[220]

"We Cannot Not Call Ourselves Christians": Vattimo, Derrida, and Universalism

In his writings on Christianity, Vattimo often quotes Croce's famous dictum, "We cannot not call ourselves Christians."[221] Although the sentence can be read to mean innocuously that, regardless of what their actual religious positions may be, those who live in a culture that includes Christianity as part of its heritage need to recognize their historical context,

Vattimo reinterprets the statement as a claim for the universalism of Christianity. He perceives Christianity not just as the historical "happy ending" to the problem of violence but as a philosophically preferable way of thinking. Because of the incarnation, Christianity in his view is inherently superior to Judaism as a philosophy. As he explains it, his own kenotic and antimetaphysical religiosity opposes what he calls the "tragic" form of Christianity, which is inspired by Aristotelian-Thomistic thought and harkens back to the "regressive" attitude of the Old Testament in emphasizing the crucifixion as "a death which testifies to God's paradoxical transcendence and alterity with respect to any mundane logic" (B, 83–84). By acknowledging kenosis as its true meaning, Christianity instead can realize the romantic vision of becoming "the universal religion" that is able to understand and "assimilate" other historical forms of religiosity (AC, 9, 27).[222]

John Caputo sharply criticizes Vattimo's privileging of Christianity, which he regards as a trap. He likens this bias to Hegel's preference for the spirit of Christianity over that of the "alienated" Jews and suggests that, on matters of religion, weak thought suddenly becomes "too strong."[223] He even charges Vattimo and Rorty with a similar chauvinism, a tendency toward overly sweeping political and religious generalizations that in Vattimo's case lead to equating Christianity with the West tout court.[224] Most importantly, Caputo objects to Vattimo's religious theory because, if we accept its terms, the process of secularization ensuing from the incarnation leads to a future where "the name of God" is behind us and all we have left "is to become what we already are."[225] This future, which reifies the conditions and limits of the present, contrasts directly with "what Derrida calls the unforeseeable 'to come' [à venir]"—a future that may fulfill the messianic dream of a democracy "in which there would be a profusion of difference" and that consequently represents "the very nature of the promise that requires faith and love and hope."[226]

Indeed, at a conference held in Capri in February 1994, Derrida elaborated a religious stance that diverges from Vattimo's in a number of important ways. Unlike Vattimo, Derrida is preoccupied with the idea of a Europe that signifies the death of God as well as a multiplicity in God (the passion, the trinity) and that therefore contrasts with both Judaism and Islam, which might revolt against this "death."[227] For Derrida, this concern becomes more pressing in light of the fact that demographic changes in world population and the influence of globalization favor growth of the Islamic faith at the expense of both Judaism and Christianity (*R*, 54). We might add that, after the events of September 11, 2001, the situation in Europe acquires an anxious biopolitical dimension that places the French philosopher's position in an ironic new light. By contrast, Vattimo fails to consider the potential weakening of Christianity as a social force because he prefers to think in the abstract terms of metaphysics and onto-theology rather than in the concrete terms of biopolitics and global culture. For him, because of the postmetaphysical condition of belief in the wake of the incarnation, Christianity can hope to read "the signs of the times" in a redemptive "light": "It is only in so far as it rediscovers its own provenance in the New Testament that this post-metaphysical thinking can take the form of a thinking of the event-like character of Being that is not simply reducible to a bare acceptance of the existent or to pure historical and cultural relativism" (*R*, 92).

Whereas Vattimo has no misgivings about ascribing to Christianity a "philosophical" privilege over other religions, Derrida is troubled by what he calls the "globalatinization" [mondialatinisation] of *religio*, or in other words a collusion of Christianity, the death of God, and "tele-technoscientific" capitalism that represents itself as the unconditional universality of Christianity (*R*, 13). Since religion itself, as Derrida reminds us, is an exclusively Latin concept that has no equivalent in other cultures, every "return to religion" should therefore be questioned about its pretended universalism: "How then to think . . . a religion which, without again becoming 'natural religion,' would today be effectively universal? And which, for that matter, would no longer be restricted to a paradigm that was Christian or even Abrahamic? Or does the idea itself remain, in its origin and in its end, Christian? And would this necessarily be a limit, a limit like any other" (*R*, 14)? This line of questioning is accompanied by an interrogation of the "kenotic horizon" of the death of God that, of course, is central to Vattimo's theory (*R*, 43). What Vattimo defines as the ability of Christianity to "assimilate" other religious paradigms, Derrida fears may be merely another manifestation of an all-too-familiar "European-colonial" sensibility (*R*, 43).[228] Derrida's quest for a religion that is not restricted to the Christian paradigm reaffirms faith and belief against the authoritarianism of knowledge and reason, albeit as a faith in the messianic without messianism and its infinite, singular promise of justice (*R*, 17–18). The space of such a faith is that of the *chora*, or the Platonic space beyond being, which is assigned to the encounter with the absolute, faceless other (*R*, 19–20). In a deliberate effort to move beyond the bounds of onto-theology, Derrida thus interprets faith as faith in what comes from the other.

Vattimo adamantly rejects any notion of religious belief that requires faith in the other and indeed admonishes both Derrida and Levinas for refusing to admit that "only in the light of the Christian doctrine of the Incarnation of the son of God does it seems possible for philosophy to think of itself as a reading of the signs of the times. . . . This problematic relation between philosophy and religious revelation is the very sense of the Incarnation" (*R*, 92). On this score, a decisive way in which philosophy responds to the signs of the times is by reading religion and technology in continuity. In *After Christianity*, the Italian philosopher in fact argues that the goal of Christianity, when properly free of dogma, is the same as that of technology, namely lightening reality (*AC*, 50–51). Yet Derrida seems to regard the prospect of this lightened reality not as a gain in self-awareness but rather as an "evil of abstraction" (*R*, 3) inasmuch as it is based on an autoimmune condition in the relationship between religion and tele-technoscience: "Religion today allies itself with tele-technoscience, to which it reacts with all its forces" (*R*, 46). Even as it ostensibly declares war on the media, religion nowadays thrives on the spectacular (in this connection, we may think again of Pope John Paul II). So although religion may promise an alternative to the uprooting forces of technology, it exploits what Derrida condemns as the abstraction, universalizing schematization, and claims to transcendence of teletechnology. Vattimo instead insists in quasi-Nietzschean parlance on the importance of "listening non-reactively to the technological destiny of Being" (*R*, 83). Yet the contrast between his credulity regarding technology's benign influence and Derrida's more sober view begs the question whether Vattimo's plea for "listening non-reactively" does not just amount to the acritical, unthinking embrace of spectacle in the name of secularization.

Christianity, Capitalism, and the Spiritual Lightening of Reality

Starting in 1998, at almost the same time as Vattimo was rediscovering a feeling of religious belief, Jean-Luc Nancy began to undertake what he defines as "the deconstruction of Christianity."[229] A brief comparison between Vattimo's and Nancy's reflections on the destiny of Christianity can be helpful in further determining the potential meanings of a contemporary return to religion. As we have noted, Vattimo's counterutopian interpretation of Christianity presumes acritical acceptance of consumerism, technology, and the "Babel" of the media, all of which he reads in continuity with Christianity itself. He does not seem at all disquieted by what Nancy defines as the "tautology of value," which is to say the static equivalence or "one-way circulation of sense" (sens unique) that arises out of the conflation of God, man, and value itself.[230] Pointedly raising critical and political questions, Nancy instead sets out to affirm Christianity as something more than a merely superstructural, accidental feature of Western civilization. Rather than the comforting idea of secularization, he turns to the concepts of monotheism, atheism, and the "monovalence of value" to analyze the conditions of Christianity in the present, to imagine an "exit from capitalism" that in his eyes can only be an "exit from nihilism."[231] It is useful by way of comparison to remember that for Vattimo nihilism, as Nietzsche and Heidegger define it, represents the "end-point of modernity" (B, 29). Nihilism and monotheism as well exemplify a perspective that, according to him, we ought to welcome. Indeed, as he sees it, the worldview of Judeo-Christian monotheism is responsible for the "rationalization of modern society" (B, 42).

The crucial equivalence for Nancy is between the "capitalist and technological economy" that enacts global rule of the law of exchange and "the general form of value or sense today."[232] This equivalence is precisely what he means by the monovalence of value, a structure that "hardly behaves otherwise than as the apparently nonreligious transcription of the monoculture whose monotheistic conception it carried: explicitly, the culture of Rome in its European and modern expansion."[233] Yet to the degree that the supposedly "atheist, atheistic, or atheological" outlook of modern culture derives from a "strictly and fundamentally monotheist provenance," the sheer dominance of globalization under "the somber wing of nihilism" makes apparent the need for a deconstruction of monotheism that aims to discover what lies beyond it.[234] The monotheism Vattimo exalts as the antithesis of the theology of God as wholly other looks to Nancy like reduction of the horizons of possibility to the One, which is the necessary unitary premise of nihilism.[235] The return to religion for the French philosopher necessitates reflection on what is new in this return and what hopeful horizon it may disclose:

> It is not our concern to save religion, even less to return to it. The much-discussed "return of the religious," which denotes a real phenomenon, deserves no more

attention than any other "return." Among the phenomenon of repetition, resurgence, revival or haunting, it is not the identical but the different that invariably counts the most. Because the identical immediately loses its identity in returning, the question should rather be asked, ceaselessly and with new risks, what an "identical secularization" might denote, invariably, other than mere transferral.[236]

Under the terms of Vattimo's theory of secularization, technology and capitalism become unproblematic "signs" of Christianity.[237] Because "the West is secularized Christianity" and therefore represents the destiny of a modernity that fundamentally affirms "scientific, economic, and technological rationality," renewal or revival of religion in Western society can only mean acceptance of the supposed truth that "Christian ethics, above all Protestant ethics, is the condition in which labor, saving, and economic success can be thought of as religious imperatives" (*AC*, 73–75). It should come as no surprise, then, that Vattimo names Max Weber's *The Protestant Ethic and the Spirit of Capitalism* (1930) as a source of inspiration in at least two works, *Belief* and *After Christianity*. Without ever directly quoting the German sociologist, Vattimo gives Weber credit for having established the genealogical continuity of Christianity and modernity. In fact, the Italian philosopher self-consciously attempts to enlarge Weber's claims by proposing that, as the alleged fulfillment of "Judaeo-Christian Scripture" and thus a defining characteristic of modernity, secularization structures capitalism and "all the principal traits of western civilization as well" (*B*, 43). One important objection to Vattimo's reappropriation of Weber's theory is that the sweeping assumption of a monotheistic, Judeo-Christian tradition flies in the face of Weber's deliberate narrowing of focus from Christianity per se down to the specific characteristics of Protestantism, with emphasis mostly on Calvinism. *The Protestant Ethic and the Spirit of Capitalism* indeed places the ethos of Protestantism in dialectical opposition to that of Catholicism, thus undermining Vattimo's attempts to bolster his own indiscriminate generalizations about Christianity and the West by invoking Weber as a model.[238] Defining the spirit of capitalism in terms of the rationalist and ascetic tendencies that gained prominence with the Reformation clearly leads Weber to distinguish between the situation of Catholic countries such as Italy and Spain, where this spirit is comparatively lacking, and that of Protestant countries such as the Netherlands and Germany, where it is predominant.[239] By contrast, Vattimo determinedly ignores the strong anticapitalist impulses in Catholicism, which can be traced back at least as far as the Franciscan tradition and continue to this day in the crucial encyclicals of Popes John Paul II and Benedict XVI.

Vattimo's argument does not become any more convincing when it is extended to modern consumerism by way of reference to Colin Campbell's *The Romantic Ethic and the Spirit of Modern Consumerism* (1987). Having been formulated "in the late modern condition in which we live," Campbell's theory is even more important than Weber's, in the eyes of the Italian thinker, to show the coincidence between the West and secularized Christianity (*AC*, 76–77). Like Weber, Campbell restricts his inquiry to specifically Protestant schools of thought, especially Calvinism, but parts ways with his predecessor in considering the development of consumerism chiefly from the late eighteenth century onward, a period on which Weber does not dwell. For Campbell, modern hedonism is based not on rational sensations but rather on emotion and presumes a self-conscious relation of internal feeling to external reality that achieves its first historically significant expression in Protestantism.[240] Although Puritanism as a form of the Protestant mentality aspired to total control of emotion, it cultivated such hostility to "natural" feeling as to cause the split between feeling and action on which hedonism is based, paradoxically encouraging the subject's ability to "manipulate the meaning of objects and events" and thus enlarging what we might call the emotional imagination.[241] On this front, however, Campbell again emulates Weber's method inasmuch as he presses his point by opposing Protestantism to Catholicism.[242] At any rate, Campbell makes clear that modern hedonism is firmly based on "a self-illusioned quality of experience" and elicits the type of longings that generally manifest themselves in daydreams and fantasies, thus resulting in the subject's permanent dissatisfaction.[243] Unlike Vattimo, he is not interested in offering an apologia for what already exists, so his "spiritualization" of consumerism does not glorify the fantasy life of consumerism as a means of weakening reality for the sake of postmodern freedom.

Of course, Vattimo never asks if it is actually a good thing for Christianity to be genealogically related to capitalism and consumerism. The closest he ever comes to admitting such a doubt is in a sentence in *After Christianity* where he speculates that, if we nowadays are unable to experience Christianity with the postmodern lightheartedness that appreciates "the appeal of aesthetic emancipation," our inability might stem from a "literalism" that fetishizes both the letter of sacred texts and the material reality of "injustices in the distribution of goods" (*AC*, 56). To be conscious of such injustices, in other words, looks to him like a sort of parochialism, a boorish concern with epiphenomena that we ought to forget rather than question or resist. According to his view, religion ultimately must be read as an epic of lightness, spirit, and fantasy that reaches its denouement with the debilitation of reality.

In this context, it makes a certain sense that he takes Joachim of Fiore (1130–1202) as an exemplar of "living postmodern religious experience" (*AC*, 26). Vattimo dedicates an entire chapter of *After Christianity* to the teaching of the twelfth-century monk, whose "spiritual posterity" includes, among others, Saint-Simon, Novalis, and Schelling, as the eminent theologian and Joachim scholar Henri de Lubac reminds us.[244] Joachim's exegetical fame is linked to a series of writings, including *Liber Concordiae Novi ac Veteris Testamenti, Expositio in Apocalypsim, Psalterium Decem Chordarum*, and *Tractatus Super Quatuor Evangilia*, in which he propounds the idea of a "Third Age" of the Spirit that would have followed those of the Father and the Son according to a logic that comprehensively transposes the eternal order of the Trinity into history.[245] Joachim's redemptive eschatology enacts transformation of the divine *oikonomia* associated with the Trinity into the providential domain of human action and thus exemplifies how trinitarian doctrine constitutes a laboratory, as Giorgio Agamben puts it in *Il Regno e la Gloria*, in which we may view the operations of the governmental machine.[246] The development of the Trinity, during the early centuries of the history of the Church, as a form of "management" (or oikonomia in its classical sense) of a divine life that no longer can be conceived of as simply monotheistic, inaugurates for Agamben articulation of power in the West in terms of economy and government.

Although Vattimo does not discuss the theological genealogy of contemporary economic categories, we may read in his enthusiasm for the "trinitarian God" something more than praise strictly for philosophical anti-foundationalism.[247] The Third Age, when "the spirit breathes where it wants," appears to signify in his eyes the epoch of the end of metaphysics when Being emerges as an elusive *Ereignis* or event rather than as a foundational paradigm (*AC*, 34).[248] Beyond the theological enigmas that Joachim has left us to ponder, what are of more interest for our purpose are the historical optimism and automatism of the transition that he envisions from the Second Age of man to the Third Age of spirit. This movement anticipates in tone and direction Vattimo's depiction of postmodernity as a postmetaphysical age of weakened Being in which "the kingdom of spirit [is] understood as lightening and poeticization of the real" (*AC*, 54).[249] Similarly, something of Joachim's mysticism resonates in Vattimo's rereading of the epoch of secularization as an "age of spirit" in which the return to religion, the end of metaphysics, and, citing a phrase from Novalis, "Europe's reconciliation and resurrection" all neatly coincide (*AC*, 35), thus bringing about an all-encompassing happy ending that deprives the "eventful" quality of Being of any opportunity to unfold or progress in unexpected dimensions.[250] Vattimo's plea for the softening of reality thus amounts to nothing less than a fully aestheticized idealism and spiritualism that belongs to the hegemonic genealogy of Italian philosophy.[251]

In a chapter of *After Christianity* titled "God, the Ornament," he declares that "the dream of Idealism," which he reminds us was advanced by Hegel but also by Marx, can be achieved only after we have embraced the Judeo-Christian revelation as it is interpreted specifically in Joachim's teaching and postmetaphysical thought, have abandoned "the 'heavy' structures in which Being has manifested itself throughout human civilization," and therefore have become "in multiple senses, spirit: spirit as pneuma, breath, the lightest breath that moves the air around us" (*AC*, 53–54). He concludes that "spiritualization," as he defines this way of thinking in light of Joachim's example and present-day conditions of "technological possibility and the evolution of ideas," may appear to be an attitude of "easiness and moral disengagement," because it carries "a densely aesthetic and poetic connotation" that allows it to "fill the otherwise empty *figure* of human history" (*AC*, 54–55). Consequently, if salvation is achievable on earth, "it has the features of lightening rather than justice" (*AC*, 55).

Whereas Derrida tried to question the binary opposition of realism and idealism through a notion of spectrality that at the same time constitutes a politically resonant utopian space, Vattimo settles for praising spirit as an aesthetic sensitivity to the "secondary qualities" of forms, lights, and colors that enables us to relinquish the real in favor of the pleasures of "phantasmagoria," thus achieving a state of perception that he associates with the Book of Revelation (*AC*, 52). Employing a turn of phrase that is evocative of Marshall McLuhan's famous dictum that the medium is the message, Vattimo claims that Christianity will realize its full antimetaphysical potential when "'reality' in all its aspects has been reduced to message," thus inaugurating the "age of interpretation."²⁵² One of the many preferred qualities that he ascribes to Christianity is its alleged antirealism. Reality for him inevitably loses its weight as Christianity introduces and enlarges the principle of "interiority."²⁵³ On this score, it is startling how radically Vattimo differs in his opinion of Christianity from Foucault, who posits in *History of Sexuality I* that, following the Council of Trent, introduction of the sacrament of confession made it possible for Christianity to work as a *dispositif* of power, as a regulative principle that controlled the discourse of sexuality.²⁵⁴

Far from considering the return to religion to be, as Derrida characterizes it in *Religion*, a reaction against "the evil of abstraction" that ensues from technological dissolution of the real, Vattimo resolutely acclaims the loss of the foundational notion of reality "since we no longer know what it actually is, subjected as we are by the world of production (merchandise), advertising, and so on to the manipulation, or better, the transformation of our imagination" (*AC*, 78). Yet the ringing declaration begs the question, Should not a philosopher interrogate the difference between manipulation and transformation? Why does he use the verb *subjected* in such nonchalant fashion, neglecting to question the political and disciplinary conditions of this subjection? In his enthusiasm for the light spirit of postmodern religion, Vattimo does not confront such "heavy" questions about our present and future condition. He affirms a concept of secularization as the ultimate ideal of his philosophy that represents the antithesis of Charles Taylor's notion of secularization as a mode of cultural innovation and creativity, that ironically resembles nothing so much as the romanticization of what Agamben condemns when he describes secularization as "a form of repression . . . [that] leaves intact the forces it deals with by simply moving them from one place to another."²⁵⁵

Ecce comu

In 1999, Vattimo was elected to serve as a senator in the European Parliament as a member of the Democratici di Sinistra (DS), which was a more centrist offshoot of the former PCI. In 2004, he began to distance himself from the party, which he accused (with good reason) of having become a form of "Craxism," which is to say a cynical, bureaucratic, light socialism.²⁵⁶ On the question of the Iraq War, the DS voted to support sending troops to that country, a decision that Vattimo judged to be an unprincipled and dangerous advancement of American imperialism. In 2007, he published a summation of his political views entitled *Ecce Comu: Come si ridiventa ciò che si era* (Ecce Comu: How to Become Again What One Was). The title, an ironic homage to Nietzsche's *Ecce Homo*, encapsulates Vattimo's central theme of "the recovered (or returned) communist hope" (*EC*, 4). Bringing original material together with articles published from 2002 to 2004 that were dedicated initially to proposing "the European ideal" as a substitute for the spent emancipatory potential of Marxism (*EC*, 9), the book offers a useful genealogy of the Italian philosopher's changing politics over several years. In fact, the reality of Europe soon disappoints him, as he is forced to recognize the hegemony of the center-right in the new political institutions of the European Union.

An important moment occurs in the book when Vattimo confronts Hardt and Negri's internationally successful *Empire* in a review originally written for *La Stampa* in 2002. Vattimo is reluctant to grant a positive value to the book, which he describes reductively as "the manifesto of the new anti-global contestation" (*EC*, 19–20). He is especially critical of Hardt and Negri's "new mythology" of the multitudes, which he ascribes to their nostalgia for an organic community (*EC*, 23). Yet he nevertheless must admit, however begrudgingly, that in Italy in particular we face the prospect of slaves whom the media encourage to identify with their masters and a society in which the majority of Italians indeed vote for Berlusconi without recognizing him as a master (*EC*, 17, 21).

The turning point in the book is represented by a speech titled "Il comunismo ritrovato" (Communism Recovered) that Vattimo delivered in 2004 at the Congress of the Partito dei Comunisti Italiani (PdCI, the Party of Italian Communists, which was established in 1998 and should not be confused with the older PCI). Following in the wake of Derrida's *Specters of Marx* (1993) and Hardt and Negri's *Empire* (2000), Vattimo laments the loss of the political perspective of the left in contemporary culture and comes close to declaring his responsibility for the undoing of emancipatory ideals: "Let me tell you, as I have been involved too in the Italian affair of the postmodern end of ideologies, that this way of interpreting the abandonment of metaphysics in politics can only originate that specific form of empiricism that was Craxism" (*EC*, 33).[257] In the speech, he includes a long citation of a letter from a philosophy teacher named Mimmo

Pichierri, whose bewildered questioning of what he dubs Vattimo's "return to strong thought" prompts Vattimo to reply, "Yes, I changed my mind, or better: many of my ideas" (*EC*, 38, 40).

In an effort to justify weak thought, however, he avoids admitting any complicity in the hegemony of neoliberalism and professes only the desire to distance himself from the violent events of 1968, which became particularly perilous in his city of Turin. He remarks that weak thought "evolved, or devolved," into a Heideggerian philosophy of history in which weakness might be considered a mode of emancipation from the history of Being (*EC*, 41). It is important to note Vattimo's ambivalence regarding the transformation of weak thought into a philosophy of history as reflected in his hesitation over whether or not to describe it as evolutionary. He draws a contrast between his approach and Rovatti's emphasis on phenomenological attention to the margins. Yet a certain doubt ultimately seems to contaminate Vattimo's sense of the meaning of his own project, which becomes particularly questionable, as we have observed, in its acritical absorption of Heidegger. In this connection, it is very interesting to note how he reverses himself in *Ecce comu* by assigning a negative value to many of the good concepts and key words that he promoted in the 1980s and 1990s. Abandonment of the reality principle that he praised in his earlier writings as a way to avoid the epistemological violence of metaphysics thus comes to characterize the "frantic behaviour" of the capital markets (*EC*, 32). He even goes so far as to observe that the current problem of Italian democracy is the degree to which it has lost touch with the "everyday reality of society" (*EC*, 50). The faith in a comprehensive weakening of ideologies to achieve peace and prosperity is now replaced by the awareness that Marx's legacy is crucial and prophetic as we are witnessing "the progressive proletarization of the world" (*EC*, 34). "Real communism is dead, long live ideal communism" becomes his new slogan, and freedom—which was one of his earlier standards and a canonical ideal of neoliberal ideology—is exchanged for equality as the value most conducive to human emancipation (*EC*, 36–37). Ultimately, however, he appears to remain eager to resuscitate his brand and insists on the need to affirm "a 'weakened' Marx" in renewing the truth of communism on nondogmatic and anti-absolutist foundations (*EC*, 41).

Most of all, Vattimo has to rethink his earlier idealization of technology and media, which reaches its zenith in *The Transparent Society*, when faced with the reality of social conditions in Italy: "Italy is the country where the mediatization of politics has manifested its effects with the greatest intensity" (*EC*, 45). Although he suggests that other nations are implicated in a global dissolution of democracy, he attributes to Italy the role of having "anticipated" and made more evident the most salient characteristic of this process, that is to say, a "mediatization" that verges on the pathological (*EC*, 44). It is significant that to describe this process in *Ecce comu* he uses for the first time a word, "spectacularization," that he carefully avoided in the past (*EC*, 44). Moreover Vattimo refers to technology and the media as "an informatic-mediatic bubble, a bubble precisely in its being a sphere that is evidently evanescent" (*EC*, 46). By decrying the false evanescence of a bubble that excludes poorer or so-called primitive social groups (*EC*, 46), he begins to deconstruct the acritical rhetoric celebrating the lightness and benevolence of the media that he helped to establish as the hegemonic Italian cultural discourse in the previous decades.

Reflecting his new disposition toward politics and the media, he pays homage to Marx, Adorno, and the value of the avant-garde (*EC*, 55). To articulate what he calls "the avantgardistic 'vocation' of politics," he avows the importance of escaping the routine of normalcy and of embracing a certain "apocalyptic" spirit, which brings him to the brink of calling for a revolutionary process of transformation (*EC*, 58–60). Apparently weary of the empty speech of reformism and of the Thatcherite slogan that there is no alternative to capitalism, Vattimo advances a case for revolution through idiosyncratic criticism of the U.S. government's handling of the siege in Waco, Texas; mild reclamation of Stalin (whom he criticizes only for having believed in the myth of progress or development); and exaltation of the new socialist societies in Latin America (*EC*, 90, 109).[258]

Unlike Negri, who has dedicated a book to Latin American politics, Vattimo's argument for a revolutionary politics seems scattered in focus and superficial. Toward the end of *Ecce comu*, he recognizes à la Hardt and Negri that the masses mobilized through the Internet to oppose the Iraq War represent a new proletariat, albeit without a class consciousness (*EC*, 79). Paying tribute to Agamben, he describes this new proletariat as the part of the population that has been reduced to *la nuda vita* or "bare life" (*EC*, 80). The future that from an earlier vantage seemed destined to witness the progressive lightening of absolutist and dogmatic structures and to achieve the triumph of irreality through the influence of the media now appears in Vattimo's eyes to be "absolutely obscure and destined to a growth of violence and to an intensification of disciplines of all sorts" (*EC*, 83). There is one philosophical principle, however, besides that of weakness that he improbably wishes to save in the process of rediscovering communism: nihilism. Now interpreting this tenet as the sign of principled renunciation of the rhetoric of development and invoking it as a guarantee of an antidogmatic freedom of mind, he still bemoans the fact that Italian leftists consistently refuse to base their political praxis on nihilism (*EC*, 97). Yet deprived of any Heideggerian raison d'être, and reformulated to give evidence of his renewed "Marxist" allegiance, Vattimo's fundamental doctrine looks more than ever like a retreat from substantive critical confrontation of the contemporary Italian social order, an empty rhetorical flourish that helps its author avoid asking hard questions of the powers that be.

4

Softness

Postcriticism

The art historian Achille Bonito Oliva helped to establish the international preeminence of a new style of painting in the 1970s when he bestowed the title Transavanguardia on an emerging group of Italian Neo-Expressionist artists. This movement succeeded the Arte Povera of the 1960s, which had emphasized art's revolutionary potential to resist the pressure of the marketplace. Gaining notoriety in no small measure thanks to its inventor's practice of "performative criticism," Transavanguardia placed the critic in the position of no longer being a mediator but rather "a constitutive subject of artistic production," in Angelo Capasso's words.[1] Bonito Oliva envisioned the critic in the role of a self-publicizing performer of music who, as Hans Belting puts it, "does not use a score but instead writes the score of how artists are to be presented and how they are to be understood."[2] On this view, Bonito Oliva played the part to the hilt in methodically "hunting" for artists who exemplified all the traits he idealized under the rubric at first of the "neoavantgarde" but shortly thereafter of the Transavantgarde.

Indeed, the four or five artists that he identifies as the main practitioners of his school exhibit a striking *air de famille*. Each is rigorously male, hails from Southern Italy as does Bonito Oliva himself, paints in a style that lends itself to easy description through applying a couple of characteristic qualifiers, and affirms an ideal of representation as "a tireless spectacle."[3] For example, Sandro Chia is preoccupied in his paintings with hedonism and embodies a genius loci that is "substantially Italian." Francesco Clemente insists on nomadism and on the encounter between the East and the West. Mimmo Paladino epitomizes a certain primitivism and Byzantine quality in his work, while the "Mediterranean artist," Enzo Cucchi, transforms Gothic verticality into horizontality (*TA*, 56–67). Trading in reductive simplifications and generalities, Bonito Oliva's approach to his subjects may be said to reflect a tendency that he himself ascribes in a complimentary tone to Chia's art, namely that it exemplifies "the inevitable consumerism of the current sensibility" (*TA*, 69).

He proclaims his disposition at various points to be that of a "Don Juan of knowledge" and a "cynic" who self-consciously cultivates a Mannerist *sprezzatura* or nonchalance. In keeping with such a temperament, Bonito Oliva applauds what Leopardi would have recognized as the paradigmatic Italian weakness for ostentation and empty spectacles; in the process he establishes the normative definition of postmodern art in Italy (*TA*, 9). In several treatises written at the end of the 1970s and the beginning of the 1980s, he pronounces the experimentalism of the historical avant-garde to be exhausted. His writings repeatedly articulate his lack of faith in "linguistic Darwinism" or the progressive evolution of artistic languages. Moreover, they presume a historical context in which the utopian promises of ideologically engaged works are no longer tenable. The derivative name *Transavantgarde* itself is meant to recall "deviously" the original's connotations of "resistance" and "political commitment," which the critic declares utterly inadequate to the "present historical context."[4]

Bonito Oliva treats the art historical situation of the 1970s and 1980s largely as a reaction against the Italian cultural condition of the 1950s, which he perceives to be dominated by a debate between committed and pure art: "Commitment had to be entirely reclaimed from the wastes of Neorealism and Communist Party bureaucrats and the autonomy of art from adherents to neoavantgarde movements" (*TI*, 46). At times, he assumes a more global view, identifying the sources of diminished optimism in the culture at large with the "catastrophic" conditions of the energy crisis of the 1970s, the Yom Kippur War, and a destabilizing of ideological models that he sees "culminating in 1977." We may surmise that this last, vague allusion to a period of political chaos during the second half of the decade refers to events such as the Solidarity movement in Poland and the season of upheaval within the Italian political Left precipitated by *Autonomia Operaia* and the Red Brigades.[5] For a critic who repeatedly boasts of breaking from received ideological pieties, Bonito Oliva displays a curious tenacity in clinging to the old Marxist idea of structure as the determining factor in the destiny of superstructure. For example, he suggests that it is on account of the energy crisis that the art world no longer finds the creative energy to sustain the original avant-garde. Furthermore, the real moment of victory for Transavanguardia in his eyes arrives in the early 1980s—as it does for American Expressionist painting in the productions of Julian Schnabel and David Salle—when the ideology of Ronald Reagan's "morning in America" comes to stand for the embrace of free-market capitalism and an accelerating redistribution of wealth in favor of the ultrarich. In this regard, then, Bonito Oliva represents the most symptomatic case of capitulation among the exemplary figures of Italian culture whom I cover in these pages, and a revealing choice of subject for the last chapter of this study.

Fredric Jameson feels that Bonito Oliva's is one of the most compelling theories of contemporary art: "What happened in the art world vindicates Bonito Oliva's diagnosis of the end of modernism as the end of the modernist developmental or historical paradigm."[6] On the other hand, Jean-François Lyotard discerns in Bonito Oliva's project a perverse attempt to eradicate the modernist heroic impulse from art: "From every direction we are urged to put an end to experimentation, in the arts and elsewhere. . . . I have read an art critic who packages and sells 'Transavantgardism' in the marketplace of painting."[7] In the preceding chapters, we have seen how interlocking artistic and philosophical disciplines in Italy from the late 1970s throughout the 1980s came to form a system that, to borrow Horkheimer's and Adorno's observation about the culture industry in general, is symptomatic of a condition of mass commerce in which "each branch of culture is unanimous within itself and all are unanimous together."[8] The hegemony of the four crucial aesthetic signifiers of sweetness, lightness, weakness, and softness in contemporary Italy reinforces an idea of culture detached from any responsibility for political or critical meaning. Vattimo's theory of weak thought and interpretation of the legacies of Nietzsche and Heidegger in a strictly apolitical vein furnish the ideological engine for the Italian culture industry, which propagates conventionality and sameness across different fields in a manner that suggests the workings of an anti-Frankfurt school of thought.

In *The Dream of Art: Between Avant Garde and Transavantgarde* (1981), Bonito Oliva proposes the concept of "the postcritical."[9] He presents the term as an idea necessitated by the natural end of belief in art's capacity to improve society and the disappearance of any strong historical project. According to his argument, the only feasible project left to today's critic, since the role of a moralist is no longer an option, is that of "accepting the lightness of his task" (*SA*, 17). Such a cultural arbiter, not alarmed by the loss of his traditional function, must learn to profit from his own "weakness" (*SA*, 20). Bonito Oliva embellishes this image of the critic finding opportunity in weakness with the iconographic trappings of martyrdom, observing that the critic's proper function no longer consists in mediating artistic judgment but rather in merely waiting to receive a strike or a blow, like Saint Sebastian (*SA*, 21). Properly speaking, the Transavanguardist critic should aim at a state of being "benumbed" (stordita, and not "bewildered" as the word has been rendered in the English translation of Bonito Oliva's book) in order to align himself with the experience of a dream or chance encounter (pensiero stordito) rather than of a dialectical, logocentric process of reasoning (*SA*, 27).[10]

"Weakness," in Bonito Oliva's sense of the word, seems to imply a Heideggerian-Deleuzian position according to which art criticism eventually becomes capable of renouncing the mirage of logical totality in favor of the "broken paths" and drifts of a newer, different way of thinking. Above all, the typical stance of this new mode of criticism is one of "tolerance," to name a concept that took on particular significance in Italian culture of the 1970s and 1980s. Vattimo celebrated tolerance as a welcome indication of metaphysical weakness, whereas Pasolini criticized the concept as an epiphenomenon of consumerism that served only to mask the oppressiveness of mass society.[11] Writing somewhat later, Bonito Oliva does not hesitate to claim Pasolini for his own cause in the guise of the patron saint of mannerism:

> But when we speak of conscience for Pasolini, we do not have to think of pure ideology or political dogma. He has always used art to represent the impossibility for life to be bent by a model. . . . Pasolini's mannerism is born exactly from these cultural roots, from the need to acquire an identity through art, from the desire for an anthropological definition that might reconcile the difficulty to exist with the gracefulness of appearance [*SA*, 121].

However, we well might ask how credible is any attempt to locate Pasolini within the genealogy of a kind of art that, as practiced by its most famous representative, Francesco Clemente, avoids all conflicts with the world in order to achieve a calm demeanor and pseudo-oriental discipline (*SA*, 247), to arrive at a "nomadism of its lightness" that corresponds to the "desire not to encounter its enemy" (*SA*, 241).

Bonito Oliva tellingly ascribes to Italian culture the specific merit of having been able to maintain at all times a detached and ironic view when confronting big issues: "This healthy kind of opportunism is only possible in cultural contexts where a tradition of this kind exists. This attitude has developed in Italy over the past few years, because Italy has always resolved its own social and natural catastrophes by taking a distance from them."[12] As we already have noted, he admires the work of Sandro Chia on the basis of the painter's ability to manifest a "substantially Italian" genius loci (*SA*, 232). In this light, Bonito Oliva may be said to be an exemplary case for Benjamin Buchloh's observation that Neo-Expressionism coincides with the return of a preoccupation with national identity. In Italy's case, far from revolving around the historical catastrophes of World War Two (as is the case with Anselm Kiefer and Gerhard Richter in Germany), this preoccupation seems to manifest itself in an enjoyment of cultural stereotypes that, I have been arguing, can be declined through the lightness, softness, sweetness, and weakness of a fundamentally nihilist collective identification.

For example, Bonito Oliva writes approvingly in *The Ideology of the Traitor* (1976) of the artist who "more than facing history, crosses the territories of art history with the attitude of a thief and with the 'sweet project' of a work that accepts staying within its frame."[13] If we follow Jameson in regarding Bonito Oliva as the paradigmatic postmodernist, it should come as no surprise that, in a recognizably postmodern fashion, he defines this sense of a framing cultural context more in terms of geography and space than of time and history. As he observes in *Achilles' Heel* (1988), the contemporary Italian artist has a Mediterranean sensibility and finds his point of reference in a benign conception of nature (*TA*, 55). With this sweeping generalization, Bonito Oliva makes clear that the character of Transavanguardia as he presents it derives in no small measure from its provincialism. Indeed, most of the artists that he names as part of the movement come like himself from the area of Naples, a locality that he conjures up via cliché references to the soccer star Diego Maradona and the comedian Totò, invocations of a type that become nearly reflexive during the 1980s: "France had Marat, whilst Italy has had Totò and the *commedia dell'arte*" ("Ital-

Tran," 42). It is not by chance, then, that he regards the perpetual insistence of Clemente's work on "stereotypes" as a praiseworthy quality (*SA*, 241). The only historical conflict to which Bonito Oliva devotes any attention is that between North and South, which in his treatment subsumes the opposition between wealth and poverty and displaces other struggles such as those between art and life, capitalism and communism, creativity and ideology, or nature and history.[14] This erasure of all differences in order to promote the importance of a tension between geographical regions has the effect of limiting discussion of contemporary Italian culture to a depoliticized, critically neutered anthropological sphere and represents one of Bonito Oliva's distinguishing ideological moves.

As we observed in the previous chapter, Gianni Vattimo defines *nihilism* in its current philosophical context as the transformation of use value into exchange value, a process he regards in a favorable light. By contrast, such a conversion marks for Adorno and Horkheimer the point at which art obediently accepts its status as a commodity.[15] Whereas they hold that the task of the intellectual is to resist this dynamic, Vattimo proposes instead that a more appropriate way of thinking is to accept nihilism by welcoming the generalization of exchange value as a symptom of a postmetaphysical age.[16] In one of the more concrete remarks that he offers during his Nietzschean ruminations, he credits a supposed reduction of violence in the historical conditions of life at large with the effect of having made superfluous any striving for the reassurance of "use value," which he associates with a "pathetic," moralizing perspective of the type that we may find in, say, Marxism.[17] One may object that Vattimo never specifies exactly in which cultural context or historical epoch life has become notably less violent, nor does he make clear where we might locate the limits or contradictions of this process of pacification. In keeping with the premise of the demise of metaphysics, he unquestioningly maintains a Nietzschean emphasis on the death of God. Yet such denial of faith seems unnecessary after the catastrophes of colonialism and the Holocaust, thus coming off as a disingenuous rhetorical gambit. What is most interesting for our immediate purposes, however, is Vattimo's ontological celebration of exchange value, which he equates with nihilism, and its consequences for meaningful discussion of the relationship between politics and aesthetics. If exchange value is all we have left, then what kind of art can best make us aware of this condition? Following Heidegger's lead in a somewhat unexpected direction, Vattimo turns not to poetry for an answer to the question but rather to decorative, ornamental art on the basis of a late, less celebrated essay by the German philosopher titled "Art and Space" (1969).[18]

If poetry is supposed to be the setting-into-work of truth, as Heidegger contends in "The Origin of the Work of Art," it cannot be a useful means of expression for the new aesthetic ideology of exchange value. The mass media and decorative art, which according to Gombrich can be only the object of "lateral" or indirect attention, are better candidates instead.[19] Claiming that the truthfulness of art happens through an event or Ereignis, which he renders in Italian as *eventualmente* or "by chance" in order to stress the accidental character of the act of opening oneself to the work of art, Vattimo sides with Yves Michaud in refuting Gombrich with the claim that contemporary art has inverted the center and periphery of its composition. What this means for Vattimo is a "weakness" of subject matter that manifests itself as a decorative attitude in contemporary art and ideally suits his reading of the state of metaphysics.[20]

In the same years during which Vattimo elucidated his theory, Bonito Oliva was defining Transavanguardia as an aesthetic system. Over the course of a series of manifestos promoting his theory, he strategically redeploys the familiar, anodyne categories of lightness, sweetness, softness, and in a slightly more complicated sense weakness, which in his handling becomes the condition of *stordita* or "being benumbed." From a holistic view of his efforts, it becomes clear that he makes purely ideological use of these signifiers, which in his work come to stand *sic et simpliciter* for an apologia of capitalism and its master figure of exchange value, thus enforcing the consumerist idealization of evanescence. He assigns a recent essay the provocative title "Bel Canto Ahead, Torture Behind," for example, in order to frame his readers' view of contemporary Italian art in terms of the antagonism between a cliché idea of pleasure attached to the productions of Transavanguardia and the laborious pathos that he ascribes to Arte Povera.[21] The dichotomy between *bel canto* and torture gives the appearance of pointedness to Bonito Oliva's incessant recurrence in the essay to the master signifier of sweetness. As he presents it, the Transavanguardist aesthetic regards the artist by definition as an achieved nihilist, presupposing an approach that is "sweet" in terms both of eclecticism of style and subject matter and also of the "de-materialization" of the concept of the artwork and the "vaporization" of its meaning.[22] This vaporization, like the debunking of all ideologies and dogmas, is emblematic for Bonito Oliva of the "lightness" of the Transavantgarde: "The artist of the new generation walks completely wrapped up in his own lightness" ("ItalTran," 28). Lightness in this sense is linked to Nietzsche's image of Zarathustra as a tightrope walker ("Man is a rope stretched between the animal and the Overman—a rope over an abyss"), as Bonito Oliva slyly acknowledges with the Nietzschean exhortation, "Every now and then, we must take repose from our own weight" ("ItalTran," 30).

Whereas we may find some philosophical value in Vattimo's call for acceptance of a postmetaphysical age, Bonito Oliva's skepticism toward foundational principles is voiced in an unabashedly capitalist language, as for example when he praises contemporary art for its "opulence." Like Vattimo, Bonito Oliva advocates a nihilism that presumes the primacy of exchange value over use value and, like Calvino, champions experiences that are the "light" or "benumbed" (stordite) productions of a "soft" subject. We remarked earlier how crucial the idea of performative criticism is for the patron of Transavanguardia. His project may be better understood, Hans Belting suggests, in specific relation to Umberto Eco's notion of an "open work," which is to say a work whose meaning is left open by its author to elicit completion through the range of readings propounded by its interpreters. Belting moreover observes that Bonito Oliva aims to produce texts about art that are "transmuted" into "an art of texts" through an elaborate process of self-dramatization: "On the cover of . . . *The Dream of Art: Between Avant Garde and Transavantgarde*, he smiles at his portrait by Sandro Chia as if staging himself not merely as the author but also as the hero of the book."[23] Although some readers may admire the entrepreneurial and performative impulses behind his criticism, the egotistical self-regard of Bonito Oliva's writing echoes the belle lettrist tone of academic French art criticism, which became notorious for a complacent mannerism that the proponents of American Modernism, in particular Clement Greenberg, rejected around the middle of the twentieth century.

As a stylistic movement dialectically opposed to the poetics of Arte Povera of the 1960s, Transavanguardia exemplifies unwavering indifference to ethical and political questions in favor of the pleasures of a hedonist imagination. If a scholar such as Heinrich Wölfflin could discuss the baroque period in art history only in opposition to the classical, Bonito Oliva's definition of Transavanguardia in polemical, "grandly" hostile tones of condescension toward Arte Povera perhaps becomes easier to explain.[24] Yet for all of his rhetorical exertions, Transavanguardia, unlike Arte Povera, seems over the intervening years generally to have disappeared from critical accounts of contemporary art. It is telling that, in a major recent study such as *Art Since 1900: Modernism, Antimodernism, Postmodernism* by Hal Foster, Rosalind Krauss, Yves-Alain Bois, and Benjamin Buchloh, Transavanguardia does not even rate consideration as a phenomenon of its own but rather is absorbed into the category of "neoconservative postmodernism."[25] In marked contrast to the strain of postmodernism derived from poststructuralist lines of inquiry, which marries a thoroughgoing critique of representation with persistent questioning of the authority of the tradition, neoconservative postmodernism as represented by Francesco Clemente, Anselm Kiefer, David Salle, and Julian Schnabel offers a pastiche of art historical references that, in the opinion of the study's authors, are organized largely in an attempt to achieve reconciliation between the public and the marketplace: "Far from democratic (as was sometimes proclaimed), this reconciliation tended to be both elitist in its historical allusions and manipulative in its consumerist clichés. . . . In this regard, neoconservative postmodernism was less postmodernism than anti-modernism."[26]

Prior to this incisive diagnosis of the antimodernist agenda of some recent painting in Italy, Germany, and the United States, Buchloh mounted a devastating critique in 1981 of the Neo-Expressionist movement in contemporary Italian and German art. In "Figures of Authority, Ciphers of Regression: Notes on the Return of Representation in European Painting," he offers an exceptionally astute reading of the political ramifications of German Neo-Expressionism and Italian Arte Cifra, which was an early label proposed by the critic Wolfgang Max Faust for Transavanguardist painting. Buchloh's analysis recalls Lukács's critique of Expressionism as a style whose abstraction from historical and material reality achieves a perverse correlative in its emptily declamatory manner, a rhetoric that ultimately lends itself to totalitarian aesthetics. The essay is particularly keen in exposing the bromides that professional commentators typically have used to discuss Neo-Expressionism, the "false naïveté" and "bloated trivialities" that undermine any effort to assess critically the authoritarian, irrational standpoint of the paintings.[27] Crucially, Buchloh asserts that on account of its theoretical and methodological inclinations, the reappearance of Expressionism often coincides with the emergence of politically repressive regimes. In the case of

Transavanguardia, the art that makes up the movement has become identical in meaning with its presentation through the lens of Bonito Oliva's acritical philosophy, which aims to de-ideologize the discourse of art criticism itself. Insofar as they enforce the standards of the marketplace through showy replication of clichés and promotion of Italy's nationalist genius loci, Transavanguardist productions thus correspond to the mixture of consumerism, jingoism, and conformism that distinguishes the governing ideology of Berlusconi's administration.

The movement may be regarded in this light as one symptom of a larger trauma of Italian culture that, according to Francesco Bonami, ought to be traced back to denial of serious thought about painting and religion and a certain dogmatism of the political left beginning in the 1970s. These failings, in his opinion, have precluded rigorous reflection on the political and cultural conditions of Italy ever since: "The denial has morphed into a society of glamour and spectacle that has transformed the television networks into the only real context accepted by Italian contemporary society."[28] Italy's transition from an alleged leftist asceticism to a society of deregulated spectacle certainly may be viewed as unfolding within a longer historical horizon and as a complex response to a broader range of contributing factors than Bonami directly addresses. Whether he would grant the Transavantgarde as central a role in this process as I have done is, moreover, unclear. However, it is revealing that when he does speak of the Transavantgarde, acknowledging it as one of only two schools of contemporary Italian art to have gained international prominence (the other being Arte Povera), he has little good to say about it:

At first, the *Transavanguardia* movement seemed like an innovative approach to painting, but that was short-lived. It was eventually devoured by a bulimic art market and destroyed by a self-referential and increasingly marginal art criticism that, rather than promise the idea of Italy as a workshop of international innovation, turned inward to focus on the self-destructive idea of the *genius loci*. . . . I find dubious that the current state of Italian culture ought to be explained only as a mere reaction to the "oppressive ideology of the '70s."[29]

One reason for his skepticism may be implicit awareness that an art that claims to have nothing to do with politics is neither less oppressive nor less ideological than the more openly politicized culture it pretends to overcome.

The limits and self-contradictions of the aspiration to de-ideologize culture are what I hope to bring to light by examining how, in pursuit of this goal, some prominent Italian thinkers have deployed the signifiers of lightness, softness, sweetness, and weakness. I have been proposing that these terms bespeak a point of view that reduces life and art to the free-floating, transposable, and evanescent status of their exchange value as commodities. In this connection, we may find helpful Jacques Rancière's position that, although no exact formula or ratio may be derived from the relationship between art and politics, it is nonetheless necessary to reject the disingenuous, habitual avoidance of the political implications of all aesthetic choices, including even the least ideological.[30] We may agree with Rancière in hoping for works of art that are "suitable" to their circumstances in the sense that they do not advance their argument through the vehicle of a didactic message; rather they elaborate an implicit political commentary through disruption and reconfiguration of perceptual form, what he calls "the distribution of the sensible."[31] The deformed physiognomies painted by Otto Dix, for example, manifest just this process of redistribution when seen within the political context of the 1920s. By contrast, we might well ask whether the artists sponsored by Bonito Oliva produced any works that were "suitable" to the milieu of the 1980s when they were painted. Not surprisingly, Bonito Oliva for his part claims that Transavanguardist art enjoys perfect autonomy and that no connection between art and politics ought to be sought: "Art has come back to being direct expression, leaving behind the business of racking one's brain and feeling guilty for being a permanent and indirect symptom of contact with the world" ("ItalTran," 28). Ultimately, he exalts works that do no more than mirror the epistemology of spectacularized consumerism.

In "The Bewildered Image," published in *Flash Art 96–97* (April 1980), Buchloh regards Bonito Oliva as a proto-fascist at heart whose criticism works by means of an eccentric pastiche of Deleuze and Guattari, Max Stirner, and Oswald Spengler.[32] In particular, Bonito Oliva appropriates the theoretical vocabulary of Deleuze and Guattari's *Anti-Oedipus* and *A Thousand Plateaus* without acknowledgment. However, he methodically repositions their concepts of intensity, drift, nomadism, minoritarianism, and even antidialecticism in a framework that sanitizes the terms of their original political valence.[33] Yet this reframing may be seen less as an exemplary act of dwelling in a magically de-ideologized domain, which is how he intimates it ought to be understood, than as surreptitious capitulation to the logic of commerce, as an unneeded apology for the marketplace. His archetypal rhetorical posture manifests itself with publication in 1979 of his first Transavanguardist manifesto, "The Italian Transavantgarde," which bears the epigraph "Art is finally returning to its internal motifs" ("ItalTran," 17). He maintains in this treatise that the internal motifs of art must be situated in a space, "the labyrinth," where the "imaginary" is allowed to "drift." Only then does art complete its return to self-reference, when the work, as he puts it in a crucial sentence, "becomes a nomad's map" ("ItalTran," 17). To compose an image of art's ideal function, he thus mobilizes the concepts of the nomad and the map, employing tropes that in contemporary discussions of philosophical questions are linked indelibly to Deleuze and Guattari's thinking. At the same time, although Bonito Oliva's evocation of the site of the labyrinth at first glance might bring to mind Calvino's association of the creative method with a "challenge to the labyrinth," the art critic instead privileges the labyrinth as a locale in which "the seeing-blind" may lose themselves, "wagging their tails around the pleasure of an art that does not stop for anything, not even history" ("ItalTran," 17).

The essay suggests a reading of Italian art history from the 1960s to the end of the 1980s that derives largely from Kleinian psychoanalytic theory. Bonito Oliva equates Arte Povera with the depressive phase on account of its allegedly "repressive and masochistic line," while aligning Transavanguardia with the schizo-paranoid manic phase owing to its "opulence" and the way it encourages the "growth and development of the capacity to become a landowner [possidente]" ("ItalTran," 17). If we take seriously the terms of his account, however, we ought to recognize that the developmental narrative he constructs is regressive, since Kleinian psychoanalysis holds that the subject overcomes the psychological fragmentation of early age on achieving the maturity of the depressive phase. Yet another potential interpretation of this narrative might be that it follows the overall course of a pathological mourning insofar as Bonito Oliva asserts that the loss of pleasure and plasticity ensuing from the rigidly ideological years of the 1960s, which he evokes with the image of a "concentration camp," led to a radiant period during the 1970s and 1980s that was dedicated to the "applied activity of desire" and achievement above all of "intensity": "Because without intensity there is no art. Intensity is the work's ability to offer itself, or what Lacan calls the 'look-tamer,' its capacity to fascinate and capture the spectator inside the intense field of work, inside the circular and self-sufficient space of art functioning according to internal laws regulated by the demi-urgic grace of the artist, by an internal metaphysics that excludes any outside motivation" ("ItalTran," 18).

The author's emphasis on the nomadism of Transavanguardia, which he juxtaposes to the poetics of the genius loci, superficially gives an impression of Deleuzo-Guattarian vitalism that he perhaps means to reinforce with the celebration of "mental and sensorial pleasure" at the end of the essay ("ItalTran," 20). Yet a harder look at his methods of argument in "The Italian Transavantgarde" reveals that he persistently retreats from this vitalist stance to the use of financial metaphors to explain the new art: "The work becomes a microcosm that grants and establishes the opulent capacity of art to repossess, to be a landowner" ("ItalTran," 18). Indeed, throughout his writings on Transavanguardia, Bonito Oliva relies on the terminology of opulence or the opulent to formulate his aesthetic principles, deploying this vocabulary in opposition to the notion of poverty on which Arte Povera is premised. We should notice in this instance the rhetorical sprezzatura with which, using another favorite word, he personifies art as "a landowner." On the evidence of such flourishes, we may wonder whether his preferred idiom is in fact as de-ideologized or politically neutral as he claims it is. Ostensibly, he applies this language to describing contemporary art, especially in the United States, to capture its aesthetic vitality and pluralism of style (*TI*, 34). However, we may remark that opulence, the spectacular surplus value of wealth, after all connotes power as much as it does affluence (see the OED's sense of "abundance of resources or power").

Bonito Oliva underscores this dominating aspect of opulence through the figure of the *possidente*, the landowner who acts perpetually to acquire property and increase its value, thus augmenting the base of capitalism as a system. The idea of an art modeled entirely on commerce seems fitting for a political culture that finds its credo in Berlusconi's glorification of opulence as a material and social ideal. Not surprisingly, then, in his admiration for contemporary art Bonito Oliva betrays not a hint of embarrassment about its condition as commodified excess: "The work becomes an opulent show which no longer tends toward economy but toward waste" (*TI*, 20). Indeed, this characterization of the artwork as "an opulent show" stands in stark contrast to a crucial rendering of Arte Povera that leaves no doubt about the critic's enjoyment of what he considers the historical triumph of capitalism in the present: "This declaration of poverty occurs in relation to the context of western society [which is] geared toward opulence and consumerism" (*TI*, 38). Such positive approval of the destiny of "western society" casts into doubt the sincerity of his contention elsewhere in the essay that the "mutations of art" depend on "the success of a different economy of life formed not through accumulation and saving but through squandering the imaginary" ("ItalTran," 36–37). It is more than a little telling that in "The Italian Transavantgarde" he manages to praise the autonomy of the imagination only by advocating a "squandering" of creativity that will establish a new "economy of life." In so doing, Bonita Oliva reinscribes the realities of capital exchange in the very act of resistance to those conditions that he supposes contemporary art to perform.

Between Lyotard and Jameson

Whether art retains its potential for political resistance in an age of mass media is a question that art critics and historians continue to confront. For David Hopkins, continuation by other means of the avant-garde project beyond its presumed dissipation in 1945 is what gives purpose to his ambitious book *After Modern Art 1945–2000*.[34] He pursues this aim through exploration of developments such as the recuperation of Marcel Duchamp's legacy by the constellation of artists revolving around Robert Rauschenberg and Jasper Johns, which he calls "the Rauschenberg-Johns Axis," and the German artist Joseph Beuys's reinterpretation of the idea of the heroic artist specific to the avant-garde. The author sets these investigations in the context of a comprehensive assessment of the major developments in art since 1945 that includes appraisals of the critical procedures of Fluxus, Minimalism, and Arte Povera.

Regarding the last group, which came into being with an exhibition organized in Genoa by Germano Celant in 1967, Hopkins observes that its practitioners assumed a neo-Romantic attitude similar to Beuys's stance, while responding with "particular poignancy" to "a set of specifically Italian circumstances" including the student riots, labor demonstrations, and terrorist bombings that took place from the late 1960s through the early 1970s.[35] His task of expanding the genealogy of the avant-garde beyond the end of its conventional period in art history seems plausible until he reaches the moment of postmodernism in the middle 1970s. Hopkins is forced to admit, on considering the work of postmodern artists, that at that time "one of art's key changes was the loss of any overall sense of an *avant garde* project."[36]

In search of a more critical notion of postmodernism, he abandons the early, neoclassical, and to some degree neoconservative definition provided by Charles Jencks in *The Languages of Postmodern Architecture* (1977), favoring instead the theoretical positions respectively taken by Jean-François Lyotard, Fredric Jameson, and perhaps most pointedly the art critics of *October*, namely Rosalind Krauss, Annette Michelson, and Hal Foster. Krauss, Michelson, and Foster propose a "postmodern of resistance," to cite Foster's explicit formulation, that rejects the reactionary politics of more complacent postmodernisms and clearly takes its inspiration from the undertaking of the Russian avant-garde in its heyday following the Communist Revolution. Eschewing modernist notions of originality and authenticity, they commend the procedures of conceptual art in general and of conceptual photography as represented by Sherrie Levine, Robert Longo, Barbara Kruger, and Jenny Holzer in particular, works that for the critics represent the contemporary equivalent of Duchamp's readymade, as Hopkins observes.[37] Whereas he finds the critics' attitude to be tinged with intellectual snobbery, we may remark that at least they have the merit of reaffirming the necessity of art that defies its complete absorption by mass culture. Conversely, we may discern in the productions of Transavanguardia the most immediate examples of an appeasing, formally purist postmodernism, a stance that Bonito Oliva took up, according to Hopkins, precisely in order to avoid the "difficulty" and "singularity of purpose" of the avant-garde.[38]

In *Postmodernism or, The Cultural Logic of Late Capitalism* (1991), Fredric Jameson names Bonito Oliva's "The Italian Transavantgarde" as an iconic critical reading of postmodern art, admiring in particular the author's rejection of the developmental narrative that typifies more conventional views of art history.[39] In his introduction to the book, Jameson declares his preference for Bonito Oliva's account over Lyotard's exposition of postmodernity. Bonito Oliva's stress on the vanishing of the modernist aesthetic paradigm strikes Jameson as more "interesting" and "plausible" than the French philosopher's more grandiose claim that the metanarratives constituting the foundations of knowledge have come to a historical end.[40] Although Lyotard has been criticized and to an extent discredited for this suggestion, he does grant to art the utopian critical purpose of presenting what is unpresentable, hence of being able to bear witness to the *differends* or political and epistemological conflicts that erupt under the postmodern condition. Jameson, on the other hand, is forced to concede that, notwithstanding Bonito Oliva's "very interesting and pertinent characterizations," the Italian art critic in his "mildness" and "neo-mannerist sensibility" epitomizes the classic postmodernist tendencies toward "de-ideologization" and antiutopianism.[41]

On this score, Jameson renders an acute judgment on the basic political inclination of postmodern art without acknowledging its implications for his endorsement of Bonito Oliva: "What is initially certain, at any rate, is that the spokespeople for postmodern painting . . . agree on the renunciation, by contemporary neo-figurative painters of painting's older (modernist) Utopian vocations."[42] Bonito Oliva's "mildness" of tone may capture the "relief of the postmodern," which is to say the relief of an art that does not "hector you for ideological purposes," to use Jameson's phrase, but it is also symptomatic of an aesthetic that encourages "dissolution into a multidimensional digression."[43] Indeed, we might take these comments as representative of Jameson's singular contribution to the definition of postmodernism, which is to have registered the convergence of aesthetic and commodity production during late capitalism. At the same time, we should not forget that he pleads for recognition of "a party of utopia" among artists and writers, a party in which he enlists postmodern photography insofar as the medium elaborates an independent vision with no external referent.[44] Yet such a plea leaves no space for an art that still aspires in some way to redeem or rectify reality and thus sustain what Bonito Oliva regards as an "old superstition" from which Lyotard is not immune (*TI*, 44).

Whereas Jameson recognizes Bonito Oliva as an effective ideologue of the postmodern, Lyotard identifies his efforts with the most regressively conformist impulses of postmodernism: "This is a period of slackening—I refer to the color of the times. . . . For all those writers [who call for suspension of artistic experimentation] nothing is more urgent than to liquidate the heritage of the *avant gardes*. Such is the case, in particular, of the so called transavantgardism."[45] According to Lyotard, Transavanguardia's "cynical eclecticism" directly reflects "the power" of capitalism "to derealize familiar objects, social roles, and institutions" by reducing art to a merely stylistic "mixing process" that avoids commitment to any specific critical viewpoint.[46] Bonito Oliva delivers his most thorough response to Lyotard in the article "A proposito di Transavanguardia," where he recapitulates the genealogy of reactionary movements against both communist bureaucrats who remain faithful to Neorealism and the experimentalism of the neoavantgarde.[47] All the while, the Italian art historian claims that the situation of "generalized catastrophe" makes it impossible to believe in progress and the future. As he declares elsewhere, it is in his eyes hypocritical for Lyotard on the one hand to posit the historical crisis of the metanarratives of knowledge and on the other to maintain the possibility of a metanarrative of sublime experimentalism in the domain of art.[48] What is most pressing for Bonito Oliva is to make clear the inadequacy of the metaphor of the avant-garde under the present historical circumstances, which he feels do not allow any sort of critical or political resistance (*Alfa*, 56). He nominates his own ideological construct of the mannerist "traitor" as the only figure of the artist that is compatible with the new, nihilist sensibility of the times: "Thus Nihilism is the only right position for the artist's point of departure, but an active nihilism, which recuperates Nietzsche without despair" (*Alfa*, 56).

Lyotard and Bonito Oliva indeed diverge apropos of the importance of nihilism for contemporary thought. Whereas the Italian critic enthusiastically affirms Vattimo's celebration of the doctrine, the French philosopher finds in the Kantian sublime a remedy to identification of historical perspectivism with a nihilism that precludes any possibility of engagement.[49] Lyotard, it is true, is acutely aware that the feelings of derealization ensuing from the incursion of technology on daily life and the crisis of historical metanarratives may be said to bear a passing resemblance to some strains of the nihilist inheritance. However, he is able to distinguish "the aesthetic of the sublime," which he regards as an "earlier modulation of Nietzschean perspectivism," from appropriation of nihilism by mouthpieces for the culture industry. Sublime feeling, as he defines it, acknowledges the failure of the imagination and thus recuperates the logic of the avant-garde in ultimately "witnessing the unpresentable."[50] This shocking capacity of the sublime to present the unpresentable "signifies an outrage to piety, a sacrilege" that, according to Lyotard, "involves an an-economy, which would be of the order of holiness."[51] In the Kantian sublime, the subject confronts the abyss between the imagination's freedom and the law of practical reason, thus entering into "a 'mediation' authorizing exalted pleasure to discover the true (ethical) destination of thought."[52] Such mediation is precisely antithetical to Bonito Oliva's emphasis on the "cordiality" between art and the consuming public, high and low culture, which

Transavanguardist nihilism achieves through a "sweet well-tempered form against the background of a tempestuous history" (*Alfa*, 56).

As Lyotard has noted, it is the dubious mark of a certain postmodernism to aim at nothing more than unmediated reflection of the market: "Artists, gallery owners, critics, and public wallow together in the 'anything goes,' and the epoch is one of slackening. But this realism of the 'anything goes' is in fact that of money."[53] Pursuing a related point, David Hopkins discusses the return to figurative style in painting as a predictable response to an "art market attuned to Reaganism."[54] Indeed, he traces the canonization of painters such as Schnabel in the United States and Chia in Italy back to the influence of Charles Saatchi, one of the two founders with his brother Maurice of the trendsetting advertising agency Saatchi and Saatchi, which in England played an influential role in the electoral success of the Margaret Thatcher-led Conservative Party during the 1980s. Charles Saatchi made and unmade the careers of certain painters by buying their productions in bulk and, in Schnabel's case, by orchestrating a major exhibition of his works at the Tate Gallery in 1982, while arranging for others such as Chia to be "strategically dropped" when it suited him.[55] If in fact the reputations of many artists belonging to what Hal Foster calls the "postmodernism of reaction" rose and fell at a meteoric rate, this was because interest in their works was often fueled by the speculative investments of buyers who were looking for short-term gains.[56] Hans Haacke's slyly titled painting "Taking Stock" (1983) skewers the sycophancy of the art community that invites precisely such violent changes of fortune. The satirical composition portrays Thatcher in a Victorian domestic scene that includes a bookcase filled with company reports and two cracked plates bearing the likenesses of the Saatchi brothers, thus reminding the viewer of their patronage of Schnabel through allusion to his "broken plate" paintings. Haacke's broadside perfectly captures the complicity between the new hegemonic style in art and the political and financial forces of the time.

In retrospect, Transavanguardia did not merely contribute to reification of certain conservative tendencies in Italian art and politics. It also clearly anticipated, almost in the manner of a teaser advertisement or movie trailer, what Guy Debord would have called the "integrated spectacle" of the Berlusconi administration's domination of media, finance, and politics, which emerged full-blown with Berlusconi's election to the office of prime minister in 1994. The kinship is striking in a number of particulars, from the shared proclivities for triumphal consumerism, ostentation and rhetorical exaggeration, and macho posturing down to the similarly folkloric nationalism of the genius loci and Forza Italia. It is far more apt, in other words, to look at the dynamic mutation of Italian culture in the 1980s as a foreshadowing of Berlusconi's success in binding together under his control the apparatuses of cultural, economic, and governmental power than as a compensatory response to the outmoded bureaucratic supremacy of the Left, which is how Bonito Oliva represents the period.[57] On this view, we may side with Buchloh, who warns that Neo-Expressionist reclamations of tradition tend to coincide with the ascendancy of regressive and nationalist politics, as demonstrated by the *rappel à l'ordre* that resulted in abandoning the avant-garde following World War I.

Bonito Oliva's constant invocation of the genius loci in his writings obviously aims at rehabilitating the categories of the local and the parochial as a corrective to the emphatic internationalism of the avant-garde. He avows that, although we may be able to speak of a Transavantgarde of the United States or of Germany, the movement produces its own identity in every nation. When pressed for examples, however, what he offers often amounts to little more than the most banal clichés:

The different arts are more or less national and are linked to the natural aspect of a people. Italians, for example, by nature possess song and melody, whereas for the Northern peoples music and opera, even if they have been carefully nurtured with great success, have never become 'natural' [autoctone] to them, just as orange trees are not natural to those lands. . . . In this way, art and its specific production are linked to the determinate nationality of different populaces. Thus improvisers generally can be found in Italy, and they are gifted with admirable talent [*TI*, 80].

By contrast, one of the more distinctive traits of Arte Povera was its challenge to the dominant national tradition in matters of aesthetics.[58] Bonito Oliva's ideology of the traitor reinscribes the figure of the contemporary artist in the Mannerist tradition and thereby reaches back to an old aesthetic and nationalist genealogy.

In this gesture we may discern one instance of a larger impulse within Italian culture, a propensity that Germano Celant has investigated with respect to art criticism between 1959 and 1981 in an essay significantly titled "For an Italian Identity," which introduces the book *Arte dall'Italia*. Anticipating the allegorical contrast that Carla Benedetti draws between the artistic examples of Calvino and Pasolini, Celant remarks that critical discourse in Italy has been divided between acceptance of the general epistemological bias of the artistic process toward fantasy (e.g., Calvino, Francesco Lo Savio) and an opposing way of thinking that aims to maintain an unremitting critical distance from the consolations of the culture industry (e.g., Pasolini, Piero Manzoni).[59] Against the historical background of de-Stalinization and postexistentialism, Italy has deteriorated into a materialist cult, according to Celant, whose preoccupation with design and décor reflects its subservience to the entrenched logic of commodification.

Celant is particularly engrossed with the way some of the Transavanguardist artists such as Chia, working under Bonito Oliva's sanction, have revived the techniques of artists such as Sironi and Carrà from the 1920s and 1930s: "Today, the audience for a citation of the dark years of European history is constantly increasing and the insouciants [arditi] of art call with a loud voice to discredit engagement and conceptualism in favor of '*pompierismo*' and populist Fauvism."[60] He recognizes in the new trend of figurative painting the symptom of a "national-patriotic" mentality that is more worrisome in Italy where painters such as Mario Sironi, Ottone Rosai, and Filippo De Pisis actively supported the Fascist régime than in Germany where the roster of past artists at least included dissenting voices such as Max Beckmann and Ernst Ludwig Kirchner.[61] Celant refuses to justify the new patriotism and nostalgia for the historical past, instead evoking once again the rejection of moral and political engagement that sustained artistic experimentation in the 1960s. This sense of commitment found its motivating inspiration not in nationalist ambition but rather in a chastening sense of shared international pathos. Consequently, Celant is hard pressed not to compare the art of the 1980s to the bane of "neo-romantic" ideology that plagued Italy and Germany after the 1920s.[62]

The Critic and the Marketplace

Both Perry Anderson and Jameson observe that although modernism was apt to show a hostile face to the market, postmodernism is likely to embrace the market.[63] In his early study of Mannerism, *The Ideology of the Traitor* (1976), Bonito Oliva attributes the dissociation and alienation of the Mannerist artist to the "internationalization of finance" (*IdeoTrad*, 19). He was one of the first Italian critics to recognize the ascendancy of postmodernism in several essays published in *Domus* in the 1970s, according to Angelo Capasso's hagiography of Bonito Oliva, and also one of the most vocal proponents of the notion of an aesthetic specific to neocapitalism (*ABO*, 17–20). Capasso originally wrote this account of Bonito Oliva's career to provide the catalogue of an exhibition organized to help circulate an idea of the critic not as a sophisticated interpreter of enigmatic works but rather as one of the constitutive subjects of artistic production.

In commemorating the advent of what Bonito Oliva defined in *The Dream of Art* as "la postcritica," Capasso welcomes the eclipsing of criticism's function as a witness to reality by the performativity of a criticism whose purpose is to facilitate transforming art into communication (*ABO*, 11–15). Bonito Oliva's various staged exploits—such as posing in the nude on the cover of the magazine *Frigidaire* accompanied by the witty Duchampian tag "The critic stripped bare by art itself"; appearing in a tutu on RomeArte; his constant appearances on television shows; and the so-called virtual interviews or imaginary encounters he has published with artists of the past—are all procedures that persuade Capasso of our finally having entered the territory of "criticism as behavior" (*ABO*, 12). Although he strains to establish an impressive genealogy for Bonito Oliva's habit of incorporating considerations extrinsic to art in his books, conjuring up Addison, Steele, and Vasari as predecessors whose writings anticipate the effects of performative criticism, it becomes clear that in Capasso's view Bonito Oliva's greatest achievement has been to repudiate any idealism that we still may naïvely attach to the role of the critic. In this regard, two of Bonito Oliva's books appear to be of particular importance to Capasso—*Art and The System of Art* (1975) and *Superart* (1988, *ABO*, 13, 17)—in which the critic redefines the "system" of art in terms of "the symbolic value of money" to erase the traditional discrepancy between art's cultural value and its market value (*ABO*, 17). Another contributor to the same volume, Gioacchino Lanzi Tomasi, takes pains to assure the reader that Bonito Oliva enjoys the present century and can be found spending his time in nightclubs, on volcanic islands or beaches, or participating in debates.[64] This adulation of the critic's worldliness culminates with the final assertion that in Bonito Oliva's example we encounter the centrality of criticism and the marginality of art (*ABO*, 33).

In an essay surveying contemporary art up to the year 2000 that he contributed to the reissue of Giulio Carlo Argan's *L'arte moderna 1770–1970*, Bonito Oliva once again dedicates ample space to the "system of art," which is to say the habitat in which the art "product" is developed.[65] Manically parodying the beginning of Marx and Engels's *Manifesto*, Bonito Oliva claims that a so-called Superart "haunts" Europe and the United States in the form of the "strong" presence of new cultural subjects beyond the artist, whom he also describes as a "soft subject" that is enabled by recognition of the symbolic value of money to disrupt idealistic hierarchies in the art world.[66] Glorifying the art consumer and the social rites of consumerism, he enthusiastically recalls the historical process of de-ideologization, which is the term he uses for the decline of Marxist ideology catalyzed by Mikhail Gorbachev's economic reforms of the 1980s.[67] This section of *L'Arte fino al 2000* clearly demonstrates the critic's bad faith in pretending that the celebration of the marketplace may be taken naïvely as "non-ideological." Bonito Oliva invents for himself an illustrious pedigree as the contemporary theorist par excellence of the equivalence between art and consumer goods, an inheritance that he traces back to Warhol and Baudelaire: "We live in times favorable to rhetoric, to the language of shop windows. Before Warhol, the noble ancestor is Baudelaire, the date of departure is that of the Universal Exposition in Paris: 1855. There the poet realizes the new objectifications of an art that acquires the characteristic of indifference and an equivalence to consumer goods."[68]

Certainly, Bonito Oliva is not alone in seeking to establish a genealogical link between Baudelaire and Warhol. Yet the conclusions he draws from the family resemblance are dubious at best. It is difficult to imagine Baudelaire, for example, equating artworks with commodities without problematizing the relationship through a mock-heroic parody of the commodity that finally leads to its mortification.[69] The French poet indeed may have cultivated an interest in fashion and in much of the contingent cultural ephemera of his day. However, he did so, Foucault points out in "What Is Enlightenment?" precisely in order to expose and release new imaginative potentialities.[70] In fact, Baudelaire's poetry as a whole ought to be understood to propound a decidedly critical view of the marketplace, as Walter Benjamin argues in "On Some Motifs in Baudelaire" and "Paris, Capital of the Nineteenth Century" (see in particular his reading of "Le Vin des Chiffoniers"). It may be said as well that Warhol's art demands to be seen as more than a mere encomium to consumer goods and celebrity culture, at least in the case of his output prior to the 1970s. The artist challenges us to approach the artwork, in Arthur C. Danto's opinion, as a transfiguration of the commonplace and the ordinary that has philosophical value.[71]

Even more than Duchamp's "Fountain" (1917) and subsequent readymades, Warhol's "Brillo Box" (1964) makes clear for Danto that the difference between art and reality can never rest on solely perceptual grounds. After all, a cardboard box of Brillo pads exhibited at the Stable Gallery in New York City may be perceptually identical to one that we encounter in the supermarket; nevertheless, it must be regarded as art.[72] In this context, the encounter with "Brillo Box" throws into question our very concept of what constitutes an aesthetic event as opposed to what constitutes mundane experience. As a consequence, it comes to exemplify Warhol's greatest achievement, which was to have redefined all art, independent of its subject matter, as conceptual art and thus to have brought "artistic practice to philosophical self-consciousness," in Danto's words.[73]

With this background in mind, Bonito Oliva's claim of kinship with Baudelaire and Warhol rings hollow. The task of Transavanguardia is to reactivate the "dream of art," as Bonito Oliva defines it in the title of one of his books, thus inhabiting an unconscious space that shares neither Baudelaire's ironic critical distance from the modern masses nor Warhol's skeptical self-awareness toward quotidian material conditions.[74] Although Warhol seems far from advocating an attitude of dissent, despite whatever particular significance might be ascribed to a specific project such as his sequence of paintings of the electric chair in contrast to, say, his series of Campbell's soup cans, his work nevertheless can be taken as a "suitable" example of the correlation between art and politics in Rancière's sense. Rather than romanticizing market culture, Warhol's method of ostentatiously, serially replicating objects and persons cannot but raise unsettling questions for the viewer. The most egregious misconception perpetuated by Bonito Oliva, however, is that, after Warhol's experimentations, our customary perceptions of the things of the world can remain unchanged.

The Achieved Nihilist

Since publication of his first essay on the Transavantgarde, Bonito Oliva has nominated Nietzsche as his personal critical exemplar, reserving special admiration for the figure of Zarathustra, who "wishes to lose nothing of mankind's past; he wishes to throw everything into the crucible" ("ItalTran," 19). The formulation of the name *Transavanguardia* itself seems suggestive of the mission that Nietzsche defined in his later writings of achieving a "transvaluation of all values" after the demise of the highest values of morality and religion: "The *Transavanguardia* spins like a fan with the torsion of a sensitivity that allows art to move in all directions, including toward the past" ("ItalTran," 19). Notwithstanding the vitalist tone of his rhetoric, which would imply a Deleuzian emphasis on Nietzsche as a thinker of transformative forces and energy, in substance Bonito Oliva affirms Nietzsche as the philosopher of so-called active nihilism whom Vattimo praises for ushering in a Heideggerian end of metaphysics.[75]

Accordingly, Bonito Oliva often quotes from the same narrow repertoire of Nietzschean aphorisms compiled by Vattimo to supply the leitmotif of his reading of the German philosopher. For example, the crucial definition of nihilism cited by Bonito Oliva from *The Will to Power* is the same one offered by Vattimo in his essay "Apology for Nihilism": "Nihilism is, then, the right starting point for the artist; an active nihilism, though, that recuperates Nietzsche without desperation. The pleasure of 'rolling from the center toward X' without grabbing hold of impossible anchorages, but sliding over all the slats of culture through shifts that increase the artwork's power to contaminate."[76] Another shared touchstone that, as we have seen in the previous chapter, furnishes Vattimo with the main focus of his reading of Nietzsche, is the declaration from *Twilight of the Idols* that the world has become a fable. That Bonito Oliva too employs this passage to revisit Nietzsche's thought through the lens of Heideggerian philosophy is especially revealing: "If Nietzsche made the prophecy of a world transformed into a fable, of truth in narratives without foundation, Heidegger confirmed the inevitability of such a destiny."[77] Nominating Nietzsche and Maradona in *Achilles' Heel* as prototypes of the modern-day cultural analyst (in the latter case, on the grounds that the soccer star embodies the interpretive ability to play the entire field), Bonito Oliva asserts that the nomadism of the critic has no affinity for places or sites but rather only for the "broken path" of Heideggerian memory, which means he is doomed to "drift within dead ends" (*TA*, 12–13). By endorsing Vattimo's reading of Nietzsche through Heidegger, Bonito Oliva eschews the Deleuzo-Guattarian notion of the philosopher as a vital catalyst of critical assemblages in favor of a view of such a thinker as the source of an achieved, enjoyed passivity.

If softness and sweetness are crucial words for the Italian art historian, another term that he privileges in his writing in order to define the ideology and practice of Transavanguardia is "cordiality." For example, he pointedly characterizes Francesco Clemente's oeuvre as an artistic "utopia" on account of the painter's "desire not to meet his enemy."[78] Bonito Oliva's attitude seems to be patterned after that of the allegorical man of "good character" and temperament whom Nietzsche depicts as being "free from emphasis" in *Human, All Too Human* (I, 34) and whom Vattimo in turn invokes with admiration at crucial moments in his own writings.[79] For both Vattimo and Bonito Oliva, this bonhomie in fact merely reinforces their allegiance to an idea of art conceived strictly in terms of exchange value and corresponding hostility to what they see as a passé, Adornian definition of culture in terms of use value. According to Vattimo, Adorno's greatest mistake was to have regarded the commercial order of the mass media with suspicion for its supposed ideological enmity toward the work of art rather than to have accepted the collaboration between art and the media (see Boyer). Such acquiescence supposedly would uphold the spirit of the age by acknowledging the end of metaphysics and helping to make manifest "the ontology of decline" that Vattimo identifies as the logical conclusion of Hegel's concept of the death of art viewed from a Heideggerian perspective.[80] Offering his own response to the suggested possibility of art's demise, Bonito Oliva likens it with cheerful resignation to the "impotent" destiny of superstructure (i.e., art) in relation to structure (economy and politics) under the conditions of capitalism ("ItalTran," 6). His willful adoption of a pre-Gramscian critical language that relegates art to the limbo of superstructure in exchange for its supposed autonomy makes his subsequent proclamation of art as a "biological activity" whose language "cannot be reduced to reality" sound desperate and defensive by comparison ("ItalTran," 8).

Bonito Oliva's reading of nihilism has remained consistent since its initial articulation in one of his earliest contributions to art criticism, the theoretical study of Mannerism titled *Ideology of the Traitor* (1976), which preceded his more mature writings on the Transavantgarde.[81] In this book we find *in nuce* many of the same concerns that motivate Bonito Oliva's subsequent critical efforts. Indeed, the critic redefines Mannerism in *Ideology of the Traitor* as a transhistorical category that informs the entirety of Italian art. After the Renaissance, Mannerism seems to represent a transvaluation of all values for Bonito Oliva. Mannerist questioning of linear perspective, in his opinion, signaled a crisis in the discourse of Renaissance aesthetics as a whole, including the "strong subject" and "strong categories" of myth, drama, and tragedy that gave the painting its formal principles. According to this argument, the decline of faith in the customary methods of visualizing natural space and conventional subject matter compelled Mannerist painters to betray these practices through acts of dissimulation and citation. By turning to such techniques, and particularly by relying on citation, Mannerism may be taken as anticipating the defining artistic processes of postmodernism in architecture, literature, and painting.

On this score, it should come as no surprise that in Mannerism, and especially in its invention of the figure of *il dicitore*, Bonito Oliva discerns the origin of the poetics of cynical distance and obliquity, which influence postmodernism's rhetorical tendency to alternate between the moods of impotence and omnipotence.[82] The dicitore was a device that Mannerist painters introduced as a means to laterally or obliquely address the viewer of the painting by depicting the character in the act of pointing with his finger to the painting's crucial action. By mediating between art and life, the dicitore for Bonito Oliva manages to "freeze" any tension that might arise from the painting's challenge to the interpretive assumptions of the viewer (*Ideo Trad*, 27). As a performative critic, the art historian indeed may be said to reserve for himself a role that in the end positions him as a dicitore of contemporary culture who freezes for us any potential space of reflection or critical thought. In his opinion, in other words, "the critic is one who lives reality as a spectacle, placed before a situation of paralyzed frontality" (*Ideo Trad*, 59).

The Mannerist artist, in this view, confronted the proper historical circumstances for inauguration of the "sweet project" that ultimately culminates in the undertaking of Transavanguardia (*Ideo Trad*, 10–13). Significantly, Bonito Oliva links the characteristic Mannerist posture of distance from the world to internationalization of the financial markets (*Ideo Trad*, 19). Even more remarkably, he explains that his master trope of the ideology of the traitor represents the system of an "already betrayed ideology, destitute of its superstructural quality . . . in order to acquire the virginal force of a subversive project" (*Ideo Trad*, 20). As Jameson has noted, the version of postmodernism advocated by Bonito Oliva in fact dogmatically insists on the de-ideologization of the work of art.[83] Notwithstanding his lip service to the "subversive project" of his creative role model, it becomes clear that the "traitor" whom he idealizes is simply a conformist, the epitome of a worldly conviction of the need to enforce the hegemonic codes of fashion, hierarchy, and rules.[84] It is noteworthy that he takes pains throughout these ruminations to dissociate the concept of *moda* from Baudelaire's exuberant love of the new, instead conveying the impression of something closer to Leopardi's nihilist view of fashion as a child of transience, hence as a sibling of death, inspiring an irrational compulsion to conform.[85]

Although acknowledging that intellectuals cannot pretend to escape the prevalent power structure, Bonito Oliva evokes an idea of ethical and political conduct in the figure of the traitor that is complicit with disavowing any basis for knowing with whom to side (*IdeoTrad*, 35, 36). This indifference of the traitor should not be mistaken for the Promethean independence of the Romantic revolutionary, but rather recognized as the sort of detachment that allows one to participate successfully in the machinations of power; follow the rules with stylistic diligence; and, assuming a Machiavellian vocabulary, to placate the prince unless it becomes necessary to assassinate him.[86] The latter possibility, however, is never seriously considered by Bonito Oliva. As he declares elsewhere: "The traitor is somebody who looks at the world, does not accept it, thinks of modifying it but does not act, because if he were to act, he would be a revolutionary."[87] In an astonishing and illuminating moment, he in fact locates his ethical ideal in Shakespeare's Iago, thanks to the character's proud self-description in *Othello* as a "critic" (*IdeoTrad*, 59). Through the art historian's various attempts to capture the mood of his own time, the figure of the traitor emerges in the end as nothing other than a latter-day courtier, a personification of cynicism, albeit in a somewhat pathetic vein, who restricts his actions to the sphere of the court and complacently obeys its codes in order to affirm the life of an empty, automated idea of "style" (*IdeoTrad*, 30, 75). As with fashion, style for Bonito Oliva does not connote an iconoclastic spirit of experimentation; rather, it is a love of decorum and conventionality pushed to an extreme of artifice. In this view, artificiality is not to be feared; it is what confers "lightness" on language (*IdeoTrad*, 76).

We noted earlier that he often borrows terms from Deleuze and Guattari such as intensity, drift, nomadism, and minoritarianism to describe artistic experience.[88] In such cases, Bonito Oliva revises Deleuze and Guattari's philosophical-political concepts into values for the aesthetics of contemporary capitalism. At a superficial first glance, one even might suppose wishfully that the art historian intended the prefix "trans-" in the name "Transavantgarde" to imply the sort of transversal movement of genealogical deconstruction that animates *A Thousand Plateaus*.[89] However, closer examination suggests that Bonito Oliva carefully reterritorializes the subversive political problematic of Deleuze and Guattari's thought. Although described as the "idea propelling the new work," for example, "drifting" in his writing comes to mean merely the freedom of a self-indulgent, subjective wandering of feeling.[90] It should be remembered that for Deleuze and Guattari, as for the Situationists and Debord, terms such as "diversion" (détournement) and "drifting" (dériver) always imply strategic deformation of orthodox or sanctioned forms of organization.[91] A case in point is the "minoritarianism" that Deleuze and Guattari originally ascribed to Kafka's "minor literature," that is, his ability as a Jew to write in German from a stranger's perspective, deterritorializing a "major language" or language of power by performing a critical, disruptive function from inside the language itself.[92] Such a development as presented in *A Thousand Plateaus* is fundamentally political in nature, since all becomings are for Deleuze and Guattari minoritarian. In their view, only minoritarian subjects can produce social changes through a micropolitics that opposes the dominating power of the majority, which conventional history enshrines.[93]

In Bonito Oliva's criticism, we first encounter the notion of a "minor subject" in *The Ideology of the Traitor*, where it signifies the artist's position in the social order after the demise of the strong subject of the Renaissance (*IdeoTrad*, 10). The condition that the English translation of "The Italian Transavantgarde" somewhat awkwardly renders as "minority" finally stands for the artist's mobility and "feminine" distance from the shackles of reality: "Minority is another value recovered by the new mentality of art, moving with almost feline grace, with a feminine and underground sensibility" (*IdeoTrad*, 68, 31). However, it should be said that this feminine awareness is in the author's eyes a proper attribute of the male artist, since, as Buchloh points out, no women have actually been admitted to the men's club of Transavanguardia. No longer suggestive of a real negotiation with power, as it is for Deleuze and Guattari, the term "minority" instead indicates for Bonito Oliva a certain aesthetic sophistication, a quasi-decadent state of sensibility. By the time of the publication of *Transavantgarde International* in 1982, the "minoritarian" has become the artist's own "ego": "In this way, the artist rediscovers a healthy working solitude, a *minority feeling* that drives him to the point of concentrating the social notion of the minority on the creative needs of the individual" (un sentimento minoritario che lo porta ad identificare la minoranza col proprio io; *TI*, 28). The original Italian asserts far more starkly the decisive coincidence of the "minority feeling" with the *proprio io* of the artist's ego. In this light, we witness the transmutation of a concept of political engagement as process into a static and overly familiar idealization of the artist's self-absorbed narcissism.[94]

The persona of the nomad, which is crucial to the poststructuralist politics of Deleuze and Guattari, also becomes utterly apolitical in Bonito Oliva's handling of it. A fundamental characteristic of the French philosophers' "nomadology" is that, as a line of inquiry, it represents the ethical and political opposite of history in the conventional sense: "History is always written from the sedentary point of view and in the name of a unitary State apparatus. . . . What is lacking is a Nomadology, the opposite of a history."[95] Their most extended reflection on nomadology occurs in a chapter significantly titled "Treatise on Nomadology—The War Machine," in which the "war machine" is "irreducible to the State apparatus . . . outside its sovereignty and prior to its law" and appears to embody the principle of transformation per se "because he sees all things in relations of becoming, rather than implementing binary distributions between 'states.'"[96] Deleuze and Guattari's emphasis on nomadology as an alternative way of thinking the political entails a serious effort to go beyond the State model and its rules, in a line of flight of continuous deterritorialization, toward an understanding of the nomad as the "de-territorialized par excellence."[97]

In a space so conceived, the archetype of the traitor, which again resonates with Bonito Oliva's rhetoric while contrasting with his logic, gains in symbolic importance. Unlike the two classic figures of political sovereignty in Indo-European mythology, the magician-king and the jurist-priest, the Deleuzo-Guattarian traitor is fundamentally an agent of deterritorialization whose appearance has accompanied the great revolutions and reformations of Christendom and modern politics. However, Deleuze and Guattari's thinking draws a crucial distinction between despotic deception and passionate betrayal, according to which betrayal has a radical, absolute quality whereas deception belongs "to the man of the court or even of the state."[98] Now when we examine Bonito Oliva's invocations of terms such as drifting and nomadism, we find that the concepts bespeak an innocuous artistic sensibility that has been thoroughly depoliticized, reduced to no more than a "mental reservoir of allegories and metaphors."[99]

His nomadism of lightness in fact seems compatible with the most obsequious possible relationship to disciplinary and coercive power (*SA*, 241).

According to his theory, the nomadism of the artist and critic has nothing to do with the flow of deterritorialization à la Deleuze and Guattari but rather involves a pseudo-Heideggerian nihilism responsive to the "broken paths" of art that lead nowhere (*TA*, 13). In this aestheticized context, the concepts of drifting and nomadism are reduced to being little more than conduits of nihilist pleasure. Consequently, Bonito Oliva writes at different points of "drifts of pleasure" and of the critic's compulsion to "nomadism and hedonism" (*SA*, 15; *TA*, 13). Elsewhere, he explicitly echoes Calvino's well-known disparagement of "i quaresimalisti della cultura di massa" when he refers to his method as "per niente quaresimale" (*TA*, 137). With his single-minded focus on pleasure, he distances himself from the productivity of desire and its utopian dimensions, claiming all the same to have widened the scope of art insofar as Transavanguardia also focuses on the moment of consumption (*TA*, 70).[100]

In the end, however, the term that most clearly betrays Bonito Oliva's antipathy toward Deleuze and Guattari's thought is his reinterpretation of the concept of the traitor, which, as we have seen, far from illustrating a reformist or revolutionary ideal, appears in his writings as a simple opportunist with respect to power who is adept at deception but incapable of absolute betrayal, who takes as his model not Luther but Iago (*IdeoTrad*, 56). Bonito Oliva could not emphasize more sharply the "qualunquismo" of the Mannerist intellectual than he does by espousing this figure, for whom "the court becomes the reality principle, the opaque space within which he is forced to live appearance as being" (*IdeoTrad*, 64). In a later essay written in the era of Berlusconi's political ascendancy, the art historian reaffirms that, even if the traitor does not like what he sees, he chooses not to act because he is not a revolutionary and prefers instead to take refuge in his reservoir of metaphors.[101] His cynical, conservative rereadings of the themes of nomadism and betrayal locate Bonito Oliva at the antipodes of Deleuze and Guattari's antiauthoritarian philosophy. For all his performative gusto, his theories reveal him ultimately to be nothing more than a dutiful courtier, obedient to the contemporary *galateo* of power.

Notes

FREQUENTLY USED ABBREVIATIONS

AC = Vattimo, *After Christianity*
AD = Vattimo, *The Adventures of Difference*
AV = Vattimo, *Addio alla verità*
BI = Vattimo, *Beyond Interpretation*
EC = Vattimo, *Ecce comu*
EOM = Vattimo, *The End of Modernity*
GF = Fellini et al., *Ginger e Fred*
"ItalTran" = Bonito Oliva, "The Italian Transavantgarde"
IdeoTrad = Bonito Oliva, *L'ideologia del traditore*
NBG = Vattimo with Paterlini, *Not Being God*
OI = Vattimo, *Oltre l'interpretazione*
PD = Vattimo and Rovatti, *Il pensiero debole*
SA = Bonito Oliva, *Il sogno dell'arte*
SM = Calvino, *Six Memos for the Next Millennium*
ST = Vattimo, *La società trasparente*, 3rd edition
TA = Bonito Oliva, *Il talone di Achille*
TI = Bonito Oliva, *Transavantgarde International*
TS = Vattimo, *The Transparent Society*
VRF = Vattimo, *Vocazione e responsabilità del filosofo*

INTRODUCTION

1. Paul Ginsborg, *Silvio Berlusconi: Television Power and Patrimony* (London: Verso, 2004), 17–18.

2. Massimiliano Panarari, *L'egemonia sottoculturale: L'Italia da Gramsci al gossip* (Turin: Einaudi, 2010), 9. Panarari's formulation, of course, pays homage to the notion of "the long twentieth century" that Giovanni Arrighi sets forth in *The Long Twentieth Century: Money, Power, and the Origins of Our Times* (London: Verso, 1994).

3. Originally a member of the wing of the Italian Socialist Party led by Bettino Craxi, Achille Bonito Oliva in my opinion provides the most fully developed case study of how pseudoleftist intellectuals have advanced the cultural politics of Berlusconism (of course, Berlusconi himself started as a protégé of Craxi). Luca Mastrantonio and Francesco Bonami thus speak derisively of Bonito Oliva's "eternal trans-avanguardia" in *Irrazionalpopolare: Da Bocelli ai Suv. Viaggio tra gli incomprensibili miracoli d'Italia* (Turin: Einaudi, 2008), 19. Panarari similarly discusses Bonito Oliva's contribution to what he defines as the "subcultural hegemony" in *L'egemonia sottoculturale*, 29. Finally, Bonito Oliva is a target of Mario Perniola, who refers to him as the "tycoon of contemporary art" in *Contro la comunicazione* (Turin: Einaudi, 2004), 22.

4. "Berlusconi didn't mind using TV contacts to advance his standing in the political world." Alexander Stille, "Letter from Rome: Girls! Girls! Girls!," *New Yorker*, November 3, 2008, 72–74.

5. Romano Luperini is one of the very few critics who have observed that "berlusconismo" was foreshadowed on the left well before the 1990s. Romano Luperini, *La fine del postmoderno* (Naples: Guida, 2008), 16, 25.

6. Perry Anderson, *The New Old World* (London: Verso, 2009), 286.

7. Ibid., 286.

8. The hegemonic position that the PCI held through the 1960s was not a given condition of ideology but rather a function of intellectual openness, as Anderson pointedly emphasizes: "Owed in part to the sociology of its leadership, which, unlike that of the French, German, British or Spanish Communist parties, was for the most part highly educated, and in part to the relatively tolerant and flexible handling of the 'battle of ideas,' its dominion in this sphere was the really distinctive asset of Italian Communism." Ibid., 327.

9. Anderson exempts Umberto Eco from responsibility for this glum state of affairs in light of his engagements with mass culture (ibid., 329). Yet Eco generally has avoided the task of criticizing the media, tending instead to encourage what Benedetti calls the "national postmodern," especially through his best-selling fiction.

10. Ibid., 328.

11. "The discourse of the left is by now perfectly integral to Berlusconi's logic. A new episteme has imposed itself, sweeping away the former culture." Carlo Freccero, *Sinistra senza sinistra: Idee plurali per uscire dall'angolo* (Rome: Feltrinelli, 2008), 51. The English translation is my own.

12. Ernesto Galli della Loggia, *L'identità italiana* (Bologna: Il Mulino, 1998), 141, 155.

13. I will not rehearse the international history of postmodernism from Jencks and Lyotard to Jameson and Harvey, as has already been done countless times. However, I would like to join Monica Jensen in noting that from its inception postmodernism in Italy was conceived as an ahistorical style. See Jensen's *Il dibattito sul postmoderno in Italia: In bilico tra dialettica e ambiguità* (Florence: F. Cesati,

2002). Omar Calabrese's framing of postmodernism in terms of the "neo-baroque" and Eco's treatment of the concept as a recurrent form of mannerism in art and literature are only the most prominent examples of this view. Eco gives his own definition of postmodernism in his *Postille a Il nome della Rosa* (Milan: Bompiani, 1984, published in English as *Postscript to The Name of the Rose* by Harcourt in 1984). One of the most comprehensive books on the topic of Italy's understanding of postmodernism is Remo Ceserani's *Raccontare il postmoderno* (Turin: Bollati Boringhieri, 1997). Ceserani offers a clear overview of the genealogy of the concept in the Italian context with specific references to the cases of Calvino, Eco, and Antonio Tabucchi. An excellent critical analysis of "national postmodernism" can be found in Carla Benedetti's *Pasolini contro Calvino: Per una lettura impura* (Turin: Bollati Boringhieri, 1998). Disenchanted views of postmodernism lately have become more common, for example in Luperini's *La fine del postmoderno*, op. cit., and Alfonso Berardinelli's *Casi critici: Dal postmoderno alla mutazione* (Macerata: Quodlibet, 2007), which characterizes postmodernism as an apology for the present that is indifferent to historical truth. In recent years, some less convincing studies of Italian postmodernism have been published in English, such as Pier Paolo Antonello and Florian Mussgnug, eds., *Postmodern Impegno: Ethics and Commitment in Contemporary Italian Culture* (Bern: Peter Lang, 2009); and Jennifer Burns, *Fragments of Impegno: Interpretations of Commitment in Contemporary Italian Narrative 1980–2000* (Leeds: Northern University Press, 2001). Both books seem to me disconcertingly naïve in their desperate attempts to reframe Italian contemporary culture in the Berlusconi era in a positive light.

14. Luperini succinctly captures the spirit of this ideology with the phrase "the luxury of lightness." *La fine del postmoderno*, 13.

15. Panarari contends that the social and cultural shift that took place in the 1980s, which he regards as a fundamental "change of paradigm," was all the more dramatic as it happened in an already highly politicized nation. *L'egemonia sottoculturale*, 20.

16. In *Pasolini contro Calvino*, Benedetti refers to a "postmoderno nazionale," as does Luperini (*La fine del postmoderno*, 25).

17. Mastrantonio and Bonami, *Irrazionalpopolare*, 12.

18. Giorgio Agamben, *The End of the Poem: Studies in Poetics*, trans. Daniel Heller-Roazen (Stanford: Stanford University Press, 1999), 1.

19. Richard Wolin, *The Frankfurt School Revisited and Other Essays on Politics and Society* (New York: Routledge, 2006), 243.

20. Luperini laments the current position of Calvino in the Italian literary pantheon as a "classic for academics and high school professors" (*La fine del postmoderno*, 128). Ceserani believes that, in *Six Memos*, Calvino provides one of the most lucid descriptions of the "postmodern world." See Ceserani's "Intellettuali liquidi o in liquidazione" in Antonello and Mussgnug, *Postmodern Impegno*, 37. Mario Perniola exempts Calvino from the decadence of postmodernity; he re-

gards Calvino's late style and reflections on aesthetics as a sort of strategic weapon against the ills of the "society of communication" (*Contro la Comunicazione*, 105). On the other hand, Carla Benedetti in *Pasolini contro Calvino* takes a much more jaundiced view of Calvino's postmodern playfulness.

21. See Zygmunt Bauman, "Foreword: On Being Light and Liquid," in *Liquid Modernity* (Cambridge, UK: Polity Press, 2000), 1–15.

22. In an article for *Il Corriere della Sera* published on August 23, 2010, that responds to relentless public attacks on the quality of Italian television, the television critic Eugenio Grasso sarcastically asks the question: "But is it not that it is the fault of Calvino's lightness?" However, we might surmise that the sarcasm itself reveals an evident discomfort that Scalfari's recent praise of Calvino as a hero of the enlightenment cannot quite dispel. See Scalfari's *Per l'alto mare aperto: La modernità e il pensiero danzante* (Turin: Einaudi, 2010), 270.

23. Carla Benedetti's *Pasolini contro Calvino* is definitive on this topic, even if the opposition between Pasolini and Calvino may seem at first glance overly schematic.

24. Leland de la Durantaye, *Giorgio Agamben: A Critical Introduction* (Stanford: Stanford University Press, 2009), 200–201.

25. Ibid., 201–7.

26. Wolin is particularly incensed about what he regards as the meager effort made by poststructuralism to discuss human rights (*The Frankfurt School Revisited*, 193).

27. I will enlarge on this point in my chapter "Weakness" but for now would like to point out that Ernesto Laclau and Chantal Mouffe's seminal *Hegemony and Socialist Strategy: Towards a Radical Democratic Politics* (London: Verso, 1985) takes its cues not only from Gramsci but also from French poststructuralism's emphasis on difference. Laclau and Mouffe's approach enables them to foster a more dynamic, pluralistic view of democratic politics. Of course, since the publication of *Hegemony and Socialist Strategy*, many readers have condemned Laclau and Mouffe's work for not being sufficiently socialist.

28. Luperini, *La fine del postmoderno*, 20. Luperini also blasts the "idiocies" promulgated by weak thought. Ibid., 14.

29. Mastrantonio and Bonami, *Irrazionalpopolare*, 19.

30. Anderson, *The New Old World*, 207.

31. Antonio Negri, *La differenza italiana* (Rome: Nottetempo, 2005).

32. In the eyes of readers from Goethe to Byron, Italy has always represented a safe island in which sensual anarchy and wisdom might coexist, as Anderson observes (*The New Old World*, 278–79).

CHAPTER 1

1. The term *Transavanguardia* was coined by the critic Achille Bonito Oliva to describe the movement in Italian art that coalesced between the end of the 1970s

and the mid-1980s and included artists such as Sandro Chia, Francesco Clemente, and Enzo Cucchi. Indiscriminately removing signifiers from their historical and cultural contexts, such artists suggest the prospect of Italy as a culture industry engaged in little more than the recycling of historical forms. A dandyish, kitschy remarketing of such forms, however, denies the historicity of the work of art and its implication in society. The notion of "weak thought" was developed by the philosopher Gianni Vattimo and has been associated as well with the work of his contemporaries Aldo G. Gargani, Pier Aldo Rovatti, and Massimo Cacciari. The principle of philosophical weakness aims at an original reinterpretation of Heidegger that essentially confines itself to a hermeneutics of existing conditions. In this sense, the project of weak thought may be contrasted to that of Derridean deconstruction, for example.

2. Fredric Jameson, *Postmodernism, or, the Cultural Logic of Late Capitalism* (Durham: Duke University Press, 1990); and David Harvey, *The Conditions of Postmodernity* (Oxford: Basil Blackwell, 1989).

3. See note 80 of this chapter.

4. See notes 115 and 116 of this chapter.

5. See my characterization of Italian national identity in the 1980s in the below section, *La dolce vita* Twenty Years Later: *Ginger and Fred*, for more on the Italian Style.

6. André Bazin, *What Is Cinema*, Vol. 2, ed. and trans. Hugh Gray (Berkeley: University of California Press, 1971), 88–89. In this first phase, the Italian leftist establishment, led in particular by Guido Aristarco, the legendary editor of the Marxist journal *Cinema Nuovo*, accused Fellini of gradually having abandoned neorealism and embraced with the making of *La strada* what Aristarco scornfully defined as "the tradition of poetry of the solitary man." See Aristarco, "Italian Cinema," in *Film Culture* 1:2 (1955), 30; reprinted in *Federico Fellini: Essays in Criticism*, ed. Peter Bondanella (New York: Oxford University Press, 1978), 60.

7. Metz's most influential essay on Fellini is "Mirror Construction in Fellini's *8½*," published in 1963 in *Études cinématographiques*. For more on Deleuze, see note 8.

8. Gilles Deleuze, *Cinema 2: The Time-Image* trans. Hugh Tomlinson and Robert Galeta (Minneapolis: University of Minnesota Press, 1989), 4–6, 88–93. Deleuze's *Cinema 2* comprises the most thoroughly considered commentary on the disjunctive, experimental narrative techniques of European cinema from the 1950s through the 1960s. Deleuze identifies the Italian films of the period as the chief instances of such techniques and reads these works in continuity with the preceding generation of neorealist films as belonging to a cinema of the "time image." As opposed to the European cinema prior to neorealism, in which meaning is achieved through a synthetic action movement, the new cinema of the time image is characterized by dispersive situations, weak plot links, the voyage or "stroll" form, and an absence of plot. The visual *flânerie* of *La dolce vita* thus provides a textbook

case for application of Deleuze's theory. Deleuze makes the point that the movies of Visconti, Antonioni, and Fellini all might be considered neorealist, as they all share what he considers the two main achievements of neorealism: a "direct image of time" and a purely optical space. This kind of cinema, which will come to encompass the French New Wave, provokes the spectator to decipher an image rather than follow an action.

9. A useful mapping of Fellini's output is provided by the editors' introduction to *Perspectives on Federico Fellini*, eds. Peter Bondanella and Cristina degli Esposti (New York: Hall, 1993), 3–21. They laconically observe that a certain disagreement persists regarding the films released after *Amarcord*.

10. The genesis of the film was Fellini's proposal of a television drama entitled "Stories of Women" that would have starred Masina and included episodes directed by Antonioni, Franco Zeffirelli, and Luigi Magni. The producer instead encouraged Fellini to expand his own segment to the length of a feature film.

11. The commentator who has expressed sharpest interest in what he calls Fellini's "postmodern reproductions" is the American critic Frank Burke. See his *Fellini's Films* (New York: Twayne, 1996), 223–89.

12. Paul Ginsborg, *Italy and Its Discontents* (New York: Penguin, 2001), 108.

13. Fellini's outrage at television's encouragement of the sheeplike conformism of the public is palpable in *Ginger and Fred*. At one point, Pippo imagines himself addressing the audience of "We Are Proud to Present" as "overgrown sheep" and indulging in a vulgar gesture toward what he calls the "teledependents."

14. Interestingly, Celentano also makes an appearance in *Ginger and Fred*, although this time as an aging pop star in his own right.

15. Tullio Kezich, "Fellini e altri: bloc-notes per *La dolce vita*" in *Il dolce cinema* (Milan: Bompiani, 1978), 25.

16. "There are always many modernisms. . . . The modernism that mattered most to me in the beginning—for years I had a blow-up from Roberto Rossellini's *Paisà* on my wall—was that of film and literature in Italy after 1945." T. J. Clark, *Farewell to an Idea* (New Haven: Yale University Press, 1999), 405.

17. "Indeed those features of style or narrative called postmodern-pastiche, self-conscious narrative, game-playing, polyvalence—which are undoubtedly present in contemporary culture—are already there from the start as part of a modern departure from the classical narratives of sound cinema, a departure which takes place towards the end of the '50s. Most are neo-modern inventions." John Orr, *Cinema and Modernity* (Cambridge, MA: Polity Press, 1993), 3. Jameson identifies three significant periods in cinematic history since the advent of sound movies, taking care to differentiate them from the literary movements of the same name: realism, modernism, and postmodernism. He defines the cinema of *auteurs* that emerged in the late 1950s and early 1960s as modernist: "It will seem appropriate to characterize the moment of modernism as the moment of emergence of the great auteurs: Hitchcock, Bergman, Fellini, Kurosawa, Renoir, Welles, Wajda,

Antonioni, Ray, etc." Frederic Jameson, *Signatures of the Visible* (London: Routledge, 1992), 199.

18. Tullio Kezich, *Fellini* (Milan: Camunia, 1987), 278.

19. The territory is highly controversial, since for certain critics cinema represents the quintessential modernist art, whereas for others such as Michael Fried film is essentially unable to fulfill canonical modernist categories: "cinema is not, even at its most experimental, a modernist art." What Fried wishes to suggest is that, being an impure medium, cinema does not possess inherent dimensions and functions. See Fried's "Art and Objecthood," originally published in the June 1967 issue of *Artforum* and reprinted in *Minimal Art*, ed. G. Battock (Berkeley: University of California Press, 1995), 141.

20. Orr, *Cinema and Modernity*, 1.

21. Ibid., 2, 6.

22. Tony Pinkney, "Editor's Introduction: Modernism and Cultural Theory," in Raymond Williams, *The Politics of Modernity* (New York: Verso, 1989), 15. Pinkney makes an important claim a little earlier in the essay: "It is, I would argue, film that is for Williams the pre-eminent Modernist medium" (ibid., 9). It should be noted, furthermore, that Williams in fact rethinks the whole of Modernism in the light of film. Woolf and Joyce too are filmmakers *manqués*, for their fragmented "stream of consciousness" is "deeply related to several characteristic forms of modern imagery, most evident in painting and especially in film which as a medium contains much of its intrinsic movement." See Raymond Williams, *The Country and the City* (London: Chatto and Windus, 1973), 290.

23. Burke, *Fellini's Films*, 267.

24. P. Adams Sitney, *Vital Crises in Italian Cinema* (Austin: University of Texas Press, 1995), 110.

25. Fredric Jameson, *The Geopolitical Aesthetic* (Bloomington: Indiana University Press, 1995).

26. In this sense, I would extend to *La dolce vita* the definition that Kezich applies generally to Fellini's cinema of the 1950s from *Luci del varietà* to *The Nights of Cabiria*. See Kezich, *Fellini*, 189.

27. For more on the significance of this structure, see note 8 above and Deleuze, *Cinema 2*, 4.

28. Robert Richardson, "*La dolce vita*: Fellini and T. S. Eliot" in *Federico Fellini: Essays in Criticism*, ed. Peter Bondanella (New York: Oxford University Press, 1978), 105–106.

29. Pier Paolo Pasolini, "The Catholic Irrationalism of Fellini" in Bondanella and degli Esposti, editors, *Perspectives*, 104.

30. It is useful in this connection to note that Stanley Cavell argues for the relevance of Baudelaire's essay "The Painter of Modern Life" to both film and film criticism, particularly with regard to the poet's identification of certain mesmerizing, iconic archetypes of modernity such as the military man, the dandy (or

flâneur), and the woman. According to Cavell, these character types play a central and recurrent role in the development of cinema. Stanley Cavell, *The World Viewed* (Cambridge: Harvard University Press, 1979), 41–60.

31. Charles Baudelaire, *The Painter of Modern Life and Other Essays*, trans. and ed. Jonathan Mayne (London: Phaidon Press, 1964), 9.

32. Ibid., 12.

33. "Of all the experiences which made his life what it was, Baudelaire singled out his having been jostled by the crowd as the decisive, unique experience. The luster of the crowd with a motion and a soul of its own, the glitter that had bedazzled the *flâneur*, had dimmed for him. To impress the crowd's meanness upon himself, he envisaged a day when even the lost women, the outcasts, would be ready to advocate a well-ordered life, condemn libertinism, and reject everything except money. . . . Baudelaire battled the crowd—with the impotent rage of someone fighting the rain or the wind." Benjamin, "On Some Motifs in Baudelaire," in *Illuminations*, ed. Hannah Arendt (New York: Schocken, 1968), 193–94.

34. Indeed, the inspiration for Fellini's chef d'oeuvre may have been a contemporary fashion style: "*La dolce vita* was inspired for him, then, by the fashion of women's sack dresses which conveyed that sense of luxurious butterflying out around a body that might be [physically] beautiful but not morally so; these sack dresses struck Fellini because they rendered a woman gorgeous who could, instead, be a skeleton of squalor and solitude inside." Franca Faldini and Goffredo Fofi, *L'avventurosa storia del cinema italiano raccontata dai suoi protagonisti 1960–1969* (Milan: Feltrinelli, 1981), 4–5.

35. Sitney, *Crises*, 112–13. Barbara Lewalski, "Federico Fellini's *Purgatorio*," in Bondanella, *Federico Fellini: Essays in Criticism*.

36. Anne Paolucci, "Italian Film: Antonioni, Fellini, Bolognini," in *Massachusetts Review* 7:3 (Summer 1966); and Sitney, *Crises*, 117–18.

37. Hollis Alpert, *Fellini: A Life* (New York: Atheneum, 1986), 151.

38. Flaiano has likened the scriptwriters' effort to find the appropriate name for the character of Paparazzo to the two years of labor spent by Flaubert to settle on "Emma" as the first name of the heroine of *Madame Bovary*. "Paparazzo," Flaiano tells us, derives from a text by George Gessing entitled *Sulle rive dello Jonio*. At any rate, the success of Fellini, Flaiano, and Pinelli at their endeavor may be judged by the thoroughness with which the plural form, "paparazzi," has penetrated the contemporary vernacular as a shorthand label for tabloid photojournalists. Ennio Flaiano, *La solitudine del satiro* (Milan: Rizzoli, 1973), 13–14.

39. Guillaume Apollinaire, "Zone" in *Alcools* (Paris: Gallimard, 1920), 9.

40. Richard Poirier regards the "appearance of bravery" and an insistence on difficulty as two sine qua non conditions of the modernist enterprise. See "Modernism and Its Difficulties" in *The Renewal of Literature* (New Haven: Yale University Press, 1987), 112.

41. Kezich, *Fellini*, 274–76.

42. Ibid., 275.

43. Manuela Gieri, *Contemporary Italian Filmmaking: Strategies of Subversion, Pirandello, Fellini, Scola and the Directors of the New Generation* (Toronto: University of Toronto Press, 1995).

44. Despite his decision not to appear in *La dolce vita*, Vittorini made a public statement following the film's release to defend the work against charges that it was a corrupting, anti-Catholic influence, accusations that Vittorini regarded as Fascist and reactionary. In fact, the Fascists did introduce a motion in the Italian parliament on February 9, 1960, accusing Fellini of desecrating the reputation of the Eternal City. Sitney, *Crises*, 111.

45. See Gottfried Boehm, "Giorgio Morandi's Artistic Concept," in *Giorgio Morandi*, eds. Ernest Gerhard Guese and Franz Armin (New York: Morat Prestel, 1999), 9–20.

46. According to Kezich, Fellini decided to cast the French actor Alain Cuny as Steiner after Pasolini described him as a "Gothic cathedral." Kezich, *Fellini*, 279.

47. "Modernism must be under the sign of suicide, an act which seals a heroic will that makes no concession to a mentality inimical toward this will." Walter Benjamin, "The Paris of the Second Empire in Baudelaire," in *Charles Baudelaire: A Lyric Poet in the Era of High Capitalism*, trans. Harry Zohn (London: NLB, 1973), 75.

48. Ibid., 99–103.

49. Discussing the characteristics of postmodern cinema, Jameson argues that the typical modernist hero of film never approaches the "bewilderment of an honest schizophrenic life." Fellini's Marcello, however, strikes Jameson as closest to the postmodern existential condition: "Nor is the chaos and bewilderment of the honest schizophrenic life really the 'problem' of modernist film makers either, having little enough to do with the obsessions of the hero of *Vertigo* (Hitchcock, 1958), or the neuroses and psychoses of Bergman and Antonioni characters, although in this last arguably we come close, and in *La dolce vita* (Fellini, 1960) we're already on our way." Jameson, *Geopolitical Aesthetic*, 42–43.

50. Federico Fellini, *La dolce vita*, in *Quattro film* (Turin: Einaudi, 1974), 204–5.

51. On the missing episodes, see Brunello Rondi, *Il cinema di Fellini* (Rome: Edizioni di Bianco e Nero, 1965), 207–8.

52. Orr, *Cinema and Modernity*, 14.

53. The phrase occurs during the description of Dorothea's honeymoon with Casaubon in *Middlemarch*. Poirier remarks on the suggestiveness of the description with regard to the short-lived nature of forms of knowledge. Poirier, *Renewal*, 154.

54. See Giorgio Ciucci, "Roma come Modello" in *Storia dell'arte italiana*, Vol. 3 (Turin: Einaudi, 1982), 373–78.

55. Rondi, *Cinema*, 227.

56. Charles Baudelaire, "Le cygne," in *Les fleurs du mal*, trans. Richard Howard (Boston: Godine, 1982), 269 (French), 91 (English).

57. Walter Benjamin, "The Return of the *Flâneur*," in *Selected Writings*, Vol. 2: *1927–1934*, eds. Michael W. Jennings, Howard Eiland, and Gary Smith, trans. Rodney Livingstone et al. (Cambridge, MA: Belknap Press, 1999), 263.

58. Sigmund Freud, "Civilization and Its Discontents," in *Standard Edition of the Complete Works*, Vol. 21, ed. James Strachey (London: Hogarth Press, 1961), 69–71.

59. Zygmunt Bauman, *Intimations of Postmodernity* (New York: Routledge, 1992), 151.

60. Jean Baudrillard, *La transparence du mal* (Paris: Galilée, 1990), 4.

61. Fellini, *Quattro film*, 277.

62. Jean Baudrillard, *L'illusion de la fin* (Paris: Galilée, 1992), 40–41. I give my own translation, because the existing English translation (Baudrillard, *The Illusion of the End*, trans. Chris Turner, Stanford: Stanford University Press, 1994, 22) unfortunately misses Baudrillard's emphasis on *douceur* in the original text: "elles repensent tout en douceur."

63. There is a similar moment in an earlier Fellini film, *The Nights of Cabiria*, when Cabiria walks through a pine forest at the end of the movie. The scene conveys an anxious expectation of a moral and aesthetic *Lichtung*.

64. Benjamin, "Baudelaire," 188.

65. Burke, *Fellini's Films*, 271.

66. We ought to bear in mind that Fellini stressed in an interview the possibly deliberate nature of Marcello's withdrawal from Paola: "It [Marcello's incomprehension] could be considered a bantering gesture: 'I do not hear you because I do not want to hear you.'" Alpert, *Fellini*, 151.

67. Michel Foucault, *The Order of Things* (New York: Random House, 1970), 387.

68. James Joyce, *A Portrait of the Artist as a Young Man*, in *The Portable James Joyce*, ed. Harry Levin (New York: Penguin, 1976), 432.

69. Ibid., 433–34.

70. Fellini, *Quattro film*, 279.

71. Ibid., 281–82.

72. In "The Painter of Modern Life," Baudelaire stresses the importance of both convalescence and childhood to the ideal artistic Bildung: "Convalescence is like a return toward childhood. The convalescent, like the child, is possessed in the highest degree of the faculty of keenly interesting himself in things, be they apparently of the most trivial nature." Baudelaire, *Painter*, 7. Paul De Man regards the figure of the convalescent as one of the archetypes that epitomize modernity. See his "Lyric and Modernity," in *Blindness and Insight* (Minneapolis: University of Minnesota Press, 1971), 157.

73. Umberto Eco, "Thoth, Fellini, and the Pharaoh," in Bondanella and degli Esposti, editors, *Perspectives*, 294.

74. Stephen Gundle, "From Neorealism to Luci Rosse: Cinema, Politics, So-

ciety, 1945–1985," in *Conflict and Culture in Postwar Italy*, eds. Zygmunt Baranski and Robert Lumley (New York: St. Martin's Press, 1990), 203, 220–21.

75. Ibid., 203–14.

76. Ibid., 276.

77. Silvana Patriarca, "National Identity or National Character: New Vocabularies and Old Paradigms," in *Making and Remaking Italy*, eds. Albert Russell Ascoli and Krystyna von Henneberg (Oxford: Berg, 2001), 302–3.

78. Ibid., 301–2.

79. On the relationship between consumption and identity in Italy, see Ginsborg, *Discontents*, 86–87.

80. Guy Debord, *Comments on the Society of the Spectacle*, trans. Malcolm Imrie (London: Verso, 1990), 8.

81. Ibid., 22.

82. Ibid., 49.

83. Richard Dienst, *Still Life in Real Time* (Durham, NC: Duke University Press, 1994), 8.

84. Ginsborg, *Discontents*, 86.

85. Ibid., 112.

86. Umberto Eco, "A Guide to the Neo-Television of the 1980s" in Baranski and Lumley, editors, *Culture and Conflict*, 251, 246.

87. Ibid., 247.

88. Pasolini, "Ampliamento del 'bozzetto' sulla rivoluzione antropologica in Italia," in *Scritti Corsari* (Milan: Garzanti: 1990), 59.

89. Federico Fellini, *Fare un film* (Turin: Einaudi, 1980), 109.

90. Ibid., 137.

91. Ibid., 137–38.

92. Ibid., 142. The translation is mine.

93. Michel Chion, "1985" in *Cahiers du Cinéma* 380 (February 1986), 16.

94. Fellini, *Fare un film*, 43.

95. Fellini, *Quattro film*, xxiv.

96. See Ginsborg, *Discontents*, 164. It is interesting to note that the first screening of *Ginger and Fred* on December 15, 1985, was organized for Francesco Cossiga, the Christian Democrat who was at the time the president of the Republic and who invited, among his other guests, the conservative ideologue Andreotti. Andreotti in fact wound up as the first reviewer of the film, writing a piece on the screening two days later that was published on the front page of *Il Corriere della Sera*. Kezich, *Fellini*, 519.

97. Jacqueline Risset, "Fellini politique," in *Cahiers du Cinéma* 479/80 (May 1994), 68.

98. Ibid., 68.

99. "Queste TV non sono degne di sopravvivere." Kezich, *Fellini*, 513.

100. Peter Bondanella, in particular, asserts that *Amarcord* and *Orchestra Re-*

hearsal represent Fellini's most political films. See his *The Cinema of Federico Fellini* (Princeton: Princeton University Press, 1992), 262–91. Bondanella's thesis, however, does not take into account certain important points. Whereas *Amarcord* deals with the memory of Fascism, *Ginger and Fred* attacks the Italian society of its day. Whereas *Orchestra Rehearsal* allegorically warns of the threat of totalitarianism, *Ginger and Fred* analytically exposes the banality of mass culture. And like his later film *The Voice of the Moon*, *Ginger and Fred* reflects on, and is linked to, Fellini's much-publicized legal disputes with Berlusconi.

101. Federico Fellini and Tatti Sanguinetti, "Fellini, intervista" in *Cahiers du Cinéma* 479/80 (May 1994), 70. The interview first appeared in Italian in *L'Europeo* when *Ginger and Fred* had its broadcast premiere on the RAI on December 5, 1987.

102. Federico Fellini, "Propos de Federico Fellini," in *Cahiers du Cinéma* 474 (December 1993), 58. For more details on Fellini's commercial spots, see Bondanella, *Films of Federico Fellini*, 40, and "Fellini e la grande tentatrice—breve storia: dai maccheroncini pop, alla Pasta Barilla al Banco di Roma" in *Lo schermo manifesto*, ed. Paolo Fabbri (Rimini: Guaraldi, 1999), 21–47.

103. Ginsborg, *Discontents*, 167.

104. Fellini and Sanguinetti, "Fellini, intervista," 71.

105. Burke, *Fellini's Films*, 266. Fellini actually had planned on lampooning Berlusconi in a far more overt manner in the film and had even requested the use of his image for this purpose. Not surprisingly, Berlusconi refused. See Fellini, "Propos," 58.

106. Federico Fellini, Tonino Guerra, and Tullio Pinelli, *Ginger e Fred* (Milan: Longanesi, 1985), 75. Hereafter all citations from this screenplay will be flagged in the notes with the abbreviation *GF*. All English translations are mine.

107. Fellini et al., *GF*, 57.

108. Pasolini, *Scritti Corsari*, 40.

109. Kezich, *Fellini*, 515. On this score, we should recall that Pasolini collaborated with Fellini on the dialogue for *The Nights of Cabiria*, contributing in particular to the exchanges between prostitutes, thanks to his knowledge of the Roman demimonde. On a less collegial note, the production company chaired by Fellini, Cineriz, rejected the script that Pasolini eventually made into his first feature film, *Accatone*.

110. Kezich, *Fellini*, 512–13.

111. Angelo Restivo, *The Cinema of Economic Miracles: Visuality and Modernization in the Italian Art Film* (Durham, NC: Duke University Press, 2002), 8.

112. Italo Calvino, "Autobiografia di uno spettatore," in Fellini, *Quattro film*, xxiii.

113. W. H. Auden, foreword to Angus Stewart, *Sense and Inconsequence* (London: Michael de Hartington, 1972), 4. Among the numerous critics who describe *Ginger and Fred* as a satire is Bondanella: "With *Ginger and Fred* the outlook on TV, seen from backstage of the TV studios, becomes very critical and rich in satire." Bondanella, "Fellini e la grande tentatrice," 40.

114. By applying this name to their works, the Roman poets playfully associated the variety of tones and forms incorporated in their writing with the *lanx satura* or "full platter" of fruits and nuts offered in ritual ceremonies. C. A. Van Rooy, *Studies in Classical Satire and Related Literary Theory* (Leiden: Brill, 1965), 1–13.

115. Giorgio Agamben, *The Coming Community*, trans. Michael Hardt (Minneapolis: University of Minnesota Press, 1993), 78–79.

116. Ibid., 79.

117. The only exception to his insistence on a minimalist style in the fake advertisements, in my opinion, is the ad for the watch Betrix, which displays a quotation of the *terzina* that starts *The Divine Comedy*. The watch is advertised as helping the fortunate owner find his or her way out of the *selva oscura* in which the poem opens. Yet even in this case what is amusing about the advertisement is not the pseudocomplexity of its premise but the sheer idiocy and bad taste of its pretension to unite high and low culture through mere invocation of Dante, the most reflexive, Pavlovian reference in the Italian cultural landscape.

118. Bondanella rightly points out that commercial ads are no longer part of the screen but that they have invaded the space surrounding the characters. However notwithstanding his sharp analysis, the conclusions he draws at the end of his essays aim at blunting the provocation of Fellini's cultural critique. Bondanella, "Fellini e la grande tentatrice," 42–43.

119. Cesare Zavattini, *Neorealismo* (Milan: Bompiani, 1979).

120. See Bazin, *What Is Cinema*, Vol. 2; and Deleuze, *Cinema 1* and *Cinema 2*.

121. Restivo, *Miracles*, 24.

122. Malcolm Bowie, *Lacan* (Cambridge: Harvard University Press, 1991), 91.

123. Jacques Lacan, *Seminar XI: The Four Fundamental Concepts of Psychoanalysis*, ed. Jacques-Alain Miller, trans. Alan Sheridan (New York: Norton, 1998), 49.

124. Lacan, *Écrits*, 388, as cited in Bowie's *Lacan*, 95.

125. Suaro Borelli, *L'Unità*, 22 January 1986, reprinted in Claudio Fava and Aldo Vagano, eds. *I film di Federico Fellini* (Rome: Gremese, 1987), 185.

126. Fellini et al., *GF*, 76.

127. Dienst, *Still Life*, 16.

128. Fellini et al., *GF*, 57.

129. Millicent Marcus maintains that in *Ginger and Fred* Fellini establishes a continuity, rather than an opposition, between cinema and television, a progression from the most to the least referential technology of visualization. For Marcus, Fellini does not see the relation between the two media as antithetical, because the imitative stage personae of "Ginger" and "Fred" cannot properly be opposed to those of the celebrity impersonators. Millicent Marcus, *After Fellini: National Cinema in the Postmodern Age* (Baltimore: Johns Hopkins University Press, 2002) 192.

130. For an authoritative discussion of the relationship between the Real and reality in Lacan, see Slavoj Žižek, *Looking Awry* (Cambridge, MA: MIT Press, 1997), 13.

131. Ibid., 6–8.

132. In this sense, we may consider the *fegatelli* to represent the equivalent of *Das Ding*, the thing that gives body to the substance of enjoyment. Ibid., 19.

133. Fellini et al., *GF*, 214.

134. Marcus, *After Fellini*, 193.

135. Fellini et al., *GF*, 215.

136. Fellini explains the connection between his insistence on Mastroianni's longish hairstyle and Pippo's cranky personality in the film: "I made him lengthen his hair to give him a seedier appearance, like an unhinged ex-protestor nourished by a ridiculous, demagogic, and messy revolt." Fellini et al., *GF*, 111. This is my translation.

137. Marcus, *After Fellini*, 182.

138. "The art of storytelling is nearing its end because the epic side of truth—wisdom—is dying out. This, however, is a process that has been going on for a long time. . . . It is . . . only a concomitant of the secular productive forces of history—a symptom that has quite gradually removed narrative from the realm of living speech and at the same time is making it possible to find a new beauty in what is vanishing. . . . It is not only a man's knowledge or wisdom, but above all his real life—and this is the stuff that stories are made of—which first assumes transmissible form at the moment of his death. Just as a sequence of images is set in motion inside a man as his life comes to an end—unfolding the views of himself in which he has encountered himself without being aware of it—suddenly in his expressions and looks the unforgettable emerges, and imparts to everything that concerned him that authority which even the poorest wretch in the act of dying possesses for the living around him. This authority lies at the very origin of the story." Walter Benjamin, "The Storyteller: Observations on the Work of Nikolai Leskov," in *Selected Writings*, Vol. 3: *1935–1938*, eds. Howard Eiland and Michael W. Jennings, trans. Edmund Jephcott, Howard Eiland, et al. (Cambridge, MA: Belknap Press, 2002), 146, 151.

139. Fellini et al., *GF*, 261.

140. Ibid., 262. Pippo's melancholic self-appraisal in these lines seems to underscore his genealogical relation to the character of Gattone, a friend of the eponymous protagonist of *Moraldo in Città*, Fellini's early draft of *La dolce vita*. Like Gattone, Pippo drinks too much, impulsively and vainly pursues women, and has spent time in a psychiatric hospital (Gattone in fact dies in an asylum). Yet the ghostly status of the two protagonists of *Ginger and Fred* relates them as well to the equally spectral Ivo and Gonnella, the lunatic central figures of *The Voice of the Moon*, who seem perpetually engaged in poetic and pathetic acts of nonsensical resistance to the larger culture.

141. Slavoj Žižek, *The Ticklish Subject: The Absent Center of Political Ontology* (New York: Verso, 1999), 195.

142. Žižek clearly elucidates the dialectic between the Real and the Symbolic in "normal" and "psychotic" contexts. See *Looking Awry*, 40.

143. Fellini et al., *GF*, 33.

144. Ibid., 152.
145. Ibid., 154.
146. T. J. Clark, "Modernism, Postmodernism, and Steam," in *October* 100 (Spring, 2002), 154–74.
147. For a succinct assessment of the neorealist inspiration behind the Quaroni, Ridolfi, and Fiorentino plan for renovating Termini station, see Manfredo Tafuri, *Storia dell'architettura italiana (1944–1985)* (Turin: Einaudi, 1982), 14–16.
148. Jean-Paul Aron, "Critica Dossier," cited in *Cinemasessanta XXVII* 2:168 (March–April 1986), 52.
149. Kezich, *Fellini*, 514.
150. Ibid., 521.
151. Ibid., 522.
152. Among American critics, Millicent Marcus's essay on *Ginger and Fred* offers one of the best and most sophisticated readings of the film and its metacinematic implications. Marcus effectively identifies all the fragments of Fellini's cinematic past that have been recycled in *Ginger and Fred*, which she defines as a "hyperfilm," a commentary on the destiny of film as an art form and on Fellini's own career. Marcus beautifully describes the casting of the leading actors in the film—Mastroianni, Masina, and Fabrizi—as part of an attempt to create a sort of "tableau vivant" of Fellini's cinematic past, as all three have played crucial roles in his most important films. Marcus also strikes me as being quite correct in her conclusion that, far from signaling Fellini's surrender, the unhappy ending of the film marks his adoption of a clearly oppositional stance (*After Fellini*, 198). But my interpretive approach to the film differs from Marcus in two important ways. I am not convinced by her attempt to discredit the suggestion that Fellini might have involved himself in anything as "silly" as a crusade against television. Marcus concedes initially that, "at its most obvious," *Ginger and Fred* portrays a battle between the cinematic past and the televisual present (ibid., 185). She proceeds inexplicably to argue that we can detect a "hidden complicity" between Fellini and the producers of commercial television programming (192). I think instead that to pose the problem in these terms begs the question the film raises about the saturation of "integrated spectacle" reached in Italian culture. That Fellini might have directed advertisements himself (famously for Barilla and Campari) and traditionally represented himself as an accomplice rather than a judge of Italian culture does not mean that something new is not at stake in *Ginger and Fred*—and this, in fact, is why the film is so important. Marcus concludes that Fellini does not fully condemn television, a medium she claims he has "transfigured" (ibid., 193). However, Fellini himself might have been perplexed by Marcus's contention that in *Ginger and Fred* the director "reinvents television, by exaggerating and distorting it, in order to reinforce his satirical and polemical discourse." In the published screenplay, Fellini confesses the fear of not having achieved in the film his goal of a sufficiently forceful satire on commercial television: "I met with some difficulty

in restraining my taste for parody, because it seems to me difficult to produce a parody of something that is already the parody of itself." Fellini et al., *GF*, 69.

153. An excerpt from Eco's article is reprinted in Fava and Vagano, *I film*, 183.

154. Ibid., 184. De Santi's review of *Ginger and Fred* originally appeared in *Cineforum* 252 (1986).

155. Ibid., 182. Grazzini's pronouncement was published initially in *Il Corriere della Sera*, June 15, 1986.

156. Carla Benedetti, *The Empty Cage: Inquiry into the Mysterious Disappearance of the Author*, trans. William Hartley (Ithaca, NY: Cornell University Press, 2005), 40–41.

157. Ibid., 48–49.

158. "Fellini e la grande tentatrice," 45.

159. See Gieri, *Lo schermo manifesto*.

160. Žižek, *Looking Awry*, 22.

161. See Jacques Lacan, *The Seminar of Jacques Lacan, Book VII: The Ethics of Psychoanalysis, 1959–1960*, ed. Jacques-Alain Miller, trans. Dennis Porter (New York: Norton, 1992), 270–87.

CHAPTER 2

1. See Lucia Re, *Calvino and the Age of Neorealism: Fables of Estrangement* (Stanford: Stanford University Press, 1990). Re's book is one of the few dedicated to the "neorealist" period in Calvino's writing. She emphasizes that the first Calvino strives to develop the notion of a committed literature that is neither didactic nor ideological.

2. John Barth, "The Literature of Replenishment," *The Friday Book* (New York: Putnam, 1984).

3. Italo Calvino, *Saggi 1945–1985*, 2 vols., ed. Mario Barenghi (Milan: Mondadori, 1995). See *Saggi* 1: 565–625 regarding his trips to Japan, Iran, and Mexico and *Saggi* 2: 2409–2679 for his accounts of his tours of what was then the Soviet Union and the United States. All further references to Calvino's journalistic and critical writings other than *Six Memos for the Next Millennium* will be keyed to this edition by volume and page number and given in the text.

4. *Six Memos for the Next Millennium* (Cambridge, MA: Harvard University Press, 1988), 8. All further citations will be from this edition; page references will be given in the text after the abbreviation *SM*.

5. Alberto Asor Rosa is right to observe that these values have one common denominator: they approximate the properties of physical objects in space. Rosa, *Stile Calvino* (Turin: Einaudi, 2001), 84. It would seem that Calvino's final text privileges those values that allow us to establish a sort of cosmic continuity between things and words. Yet the relentless emphasis on the material quality of these values makes them abstract, remote, and inhuman without being sublime.

6. Even the first Calvino, as Re points out, refrains from a stridently "realist" rhetoric and presents the mythical experience of *Resistenza* in the mode of a fairy tale. Re, *Neorealism*, 157–58.

7. See the second paragraph of the below section, "The Lightness of Nihilism."

8. In Italian, the titles of these novels are *Il sentiero dei nidi di ragno, Ultimo viene il corvo, Il visconte dimezzato, L'entrata in guerra, Fiabe italiane,* and *Il barone rampante*.

9. For a good analysis of the power split between right and left in Italy after World War Two, see Remo Bodei, *Il noi diviso: ethos ed idee dell'Italia repubblicana* (Milan: Einaudi, 1998), 21–22.

10. On the significance of this change in the tone and rhetoric of Calvino's essays, see Barenghi, "Introduzione," *Saggi* I: xvii–xxiii.

11. For Calvino's consideration of the dangers implicit in the Italian economic miracle, see "Un'amara serenità," an article written in 1961: "The man who wants to see beyond today suspects the euphoria of so many who, happily wallowing in the flood of mass production and consumerism, . . . run at the facile, feverish rhythm of business affairs and holidays, thus losing their soul" (*Saggi* I: 125). My translation.

12. The lectures were published in English first, with the title *Six Memos for the Next Millennium* (Cambridge, MA: Harvard University Press, 1988), and then in Italian with the title *Lezioni Americane. Sei proposte per il prossimo millennio* (Milan: Garzanti, 1988).

13. The Norton series invites speakers to deliver a minimum of six lectures at Harvard in the course of an academic year. At the time of his death, Calvino had completed the first five of his talks and was planning a sixth on the value of "consistency." Although some initial notes toward this sixth memo have survived, the extant draft material is incomplete.

14. See the "Introduction" to Antonio Gramsci, *Selections from Cultural Writings*, eds. David Forgacs and Geoffrey Nowell-Smith, trans. William Boelhower (Cambridge, MA: Harvard University Press, 1985), 4.

15. Ibid., 108.

16. Ibid., 98.

17. Jacques Rancière, *The Politics of Aesthetics*, trans. Gabriel Rockwill (London: Continuum, 2004), 60.

18. Piacentini rightly has pointed out that, more than adhering to a logic of polarity or of the oxymoron, Calvino adopts an ambivalent stance when confronting opposing values. Piacentini, however, considers the ambivalence a positive feature of Calvino's rhetoric. See Adriano Piacentini, *Il cristallo e la fiamma* (Florence: Atheneum, 2002), 23.

19. Asor Rosa, *Stile*, 81.

20. "The strategies of reframing Leopardi's thought advanced by an imposing number of publications of the last decade are different and of a different level;

and yet are all homogeneous among themselves and, as we have said, are responsive most of all to the consolidated schemes of the Italian ideology in their search for equilibrium, compromise, and mediation." Massimiliano Biscuso and Franco Gallo, *Leopardi antitaliano* (Rome: Manifesto Libri, 1999), 42. The English translation is mine.

21. G. Bollati, "L'italiano" in *Storia d'Italia I: I caratteri originali* (Turin: Einaudi, 1972), 949–1022.

22. Ibid., 1015.

23. Cesare Luporini, "Leopardi moderno," interview with Ferdinando Adornato in *L'Espresso*, March 1, 1987, 108–16.

24. We might well recollect how, at an earlier point in his career, he instead stressed the revolutionary necessity of thinking against the grain of received ideas. As he put it in an interview in 1968: "A Marxist is a man who knows that in the process of history every value can be denied (or confirmed) by an antithetical value. Much of the work of Bertolt Brecht is based on this pitiless reversal." And in an essay published a year earlier in the *Times Literary Supplement*, he made clear that he considered Brecht the only authentic Marxist writer, because of the German playwright's disdain for superficial realism and preference for a provocative, paradoxical didacticism aimed at the "overturning of values." See "Two Interviews on Science and Literature" and "Philosophy and Literature," in *The Uses of Literature*, trans. Patrick Creagh (New York: Harcourt Brace, 1986), 36, 43.

25. Rancière, *Politics*, 61–62.

26. *The Uses of Literature*, 97.

27. Ibid., 98.

28. Asor Rosa, *Stile*, 129.

29. In the text itself, Calvino never makes reference to any non-Western art, with the sole exception of the anecdote of a Chinese painter that ends the memo "Quickness." The story recounts how Chuang-tzu, when commissioned by the king to draw a crab, asked for ten years of preparation time, after which he took up a brush and in one move drew "the most perfect crab ever seen" (*SM* 54). Calvino's emphasis on the uniformity, simplicity, and aesthetic perfection of the painting draws on the most entrenched Western clichés regarding the semiotic potential of Asian art.

30. Citati condemns *Six Memos* for its sterile approach to reality. See Pietro Citati, "Calvino così perspicace così cieco" in *Corriere della Sera*, June 4, 1988.

31. Benedetti's notion of "il postmoderno nazionale" may be meant to sum up not only the state of literature but of philosophy as well, particularly the contributions of Gianni Vattimo, Massimo Cacciari, and Aldo Gargani to the constellation of ideas that has been called "Weak Thought."

32. Benedetti, *Pasolini contro Calvino* (Turin: Bollati Boringhieri, 1998), 56–57. The English translation is mine.

33. Moresco, *Il vulcano* (Turin: Bollati Boringhieri, 1999), 21.

34. Ibid., 14.

35. In line with such a hermeneutics, the concluding paragraph of the lecture chillingly presents an idea of writing that strips language of everything but its typographical form and reduces all utterances to an empty, illegible, purgatorial spectacle: "Still, all 'realities' and 'fantasies' can take on form only by means of writing, in which outwardness and inwardness, the world and I, experience and fantasy, appear composed of the same verbal material. The polymorphic visions of the eyes and the spirit are contained in uniform lines of small or capital letters, periods, commas, parentheses—pages of signs, packed as closely together as grains of sand, representing the many-colored spectacle of the world on a surface that is always the same and always different, like dunes shifted by the desert wind" (*SM* 99).

36. Moresco, *Il vulcano*, 14.

37. Benedetti has criticized the assertion that the Italian tradition possesses no great novelists. See her *Il tradimento dei critici* (Turin: Bollati Boringhieri, 2002).

38. Giacomo Leopardi, *Discorso sopra lo stato presente dei costumi degli Italiani* ed. Maurizio Moncagatta (Milan: Feltrinelli, 1991), 49. When Gramsci complains about the lack of a national-popular culture in Italy, his comments in fact echo Leopardi's position. According to Gramsci, "A work of art is even more 'artistically' popular if its moral, cultural, and sentimental content adheres to the morality of culture, to national feelings, not meant as something static but as an activity in constant development." Antonio Gramsci, *Letteratura e vita nazionale* (Rome: Editori Riuniti, 1987, 27); my translation. What Gramsci means by the appellation "national-popular" is not, of course, a nationalistic and populist literature in the Fascist sense, but a literature that resists individualist and elitist positions in order to promote the general values and interests of the nation. For a useful commentary on the Gramscian notion of nazional-popolare, see Sanguinetti's "Introduzione," ibid., xxiv.

39. Leopardi, ibid., 49.

40. Gramsci, *Selections*, 236–37.

41. Ibid., 255.

42. Camus, *The Rebel* trans. Anthony Bower (New York: Knopf, 1954).

43. Walter Benjamin, "The Storyteller: Observations on the Works of Nikolai Leskov" in *Selected Writings*, Vol. 3: *1935–1938* ed. Howard Eiland and Michael Jennings, trans. Edmund Jephcott, Howard Eiland, et al. (Cambridge, MA: Belknap Press, 2002), 144.

44. Ibid., 145.

45. Ibid., 144.

46. Ibid., 146.

47. At that point, only the last lecture was still unfinished. Calvino was thinking of devoting it to the topic of "openness" (in the sense of frankness).

48. "The *Operette morali* is the book from which all I write derives" (*Saggi* I: xlviii). My translation.

49. Asor Rosa, *Stile*, 122–23. *Six Memos for the Next Millennium* may have been

modeled after Leopardi's text "Lettera a un giovane del ventesimo secolo." See Giacomo Leopardi, *Tutte le opere*, eds. Walter Binni and E. Ghidetti (Florence: Sansoni, 1969), I: 371.

50. Cesare Luporini, *Leopardi progressivo* (Rome: Editori Riuniti, 1980), 5.

51. Leopardi, *Tutte le Opere*, I: 1109. The letter is dated September 4, 1820, and makes reference to the first drafts of the *Operette*.

52. Giacomo Leopardi, *Zibaldone*, ed. Rolando Damiani (Milan: Mondadori, 1997), I: 1004. The translation is mine.

53. Giacomo Leopardi, *Operette morali*, ed. Antonio Prete (Milan: Feltrinelli, 1972), 59. All further citations will be from this edition; page references will be given in the text after the abbreviation *OM*.

54. Novella Celli Bellucci, *G. Leopardi e i contemporanei. Testimonianze dell'Italia e dell'Europa in vita e in morte del poeta* (Florence: Ponte alle Grazie, 1996), 237, 367.

55. Benedetto Croce, "Leopardi," in *Poesia e non poesia* (Bari: Laterza 1942), 98–99. For a criticism of the Crocean interpretation of Leopardi, see Giulio Bollati, *Crestomazia italiana la prosa* (Turin: Einaudi, 1978).

56. Croce, ibid., 98–99.

57. See Cesare Luporini, *Leopardi progressivo* (1947), and Walter Binni, *Nuova poetica leopardiana* (1947).

58. Antonio Negri, *Lenta ginestra. Saggio sull'ontologia di Giacomo Leopardi* (Milan: Mimesis Eterotopia, 2001), 53.

59. Even Calvino's distaste for an "anthropocentric" point of view should be read in continuity with Leopardi's lesson. Like Leopardi, Calvino privileges Galileo's precedent in the Italian cultural tradition as a critic of an anthropocentric metaphysics. For an incisive example of Leopardi's aggressively antianthropocentric stance, see "Dialogo di un folletto e di uno gnomo" and "Dialogo della terra e della luna" (*OM* 81–85, 91–97).

60. On Leopardi's interpretation of the Enlightenment, see Luporini, *Leopardi progressivo*, 45, 62–69.

61. Ibid., 18.

62. Negri, *Lenta ginestra*, 59.

63. Guido Guglielmi, *L'infinito terreno* (Florence: Piero Manni, 2000), 13.

64. Ibid., 69.

65. Ibid., 84.

66. Ibid., 90.

67. Calvino applies the same interpretive scheme to Balzac, whom he portrays as a convert from the "intensive" effort to capture "the world soul in a single symbol" to the "extensive" attempt "through writing to embrace the infinite stretch of space and time, swarming with multitudes, lives, and stories" (*SM* 98).

68. Giacomo Leopardi, *Canti*, ed. Fernando Bandini (Milan: Garzanti, 1975), 120.

69. See note 20 above.

Notes to Chapter 2   261

70. Walter Benjamin, *Arcades Project*, ed. Rolf Tideman, trans. Howard Eiland and Kevin McLaughlin (Cambridge, MA: Harvard University Press, 1999), 8, 18, 62, 894.

71. See his declaration that "melancholy is sadness that has taken on lightness" (*SM* 19) as well as his avowal that "I am a Saturn who dreams of being a Mercury, and everything I write reflects these two impulses" (*SM* 52).

72. "In this preference for short literary forms I am only following the true vocation of Italian literature, which is poor in novelists but rich in poets, who even when they write in prose give of their best in texts where the highest degree of invention and thought is contained in a few pages. This is the case with a book unparalleled in other literatures: Leopardi's *Operette morali*" (*SM*, 49).

73. Leopardi, *Epistolario* in *Tutte le Opere*, ed. Walter Binni (Florence: Sansoni, 1969), 1: 1109.

74. Ibid., 1: 1274.

75. Biscuso and Gallo, *Leopardi antitaliano*, 151.

76. As Guglielmi notices, the two characters in Leopardi always participate in a discursive process, opening themselves to the truth of the other. The resulting truth is therefore offered not in the guise of logical reasoning but in that of communicative reason (*L'infinito terreno*, 72).

77. I am referring to Giorgio Agamben's influential interpretation of Melville's story, "Bartleby, or On Contingency" in *Potentialities*, trans. Daniel Heller-Roazen (Stanford: Stanford University Press, 1999), 243–75.

78. Walter Binni, *Lettura delle Operette morali* (Genova: Marietti, 1987), 79.

79. Rainier Maria Rilke, *Letters to a Young Poet*, trans. Stephen Mitchell (New York: Modern Library, 1984), 37–38.

80. Sigmund Freud, *Collected Papers*, Vol. 5, ed. James Strachey (London: Hogarth Press, 1959), 105–6.

81. It is important on this score to compare Calvino's dismissal of the ethnic roots of Italian culture to Gramsci's pleas in favor of folklore and popular literature as the privileged expressions of a people. An attentive reading of Leopardi's *Zibaldone* makes clear that, like Gramsci, the Italian poet was chiefly interested in the national-popular dimension of Italian culture. On this point, see Luporini, 15.

82. Calvino gloomily draws the conclusion in "Visibility" that "our imagination cannot be anything but anthropomorphic" (*SM* 90). More than an anthropological impulse to literary creation, however, we encounter here a sort of anthropocentric compulsion.

83. Franz Kafka, "Der Kübelreiter," *Gesammelte Schriften*, Vol. 5, ed. Max Brod (New York: Schocken Books, 1937) 126; "The Bucket Rider," *The Complete Stories*, ed. Nahum N. Glatzer, trans. Willa and Edna Muir (New York: Schocken Books, 1971), 414.

84. Ibid., 413.

85. Ibid., 136.

86. In Italian the title of Kafka's story is translated "Il cavaliere del secchio," because in Italian there is no other way of translating *Reiter*. Calvino may have been misled by the Italian translation.

87. Walter Benjamin, "Franz Kafka on the Tenth Anniversary of His Death," *Illuminations*, ed. Hannah Arendt, trans. Harry Zohn (New York: Schocken Books, 1968), 138–39.

88. Benjamin, "Some Reflections on Kafka," *Illuminations*, 144.

89. Perhaps the one significant philosophical consequence of Calvino's conception of lightness is a deconstruction of materialism meant as a philosophy of ontological and ethical resistance. In this regard, Calvino's ascription to Lucretius of the merit of having written the kind of poetry in which knowledge of the world entails dissolution of the very texture and consistency of the cosmos is exemplary. In contrast to Calvino, Antonio Negri singles out Lucretius as the first philosopher to have raised the question of freedom and innovation in the materialist tradition through the notion of *clinamen*, which was his term for the random swerving of atoms that in his view made manifest the free will of living beings. Calvino instead confines Lucretius to a fulfilled, light ontological ground where ethical problems cannot emerge. For Negri's thinking on this topic, see his *Kairós, Alma Venus, Multitudo* (Rome: Manifesto Libri, 2000).

90. Milan Kundera, *The Unbearable Lightness of Being* trans. Michael Henry Heim (New York: Harper, 1984), 3.

91. Ibid., 4.

92. Ibid., 5.

93. Oliver Goldsmith's *The Vicar of Wakefield*, Kafka's *Amerika*, and Melville's "Bartleby, the Scrivener" are the three texts that Calvino mentions in draft notes in connection with his intended discussion of the question of intersubjectivity. However, Barenghi believes that only "Bartleby" would have remained in the final version of "Consistency."

94. "Mondo scritto e mondo non scritto" in *Saggi* 2: 1865–75.

95. Benedetti, *Pasolini contro Calvino*, 126. Toward the end of *Invisible Cities*, Calvino makes gestures toward a more ethical point of view. Yet such gestures operate negatively by simply associating literature with everything that is "not inferno," a strategy that seems merely opportunistic.

96. In the Italian text, it should be noted, the last word is *estraneazione* (estrangement) rather than *alienazione* (alienation; *Saggi* I: 711).

97. "Probably for the first time in the history of the world, there is an author who recounts the exhaustion of all stories" (*Saggi* 1: 753; my translation).

98. On irony as a mere mode of citation, see Benedetti, *Pasolini contro Calvino*, 95.

99. Umberto Eco, "Author's Postscript" to *The Name of the Rose*, trans. William Weaver (San Diego: Harcourt, 1994), 530–31.

100. From the beginning, the narrator presents himself as a powerbroker

complimented by Wall Street royalty such as John Jacob Astor for his "prudence" and "method" (40). It is worth recalling as well that the full title of the story is "Bartleby, The Scrivener: A Story of Wall Street." Herman Melville, *Great Short Works*, ed. Warner Berthoff (New York: Perennial Classic, 1969), 39. All further citations will be from this edition; page references will be given in the text after the abbreviation *GSW*.

101. Agamben, "Bartleby, or on Contingency," in *Potentialities*, trans. Daniel Heller-Roazen (Stanford: Stanford University Press, 1999), 243–71. Agamben's invocation of "pure, absolute potentiality" and protest against the "perpetual illusion" of the ethical tradition, which he believes has unduly transformed potentiality into will, occur on page 254.

102. Ibid., 254.

103. Ibid., 259.

104. Agamben's work does not belong to the school of "Weak Thought" chiefly epitomized by Gianni Vattimo, Pier Aldo Rovatti, and Massimo Cacciari. However, Agamben's interpretation of "Bartleby" enforces a nihilistic position that is very close to the philosophical style of the weak philosophers.

105. Michael Hardt and Antonio Negri, *Empire* (Cambridge, MA: Harvard University Press, 2000), 203.

106. Ibid., 204.

107. Ibid., 204.

CHAPTER 3

1. Gianni Vattimo and Pier Aldo Rovatti, eds., *Il pensiero debole* (Milan: Feltrinelli, 1983). The other contributors were Leonardo Amoroso, Gianni Carchia, Giampiero Comolli, Filippo Costa, Franco Crespi, Alessandro Dal Lago, Umberto Eco, Maurizio Ferraris, and Diego Marconi. All further page references for this text will follow the abbreviation *PD*; all translations into English are mine.

2. Italy has been an important site for Nietzsche studies ever since the scholars Giorgio Colli and Mazzino Montanari began curating what has become the philologically definitive edition of Nietzsche's works. Adelphi started publishing this edition in Italian in 1963, followed by Gallimard in French, and Walter de Gruyter in German.

3. Fond of the passage in *Twilight of the Idols* in which Nietzsche declares that the "'Real World' at last became a myth," Vattimo concludes in *The Adventure of Difference* that "What Nietzsche calls the world as will to power is this play of 'interpretations' imposing themselves without any 'facts'. . . . This world is like a 'work of art that creates itself.'" Gianni Vattimo, *The Adventure of Difference: Philosophy After Nietzsche and Heidegger*, trans. Cyprian Blamires with the assistance of Thomas Harrison (Baltimore: Johns Hopkins University Press, 1993), 92. Hereafter, citations of this edition will be denoted by the abbreviation *AD*.

Only relatively recently has Vattimo overturned his previous position, affirming that the task of philosophy is neither artistic nor literary, but rather edifying and persuasive. Vattimo, *Vocazione e responsabilità del filosofo*, ed. Franca D'Agostini (Genoa: Il Melangelo, 2000), 77. Further references to this text will use the abbreviation *VRF*.

4. Rovatti's "Narrare un soggetto," which is collected in *Elogio del pudore: Per un pensiero debole*, eds. Alessandro Dal Lago and Pier Aldo Rovatti (Milan: Feltrinelli, 1989), 117–23, is dedicated to a celebration of Calvino's *Palomar*.

5. Ibid., 117.

6. Ibid., 118–19.

7. Ibid., 123.

8. Mario Perniola, *Contro la comunicazione* (Milan: Einaudi, 2004), 105.

9. Ibid., 106–7.

10. Eco, "L'antiporfirio" in *PD*, 52–90.

11. Carlo Augusto Viano, *Va pensiero: Il carattere della filosofia italiana contemporanea* (Turin: Einaudi, 1985), 15. Further citations from this edition will use the abbreviation *VP*.

12. Perry Anderson, "An Invertebrate Left," in *London Review of Books*, 31:5 (March 12, 2009), 12–18.

13. Aldo Giorgio Gargani, *Crisi della ragione: Nuovi modelli nel rapporto tra sapere e attività umane* (Turin: Einaudi, 1979). The volume contains essays by Gargani, Carlo Ginzburg (who contributed an influential essay titled "Spie: Radici di un paradigma indiziario"), Giulio Lepschy, Francesco Orlando, Franco Rella, Vittorio Strada, Remo Bodei, Nicola Badaloni, Salvatore Veca, and Carlo Augusto Viano. All further citations will feature page references following the abbreviation *CR*.

14. On this issue, see Gargani's introduction (*CR*, 3–57).

15. The abandonment of Marxism by Vattimo, Rovatti, and their associates played an exemplary role in its cultural moment: "The late 'renaissance' of Heideggerian and Nietzschean studies, the dissemination of French poststructuralism, the renewed interest in the culture of Vienna of the first decades of our century and in some themes of the Frankfurt School, all coincide in contemporary Italy with the crisis of Marxist historicism, which had been a kind of common ground for most Italian thinkers in the fifties and sixties, prior to the pervasive diffusion of structuralism." Steffano Rosso, "Postmodern Italy: Notes on the 'Crisis of Reason,' 'Weak Thought,' and *The Name of the Rose*," in *Exploring Postmodernism: Selected Papers Presented at a Workshop on Postmodernism at the 11th International Comparative Literature Congress, Paris, 20–24 August 1985*, eds. Matei Calinescu and Douwe Fokkema (Amsterdam and Philadelphia: John Benjamins, 1987), 80. It is telling that Rosso places the Heideggerian and Nietzschean concerns of weak thought in the lead position in his list of contemporary Italian philosophical currents.

16. Gianni Vattimo, *The End of Modernity*, trans. Jon R. Snyder (Baltimore:

Johns Hopkins Press, 1985), 164. Hereafter, page references from this edition follow the abbreviation *EOM*.

17. Gianni Vattimo, *The Transparent Society*, trans. David Webb (Baltimore: Johns Hopkins Press, 1992), 46. Cf. Vattimo's reference to "the critical power of the work vis-à-vis the existing reality" in *La società trasparente*, 3rd ed. (Milan: Garzanti, 2000), 65 (my translation). Additional citations will denote these editions with the abbreviations *TS* and *ST*. It is important to be aware that the third Italian edition substitutes a new final chapter for the last three chapters of Webb's translation. Wherever possible, I cite Webb's translation, but where doing so is not possible, I cite the Garzanti edition published in 2000 and give my own translation.

18. Nietzsche, *The Will to Power*, trans. Walter Kaufmann and R. J. Hollingdale (New York: Vintage, 1968), 4.

19. See Heidegger, *Nietzsche*, vol. II: *The Eternal Recurrence of the Same* (1961), trans. David F. Krell (New York: Harper and Row, 1984).

20. See note 17 regarding Italian-only citation of this text. Not surprisingly, Vattimo accuses Jameson of still being conditioned by Adornian presuppositions (*ST*, 204).

21. For an excellent study of the limits of secularism as an intellectual position, see William E. Connolly, *Why I Am Not a Secularist* (Minneapolis: University of Minnesota Press, 1999). Connolly is also the author of *Capitalism and Christianity, American Style* (Durham, NC: Duke University Press, 2008), which, though obviously analyzing the specific religious logic of contemporary American culture, makes several points that in my opinion are highly relevant to a diagnosis of the Italian situation.

22. Gianni Vattimo with Piergiorgio Paterlini, *Not Being God: A Collaborative Autobiography*, trans. William McCuaig (New York: Columbia University Press, 2009), 107. Further citations of this edition will be denoted with the abbreviation *NBG*.

23. Gianni Vattimo, *Ecce comu: Come si ridiventa ciò che si era* (Rome: Fazi, 2007). Hereafter, all references from this edition are abbreviated *EC*; all translations into English are mine. Negri has recognized Vattimo's recent efforts at self-critique but observes that Vattimo's attempts in the 1970s to weaken Marxism by depriving it of a teleology and of any belief in historical progress denies Marxism its potential as a strategy of resistance. According to Negri, Vattimo's position surrenders to a notion of Being that ultimately views the market as a form of nature. See Antonio Negri, *Movimenti nell'impero: Passaggi e paesaggi* (Milan: Raffaello Cortina, 2006), 258.

24. Vattimo goes so far as to assign to the term *postmodernity* not only a descriptive function but also the role of a "normative ideal." See *Nihilism and Emancipation: Ethics, Politics, & Law*, ed. Santiago Zabala, trans. William McCuaig (New York: Columbia University Press, 2004), 11. Hereafter, I give page references from this edition following the abbreviation *NE*.

25. William McCuaig renders Vattimo's sentence "io posso dire di essere l'unico vero filosofo italiano popolare" with misleading blandness as "what they've achieved [i.e. Vattimo's detractors] is to make me the only Italian philosopher well known to the public" (*NBG*, 92). McCuaig's translation suppresses the first-person assertiveness of "io posso dire" and wrongly avoids using the cognate "popular" for the crucial adjective "popolare," which, in addition to being more direct than the epithet "well known to the public," evokes Gramsci's terminology and thus suggests Vattimo's desire to affirm weak thought as the democratic expression of a national-popular culture.

26. Giovanna Borradori has explicitly linked weak thought to the Transavanguardia's practice of "radical quotationism." Her book is a helpful overview of Italian poststructuralist thought, although at times perhaps a bit too celebratory of its topic. Borradori, ed., *Recoding Metaphysics: The New Italian Philosophy* (Evanston, IN: Northwestern University Press, 1988), 5.

27. It might be helpful to consider why Vattimo avoided the category of "lightness" and instead settled on that of "weakness" as his master signifier. From a genealogical perspective, the former category attains a positive valence in Nietzsche's philosophy that the latter does not possess. In this connection, we ought to recall that Nietzsche opposes a semiotics of heaviness to that of lightness, interpreting the latter as the quality of the will to power that is linked to a noble, affirmative, and light soul ("Beyond Good and Evil" BGE 287, French p, 196). In a somewhat cryptic passage in *Thus Spoke Zarathustra*, Nietzsche appears to redescribe the *Übermensch* as "he who will one day teach men to fly," as a figure who "will rebaptize the earth('the light one.'" *Thus Spoke Zarathustra*, trans. Walter Kaufmann (New York: Viking Penguin, 1966), 192 (cf. p. 210, French). Unlike weakness, "lightness" in Nietzsche's writing signifies the dancing, affirmative joy of the active nihilist. As Deleuze puts it, "*High* and *noble* designate for Nietzsche the superiority of active forces, their affinity with affirmation, their tendency to ascend, their lightness. *Low* and *base* designate the triumph of reactive forces, their affinity with the negative, their heaviness and clumsiness." Gilles Deleuze, *Nietzsche and Philosophy*, trans. Hugh Tomlinson (London: Athlone Press, 1983), 86. As is well known, weakness for Nietzsche is linked to the moralist mentality of *ressentiment* and is a symptom of decadence. By choosing weakness as a master signifier, Vattimo implicitly seems to criticize the vitalist Nietzsche, who perpetually engages in critical evaluation and transvaluation of cultural conventions, preferring instead a tamer view of Nietzsche as a strictly metaphysical thinker.

28. See Jacques Rancière, *The Politics of Aesthetics: the Distribution of the Sensible*, trans. Gabriel Rockhill (New York: Continuum, 2004). Among the books that have insisted on a revival of aesthetics over the last dozen years or so, see Jonathan Loesberg, *A Return to Aesthetics: Autonomy, Indifference, and Postmodernism* (Stanford: Stanford University Press, 2005); Arthur C. Danto, *The Abuse of Beauty: Aesthetics and the Concept of Art* (Chicago: Open Court, 2003); Brian

Massumi, *Parables of the Virtual: Movement, Affect, Sensation* (Durham, NC: Duke University Press, 2002); Isobel Armstrong, *The Radical Aesthetic* (Oxford: Blackwell, 2000); and Elaine Scarry, *On Beauty and Being Just* (Princeton: Princeton University Press, 1999).

29. Early on, some philosophers such as Philippe Lacoue-Labarthe expressed dismay over the complacency of weak thought. See Lacoue-Labarthe's *Heidegger, Art and Politics: The Fiction of the Political*, trans. Chris Turner (Oxford, UK: Blackwell, 1990), 6. By contrast, Richard Rorty considered his own neopragmatism to be similar to weak thought and declared himself at a conference in London to be a weak thinker (*NBG*, 99).

30. His most prominent critics in Italy have been Carlo Augusto Viano, Massimo Cacciari, Carlo Sini, and Antonio Negri.

31. Borradori succinctly explains how important the historicist interpretation of hermeneutics and the anti-Cartesian, antirationalist stance have been to the genealogy of weak thought. She observes that in Italy philosophy per se was relegated to a marginal position in the twentieth century as a result of the lingering influence of Vico's "anti-Enlightenment" historicism and Croce's rereading of Hegel's idealism in a historicist key (*Recoding Metaphysics*, 1–9). In both cases (Vico and Croce), we are dealing with anticritical thinkers who wish to avoid methodologically and ideologically problematic questions. Borradori observes, for example, how in Croce's thought there was no real critical problem involved even in consideration of historiography, as "life" and "reality" for him were synonymous with history (ibid., 9). Whereas the French poststructuralists were proposing a more radical dissolution of metaphysics on a variety of fronts, the Italian thinkers were content with a nihilistic historicism (ibid., 17).

32. Jürgen Habermas, *The Philosophical Discourse of Modernity*, trans. Frederick G. Lawrence (Cambridge, MA: MIT Press, 1987). In the ninth and tenth chapters of his *Discourse*, Habermas criticizes Foucault's claims of offering an emancipatory project, because the French philosopher's proposition that truth and power are interconnected allegedly leaves little logical space for an oppositional politics. Richard Rorty is fully in agreement with Habermas on this point; cf. Rorty's *Truth and Progress: Philosophical Papers, Vol. 3* (Cambridge, UK: Cambridge University Press, 1998), 310.

33. In a pamphlet entitled *La pensée 68*, Luc Ferry and Alain Renault tried to dismiss the merits of French poststructuralism as a "hyperbolic" recapitulation of German nihilism by identifying the supposedly exclusively German pedigree of both Derrida (Heidegger) and Foucault (Heidegger plus Nietzsche). Yet neither Derrida nor Foucault functions as a philosophical ventriloquist or pretends to "correspond" with his sources in a state of philosophical empathy.

34. Jacques Derrida and Elisabeth Roudinesco, *For What Tomorrow*, trans. Jeff Fort (Stanford: Stanford University Press, 2004), 124. For both Derrida and Foucault, it is important to identify strategies of resistance, as Foucault states in *Dits et*

écrits, tome 2: 1976–1988 (Paris: Gallimard, 2001), 1560, and Derrida in *Résistances de la psychoanalyse* (Paris: Galilée, 1996).

35. After the "epic" experience of discovering Nietzsche, Vattimo counts the study of Heidegger as, in his words, "the second great erotic-philosophical adventure of my life" (*NBG*, 15). After a youth of active participation in Catholic groups, Vattimo was hired by the RAI in 1955 along with Umberto Eco and Furio Colombo, where they developed a successful pedagogical television show about contemporary Italian culture titled *Orizzonte* (Horizon). After studying in Heidelberg with Karl Löwith and Hans-Georg Gadamer, whose magnum opus *Truth and Method* he began translating in the early 1960s, Vattimo published *Essere, storia e linguaggio in Heidegger* with Edizioni di Filosofia in 1963, a text that inaugurates his lifelong project of "urbanizing" Heidegger beyond Gadamer's wildest dreams. In 1964, he started his academic career as an assistant professor of aesthetics at the University of Turin. That same year, he participated in a colloquium on Nietzsche at the Abbaye de Royaumont that was widely held responsible for the renaissance of Nietzsche's thought in Europe in the following years. For a more detailed account of these years, see *NBG*, 14–54.

36. Vattimo characterizes Heidegger's apologetic attitude as "scandalous" and "problematic," only to proclaim (with a vengeance) Heidegger's philosophical victory over the likes of Adorno, whom Vattimo condemns for being attached mistakenly to a "dialectical notion of the subject." Vattimo instead supposes the Heideggerian notion of *Ge-stell* to dissolve any categorical opposition between subject and object. As is frequently the case, Vattimo seems here to grant Heidegger a philosophically Pyrrhic victory. See Vattimo's "Metaphysics and Violence" in *Weakening Philosophy: Festschrift in Honor of Professor Gianni Vattimo*, ed. Santiago Zabala (Montreal: McGill-Queen's University Press, 2007), 418.

37. Ibid., 418.

38. It is useful on this question to compare the position of Vattimo's philosophical ally Richard Rorty, who in *Truth and Progress* defines the question of power as a useless remainder of a metaphysical past. Rorty holds that Foucault views modern Western society as a panopticon in which individuality and rationality increasingly have become impossible, whereas Dewey recognizes the wealth, technology, and security of modernity as means that make it easier to achieve the ends of individuality and rationality. Rorty, *Truth and Progress*, 198.

39. Vattimo dedicated one of his early books, *Il soggetto e la maschera* (1974), to a more Dionysian reading of Nietzsche that at one point interprets the Übermensch as a revolutionary subject. However, this thesis is quickly abandoned in the course of the book's argument.

40. According to Vattimo, "we still require an ontology, if for no other purpose than to demonstrate that ontology is headed toward disintegration" (*NE*, 19).

41. *Weakening Philosophy*, 17.

42. Ibid., 81.

43. Ibid., 13. Cf. "Revolutionary Moralism" in *NBG*, 84–85.

44. Tronti authored the groundbreaking book *Operai e capitale* (1966), in which he calls for redirection of attention from the operation of capital to the workers' role within this system. Tronti thus helps to usher in a new logic of empowerment that leads to the movement of *Autonomia Operaia* and represents, along with Negri's pioneering work, the first inklings of the changed physiognomy and rhythm of contemporary labor. Despite being suspicious of some *autonomi* who did not shrink from revolutionary acts of violence, Vattimo confesses in his autobiography to being fond generally of the term *autonomy*, which evokes "a different notion of politics" from the one he now holds. In his opinion, the notion of autonomia also subtly hints at the idea of "weakening as a way of eluding power" (*NBG*, 84–85).

45. Occasionally, Vattimo has proposed to read Heidegger in continuity with Marx, a project that he admits might seem "incredible." He suggests a spurious correspondence between Heidegger's forgetting of Being and Marx's alienation (*NBG*, 60). Cf. also Vattimo, *Addio alla verità* (Rome: Meltemi, 2009) 13, 30–34, which I will cite hereafter using the abbreviation *AV*, and *Ecce comu*.

46. See in particular "I limiti della derealizzazione" (The Limits of Derealization), the final chapter of the third edition of *La società trasparente*, which is available only in Italian (*ST*, 101–121). Also, see note 17 for more on the discrepancy between the third Italian edition and the currently available English translation by David Webb.

47. Antonio Negri, *La differenza italiana* (Rome: Nottetempo, 2005), 6–8.

48. As Samuel Weber has pointed out, Derrida started in the 1970s to pursue political projects revolving around local, institutional practices. For example, he and other intellectuals in France worked to found an organization of teachers in 1975 whose purpose was to expand the limited role of philosophy in the secondary school curriculum, thus resisting government plans to eliminate the teaching of philosophy in the last year of the *lycée* in favor of more technocratic training. From these interventions at what Weber calls the "micropolitical" level, Derrida moved to address more broadly conceived, "macropolitical" questions in the writings that he published in later years, beginning with *On Spirit* (1987) and *On the Right to Philosophy* (1988). Samuel Weber, "Rogue Democracy and the Hidden God," in *Political Theologies: Public Religions in a Post-Secular World*, eds. Hent de Vries and Eugene Sullivan (Bronx: Fordham University Press, 2006), 382–84.

49. Paul Patton, *Deleuze and the Political* (New York: Routledge, 2000).

50. Zygmunt Bauman, *Liquid Modernity* (Cambridge, UK: Polity, 2000), 1–15. Bauman suggests that our society is no longer hospitable to the kind of "solid," "heavy" critique practiced by Adorno and Horkheimer, because the frame of contemporary life has changed, so that critical theory no longer needs to define its purpose as the defense of individual autonomy and freedom of choice against the threat of totalitarianism (ibid., 25–26). For Bauman, the overridingly important task of critical theory today is, instead, the defense of the vanishing public realm.

51. See Viano's *Va pensiero* as cited in note 11. Vattimo in fact coined the term *weak thought* in response to Viano's essay "La ragione, l'abbondanza e la credenza," which was published in *Crisi della ragione* (1979), the anthology edited by Aldo Giorgio Gargani; see note 13 for more on this volume. The origin of the name is recounted by Vattimo in *Belief*, trans. Luca D'Isanto and David Webb (Stanford: Stanford University Press, 1999), 34–35. References hereafter to this edition will be denoted by the abbreviation *B*. It might be observed as well that Vattimo's first statement of something resembling his mature theory of weakness occurs in 1979 in the essay "Verso un'ontologia del declino," where he describes Heidegger's philosophy as an "ontology of decline." For the English translation of this essay, see "Toward an Ontology of Decline," in Borradori, *Recoding Metaphysics*, 63–75.

52. Viano offers as a prominent example Croce's and Gentile's brand of idealism, which claimed to resolve the contradictions of Hegelian philosophy (*VP*, viii–ix).

53. Viano, *VP*, 6–8. For Viano, one of the most disconcerting positions of the gentle and hypertolerant *flebili* is their determination to present even the "terrible" Heidegger as a "benevolent grandpa," an attitude that symptomizes the school's general indifference to ethical and political questions (*VP*, 8).

54. Consider also this statement: "We should promote a free and intense coexistence of multiple symbolic universes in a spirit of hospitality that well expresses the lay orientation of western culture, and its deeply religious origin, perhaps taking the museum, with its juxtaposition of different styles, tastes and culture, as a symbolic model of democracy." Vattimo, *After Christianity*, trans. Luca D'Isanto (New York: Columbia University Press, 2002), 102. Further citations of this edition will give page references following the abbreviation *AC*.

55. Theodor W. Adorno, *Prisms*, trans. Samuel M. Weber (Cambridge, MA: MIT Press, 1981), 176. Adorno's essay, which was a response to Valéry's "Le problème des musées," has been developed in a more critical direction by Baudrillard, who defines the museum in "Le système des objets" (1968) as the main method of transition from use value to the wish fulfillment of advertising. Baudrillard's essay has been reprinted in English in his *Selected Writings*, ed. Mark Poster (Stanford: Stanford University Press, 2001), 13–31. More recently, Douglas Crimp in *The Museum's Ruins* (Cambridge, MA: MIT Press, 1993) advances the line of critical questioning yet further. In an incisive study, Chantal Georgel points out that the museum actually follows the logic of the department store. See Georgel, "The Museum as a Metaphor in Nineteenth-Century France," in *Museum Culture: History, Discourses, Spectacles*, eds. Irit Rogoff and Daniel Sherman (London: Routledge, 1994), 119. In their introduction to the volume, Sherman and Rogoff observe that in both America and Europe the museum has been used by the bourgeois élite to legitimate their political power through institutionalization of cultural hegemony (ibid., xvi).

56. Cf. Salvatore Settis, *Italia S.P.A.: L'assalto al patrimonio culturale* (Turin: Einaudi, 2002); and *Battaglie senza eroi: I beni culturali tra istituzioni e profitto* (Milan: Electa, 2005).

57. "Where there is power, there is resistance, and yet, or rather consequently, this resistance is never in a position of exteriority in relation to power." Michel Foucault, *The History of Sexuality*, Vol. 1: *An Introduction*, trans. Robert Hurley (New York: Vintage Books, 1978), 95. Derrida first introduced the term *différance*, spelled eccentrically with an *a*, in an essay on Artaud, "La parole soufflée," in 1965, and then in a longer essay, "Différance," which was presented as a lecture on January 27, 1968, to the Société française de philosophie. See also note 106 of this chapter.

58. Theodor W. Adorno, *The Jargon of Authenticity*, trans. Knut Tarnowski and Frederic Will (Evanston, IN: Northwestern University Press, 1993), xxii. I give page references in further citations of this edition following the abbreviation *JA*.

59. For example, Adorno pointed out how obsessive use of the word *shelter* was indeed linked to the fear of unemployment (*JA*, 34).

60. D. Medina Lasansky traces the origins of this strategy back to Fascism but notes that in the postwar years it metastasized into nothing less than a celebration of Italian capitalism: "The Italian government's interest in the Middle Ages and Renaissance continued after the fall of Mussolini's government. During the post–World War II period, the celebration of this past played an important role in re-establishing economic stability and physical rejuvenation. In David Lowenthal's words, 'heritage is entrepreneurial.' Towns throughout the country, particularly those ravaged by the war, realized that they could capitalize on the broad-based appeal of the Italian Middle Ages and Renaissance. Tourist initiatives launched during the Fascist regime were restaged, depoliticized, and marketed with the objective of achieving commercial success." Lasansky, *The Renaissance Perfected: Architecture, Spectacle, and Tourism in Fascist Italy* (University Park: Pennsylvania State University Press, 2004), 217. One well may ask in response to this analysis if it is realistic to believe that such initiatives actually can be "depoliticized" or if, in fact, their politics for the most part have been ignored.

61. Verwindung is a concept that appears only a few times in Heidegger's work, in particular in *Holzwege*, *Vorträge und Aufsätze*, and *Identity and Difference*. Vattimo discusses the concept in terms of resignation (*EOM*, 172–73).

62. In my analysis of the auratic function of certain words, I am inspired by Adorno's reflections (*JA*, 9–14).

63. Here I am using an expression first employed by Adorno vis-à-vis Heidegger. Adorno pointed out that Heidegger was not, in his opinion, the worst offender or "matador" of the political strategy enacted by the jargon of authenticity (*JA*, 49).

64. Vattimo might be thinking of Cacciari's work in particular, but more recently I would suggest that the work of Giorgio Agamben best corresponds to Vattimo's characterization.

65. In *Vocazione*, Vattimo argues that the exhortative aims of philosophy may have important consequences because what is at stake is not only an exercise of

style but also a call to responsibility (*VRF*, 65). One might well ask, however, whether exhortation through reiteration rather than through analysis, criticism, or argumentation is really the best vehicle for authentic affirmation of responsibility.

66. "What Is Critique?" in Michel Foucault, *The Politics of Truth*, eds. Sylvère Lotringer and Lysa Hochroch (New York: Semiotext(e), 1997), 37.

67. Gianni Vattimo, *Beyond Interpretation: The Meaning of Hermeneutics for Philosophy*, trans. David Webb (Cambridge, UK: Polity Press, 1997), ix–x. Cf. Vattimo, *Oltre l'interpretazione: Il significato dell'eremeneutica per la filosofia* (Rome-Bari: Editori Laterza, 1994), ix–xi. Additional citations of these editions will give page references following the abbreviations *BI* and *OI*.

68. Jacques Derrida, *Writing and Difference*, trans. Alan Bass (Chicago: University of Chicago Press, 1978), 20. For a closer look at Derrida's exploration of the legacy of structuralism, see the section "Choosing One's Heritage" in Jacques Derrida and Elizabeth Roudinesco, *For What Tomorrow: A Dialogue*, trans. Jeff Fort (Stanford: Stanford University Press, 2004), 7.

69. Gilles Deleuze, *Nietzsche and Philosophy*, trans. Hugh Tomlinson (New York: Columbia University Press, 1983), 89.

70. Ibid., 1.

71. The citation of Nietzsche is from *La Volonté de puissance, tome 2*, trad. Geneviève Bianquis (Paris: Gallimard, 1995), 29. The citation of Deleuze is from *Nietzsche and Philosophy*, 6.

72. See in particular Foucault's "What Is Enlightenment?" in *The Foucault Reader*, ed. Paul Rabinow (New York: Pantheon Books, 1984), 32–50.

73. Deleuze helps us understand what impulses lie behind the conservative reading of Nietzsche. In Deleuze's eyes, the German philosopher's "most general project was the introduction of the notion of sense and value into philosophy" (*Nietzsche and Philosophy*, 1). However, some readers have absorbed the notion of value as the basis of philosophy without also recognizing that value itself arises from the strife of critical evaluation, thus placing themselves "at the service of modern conformism" (ibid., 1). These readers fail to grasp that Nietzsche's emphasis on the relation between evaluation and value aims to rebuke, among others, "those who remove values from criticism, contenting themselves with producing inventories of existing values or with criticising things in the name of established values" (ibid., 2). As Deleuze aptly puts it, "With Nietzsche, we must begin with the fact that the philosophy of values as envisaged and established by him is the true realisation of critique and the only way in which a total critique might be realised" (ibid., 1).

74. Luperini, *La fine del postmoderno* (Naples: Guida, 2008), 22.

75. Only lately has Vattimo acknowledged that Italy is the country where the influence of the mass media on politics has manifested its effects most intensely (*EC*, 45). Indeed, he even admits in *Ecce comu* that, by promoting the supposed demise of ideologies under postmodernity, he contributed to the specific form of empiricism in Italy that ultimately led to "Craxism," which is to say the corrupt

opportunism that was characteristic of Bettino Craxi, who was Berlusconi's early political patron (*EC*, 33). Already in 1990, Philippe Lacoue-Labarthe had exposed the complacency of weak thought sponsored by Vattimo and Rovatti, which he rightly inscribes in a rejection of the heroism of modernity advocated by Baudelaire and Benjamin. Lacoue-Labarthe, *Heidegger, Art and Politics*, 6.

76. Nietzsche named Cesare Borgia as a type of the Übermensch in *Beyond Good and Evil*. See section 197 in Friedrich Nietzsche, *Beyond Good and Evil: Prelude to a Philosophy of the Future*, trans. Walter Kauffman (New York: Vintage, 1966), 108. For discussion of the Renaissance as a "strong age" and Borgia as one of its exemplary figures, see Friedrich Nietzsche, *Twilight of the Idols* and *The Anti-Christ*, trans. R. J. Hollingdale (London: Penguin, 1968), 89–92, section 37 of *Twilight of the Idols*.

77. For an interesting collection of studies of the relation between Nietzsche and Italian culture, see Thomas Harrison, ed., *Nietzsche in Italy* (Saratoga, CA: Anma Libri, 1988).

78. Luigi Barzini, *The Italians: A Full-Length Portrait Featuring Their Manners and Morals* (New York: Simon and Schuster, 1996), 12.

79. Ibid., 56–57.

80. Ibid., 72.

81. In fact, the first section of *The End of Modernity* is titled "Il nichilismo come destino" (Nihilism as Destiny).

82. In a dialectical move, Vattimo proposes that accomplishment of nihilism, broadly defined as loss of value in the world, is also the first step in overcoming it. Vattimo, *Dialogue with Nietzsche*, trans. William McCuaig (New York: Columbia University Press, 2006), 35.

83. See for example Heidegger's *Nietzsche*, where Heidegger characterizes Nietzsche's thought, precisely because of its nihilist inclinations, as the end of Western philosophy in the sense of being both the completion and the exhaustion of the possibilities of metaphysics.

84. For a cogent analysis of the distance between the Heideggerian and Nietzschean definitions of nihilism, see Giacomo Marramao, *Kairós: Apologia del Tempo Debito* (Bari: Laterza, 1992).

85. Rorty translates "the Heideggerian left" as "commonsense Heideggerianism" in the Foreword to the English edition of *Nihilism and Emancipation* (*NE*, ix). Derrida instead explicitly attacks the idea of "a Heideggerianism of the left" in *Points*, arguing that it is a mistake to grant any credibility, even in reserve, to the possibility of a "good and reassuring politics" in the German philosopher's work. See Jacques Derrida, *Points . . . Interviews, 1974–1994*, ed. Elisabeth Weber, trans. Peggy Kamuf and others (Stanford: Stanford University Press, 1995), 182–183.

86. Martin Heidegger, *Nietzsche*, Vol. IV: *Nihilism*, ed. David Farrell Krell, trans. Joan Stambaugh, David Farrell Krell, Frank A. Capuzzi (New York: Harper & Row, 1982), 201.

87. Published in 1961, Heidegger's *Nietzsche* gathers lectures on Nietzsche from the 1930s and 1940s. The study focuses in particular on Nietzsche's late writings and the two fundamental notions of the will to power and the eternal recurrence of the same. Heidegger regards Nietzsche as the philosopher whose thought represents the culmination of metaphysics, as a thinker of Being rather than as a cultural critic. On this reckoning, Nietzsche's biologism is a symptom of his metaphysical equation of life with will to power. For Heidegger, the Greeks were the first to define Being as the permanence of presence, a notion that he believes Nietzsche carries to its ultimate conclusion in the will to "permanentize" becoming into presence, which is to say in the will to power, by affirming the eternal return. To substantiate his assertion that Nietzsche's philosophy aims at "the permanentizing of the absolute essence of will to power as the fundamental character of beings," Heidegger cites a note that Nietzsche wrote in 1888, the last year of his life: "To *stamp* becoming with the character of being—that is the supreme *will to power.*" Heidegger, *Nietzsche*, Vol. III: *The Will to Power as Knowledge and as Metaphysics*, ed. David Farrell Krell, trans. Joan Stambaugh, David Farrell Krell, Frank A. Capuzzi (New York: Harper & Row, 1987), 245. Cf. Heidegger, *Nietzsche*, Vol. II: *The Eternal Recurrence of the Same*, trans. David Farrell Krell (New York: Harper & Row, 1984), 200–201.

88. Ibid., 189.

89. Vattimo, *Dialogue with Nietzsche*, 186–87.

90. Ibid., 187.

91. A few paragraphs later, rhapsodizing in Lacanian lingo about the benefits of exchange value, Vattimo concludes that "the world of exchange value is not only, and necessarily, the Imaginary in the Lacanian sense of the term—for it is not only an alienated rigidity, but may assume the peculiar mobility of the symbolic (though this indeed still depends upon an individual or social decision)" (*EOM*, 27).

92. Adorno, *Negative Dialectics*, 94. According to Martin Jay, Adorno was much keener in criticizing the role of exchange value in a capitalist culture than reification, as Lukács had done. See Jay's *The Dialectical Imagination: A History of the Frankfurt School and the Institute of Social Research* (Berkeley: University of California Press, 1996).

93. Vattimo, *Dialogue with Nietzsche*, 134–35. For Heidegger, one of the characteristics of active, "classical" nihilism in Nietzsche is the claim that will to power opens paths to new possibilities of the world through analysis. On the other hand, Heidegger also notes that there is a weak form of nihilism that is doomed to embrace decay, is obsessed with historicist explanations, and typically adopts an attitude of resignation (*Nietzsche*, Vol. II, 206; *Nietzsche*, Vol. IV, 54). Vattimo's collapsing of active and passive nihilism is of fundamental importance to understanding the "reactive," ultimately apologetic stance of his philosophy. In *Nihilism and Emancipation*, Vattimo makes a cursory reference to active nihilism by saying that when he speaks of nihilism he refers both to the "solvent of all principles and values" and to active nihilism, the "chance to begin a different history" (*NE*, 40).

94. Deleuze, *Nietzsche and Philosophy*, 174.

95. Vattimo, *Dialogue with Nietzsche*, 140. As Vattimo is forced to admit, however, the model of "moderation" for Nietzsche is the tragic, Dionysian artist who reacts with experimental hubris to the agony of life (ibid., 139). Nietzsche, *Writing from the Late Notebooks*, 116–121, June 10, 1887.

96. Vattimo, *Dialogue with Nietzsche*, 140. Vattimo wishes to undermine the two most influential readings of Nietzsche, which have been offered by Deleuze and Foucault: "The vitalistic image, which defines active nihilism in terms of energy and vital force, entails grave difficulties as well, although it is popular with a whole raft of Nietzschean interpreters, and not just ones on the right but Deleuze and Foucault as well. I am thinking of the 'flows' of Deleuze, which it is our task to set free from repressive canalizations and reterritorializations; or of Foucault's idea that *epistemai* are, in the last analysis, effects of power, products of acts of discipline. . . . To say that active nihilism is definable as that which actuates (or frees up etc.) the vital force would imply a 'metaphysical' notion of life that is incompatible with Nietzsche's perspectivism" (ibid., 137).

97. Ibid., 199.

98. Heidegger, *Nietzsche*, Vol. IV, 4.

99. Elena Ferrante, *La frantumaglia* (Rome: E/O, 2003), 116–18.

100. It is incongruous and bittersweet to observe Vattimo's late-blooming activism against Berlusconi, given how careless the philosopher has been until very recently when it comes to political questions. Santiago Zabala reports that on July 2, 2003, the day before Berlusconi started to serve his term in the rotating European Union presidency, Vattimo distributed to all European parliaments a pamphlet detailing the lengthy list of criminal charges that had been made against Berlusconi in Italy, from bribery to tax evasion. Zabala, ed., *Weakening Philosophy: Essays in Honour of Gianni Vattimo* (Montreal and Kingston: McGill-Queen's University Press, 2007), 27.

101. If we were to call into question Heidegger's vocabulary and framework, we might conclude with Adorno that, although the dialectic between Being and entity ought to be considered a "strategic masterpiece," it is also "a fake, a 'Potemkin's village'" (*Negative Dialectics*, 116).

102. Martin Heidegger, *Basic Writings*, ed. David Farrell Krell (New York: Harper & Row, 1977), 240.

103. Jacques Derrida, *Spurs: Nietzsche's Styles/Éperons: Les Styles de Nietzsche*, trans. Barbara Harlow (Chicago: University of Chicago Press, 1979), 108–9. See also Derrida's "Geschlecht, différence sexuelle, différence ontologique," which has been published in English as "Geschlecht II: Heidegger's Hand," in *Deconstruction and Philosophy*, ed. John Sallis (Chicago: University of Chicago Press, 1986).

104. Gilles Deleuze, Félix Guattari, *A Thousand Plateaus: Capitalism and Schizophrenia*, trans. Brian Massumi (Minneapolis: University of Minnesota Press, 1987), 277.

105. Vincent Descombes, *Modern French Philosophy*, trans. L. Scott-Fox and J. M. Harding (Cambridge and New York: Cambridge University Press, 1980), 136.

106. For Derrida on Artaud, see his "La parole soufflée," 1965, and his longer essay, "Différance," 1968. The latter essay is reprinted in Jacques Derrida, *Margins of Philosophy*, trans. Alan Bass (Chicago: University of Chicago Press, 1982), 1–27. Recall also note 57 of this chapter.

107. Gilles Deleuze, *Nietzsche and Philosophy*, trans. Hugh Tomlinson (New York: Columbia University Press, 1983), 9. Originally published in French in 1962.

108. Patton, *Deleuze and the Political*, 30.

109. In one of his most pointed definitions of deconstruction, Derrida directly challenged the idea that a deconstructive reading of Plato, Aristotle, and the philosophers of the canonical tradition might be undertaken in the spirit of preserving their legacy: "The way I tried to read Plato, Aristotle and others, is not a way of commanding, repeating or conserving this heritage. It is an analysis which tries to find out how their thinking works or does not work, to find the tensions, the contradictions, the heterogeneity within their own corpus." John D. Caputo, ed., *Deconstruction in a Nutshell: A Conversation with Jacques Derrida* (Bronx: Fordham University Press, 1997), 9–10.

110. Patton, *Deleuze and the Political*, 29.

111. As Franca D'Agostini suggests, in a decisive essay on Vattimo, the concept of difference in Deleuze's thought can be said to work as an alternative to that of dialectic (*VRF*, 33). For Vattimo, weak thought instead is the logical response to "a tendency to dissolve" on the part of the basic scheme of dialectic, a tendency that he claims becomes "visible in Benjamin's micrologies, in Adorno's 'negativity,' and in Bloch's utopianism" (*PD*, 17). As he puts it, the movement of the overcoming of metaphysics or Verwindung (a sort of weak *Aufhebung* that makes it possible to remember ontological difference through the distortion of foundational claims) can be conceived only as the legacy of dialectic (*PD*, 21).

112. For Heidegger's use of the phrase, see his *Basic Writings*, 295, 315.

113. "The destiny of human existence in technological society, if it is not viewed through a theoretical critique of the subject [such as Heidegger's], can only appear as(and be(the inferno of a wholly administered and regulated society as it is described by the Frankfurt School" (*EOM*, 46).

114. Hubert L. Dreyfus observes that, although Heidegger often emphasized the antitechnological implications of his thinking by, for example, writing repeatedly in a mystical register about Germany's Schwartzwald region, the ultimate philosophical issue for him was not one of controlling and mastering technology but rather the ontological condition that technology enframes. See Dreyfus's "Heidegger on Gaining a Free Relation to Technology," in *Heidegger Re-Examined*, eds. Hubert L. Dreyfus and Mark A. Wrathall (New York: Routledge, 2002), 163–65. The fundamental problem identified by Dreyfus in Heidegger's last reflections on technology is to keep "meditative thinking" (as opposed to "calculative think-

ing") alive by reflecting on the mystery of modern technology in its being immediately at hand and efficient for its own sake (ibid., 164–70).

115. Heidegger, *Basic Writings*, 287, 309. Heidegger's clearest statement of his views regarding technology occurs in "Only a God Can Save Us," an interview originally conducted on September 23, 1966, at a time when new charges of his involvement with Nazism had just surfaced. The imbroglio prompted him to stipulate that the interview could be published only after his death; it thus first appeared in print in *Der Spiegel* on May 31, 1976, and has been made available in English in Günther Neske and Emil Kettering, eds. *Martin Heidegger and National Socialism: Questions and Answers*, introduction by Karsten Harries, trans. Lisa Harries (New York: Paragon House, 1990), 41–66. In the interview, Heidegger starts by admitting that a path conducive to the essence of technology has not been identified as of yet. Throughout the interview Heidegger expresses the idea that the greatness of what has to be thought is daunting, which explains for him even the paucity of great art. As formulated in "The Principle of Identity" (1957), in a world where cybernetics takes the place of philosophy, the task of thinking in a manner adequate to the essence of technology would consist of keeping open the possibility that human beings in the technological age "experience a relationship to a demand that they can not only hear but to which they also belong" (*"Der Spiegel* Interview with Martin Heidegger," in Neske and Kettering, *Martin Heidegger and National Socialism*, 62). The gist of Heidegger's claim, in my opinion, is in an analogy: for Heidegger, the fact that *Gestell* reveals human beings as claimed and challenged by a technological power that they cannot control mirrors in turn the possibility of "the insight that humans are needed by Being" (*"Der Spiegel* Interview," 57).

116. Heidegger, *Basic Writings*, 307.

117. Ibid., 307.

118. In experimenting with the limits of thinking about modern technology, Heidegger emerges at best perplexed with regard to technology per se. Ultimately, the potentially revelatory character of technology in his eyes ensues from its condition as *techne*, that is as art, language, poetry (ibid., 315–17). In "The Question Concerning Technology," he assesses the danger as well as the saving power of Gestell through an *Erorterung* of Hölderlin's "Patmos" (ibid., 310). At the end of this essay, he proposes, albeit with a crucial sense of "ambiguity" (ibid., 314), that the essence of technology is ultimately revealed in the work of art. However, it is important to note that he has in mind an idea of art that renews its classical role as techne. He thinks of art in a manner that deprives it of a strictly aesthetic function as the object of *Erlebnis* (i.e., experience as an event, versus *Erfahrung* or experience as a process) and thus as endowed with a fundamental task of revelation: the "coming-to-pass of truth" (ibid., 317).

119. Vattimo, "The End of (Hi)story" in Ingeborg Hoesterey, ed., *Zeitgeist in Babel: The Postmodernist Controversy* (Bloomington: Indiana University Press, 1991), 132–41.

120. Martin Heidegger, *Identity and Difference*, trans. Joan Stambaugh (Chicago: University of Chicago Press, 2002), 41. For the technological examples in "The Question Concerning Technology," see *Basic Writings*, 288.

121. Even in "The Question Concerning Technology," Heidegger's criticism of how modern science entraps nature as a calculable entity indicates his awareness that modern physics, although in some sense very different from machine-powered technology, cannot refrain from approaching nature as an orderable "system of information" and thus in the end represents a "retreat from representation" (ibid., 302–3).

122. Heidegger, *Identity and Difference*, 38. Also, cf. Vattimo, *BI*, 24 and 110, and *NE*, 14.

123. Vattimo tries to reinforce his point by relating that Gadamer told him privately that Heidegger was much more tortured in the end by his inability to provide a definite narrative about technology and the overcoming of metaphysics than by his involvement with Nazism (*NE*, 14).

124. Heidegger, *Identity and Difference*, 41.

125. Ibid., 37.

126. Ibid., 40.

127. Ibid., 40.

128. Ibid., 41.

129. By "late" I mean in the technical sense of occurring after the so-called Kehre (turn) of *Being and Time*.

130. It is interesting that, in the original Italian, Vattimo's phrase for the principle of reality is "principio di realtà," which unlike "the principle of reality" in English is also used for the standard Italian translation of Freud's famous concept. Vattimo never acknowledges the unmistakable Freudian halo of the concept as he articulates it.

131. Vattimo never truly renounces ontology. Although he speaks of the dissolution of Being, weak ontology somehow manages for him to be conducive to a more liberal, tolerant, and democratic society (*NE*, 19–20).

132. Jacques Derrida, "Artifactualities," in Derrida and Bernard Stiegler, *Echographies of Television: Filmed Interviews*, trans. Jennifer Bajorek (Cambridge, UK: Polity, 2002), 3.

133. Ibid., 42.

134. Ibid., 9.

135. Ibid., 36–46.

136. Ibid., 5.

137. Ibid., 3–6.

138. Ibid., 22.

139. Vattimo, however, prides himself on not distinguishing, as Benjamin does, between a "good," socialist aestheticization of experience and a "bad," fascist one (*EOM*, 553).

140. Berlusconi established his media company, Fininvest, in 1978 and founded Italy's first national private television network, Canale 5, in 1980.

141. It never seems to bother Vattimo that certain phenomena of the mediatization of society have obscured the hidden cost of historically problematic events such as war. Not all contemporary thinkers, however, have maintained such a sense of ease with the media. In a famous pamphlet titled *The Gulf War Did Not Take Place*, Baudrillard undertook to identify the risks of an event experienced by most people around the world only through its televised simulacrum.

142. "In 1967, with a diagnosis that appears even too obvious to us in its correctness, Guy Debord recognized the transformation of capitalist politics and economy on a planetary scale into 'an immense accumulation of spectacles.' If we join Debord's analysis to the Schmittian thesis of public opinion as a modern form of acclaim, the whole problem of the contemporary, spectacular dominion of media over every aspect of social life appears in a new dimension. . . . Contemporary democracy is a democracy integrally founded on glory." Giorgio Agamben, *Il Regno e la Gloria: Per una genealogia teologica dell'economia e del governo, Homo sacer, II, 2* (Milan: Neri Pozza, 2007), 280; the English translation is my own. "We start from the premise that certain concepts and descriptions put forward forty years ago by Guy Debord and the Situationist International, as part of their effort to comprehend the new forms of state control and social disintegration then emerging, still possess explanatory power—more so than ever, we suspect, in the poisonous epoch we are living through." Retort collective (Iain Boal, T. J. Clark, Joseph Matthews, Michael Watts), *Afflicted Power: Capital and Spectacle in a New Age of War* (London: Verso, 2005), 17.

143. Guy Debord, *The Society of the Spectacle*, trans. Donald Nicholson-Smith (New York: Zone Books, 1995), 14, 15.

144. Guy Debord, *Comments on the Society of the Spectacle*, trans. Malcolm Imrie (London: Verso, 1998), 3–4.

145. Ibid., 9.
146. Ibid., 10.
147. Ibid., 10–11.
148. Ibid., 21–22.
149. Ibid., 65–66.
150. Ibid., 24.

151. Currently, Vattimo proposes an avant-gardist experience of politics that has to be rethought according to Adorno's definition of the avant-garde as the art that poses the problem of the essence of art itself (*EC*, 58).

152. Farias's book is largely credited with giving a more sensational tone to Hugo Ott's earlier findings about Heidegger's involvement with Nazism. Cf. Victor Farias, *Heidegger and Nazism*, eds. Joseph Margolis and Tom Rockmore, trans. Paul Burrell with Dominic Di Bernardi (French) and Gabriel R. Ricci (German; Philadelphia: Temple University Press, 1989); and Hugo Ott, *Martin Heidegger: A Political Life*, trans. A. Blunden (London: Fontana, 1994).

153. In addition to Farias's and Ott's efforts, several serious studies have been dedicated to *l'affaire Heidegger*. An important contribution to the interrogation of Heidegger's positions and the more sinister implications of his thought that nevertheless refuses to accept a deterministic or causal relationship between Nazi ideology and Heideggerian philosophy is Hans Sluga's *Heidegger's Crisis: Philosophy and Politics in Nazi Germany* (Cambridge, MA: Harvard University Press, 1993). Also useful to a critical assessment of the controversy is Julian Young, *Heidegger, Philosophy, Nazism* (Cambridge, UK: Cambridge University Press, 1997). A fundamental resource is the volume edited by Richard Wolin, *The Heidegger Controversy: A Critical Reader* (Cambridge, MA: MIT Press, 1993). The collection includes Heidegger's famous last interview with *Der Spiegel*, essays by Karl Löwith, and letters by Karl Jaspers, Herbert Marcuse, and Paul Celan. Also important is Thomas Sheehan's article "Heidegger and the Nazis" in *The New York Review of Books*, 35:10 (June 16, 1988), 38–47. A number of philosophers, among them Derrida, Lacoue-Labarthe, and Lyotard, also responded in their writings to the belated revelation of Heidegger's politics, as I note elsewhere in this chapter.

154. Julian Young, *Heidegger, Philosophy, Nazism*, op. cit., 3.

155. Martin Heidegger, "'Only a God Can Save Us': *Der Spiegel*'s interview with Martin Heidegger (1966), in *The Heidegger Controversy*, 91–116.

156. Cf. Löwith's account of Heidegger's appearance at a conference in Rome wearing a swastika on his lapel (ibid., 141).

157. See Marcuse's letter of August 28, 1947, asking Heidegger to criticize his Nazi past; and Celan's poem "Todtnauberg" requesting an "undelayed word," presumably of repentance, in *The Heidegger Controversy*, 160, 198.

158. It is revealing to compare Vattimo's position to Lacoue-Labarthe's criticism of "Heideggerianism." The French philosopher observes that, although he subscribes to Heidegger's thesis, there is little point in thinking that at the end of philosophy the question of Being might produce a new thesis on Being. *Heidegger, Art and Politics*, 9.

159. Jacques Derrida, *Of Spirit: Heidegger and the Question*, trans. Geoffrey Bennington and Rachel Bowlby (Chicago: University of Chicago Press, 1989), 5. Derrida shows how, starting in *Being and Time*, Heidegger deconstructs the concept of spirit in order to celebrate it, at the time of the rectorship address, in the guise of the historical, spiritual mission of the German nation and university. Yet Derrida finds the same fiction of the spiritual reawakening of a destitute Europe in the hands of the German language informing Heidegger's later essays on Hölderlin and Trakl, where he suggests a more originary, pre-Greek, pre-Christian, German meaning for *spirit*, which he defines as "being-resolved to the essence of Being" or a condition of existence no longer as *pneuma* ("breath" or "spirit" in Greek) or *spiritus* ("breath" or "spirit" in Latin) but rather as "fire, flame, burning, conflagration" (ibid., 67, 82–83).

160. Lacoue-Labarthe, *Heidegger, Art and Politics*, 13, 53. For Lacoue-Labarthe,

if Heidegger actually joined Nazism because of the rapid transformation of techne into technology, in his later life he recuperated this preoccupation philosophically by sanctifying techne in his writings as the essence of art, aestheticism, or the setting-to-work of *aletheia*, i.e., the "unconcealment" or disclosure of the truth of Being. By defining *techne* as the mode of unconcealing, or as Lacoue-Labarthe prefers to put it by thinking of the technical or the political as fiction, the truth of National Socialism as national aestheticism becomes inscribed in the very fabric of Heidegger's thought (ibid., 84–86).

161. Derrida, *Of Spirit*, 74.

162. Jacques Derrida and Elisabeth Roudinesco, *For What Tomorrow*, 14–15. Derrida has often described his attitude in reading certain Heideggerian themes as one of being "actively perplexed." See for example "Heidegger, the Philosophers' Hell," in *Points*, 183. Discussing Heidegger's metaphysical sanctioning of National Socialism, Derrida describes the experience of "thinking about him" as "horribly dangerous and wildly funny, certainly grave and a bit comical" (*Of Spirit*, 68).

163. Christian Jambet, "Preface" to Farias's *Heidegger and Nazism*, 4.

164. For Derrida's objection, see his *Points*, 187.

165. In thinking both Nazism and Heidegger, which is to say not just condemning them but attempting to understand them as well, Derrida writes: "Is not the task, the duty, and in truth the only new or interesting thing to try to recognize the analogies and the possibilities of rupture between, on the one hand, what is called Nazism—the enormous, plural, differentiated continent whose roots are still obscure—and, on the other hand, a Heideggerian thinking that is also multiple and that, for a long time to come, will remain provocative, enigmatic, still to be read? Not because it would hold in reserve, still encrypted, a good and reassuring politics, a 'Heideggerianism of the left,' but because it opposed to actual Nazism, to its dominant strain, only a more 'revolutionary' and purer Nazism!" (ibid., 182–83) Richard Rorty, who does not hesitate to define Heidegger as a "passionately committed Nazi and a thoroughly dishonest man," attempts to justify Vattimo's "commonsense Heideggerianism" as a philosophically cogent account of modernity. Rorty describes Vattimo's achievement as the important recognition that the rise of modern Western democracies is a sign that human beings are losing the need to feel themselves subject to the eternal and are becoming courageous enough to endure the thought of their own mortality. He admits, however, that readers may find it ludicrous to use Heidegger as the basis of a leftist political program. See Rorty's "Foreword" to the American edition of Vattimo's *Nihilism and Emancipation*, xi.

166. Cf. Derrida, *Points*, 182; and Lacoue-Labarthe, *Heidegger, Art and Politics*, 22.

167. Ibid., 39.

168. Lacoue-Labarthe notes that the lecture is still unpublished, although it is quoted by Wolfgang Schirmacher in *Technik und Gelassenheit* (Freiburg: Karl

Alber, 1984) and is also mentioned in a book by Otto Pöggeler (Lacoue-Labarthe, ibid., 34).

169. Ibid., 35.

170. On the teleological character of the notion of epochality in Heidegger, see Derrida, *Of Spirit*, 12.

171. As we will see in the next chapter, Achille Bonito Oliva espouses a similarly regressive admiration of the Baroque.

172. Vattimo concedes that he naturally agrees with the verdicts in Nuremberg but only in the name of a "determined historical situation" rather than the truth. He even declares that we ought to prefer Heidegger to have achieved purification by distancing himself from his positions of 1933. His incidental concession to political common sense, however, fails to acknowledge what Lacoue-Labarthe calls the "abyss" of Auschwitz, settling on the anodyne euphemism "determined historical situation," which in its normalcy seems to disavow and urbanize the fact of genocide. Moreover when Vattimo once again resorts to scare quotes in advocating what he regards as an ultimately beneficial "purification" of Heidegger, his bad consciousness or bad humor is glaringly prominent. Given Nazi ideology's call for purification of the race, employing this term as the *terminus ad quem* of Heidegger's potential political conversion indicates Vattimo's lack of serious reflection on the terms of the problem.

173. I find troubling as well Vattimo's perplexed tone when he remarks that the Holocaust is for both Adorno and Levinas the "biographical" event, as opposed to the theoretical, philosophical argument, that allowed them to unmask the connection between metaphysics and violence. It is almost as if Vattimo does not approve of the "qualitative" importance of Auschwitz involved in Adorno's and Levinas's critiques of violence. Vattimo criticizes the "promesse de bonheur" that legitimates every critical act of distancing oneself from the present, and thus Adorno's and Levinas's philosophies, as proof of a lingering fidelity to "transcendental metaphysics." Vattimo, "Metaphysics and Violence," in *Weakening Philosophy*, 409–10.

174. Michel Foucault, "Leçon du 5 janvier 1983," in *Le gouvernement de soi et des autres: Cours au Collège de France (1982–1983)*, ed. Frédéric Gross under the direction of François Ewald and Alessandro Fontana (Paris: Gallimard/Le Seuil, 2008), 3–22; Foucault, "What Is Enlightenment?" in *Michel Foucault: Ethics, Subjectivity and Truth*, ed. Paul Rabinow (New York: New Press, 1997), 303–20; "What Is Critique?," 23–82.

175. Ibid., 95.

176. Foucault, "Leçon du 5 janvier 1983," 22. (The translation is mine.)

177. "What Is Critique?" 43.

178. Ibid., 47.

179. Ibid., 43–44.

180. Ibid., 118.

181. Ibid., 113.

182. As early as 1987, Vattimo had already written an essay titled "Ontology of Actuality"; see *Filosofia 87*.

183. In the very same book in which Vattimo affirms the utility of an ontology of actuality, he does not hesitate to criticize the French philosopher for having supposedly reduced all interpersonal relationships to "no more than a sophisticated way of affirming a wide-reaching disciplinary structure in society" (*BI*, 51).

184. In this connection, we ought to recall that the series of lectures at the Collège de France with which Foucault's career ends are devoted to topics such as the courage of truth and the Greek concept of *parrhesia* or truth telling. Indeed, in "What Is Critique?" he even goes so far as to define criticism as a kind of "politics of truth" (op. cit., 47). By contrast, one of Vattimo's most recent works, *Addio alla verità*, is a manifesto for abandoning the very notion of truth.

185. On this issue, see Santiago Zabala, *The Remains of Being: Hermeneutica Ontology After Metaphysics* (New York: Columbia University Press, 2009).

186. "What Is Enlightenment?" 181.

187. Martin Heidegger, "The Origin of the Work of Art" in *Off the Beaten Track* (Holzwege), ed. and trans. Julian Young and Kenneth Haynes (Cambridge, UK: Cambridge University Press, 2002), 37, as cited in Vattimo, *NE*, 12 and 174 n4, and *NEI*, 24 n3. Compare also Vattimo's statement: "In the epoch of the end of metaphysics, we can no longer look for the event of Being, as Heidegger did, in those privileged moments to which he always turned his attention: the inaugural great works of poetry, the inaugural words such as Anaximander's 'saying' or Parmenides' poem, or Hölderlin's verses. These texts still function like essences, Platonic ideas, that only philosophers recognize and which they once again make into 'sovereign' voices. In the epoch of democracy, the event of Being toward which thought has to turn its attention is something probably far wider and less defined, probably closer to politics. Only an expression of late Foucault can help us to think about it, an expression, however, that we reconsider according to an autonomous meaning: *ontology of actuality*" (*AV*, 35). The English translation is mine.

188. Martin Heidegger, *Being and Time*, trans. John Macquarrie and Edward Robinson (New York: Harper, 2008), 211–14.

189. Heidegger, *Off the Beaten Track*, 242–81.

190. Ibid., 254.

191. Ibid., 280.

192. Foucault, "What Is Critique?" 105. It is important to observe that, except for Lyotard, Vattimo has been the only one among the poststructuralists to retain the concept of postmodernity. Neither Derrida nor Deleuze nor Foucault shows the slightest interest in it.

193. Roberto Esposito, "Interview with Timothy Campbell," in *Diacritics*, 36:2 (2006).

194. "What Is Critique?" 99.

195. It is doubtful that Foucault would have accepted Vico or Croce into his pantheon of critical thinkers, given their allegiance to what might be defined as the genealogy of the counter-Enlightenment. Notwithstanding Croce's reputation for antifascism, both thinkers ultimately urge compliance with tradition and authority and insist on the paralyzing "practices" of Italian culture: historicism and spiritualism.

196. Vattimo dedicated *Filosofia 86*, the 1986 issue of the annual yearbook under his editorship, to the question of secularization. In considering the sources of Vattimo's return to religion, we should not underestimate Luigi Pareyson's influence. Vattimo's teacher in fact identified Christianity as the central question of philosophy in books such as *Esistenza e persona* (1950) and *Ontologia della libertà* (1995). See Carmelo Dotolo, *La teologia fondamentale: Davanti alle sfide del "pensiero debole" di G. Vattimo* (Rome: LAS, 1999), 425–26.

197. In *After Christianity*, Vattimo recounts the narrative of his religious life, which started when he was a ten-year-old boy frequenting the parish, continued through his upbringing in Catholic values, and persisted in his career as a philosopher who initially was drawn to the works of the Thomist philosopher Jacques Maritain, the author of *Integral Humanism*. Vattimo admits to cultivating an early attitude of antimodernism by immersing himself in Nietzsche's and Heidegger's harsh criticisms of modernity and Christianity, only to find his way back to his original faith in a late-career coup de théâtre (*AC*, 2–3).

198. Cf. also *AC*, 18, 77.

199. In an amusing aside, Vattimo confesses in his autobiography to having written *Belief* as a diatribe against the self-contradictions of Massimo Cacciari, the Italian philosopher who "was always talking about angels while insisting he was not a believer" (*NBG*, 119).

200. We might want to remember that Pareyson, Vattimo's professor of philosophy in Turin, was the author of a monograph on Dostoevsky.

201. Although he maintains in *After Christianity* that the expression "believing that one believes" is "widespread" and "comprehensible," Vattimo is compelled to point out the confusing double meaning of believing: "The expression 'believing that one believes' sounds paradoxical in Italian too: to believe means having faith, conviction or certainty in something, but also to opine—that is, to think with a certain degree of uncertainty. . . . This sounds unclear as well as suspicious" (*AC*, 1). However, Vattimo concludes that for those who have familiarity with postmodern life, religious belief can be characterized only by the deep uncertainty of opinion (*AC*, 2).

202. Peter Sloterdijk, *Critique of Cynical Reason*, trans. Michael Eldred (Minneapolis: University of Minnesota Press, 1987), 5–6.

203. See Richard Rorty, "Anticlericalism and Atheism," in Rorty and Gianni Vattimo, *The Future of Religion*, ed. Santiago Zabala (New York: Columbia University Press, 2005), 35.

204. To a large extent, Vattimo's thesis is anticipated in the *Phenomenology of Spirit*, where Hegel defines the death of God in terms of the kenosis of substance and reinterprets substance as the subject, thus divesting the concept of its abstraction. G. W. F. Hegel, *Phenomenology of Spirit*, trans. A. V. Miller with analysis of the text and foreword by J. N. Findlay (New York: Oxford University Press, 1977), 478. However, as Rorty remarks, though Hegel was able to recognize human history as the incarnation of Spirit, he was unwilling "to put aside truth in favor of love" (Rorty and Vattimo, *The Future of Religion*, 35).

205. Zabala, ed., *Weakening Philosophy*, 84.

206. Carmelo Dotolo, "The Hermeneutics of Christianity and Philosophical Responsibility," in Zabala, ibid., 357.

207. Frederick Depoortere criticizes the partiality of Vattimo's reading of kenosis in Philippians 2 and points out that he skips the part of the Christological hymn in which exaltation of Christ becomes the focus. Frederick Depoortere, *Christ in Postmodern Philosophy: Gianni Vattimo, René Girard, Slavoj Zizek* (London: Clark, 2008), 21.

208. In a book that is largely sympathetic to Vattimo's philosophical reading of Christianity, Dotolo nonetheless raises some objections to Vattimo's version of Christology, noticing in particular that his view of incarnation downplays the importance of revelation and thereby undermines the radicality of the question of faith. Dotolo, *La teologia fondamentale*, 429–30.

209. Gianni Vattimo, "Toward a Non-Religious Christianity," in John. D. Caputo and Gianni Vattimo, *After the Death of God*, ed. Jeffrey W. Robbins (New York: Columbia University Press, 2007), 27–47.

210. Having downplayed consistently the seriousness of Heidegger's allegiance to Nazism, Vattimo curiously mobilizes Hitler to criticize Derrida's belief in the Messiah: "I always used to ask Derrida in person, and not in jest, 'How do you distinguish between Hitler and the other who is yet to come?'" (*NBG*, 151).

211. René Girard, *Violence and the Sacred*, trans. Patrick Gregory (London: Athlone Press, 1988); and *Things Hidden Since the Foundation of the World*, trans. Stephen Bann and Michael Metteer (Stanford: Stanford University Press, 1987).

212. René Girard and Gianni Vattimo, *Verità o fede debole? Dialogo su cristianesimo e relativismo*, ed. Pierpaolo Antonello (Massa: Transeuropa, 2006), 71.

213. Ibid., 79. In *After Christianity*, Vattimo claims that the mechanism of scapegoating excludes the possibility of self-sacrifice, thus concluding that Jesus' self-sacrifice cannot be interpreted by means of a victim-based logic (*AC*, 120).

214. *Verità o fede debole*, 77.

215. Ibid., 17–18.

216. Ibid., 22.

217. It is interesting to notice how Vattimo brushes off the objections of the Catholic theologian Sergio Quinzio, who criticizes the idea of retaining only the loving and merciful aspect of God and not also his figure as a judge (*B*, 89). Vattimo

thinks that the merciful God is indeed a secularized version of the more primitive, terrible deity, that "divine justice . . . must be 'secularized' precisely in the name of the commandment of love" (B, 89–90).

218. Charles Taylor, *A Secular Age* (Cambridge, MA: Harvard University Press, 2007), 565.

219. Ibid., 577.

220. Hannah Arendt, *On Revolution* (London: Penguin Books, 1990), 81–82.

221. Rorty and Vattimo, *The Future of Religion*, 54.

222. Vattimo praises his teacher Luigi Pareyson for having suggested that the dogma of incarnation does not delegitimize other religions. On the contrary, for Pareyson (and Vattimo) it validates them insofar as it raises the possibility that any natural and historical symbol might symbolize God (AC, 27).

223. *After the Death of God*, 77–85.

224. Cf. Vattimo, "The West or Christianity" in *AC*, 60–83.

225. *After the Death of God*, 150.

226. Ibid., 48, 122–23.

227. Jacques Derrida and Gianni Vattimo, eds., *Religion*, trans. David Webb and others (Stanford: Stanford University Press, 1998), 12. All further page references from this edition will follow the abbreviation *R*. We ought to recall that Derrida regards Europe in the essay in all its painful complexity and contradiction: "Difficult to say 'Europe' without connoting: Athens-Jerusalem-Rome-Byzantium, wars of Religion, open war over the appropriation of Jerusalem and of Mount Moriah, over the 'here I am' of Abraham or of Ibrahim, before the extreme 'sacrifice' demanded of him" (*R*, 4).

228. In the essay, after having explored the deeply Christian and colonial genealogy of the concept of tolerance, Derrida actively searches for a notion of non-Christian tolerance, as concerned by the necessity of "respecting the infinite alterity and singularity" (*R*, 21–22).

229. The crucial issue for both Vattimo and Nancy is that of Christology and the meaning of *kenosis* within Christian theology. However, Nancy approaches this problematic through searching exploration of the question of *parousia*, which traditionally is defined as the second coming of Christ, but which he defines less as the recovery of the presence of the Messiah than as the announcement of a Christ to come. By contrast, Vattimo grants a decisive status to kenosis as the basis of incarnation, ongoing secularization, nihilism, etc., that makes it impossible for him to allow what Nancy refers to as the opening of "dis-enclosure" or the "Open as such," which is to say the project made possible by the "living God" at the heart of Christianity. Jean-Luc Nancy, *Dis-Enclosure: The Deconstruction of Christianity*, trans. Bettina Bergo, Gabriel Malenfant, and Michael B. Smith (Bronx, NY: Fordham University Press, 2008), 156.

230. Ibid., 31.

231. Ibid., 20, 31.

232. Ibid., 31.
233. Ibid., 31.
234. Ibid., 31–32.
235. Ibid., 23.
236. Ibid., 1.
237. Vattimo criticizes Blumenberg's argument in *The Legitimacy of the Modern Age* that modernity represents an epistemological break with, and a completely new beginning vis-à-vis, Christianity (*AC*, 71). Cf. Hans Blumenberg, *The Legitimacy of the Modern Age*, trans. Robert M. Wallace (Cambridge, MA: MIT Press, 1983).
238. This is how Weber's book starts: "A glance at the occupational statistics of any country of mixed religious composition brings to light with remarkable frequency a situation which has several times provoked discussion in the Catholic press and literature, and in Catholic congresses in Germany, namely, the fact that business leaders and owner of capitals, as well as the higher grades of skilled labour, and even more the higher technically and commercially trained personnel of modern enterprises, are overwhelmingly Protestant." Max Weber, *The Protestant Ethic and the Spirit of Capitalism*, trans. Talcott Parsons (New York: Routledge, 2001), 3.
239. Ibid., 21, 37–38.
240. Colin Campbell, *The Romantic Ethic and the Spirit of Modern Consumerism* (Great Britain: Alcuin Academics, 2005), 74.
241. Ibid., 74.
242. "That individualism was carried to unprecedented lengths in Protestantism is particularly significant in relation to this last point, for whilst in Roman Catholicism symbols also served to arouse (and allay) powerful emotions, their control was kept firmly in the hands of the priesthood, and hence situationally located in communal ritual. In Protestantism, by contrast, not only was there no one to act as mediator between the individual and the divine, but both 'magical' rituals and the use of idols were proscribed" (ibid., 74–75).
243. Ibid., 90.
244. Cf. Henri de Lubac, *La postérité spirituelle de Joachim de Flore*, 2 vols. (Paris: Letheleux, 1980). It is interesting that Vattimo prefers to rely on Ernesto Buonaiuti's reading of Joachim rather than on de Lubac's, accusing the French theologian of being more concerned with defending Catholic orthodoxy than with properly appreciating Joachim's importance in affirming the historical character of salvation (*AC*, 32). Buonaiuti, an excommunicated modernist theologian, emphasizes the critical side of Joachim, which Vattimo perhaps regards as a source of inspiration for his own equally critical attitude toward the institution of the Catholic Church.
245. Henri de Lubac, *La postérité spirituelle*, 1:53. Joachim saw the first sign of incipient realization of the Third Age in the Cistercian movement of his time. For

Joachim, as Vattimo points out, the First Age was one of calamity characterized by law, slavery, and awe; the Second was an age of action characterized by grace, filial slavery, and faith. The Third would have been an age of contemplation characterized by freedom, friendship, and charity (*AC*, 29–30). Joachim's point of departure are two passages from Scripture, Paul 1 Corinthians 13:12 and John 16:13, which he freely interprets as articulating the possibility of achieving perfect knowledge at the moment of the realization and fulfillment of the Third Age. Frank Kermode offers one of the best summations of Joachim's importance with the observation that the Third Age provides a seminal example of "the myth of Transition." See Kermode's *The Sense of an Ending: Studies in the Theory of Fiction* (Oxford, UK: Oxford University Press, 1967), 12. By "transition," Kermode means the notion of a historical period that belongs neither to the End nor to the *saeculum* preceding it, and that in Revelation is associated with the reign of the Beast: "This period of Transition seems not to have been defined until the end of the twelfth century; but the definition then arrived at—by Joachim of Flora—has proved to be remarkably enduring" (ibid., 12). Joachim's doctrine was condemned after his death in 1260, but his ideas survived philosophically and culturally. Kermode reminds us of some of the most important inheritors of Joachim's legacy, from Dante and radical Puritan sects down to Hegel, D. H. Lawrence, and Hitler; as Kermode observes, "'the Third Reich' is itself a Joachite expression" (ibid., 13).

246. "The *dispositif* of the trinitarian *oikonomia* may represent a privileged laboratory to observe the functioning and articulation—both internal and external—of the governmental machine" (*Il Regno e la Gloria*, op. cit., 9). My translation.

247. Rorty and Vattimo, *The Future of Religion*, op. cit., 90.

248. In theological terms, however, it does not seem likely that Vattimo's emphasis on Joachim of Fiore helps his case. Even setting aside the serious hermeneutical perplexities that confront most theological interpreters of his work, Joachim's Third Age of spirit is conceivable only at the expense of any emphasis on the ongoing meaning of incarnation, as de Lubac suggests. Such loss of emphasis is of strategic importance for Vattimo's theory of secularization, for if we must wait for the Third Age then the incarnation loses its claim to being a definitive event. De Lubac argues pointedly that under such conditions Christ becomes merely the "penultimate" word of God's love for humanity (*La posterité spirituelle*, 2:473). In Joachim's thinking, as de Lubac rightly observes, it becomes difficult to understand the function of the death and resurrection of Christ, since all attention is focused on the Third Age.

249. According to de Lubac, Joachim redoubles the wait for Apocalypse with a stronger form of optimism linked to the historical, secular time of spiritual renewal (ibid., 1:61).

250. Girard criticizes the unduly optimistic tone of speculation in Vattimo's thought.

251. For Vattimo, Croce is responsible for having "reformed" Hegel's philoso-

phy of objective spirit in a more sophisticated direction that leads to "the historical spirit" (Rorty and Vattimo, *The Future of Religion*, 80).

252. Ibid., 45.

253. Ibid., 46–47.

254. Michel Foucault, *The History of Sexuality I: An Introduction*, trans. Robert Hurley (New York: Vintage, 1990), 18–19.

255. Giorgio Agamben, *Profanations*, trans. Jeff Fort (New York: Zone Books, 2007), 77.

256. Bettino Craxi was the secretary of the PSI (Italian Socialist Party), which dissolved in the wake of the "Mani Pulite" or "Clean Hands" scandal, when several judges investigated and indicted some of the highest officials of the Democrazia Cristiana (DC or Christian Democracy) and the PSI for appalling acts of corruption. During the 1980s and the beginning of the 1990s, at the time of the "second Italian miracle," Craxi achieved an imposing cultural and political hegemony in the form of a hyperspectacularization of politics that was predicated on the abandonment of any leftist emancipatory ideals. One of the most notable features of Craxi's government certainly was his ardent support of Berlusconi's real estate and media ventures in Milan and throughout the nation. In this sense, Craxi was the direct progenitor of Berlusconi as a cultural and political figure.

257. Vattimo titles one of his chapters "Lo 'spettro' di Marx" (The Specter of Marx) without even acknowledging Derrida's prior use of the same formulation in a related philosophical context (*EC*, 107–10).

258. Vattimo attempts to demonstrate that the rhetoric of reformism does not take into account contemporary violence. Following Gore Vidal's suggestion, Vattimo regards the Oklahoma City bombing as a more telling event than September 11. As a reaction to the FBI's use of force in Waco, Texas, the Oklahoma City bombing leads Vattimo back to recognizing the strategic importance of the federal government's role in the deaths of "relevant numbers of squatters" (*EC*, 76). In calling the armed militia men "squatters" and thus implying that they were killed for not having paid their taxes, Vattimo once again demonstrates a tin ear for, and questionable attention to, the nuances of historical realities in international politics.

CHAPTER 4

1. Angelo Capasso, *A.B.O.: Le arti della critica* (Milan: Skirà Editore, 2001). Further citations will be flagged with the abbreviation *ABO*. All English translations are mine.

2. Hans Belting, *Art History After Modernism*, trans. Caroline Saltzwedel, Mitch Cohen, and Kenneth J. Northcott (Chicago: University of Chicago Press, 2003), 177.

3. Achille Bonito Oliva, *Il tallone di Achille: Sull'arte contemporanea* (Milan:

Feltrinelli, 1988), 71. Hereafter all references to this edition follow the abbreviation *TA*. All English translations are mine.

4. Bonito Oliva, *Transavantgarde International* (Milan: Giancarlo Politi Editore, 1982), 48. Subsequent page references are flagged with the abbreviation *TI*. All English translations are mine. One of Bonito Oliva's early fundamental essays on mannerism was titled "La citazione deviata: L'ideologia." See Capasso.

5. "In a generalized situation of catastrophe, the recovery of previous associations . . . does not seem possible" (ibid., 48, 42).

6. Fredric Jameson, *Postmodernism or the Cultural Logic of Late Capitalism* (Durham, NC: Duke University Press, 1991), 324.

7. Cf. Jean-François Lyotard, "Answering the Question: What Is Postmodernism?" trans. Régis Durand, in *The Postmodern Condition: a Report on Knowledge*, trans. Geoff Bennington and Brian Massumi (Minneapolis: University of Minnesota Press, 1984).

8. Max Horkheimer and Theodor W. Adorno, *Dialectic of Enlightenment*, ed. Gunzelin Schmidd Noerr, trans. Edmund Jephcott (Stanford: Stanford University Press, 2002), 94.

9. Bonito Oliva, *Il sogno dell'arte: Tra avanguardia e transavanguardia* (Milan: Spirali/Vel, 1990). Hereafter, all citations follow the abbreviation *SA*. All English translations are mine.

10. It is interesting to note that many qualifiers used by Bonito Oliva compel the English translator to shift the original, more "nihilistic," and passive meaning of the terms into a different register. Thus *stordito* becomes "bewildered," *dolcezza* becomes "mildness" (which Jameson favors in his critical remarks on Transavanguardia in *Postmodernism*), and *leggere* is rendered as "fanciful" or "small" (e.g., "small adventures" for *peripezie leggere* and "fanciful motifs" for *motivi leggeri* in the essay "Transitional Art" in *Transavantgarde International*, trans. Dwight Gast and Gwen Jones). In particular, dolcezza undergoes different renderings in the same essay. "Il soggetto dolce della transavanguardia" thus becomes first "the soft subject" (*SA*, 62) and then, in a new *stilnovistic* effort, a "gentle subject" (*SA*, 72). It is almost as if the ineffable vocabulary that Bonito Oliva favors is forced in English to become more concrete and active.

11. Many critics have written recently against tolerance, from Derrida (in Jürgen Habermas, Giovanna Borradori, and Jacques Derrida, *Philosophy in a Time of Terror: Dialogues with Jürgen Habermas and Jacques Derrida*, Chicago: University of Chicago Press, 1994) to Wendy Brown.

12. Bonito Oliva, "The Italian Transavantgarde," trans. Michael Moore, in *Flash Art*, 92–93: October–November 1979, 40. Further page references to this article are flagged with the abbreviation "ItalTran."

13. Bonito Oliva, *L'ideologia del traditore: Arte, maniera, manierismo* (Milan: Biblioteca Electa, 1998), 18. Subsequent citations follow the abbreviation *IdeoTrad*. All English translations are mine.

Notes to Chapter 4   291

14. Bonito Oliva and Giulio Carlo Argan, *L'arte fino al 2000* (Milan: Sansoni, 1991), 334.
15. Horkheimer and Adorno, *Dialectic*, 128.
16. Vattimo, *La fine della modernità* (Milan: Garzanti, 1985), 53.
17. Ibid., 32–34.
18. See "Ornamento, Monumento," in *La fine della modernità*.
19. Ernst Hans Gombrich, *The Sense of Order* (Ithaca, NY: Cornell University Press, 1984), 99.
20. See "Ornamento, Monumento," in *La fine della modernità*.
21. "Davanti c'è il bel canto, dietro la tortura," in *Transavanguardia* (Milan: Skira Editore, 2002).
22. *Catalogo Castello di Rivoli*, 18–19.
23. Belting, 177.
24. Ibid., 178.
25. Hal Foster, Rosalind Krauss, Yves Alain Bois, and Benjamin H. D. Buchloh, *Art Since 1900: Modernism, Antimodernism, Postmodernism* (New York: Thames and Hudson, 2004), 597.
26. Ibid., 597.
27. Benjamin Buchloh, "Figures of Authority, Ciphers of Regression: Notes on the Return of Representation in European Painting," in *October* 16, Spring 1981, 64–65.
28. See Francesco Bonami's introductory essay, "An Ancient Contemporary Civilization," for the catalogue of the 2008 exhibition, "Italics: Italian Art Between Tradition and Revolution, 1968–2008" at the Palazzo Grassi in Venice in 2008. *Italics* (Milan: Electa, 2008), 30.
29. Bonami, *Italics*, 29.
30. In an interview for the English edition of his book, Rancière suggests: "The core of the problem is that there is no criterion for establishing an appropriate correlation between the politics of aesthetics and the aesthetics of politics. This has nothing to do with the claim made by some people that art and politics should not be mixed. They intermix in any case; politics has its aesthetics and aesthetics has its politics." Jacques Rancière, *The Politics of Aesthetics: The Distribution of The Sensible* trans. Gabriel Rockhill (New York: Continuum, 2006), 62.
31. Ibid., 63.
32. For more on Bonito Oliva's debts to Deleuze, Stirner, and Spengler, see Max Faust, *October 16*, 66, as cited by Buchloh in "The Bewildered Image."
33. Bonito Oliva's ability to distort Deleuze's concepts seems to confirm Jameson's interpretation of Deleuze's philosophy as postmodernist. See *Postmodernism*.
34. Hopkins more specifically shows how postwar avant-gardes measured their achievement against the horizon of a self-referential modernism articulated by Clement Greenberg and Michael Fried. David Hopkins, *After Modern Art 1945–2000* (Oxford: Oxford University Press, 2000), 197.

35. Ibid., 170.
36. Ibid., 197.
37. Ibid., 211.
38. Ibid., 205.
39. Jameson, 324.
40. Ibid., xi.
41. Ibid., 159, 174–75. It is interesting to observe that, in advocating a "party" of postmodern yet utopian artists, Jameson elsewhere characterizes the historical period not as one of de-ideologization but as a time "when we have agreed that everything is ideology" (ibid., 180).
42. Ibid., 174.
43. Ibid., 175.
44. Ibid., 180.
45. Lyotard, *The Postmodern Condition*, 71, 73. Cf. "Answering the Question: What Is Postmodernism?" in *The Postmodern Condition*.
46. Ibid., 76.
47. Bonito Oliva, "A proposito di Transavanguardia," in *Alfabeta* (April 1982), 35: 25. Subsequent citations from this article follow the abbreviation *Alfa*. All English translations are mine.
48. See *TI*, 44, 46.
49. Lyotard, *The Postmodern Condition*, 77.
50. Ibid., 81.
51. Lyotard, *Lessons on the Analytic of the Sublime*, trans. Elizabeth Rottenberg (Stanford: Stanford University Press, 1994), 190.
52. Ibid., 187.
53. Lyotard, *The Postmodern Condition*, 76.
54. Hopkins, 206.
55. Ibid., 208.
56. Foster, *The Anti-Aesthetic: Essays on Postmodern Culture* (Seattle: Bay Press, 1983), xii.
57. This is Bonito Oliva's line of justification even as he mentions, in addition to the negative effects of Neorealism and the bureaucrats of the Communist Party, the intransigence of the neoavantgarde. See *TI* and also *Alfa*, 25.
58. Hopkins, 169.
59. *Arte dall'Italia*, 13.
60. Ibid., 39.
61. Ibid., 40. However, Buchloh has also recognized in Kiefer, and others, traits of an archetypal, nationalist expression.
62. Ibid., 41.
63. Jameson, 304.
64. Gioacchino Lanza Tomasi, "Ritratto di A.B.O." (*ABO*, 32). The English translation is mine.

Notes to Chapter 4   293

65. Bonito Oliva and Argan, 330.
66. Ibid., 330.
67. Ibid., 332.
68. Ibid., 333.
69. For a much more insightful discussion of the Baudelaire-Warhol genealogy, see Jean Baudrillard, *The Conspiracy of Art* (Cambridge: Semiotext(e), 2005), 99–102. Although Baudrillard thinks that Baudelaire, like Warhol, was interested in advancing art as "the absolute commodity," he adds that for Baudelaire what was at stake in so doing was to produce a "radical denial" and "parody" of the commodity. He thus ascribed to the commodity a heroic status that opposed the "sentimental value" conferred on it by the bourgeoisie through advertising. Moreover, Baudrillard observes that, after Warhol, we may be said to live in the time of the "Transaesthetic." Under this condition, art is no longer interested in form but in value, especially exchange value. Ibid., 57.

70. Michel Foucault, "What Is Enlightenment?" in *Ethics: Subjectivity and Truth*, ed. Paul Rabinow, trans. Robert Hurley et al. (New York: New Press, 1997), 310–12.

71. Arthur C. Danto, "The Philosopher as Andy Warhol," in *Philosophizing Art* (Berkeley and Los Angeles: University of California Press, 1999), 61–83.

72. Ibid., 65.
73. Ibid., 63.
74. Also, Bonito Oliva claims Warhol as a model for the critic insofar as the latter increasingly is transformed into a public figure ("from Warhol, the critic procures the model of publicity," *TA*, 12; my translation).

75. In his essay on the Italian art movements of the time, Bakagiev mentions the importance in those years of Vattimo's weak thought and relativism. Bakagiev, "La transavanguardia italiana: Una rilettura 1979–1985," in *Transavanguardia*, Catalogo Castello di Rivoli, 68.

76. Achille Bonito Oliva, "The Achieved Nihilist," in *Transavanguardia: Italia/America* (Modena: Assicurazioni Unipol, 1982), 13. Cf. Vattimo's insistence on "the situation in which man rolls away from the center toward X" in *The End of Modernity*, trans. Jon R. Snyder (Baltimore: Johns Hopkins University Press, 1991), 27. The key citation for both commentators derives from the opening of Book One of *The Will to Power*, where Nietzsche includes in his list of the philosophical causes of nihilism "the nihilistic consequences of contemporary natural science (together with its attempts to escape into some beyond). The industry of its pursuit eventually leads to self-disintegration, opposition, an antiscientific mentality. Since Copernicus man has been rolling from the center toward X." Friedrich Nietzsche, *The Will to Power*, trans. Walter Kaufmann and R. J. Hollingdale (New York: Random House, 1967), xx.

77. Bonito Oliva and Argan, 333.
78. *Catalogo, Castello di Rivoli*, 25.

79. See for example *La fine della modernità*, 69.
80. Vattimo, 72.
81. See *L'ideologia del traditore*.
82. "Thus, the ideology of the traitor (pathetic or cynical as he may be), the style of loss, the distance, the very oblique positioning of the 'sayer,' are all signs of omnipotence and, at the same time, of impotence, which often are dramatic and so completely discomposed as to verge upon, or commingle with, areas of folly" (*IdeoTrad*, 31). My translation.
83. Jameson, 160.
84. "To the elusive quality of existence the traitor responds with his own optics of the oblique and with the ambivalent assumption of *fashion*, meant specifically as acceptance of the whole codification of the web of worldly relationships. Fashion, however, also marks a distance, the cynical employment of convention because, in effect, one is above convention itself: here betrayal once again assumes a double meaning" (*IdeoTrad*, 30–31). My translation.
85. See "Dialogo della Moda e la Morte," in Giacomo Leopardi, *Operette morali*, ed. Antonio Prete (Milan: Feltrinelli, 1972).
86. Ibid., 84.
87. Achille Bonito Oliva, *Gratis a bordo dell'arte* (Milan: Skira, 2000), 12. The English translation is mine.
88. The concepts of intensity, flow, deterritorialization, and nomadism are already present in *The Anti-Oedipus*, published in 1972, well before Bonito Oliva's tracts on the Transavantgarde. (See the Italian translation.) Deleuze and Guattari's *A Thousand Plateaus* (1980) completes the project initiated in *The Anti-Oedipus* (1972) and renews the ongoing process of reflection on questions of intensity, nomadism, drift, and being minoritarian, the last of which is already present in *Kafka: Toward a Minor Literature* (1975).
89. Deleuze and Guattari, *A Thousand Plateaus*, 11.
90. "The Italian Transavantgarde," 19.
91. *After the End of Art*, 63.
92. Gilles Deleuze and Felix Guattari, *Kafka: Toward a Minor Literature*, trans. Dana Polan (Minneapolis: University of Minnesota Press, 1986).
93. It might be worth remembering that the idea of minoritarian subjects for Deleuze-Guattari is qualitative, not quantitative, and designates a process rather than an aggregate. Although women may be the majority numerically (like animals, or molecules), they are still "minoritarian" vis-à-vis the social and political establishment. "When we say majority, we are referring not to a greater relative quantity but to the determination of a state or standard in relation to which larger quantities, as well as the smallest, can be said to be minoritarian: white-man, adult-male, etc. . . . Majority implies a state of domination, not the reverse." Deleuze and Guattari, *A Thousand Plateaus*, 291.
94. Making reference to the text *The Italian Transavantgarde*, Jameson curi-

ously sustains in *Postmodernism* that Bonito Oliva implies, but does not address, the important feature of the postmodern condition that is the "death of the subject" (Jameson, 174). However, a more careful reading of the text shows that we certainly do not find the end of individuality, because the subject, if fashionably soft, is alive and self-absorbed.

95. Deleuze and Guattari, *A Thousand Plateaus*, 23.
96. Ibid., 351.
97. Ibid., 381.
98. Ibid., 125–26.
99. *Gratis a bordo dell'arte*, 12.
100. Deleuze waged a polemic in favor of desire against pleasure, which he considered a conservative reterritorialization.
101. *Gratis a bordo dell'arte*, 12.

Index

In this index "f" after a number indicates a separate reference on the next page and "ff" indicates a separate reference on the next two pages. A continuous discussion over two or more pages is indicated by a span of numbers. "Passim" is used for a cluser of references in close but not consecutive sequence.

Addison, Joseph, 231
Adorno, Theodor, 1, 15, 100f, 129, 132, 135, 137, 142, 144–48, 152, 161f, 166, 168f, 176, 178, 182, 208, 213, 216, 235, 274n92, 282n173; *Minima Moralia*, 1; with Max Horkheimer, *Dialectic of Enlightenment*, 100f, 182; *Jargon of Authenticity*, 145; "The Valéry Proust Museum," 144
Agamben Giorgio, 7, 12, 16, 20, 57, 123, 170, 203, 205, 208, 263n104; *The Coming Community*, 20; *The End of the Poem*, 243n18; *Homo sacer*, 12; *Il Regno e la Gloria*, 203, 279n142
Alfieri, Vittorio, 107
Althusser, Louis, 129
Anderson, Benedict, 59
Anderson, Perry, 3f, 8, 16, 127, 230, 242n8, 242n9
Andreotti, Giulio, 53, 172, 251n96
Andrews, Geoff, 3, 8
anti-Frankfurt School: *See* Frankfurt School
Antonello, Pier Paolo, 243n13
Antonioni, Michelangelo, 1, 26, 37, 39, 48, 246n8; *The Eclipse*, 40; *La Notte*, 1
Apel, Karl-Otto, 170
Apollinaire, Guillaume, 32; "Zone," 32
Arendt, Hannah, 196; *On Revolution*, 196
Argan, Giulio Carlo, 231; *L'arte moderna 1770–1970*, 231. *See also* Bonito Oliva
Aristarco, Guido, 245n6
Aristotle, 137, 188, 276n109
Armani, Giorgio, 49

Aron, Jean-Paul, 74
Arrighi, Giovanni, 8, 16; *Chaos*, 16
Arte Povera, 211, 217–20, 222–24, 229
Asor Rosa, Alberto, 88, 90, 97
Astaire, Fred, 56, 64
Auden, W. H., 57
Augustine, Saint, 19
Auschwitz, 178f
Autonomia Operaia, 140, 213, 269n44
Avenue Cristoforo Colombo, 71

Bach, Johann Sebastian, 33; Toccata and Fugue in D minor (BWV 565), 33
Badaloni, Nicola, 127
Banco di Roma, 54, 58
Barenghi, Mario, 82, 109f, 120
Barilla, 58
Barth, John, 81, 83
Barth, Karl, 184
Barthelme, Donald, 92f
Barthes, Roland, 90; *Empire of Signs*, 90
Barzini, Luigi, 149
Bassano di Sutri, Odelscalchi castle at, 25, 41, 68
Baudelaire, Charles, 30f, 40, 100, 103, 232f, 237, 247n30, 250n72, 273n75, 293n69; "Le Cygne," 41 ; "Spleen," 30
Baudrillard, Jean, 19, 43f; *The Gulf War Did Not Take Place*, 279n141; *The Conspiracy of Art*, 293n69
Bauman, Zygmunt, 11, 143
Bazin, André, 21, 59, 245n6

Beckett, Samuel, 64, 90, 119f
Beckmann, Max, 230
Belting, Hans, 211, 218
Benedetti, Carla, 6, 77, 92f, 118, 229, 243n13; *Pasolini contro Calvino*, 92, 243n13
Benedict XVI, Pope (Joseph Aloisius Ratzinger), 202
Benjamin, Walter, 11, 31, 36, 41f, 44, 67, 95, 103, 115, 129, 169, 232, 273n75; and storytelling, 95f; "On Some Motifs in Baudelaire," 232; "Paris, Capital of the Nineteenth Century," 232; "The Return of the Flâneur," 41f; "The Work of Art in the Age of Its Mechanical Reproduction," 169
Berardinelli, Alfonso, 3, 243n13
Bergman, Ingmar, 37
Berlinische Monatsschrift, 184
Berlusconi, Silvio, 1–5, 7–11 passim, 15, 20, 22–24, 47, 50f, 53–55, 59, 61, 63, 73–75, 133–36, 144, 149, 155, 169, 172, 206, 220, 223, 228f, 240, 242n3, 252n105, 273n75, 289n256; and acquisition of rights to Fellini's films, 54f, 75; and commercial television, 2, 4f, 9, 20, 22–24, 47–51, 61, 73–6, 119, 136, 220; and Forza Italia, 3–5 passim, 172, 229
Bertolucci, Bernardo, 40; *The Conformist*, 40
Beuys, Joseph, 224
The Bicycle Thief. See De Sica, Vittorio
Binni, Walter, 99, 107
Biscuso, Massimiliano and Franco Gallo, 89, 99, 102, 106; *Leopardi antitaliano*, 99
Bloch, Ernst, 182
Boccaccio, Giovanni, 96; *Decameron*, 96
Bois, Yves-Alain, 219. See also Foster, Hal
Bollatti, Giulio, 89
Bologna, University of, 136
Bonami, Francesco, 7, 16, 220, 242n3
Bondanella, Peter, 59, 66, 77, 251n100, 253n118
Bonhöffer, Dietrich, 194
Bontadini, Gustavo, 191
Bonito Oliva, Achille, 4, 6, 10f, 15f, 130, 135, 211–40, 290n10; and artistic or apolitical nomadism, 212, 215, 221–23, 234, 237, 239f; and *il dicitore* ("the sayer"), 236, 294n82; and idealization of Shakespeare's Iago, 237, 240, 244n1; and *il possidente* ("the landowner"), 222f; and opulence, 218, 222–24; and Transavanguardia, 4, 15, 19, 130, 211–40, 244n1; and the traitor, 215, 227, 239f, 294n82, 294n84; "A proposito di Transavanguardia," 226; "The Achieved Nihilist," 15, 293n76; *Achilles' Heel*, 215, 234; *Art and the System of Art*, 231; "Bel Canto Ahead, Torture Behind," 217; *The Dream of Art: Between Avant Garde and Transavantgarde*, 214, 218, 231; *The Ideology of the Traitor*, 215, 230, 235, 238; "The Italian Transavantgarde," 222–25, 238, 295n94; *Superart*, 231, *Transavantgarde International*, 238; with Giulio Carlo Argan, *L'arte fino al 2000*, 232
Borges, Jorge Luis, 90
Bosch, Hieronymus, 75
Bourdieu, Pierre, 134
Bowie, Malcolm, 59
Brecht, Bertolt, 120, 258n24; Brechtian alienation effect and modes of critique, 67f, 79, 120
Buchloh, Benjamin, 215, 219, 229, 238; "The Bewildered Image," 221; "Figures of Authority, Ciphers of Regression: Notes on the Return of Representation in European Painting," 219. See also Foster, Hal
Burke, Frank, 27, 44
Burns, Jennifer, 243n13
Butler, Judith, 157

Cacciari, Massimo, 245n1
Calabrese, Omar, 6, 243n13
Calvino, Italo, 4, 6, 10–12, 16, 19, 22, 28, 52, 81–126, 135, 144, 146, 218, 229f, 240, 242n3, 243n13, 257n11; and aesthetic formalism, 81, 83, 87f, 92, 259n35; and attitude toward sexual and cultural difference, 90–92, 111f, 258n29; and the Enlightenment, 99–101; and etymology of "memos," 85–87; and rejection of the idea of politically engaged art, 81–85, 88, 90, 107, 109–12, 258n24, 262n89; and the subject's relation to others, 109f, 116f, 124, 262n93; *The Baron in the Trees*, 83; "I beatniks e il sistema," 93; "*La belle époque* inaspettata," 85; "Challenge to the Labyrinth," 101; *The Cloven*

Viscount, 83; "Cominciare e finire," 120; *Cosmicomics*, 81, 117; *The Crow Comes Last*, 83; "Cybernetics and Phantasms," 82; "Definitions of Territories: Comedy," 104; *Entering the War*, 83; "I Will Not Give Breath to My Trumpet Again," 85; *If on a winter's night a traveler*, 93, 117; *Invisible Cities*, 81, 93; *Italian Folktales*, 110; "The Lost Fortune of the Italian Novel," 95; "The Marrow of the Lion," 84; *Mr. Palomar*, 81, 117f, 125f; *The Path to the Spiders' Nests*, 83, 117, 123; "Right and Wrong Political Uses of Literature," 90; *Six Memos for the Next Millennium*, 4, 6, 10–12, 82–124; "Three Currents in Italian Novels of Today," 84; *Trilogy*, 117; "Two Interviews on Science and Literature," 101; "Whom Do We Write For?," 90
Campari, 58
Campbell, Colin, 202; *The Romantic Ethic and the Spirit of Modern Consumerism*, 202
Camus, Albert, 95
Capasso, Angelo, 211, 231
Caputo, John D., 194, 197
Caracalla, 25; and Caracalla baths, 41
Carrà, Carlo, 230
Cartland, Barbara, 120
Catholic Church, 19, 159; and Catholicism and/or Catholic mentality, 31, 40, 48, 51, 146, 191, 195, 201
Cavell, Stanley, 244n30
Cecchi Gori, Mario and Vittorio, 54
Celan, Paul, 175, 178, 280n153
Celant, Germano, 224, 229f; "For an Italian Identity," 229
Celentano, Adriano, 25, 62
Celli Bellucci, Novella, 99
Centro Spaziale Televisivo, 68, 72, 76
Centro Sperimentale di Cinematografia, 31
Ceserani, Remo, 243n13
Cézanne, Paul, 34
Chaplin, Charlie, 58; *City Lights*, 58
Charles Eliot Norton Lectures in Poetry, see "Harvard University"
Chavez, Hugo, 134
Chia, Sandro, 15, 211, 215, 218, 228f, 245n1
Chion, Michael, 52
Cinecittà, see "Fellini, Federico; and Cinecittà"

Cinema Nuovo, 245n6
Cineriz. See Fellini, Federico"
Citati, Pietro, 85
Clark, T. J., 25, 72
Clemente, Francesco, 15, 212, 215f, 219, 235, 245n1
Columbia University, 84
Columbus, Christopher, 95
Il Contemporaneo, 83, 90
Copernicus, Nicolaus, 132
Il Corriere della Sera, 55, 74
Cossiga, Francesco, 251n96
Craxi, Bettino, 5, 242n3, 273n75, 289n256; and Craxism, 205f, 272n75
Croce, Benedetto, 99, 149, 190, 196, 267n31, 284n195
Cubism, 21, 25, 28, 34
Cucchi, Enzo, 15, 212, 245n1

D'Agostini, Franca, 152, 161
Dante Alighieri, 7, 31, 34, 253n117; *La Divina Commedia*, 31, 253n117
Danto, Arthur C., 232f
Daumier, Honoré, 75
de Bergerac, Cyrano, 111f
Debord, Guy, 9, 20, 49, 75, 139, 161, 166, 170–72, 228, 238, 279n142; and Italy as society of integrated spectacle, 9, 20f, 23f, 49, 61, 63, 75, 170–72, 228; and the Situationists, 238, 279n142; and society of spectacle generally, 7, 20, 49, 57f, 66, 75f, 79 120, 139, 148, 161, 166, 170–72, 279n142; *Comments on the Society of Spectacle*, 9, 49, 170; *The Society of Spectacle*, 170
de Chirico, Giorgio, 34f
De Laurentiis, Dino, 33
Deleuze, Gilles, 5, 12f, 15, 21, 59, 61, 138, 141–44 passim, 148, 152f, 156, 158, 160f, 182, 221f, 237–40, 245n8, 266n27, 272n73; and becoming minoritarian, 141, 157f, 160, 221, 237–39, 294n88, 294n93; and nomadism or nomadology, 141, 221, 223, 237, 239f; and the time-image, 21, 245n8; *Nietzsche and Philosophy*, 148, 266n27; with Félix Guattari, *Anti-Oedipus*, 221; *A Thousand Plateaus*, 157, 221, 237f; "Treatise on Nomadology—The War Machine," 239
Della Casa, Giovanni, 93; *Galateo*, 93

de Man, Paul, 30
Democratici di Sinistra, 13, 134, 205
Democrazia Cristiana, 3f, 48, 134, 289n256
De Pisis, Filippo, 230
Derrida, Jacques, 5, 8, 12–14 passim, 137–39, 141, 144, 147f, 155–57, 171, 173f, 176–78, 190, 197–9, 204–6 passim, 273n85, 280n153; and deconstruction, 12–14 passim, 138, 141, 143, 156f, 167f, 182, 190, 245n1, 276n109; and faith in the other, 197–9; *Échographies*, 14, 167; "Faith and Knowledge," 141; "Force and Signification," 147; *Of Grammatology*, 139; *Of Spirit: Heidegger and the Question*, 141, 174f, 280n154, *Politics of Friendship*, 157; *Religion*, 205;, *Rogues*, 141; *Specters of Marx*, 14, 141, 206
De Sanctis, Francesco, 99, 101
de Santi, Gualtiero, 75
Descombes, Vincent, 157
De Sica, Vittorio, 59; *The Bicycle Thief*, 23; *Umberto D.*, 59
de Staël, Madame (Anne Louise Germaine de Staël-Holstein), 149
Dickinson, Emily, 90f
Dienst, Richard, 50, 62
Dix, Otto, 221
Domus, 230
Donati, Danilo, 73
Dos Passos, John, 27
Dotolo, Carmelo, 193
Duchamp, Marcel, 224f, 233; "Fountain," 233

Eco, Umberto, 6, 19, 22, 46, 51, 75f, 120, 126, 135–37, 144, 218, 242n9, 243n13; *Apocalittici e integrali*, 126, *The Name of the Rose*, 6; *Opera aperta*, 126, 168; "Postface to The Name of the Rose," 19, 243n13; *La struttura assente*, 126
economic miracle and/or boom, Italian, 20–22 passim, 26, 28, 56, 83f, 257n11; second economic miracle, 3, 127
The Economist, 4
Einaudi, Giulio editore (publishing house), 94
Einstein, Albert, 127
Eisenstein, Sergei, 26, 58; *Potemkin*, 58
Ekberg, Anita, 25
Eliot, George, 39
Eliot, T. S., 27, 29; *The Waste Land*, 29f
Elizabeth II, Queen of England, 62
energy crisis of the 1970s, 212f
Engels, Friedrich, 142, 232. *See also* Marx, Karl
Esposito, Roberto, 16, 190
L'Espresso, 75
EUR (Esposizione Universale Roma) district, 37, 39–41
L'Europeo, 53
exchange value, 11, 13, 127, 129, 132f, 150–2, 169, 216, 218, 235, 274n91, 274n92, 293n69
Expressionist painting, American, 213

Farias, Victor, 173f, 177, 179; *Heidegger and Nazism*, 173
Fascism, 7, 21, 39f, 59, 134, 151f, 175f
Faust, Wolfgang Max, 219
Fellini, Federico, 9f, 19–79, 137, 145, 245n6, 246n8, 249n49; and Cinecittà, 71; and Cineriz, 54; and criticism of commercial television and Italian consumerism, 9f, 49–59, 62–64, 66, 73–79, 252n105, 253n118, 255n152; and Fascist attacks against *La dolce vita*, 249n44; and Fellinian "neo-Realism," 59–61, 70, 76; and lawsuits against Silvio Berlusconi, 10, 53–54, 59, 63, 73; *8½*, 21, 25, 34, 37, 46f, 54, 66, 69, 72, 76, 78; *Amarcord*, 53, 249n100; *And The Ship Sails On*, 21f; *Il bidone*, 26; *Block Notes*, 51; *I clowns*, 51; *La dolce vita*, 9, 20–50, 54, 58, 61, 66, 68–71 passim, 137; *Fare un film*, 51; "Fellini Gets Angry," 55; *Ginger and Fred*, 9f, 20–24, 32, 40, 42, 47–79, 251n96, 252n100, 255n152; *Juliet of the Spirits*, 54, 78; *Moraldo in città*, 33; *The Nights of Cabiria*, 21, 26, 40, 49, 61, 69; *Orchestra Rehearsal*, 21f, 53, 251n100; *Roma*, 71; *Satyricon*, 71; *La strada*, 21f, 26, 49, 61, 66, 69, 245n6; *I Vitteloni*, 33, 54; *The Voice of the Moon*, 21, 54, 57, 73, 252n100
Ferrante, Elena, 155
Ferretti, Dante, 73
Feyerabend, Paul, 127
Financial Times, The, 4
Flaiano, Ennio, 29, 33
Flash Art, 221

Fluxus, 224
Fontana di Trevi, 30, 41, 54, 61, 70
Fortunato Stella, Antonio, 105
Foster, Hal, 219, 225, 228; with Rosalind Krauss, Yves-Alain Bois, and Benjamin Buchloh, *Art Since 1900: Modernism, Antimodernism, Postmodernism*, 219
Foucault, Michel, 5, 8, 12–14 passim, 17, 45, 137f, 141–44 passim, 146, 148, 151–53, 155, 161, 164, 173, 182–86, 188–90, 205, 232; and the Enlightenment, 183f, 186, 190, 284n195; and genealogy, 190; and ontology of actuality, 14, 134, 173, 179, 181–90, 192, 283n187; *History of Sexuality, Vol. 1*, 205; lecture to the Collège de France, January 5, 1983, 182, 184; "The Masked Philosopher," 22; "What Is Critique?," 182f, 283n184; "What is Enlightenment?," 182, 184, 232; "What is Revolution?," 182f
Frankfurt School, 5f, 15, 99, 133, 140, 142, 166, 183; and "anti-Frankfurt School," 8, 213
Freiburg, University of, 174
French Revolution, 100
Freccero, Carlo, 5
Freud, Sigmund, 42, 78; and Freudianism, 131; and reality principle, 41, 60, 70f, 207, 278n130; *Civilization and its Discontents*, 42
Fried, Michael, 247n19
Frigidaire (Italian art magazine), 231

Gable, Clark, 62
Gadamer, Hans-Georg, 159f, 162, 179f; *Truth and Method*, 160
Gadda, Carlo Emilio, 30, 90, 94
Galli della Loggia, Ernesto, 5
Gargani, Aldo Giorgio, 127f, 245n1; *Crisis of Reason*, 127f
Gentile, Giovanni, 149
Ghelen, Arnold, 190
Gieri, Manuela, 34
Ginsborg, Paul, 23, 50
Ginzburg, Carlo, 127
Giordani, Pietro, 98, 105
Girard, René, 134, 193–95; *Things Hidden Since the Foundation of the World*, 194; *Violence and the Sacred*, 194
Godard, Jean-Luc, 77

Goethe, Johann Wolfgang von, 149
Goldsmith, Oliver, 117, 262n93; *The Vicar of Wakefield*, 117, 262n93
Gombrich, Ernst Hans Joseph, 217
Gorbachev, Mikhail, 232
Gramsci, Antonio, 2, 8, 19, 23f, 82, 87, 90, 95, 127f, 133, 140, 190, 259n38, 261n81; and hegemony, 8, 127; and the national-popular, 3, 8f, 23f, 90, 95, 259n38, 261n81; *Letters from Prison*, 2; *Prison Notebooks*, 2, 8, 19, 87
Grazzini, Giovanni, 76
Greenberg, Clement, 218
Grosz, George, 75
Guattari, Félix, 15, 141, 156, 158, 169, 221f, 237–40. *See also* Deleuze, Gilles
Guerrini, Giovanni, 40
Guglielmi, Guido, 100, 105
Gundle, Stephen, 47
Gutierrez, Pedro, 95

Haacke, Hans; 228; "Taking Stock," 228
Habermas, Jürgen, 137, 183; *The Philosophical Discourse of Modernity*, 137, 183
Hardt, Michael, 16, 141, 170, 206, 208. *See also* Negri, Antonio
Harvard University, 84–86, 116; and Charles Eliot Norton Lectures in Poetry, 85f
Harvey, David, 19, 242n13
Haussmann, Georges-Eugène, Baron, 30, 41
Hegel, Georg Wilhelm Friedrich, 129, 183f, 188f, 197, 204, 235, 267n31, 285n204
Heidegger, Martin, 13f, 99, 125, 129–32, 134, 137–39, 142 146f, 149f, 155f, 160–63, 169, 173–82, 185–89, 192–94, 200, 207, 213, 216f, 234, 273n83; and end of metaphysics, 125, 129f, 138, 150, 153, 155–57 passim, 160, 162, 187, 192, 234, 273n83, 283n187; and *Ereignis*, 14, 134, 164, 179, 189, 203, 217; and Heideggerian left, 138, 151, 273n85, 281n165; and Nazism, 128–30, 134, 161, 173–82, 277n115, 280n153, 280n160, 281n165; and silence regarding death camps, 178f; and *Verwindung*, 129–32, 138f, 146, 150, 192f, 276n111; and Western history, 154, 175, 178f; "The Age of the World Picture," 165; "Anaximander's Saying," 187; "Art and Space," 217; *Being and Time*, 155,

280n154; *Holzwege*, 130, 187; *Identität und Differenz*, 130, 162, 164, 179, *Introduction to Metaphysics*, 128, 177; *Letter on Humanism*, 156; *Nietzsche*, 132, 151, 273n83; "Origin of the Work of Art," 169, 187, 217; "The Principle of Identity," 164f, 277n115; "The Question Concerning Technology," 161f, 277n118; "The Self-Assertion of the German University," 174; *Der Spiegel* interview, 162, 174, 277n115, 280n153; *Vorträge und Aufsätze*, 130
Hitler, Adolf, 116, 174, 181, 285n210
Hölderlin, Friedrich, 169, 177
Holocaust, the, 138f, 178f, 216, 282n173
Holzer, Jenny, 225
Hopkins, David, 224f, 228; *After Modern Art 1945–2000*, 224
Horkheimer, Max, 100f, 182, 213, 216; with Theodor Adorno, *Dialectic of Enlightenment*, 100f, 182

Iraq War, 205, 208
Irigaray, Luce, 157
"Italian Style," 21f, 49, 71. *See also* "Made in Italy"

Jameson, Fredric, 6, 11, 19f, 25, 28, 37, 213, 215, 225f, 230, 236, 242n13, 246n17, 249n49, 292n41; *Postmodernism or, The Cultural Logic of Late Capitalism*, 225, 295n94; *Valences of the Dialectic*, 11
Jaspers, Karl, 280n153
Jay, Martin, 274n92
Jencks, Charles, 225, 242n13; *The Languages of Postmodern Architecture*, 225
Jensen, Monica, 242n13
Joachim of Fiore, 203f, 287n245; *Liber Concordiae Novi ac Veteris Testamenti*, 203; *Expositio in Apocalypsim*, 203; *Psalterium Decem Chordarum*, 203; *Tractatus Super Quatuor Evangilia*, 203
John Paul II, Pope (Karol Józef Wojtyla), 191, 199, 202
Johns, Jasper, 224
Joyce, James, 27, 29, 91, 247n22; *A Portrait of the Artist as a Young Man*, 45, *Ulysses*, 29
Jung, Carl, 78

Kafka, Franz, 11, 62, 110, 113–17, 238, 262n93; *Amerika*, 110, 117, 262n93;

"The Bucket Rider," 11, 113–16; "The Metamorphosis," 114
Kant, Immanuel, 132, 148, 184, 186, 190; and Kantian sublime, 227
Kezich, Tullio, 33, 55, 74f
Kiefer, Anselm, 215, 219
Kirchner, Ernst Ludwig, 230
Kleinian psychoanalysis, 166, 221
Kracauer, Siegfried, 46, 62
Krauss, Rosalind, 219, 225. *See also* Foster, Hal
Kruger, Barbara, 225
Kundera, Milan, 11, 28, 103, 115f, 146; *The Unbearable Lightness of Being*, 103, 115f

Lacan, Jacques, 32, 58–63, 70, 78, 131, 222; and the Real, 37, 49, 59–61, 64, 67, 69f, 72f, 78f; and seminar on *Antigone*, 78
Laclau, Ernesto, 244n27; with Chantal Mouffe, *Hegemony and Socialist Strategy*, 244n27
Lacoue-Labarthe, Philippe, 174–76, 178f, 273n75, 280n153
Lang, Fritz, 26
Lanzi Tomasi, Gioacchino, 231
La Padula, Ernesto, 40
La Rochefoucauld, François de, 99
left and/or leftism, political, 2–8, 10, 13, 16, 83f, 127, 133, 136–38, 140, 154f, 170, 206, 212, 220, 229, 245n6
Lega Nord, 136
Legge Mammì, 50, 53f
Leibniz, Gottfried Wilhelm, 99
Leopardi, Giacomo, 7, 49, 89, 91, 94f, 97–108, 212, 237, 259n38, 261n81; "The Broom," 100; "Dialogue Between Fashion and Death," 100, 102f; "Dialogue Between Hercules and Atlas," 98, 105; "Dialogue Between Nature and an Icelander," 100; "Dialogue Between Plotinus and Porphyry," 107; "Dialogue Between Tristan and a Friend," 104; *Discourse on the Present State of the Customs of the Italians*, 7, 49, 94, 102, 259n38; "The History of the Human Race," 105; "The Infinite," 97, 102; *Operette morali*, 95, 97–107; "Parini's Discourse on Glory," 107; "The Wager of Prometheus," 105; *Zibaldone*, 98, 100, 102, 107, 261n81

Levinas, Emmanuel, 194, 199, 282n173
Levine, Sherrie, 225
Lewalski, Barbara, 31
Liberation, 4, 11
Longo, Robert, 225
Lo Savio, Francesco, 230
Löwith, Karl, 176
Lucretius, 92
Lukács, György, 87, 138, 182, 219, 274n92
Luperini, Romano, 6, 10, 144, 243n13, 243n20
Luporini, Cesare, 89, 99, 100
Luther, Martin, 240
Lyotard, Jean-François, 14, 28, 92, 150, 161, 168, 190, 213, 225–27, 242n13, 280n153

Mach, Ernst, 127
Machiavelli, Niccolò, 180, 190, 237
"Made in Italy," 9, 49, 143. *See also* "Italian Style"
Mani pulite, 180, 289n256
Mann, Thomas, 46
mannerism and/or "the Mannerist" in art, 212, 214, 218, 226f, 229f, 235f, 240
Manzoni, Piero, 230
Maradona, Diego, 215, 234
Marat, Jean-Paul, 215
Marcus, Millicent, 66, 253n129, 255n152
Marcuse, Herbert, 175, 280n153
Marinetti, Filippo Tommaso, 32; "The Pope's Monoplane," 32
Marramao, Giacomo, 139, 192
Marx, Karl, 127–29, 132f, 143, 148, 177, 181, 204, 207f, 232; and Marxism, 2f, 13, 82, 87, 127–29, 131, 133f, 138, 177, 209, 213, 216, 232, 258n24, 265n23; *Capital*, 128, 177; with Friedrich Engels, *The Communist Manifesto*, 143, 232
mass culture, media, and/or society, 2, 4–5, 8–10 passim, 12–15 passim, 19f, 22, 24–28 passim, 32, 42, 49, 54–56, 61, 63f, 66, 70, 74–76, 86f, 93, 96, 118–20, 126f, 133, 136f, 140, 143–45, 150, 156, 162, 166, 168f, 179, 208, 213, 217, 224f, 272n75
Masina, Giulietta, 21, 56, 66
Mastrantonio, Luca, 7, 16, 242n3
Mastroianni, Marcello, 21f, 50, 54, 56, 66
Mazzoni, Angiolo, 73
McLuhan, Marshall, 204
Melville, Herman, 107, 116f, 121–24, 262n93;

and Bartleby (character), 107, 121–24; "Bartleby, the Scrivener," 116f, 121, 123, 262n93
Metz, Christian, 21
Michaud, Yves, 217
Michelson, Annette, 225
Minimalist art, 224
modernism, 11, 21f, 24–42, 45–47, 48, 55, 70, 77, 81–3 passim, 88, 91, 115, 213, 218, 225, 230, 246n17, 247n19, 247n22, 249n49
Mollica, Vicenzo, 54
Montale, Eugenio, 91
Montesquieu, Baron de la Brède et de (Charles-Louis de Secondat), 149
Moore, Marianne, 90f
Morandi, Giorgio, 34–6, 39
Moravia, Alberto, 11, 50, 54
Moresco, Antonio, 93f
Moretti, Nanni, 9
Mouffe, Chantal, 244n27. *See also* Laclau, Ernesto
Muir, Willa and Edna, 114
Muraro, Luisa, 16
Murnau, F. W., 26
Musil, Robert, 91, 94
Mussgnug, Florian, 243n13
Mussolini, Benito, 4, 40

Nancy, Jean-Luc, 190, 199f, 286n229
Naples, 215
Negri, Antonio, 8, 16, 99, 140f, 170, 206, 208, 262n89, 265n23; "The Italian Difference," 16; *Lenta ginestra*, 99; with Michael Hardt, *Empire*, 16, 123, 140, 206
Neo-Expressionist painting, Italian and German, 211, 215, 219, 229
neorealism, cinematic, 9f, 21, 23, 25, 29, 48, 59, 70, 245n6, 245n8
Neorealist painting, 212, 227
Nico, 25
Nietzsche, Friedrich, 9, 13–15 passim, 28, 116, 125, 128f, 131f, 134, 138, 142, 149–51, 153, 158, 160–62, 168, 175, 183, 193, 195, 200, 206, 213, 216, 218, 227, 233–35, 266n27, 272n73, 273n83; and eternal return, 116; and Nietzschean superman/overman, 139, 144, 149, 218, 266n27; and Zarathustra, 218, 233; *Ecce Homo*, 206, "European Nihilism," 161; *The Gay Science*, 14; *Human, All Too Human*,

9, 162, 235; *Thus Spoke Zaarathustra*, 266n27; *The Twilight of the Idols*, 14, 150, 168, 234; *The Will to Power*, 132, 153, 234, 293n76
nihilism, 13f, 28, 52, 64, 69, 83, 92, 97, 104, 115f, 121, 123, 125, 128, 132–34, 139f, 147, 150–55, 161, 175, 186, 192, 200, 209, 216, 218, 227f, 235, 240, 267n31, 273n83, 293n76
Nouvelle Vague, 77, 246n8
Novalis (pen name of Georg Philipp Friedrich Freiherr von Hardenberg), 204
Nuovi Argomenti, 84
Nuremberg trials, 181, 282n172

October, 225
O'Grady, Desmond, 34
Oklahoma City bombing, 289n258
Orlando, Francesco, 127
Orr, John, 25, 27, 246n17
Ovid, 92

P2 (Potere Due), 49, 172
Paisà. See Rosselini, Roberto
Palais de Chaillot, 74
Palazzo della Civiltà Italiana, 40
Palladino, Mimmo, 15, 212
Panarari, Massimo, 3, 242n3
Paolucci, Anne, 31
Paparazzo, name of character, 245n38
Pareyson, Luigi, 137f, 193, 284n196
Parini, Giuseppe, 107
Partito Comunista Italiano (PCI), 2, 4, 8, 10f, 48, 53, 82, 107, 127, 135, 205, 212, 242n8
Partito dei Comunisti Italiani (PdCI), 206
Partitio Socialista Italiano (PSI), 3, 5, 48, 53, 74, 289n256
Pasolini, Pier Paolo, 2f, 11, 13, 16, 30, 35, 50, 54f, 78, 101, 108, 158, 214, 229f; and anthropological mutation, 2, 54f; *Accatone*, 35; *Corsair Writings* (*Scritti corsari*), 2, 54; "Gli Italiani non sono più quelli" ("Studio della rivoluzione antropologica in Italia"), 54; *The Hawks and the Sparrows*, 2; *Lutheran Letters*, 2f, 108
Patriarca, Silvana, 48
"Patricia" (pop song), 25, 39
Patton, Paul, 141, 158, 160
Paul, Saint, 147, 195

Pavese, Cesare, 11
Peanuts, 126
Perec, Georges, 92
Perniola, Mario, 126, 242n3
Petrarch (Francesco Petrarca), 145
Piacentini, Marcello, 40
Picasso, Pablo, 25, 32, 70
Pichierri, Mimmo, 206f
Pinelli, Tullio, 29
Pinkney, Tony, 27, 247n22
Plato, 276n109
Pollock, Jackson, 101
postmodernism, 3, 6f, 14, 19, 24–28 passim, 30, 42f, 47, 63, 70, 75, 81, 92f, 97, 103, 116, 119f, 131f, 134, 137, 140f, 143, 150, 152, 154, 156, 161, 166, 171, 179, 181, 189f, 202–6 passim, 212, 215, 219, 224–228, 230, 236, 242n13, 246n17, 249n49; and simulacrum, 25, 36, 56, 69f, 73, 156, 167, 279n141
poststructuralism, 3, 6f, 8, 12–15, 103, 129, 141f, 144f, 147f, 153, 155, 160, 177, 182, 219, 239, 267n31
Prete, Antonio, 99; *Il pensiero poetante*, 99
Protestantism and/or Protestant mentality, 201f
Proust, Marcel, 36, 91; *À la recherche du temps perdu*, 45
Pynchon, Thomas, 92

"Quelli della Notte," 135

RAI (Radio Televisione Italiana), 48, 50, 53
Rainer, Louise, 38
Rancière, Jacques, 11, 88f, 136, 221, 291n30
Rapaci, Leonida, 34
Rauschenberg, Robert, 224
Reagan, Ronald, 62, 191, 213; and Reaganism or "the Reaganite," 135, 228
Red Brigades, the, 139f, 213
Real, the. *See* Lacan, Jacques
Rella, Franco, 127
Resistenza, 73, 123
Restivo, Angelo, 54, 59
Retort (Iain Boal, T. J. Clark, Joseph Matthews, Michael Watts), 170, 279n142
Richardson, Robert, 29f
Richter, Gerhard, 215
right and/or conservatism, political, 2, 4f, 48, 84, 138, 206

Rilke, Rainer Maria, 108; *Letters to a Young Poet*, 108
Rinascita, 83
Risorgimento, il, 48, 59, 89
Risset, Jacqueline, 53
Rizzoli (publishing house), 54
Rizzoli, Angelo, 33
Rogers, Ginger, 56, 64
Romano, Mario, 40
Rome, 24, 30–33 passim, 37, 39–42, 56f, 59, 61, 64, 71, 73, 200
Rome, Open City. See Rossellini, Roberto
Rondi, Brunello, 40
Rorty, Richard, 136, 192, 197, 273n85, 281n165
Rosai, Ottone, 230
Rossellini, Roberto, 59; *Paisà*, 23, 59; *Rome, Open City*, 23
Rota, Nino, 26, 46
Rouault, Georges, 36
Rousseau, Jean-Jacques, 149
Rovatti, Pier Aldo, 125f, 128f, 142, 207, 245n1; *Elogio del pudore*, 157
Rugafiori, Claudio, 12

Saatchi, Charles, 228
Salle, David, 213, 219
Salvatore, Anna, 34
Sartre, Jean-Paul, 112
Saussure, Ferdinand de, 158
Schlegel, Friedrich, 120; *Lyceum* fragments, 120
Schleiermacher, Friedrich, 193
Schnabel, Julian, 213, 219, 228
Schocken Books, 114
Scholem, Gershem, 115
Sebastian, Saint, 214
second economic miracle. *See* economic miracle
Shakespeare, William, 23; *Othello*, 237
simulacrum. *See* postmodernism
Sironi, Mario, 230
Sitney, P. Adams, 31
Slave Act of 1740, 65
Sloterdijk, Peter, 192
Sluga, Hans, 175, 280n153
Solidarity movement, 212
Spadini, Letizia, 34
Spengler, Oswald, 221
Stable Gallery, 233

Stalinism, 182, 208
La Stampa, 206
Steele, Richard, 231
Stella, Antonio Fortunato, 105
Steve Canyon, 126
Stendahl (pen name of Marie-Henri Beyle), 149
Stiegler, Bernard, 13
Stille, Alexander, 3
Stillman, Charles, 86
Stirner, Max, 221
Strada, Vittorio, 127
Superman, 126

Tabucchi, Antonio, 243n13
Tate Gallery, 228
Taylor, Charles, 196, 205; *A Secular Age*, 196
technology, 14, 32, 87, 118, 133, 136, 144, 161–7, 174, 176, 178–80, 186, 199–201, 204f, 207, 227, 276n114, 277n115, 277n118, 281n153
Termini station, 64, 70f, 73, 75
Thatcher, Margaret, 228
time-image. *See* Deleuze, Gilles
Togliatti, Palmiro, 2
Totò, 2, 215
Transavanguardia. *See* Bonito Oliva, Achille
Tree, Iris, 34
Tronti, Mario, 16, 140, 269n44
Turin, University of, 137f, 207

L'Unità, 83

Vasari, Giorgio, 231
Vattimo, Gianni, 4, 6, 10–16 passim, 28, 125–209, 213, 216–18, 227, 234f, 245n1, 266n27, 272n75, 274n91, 281n165, 289n258; and abandonment of Marxist thought, 128–31, 133, 138, 264n15; and avoidance of criticism, 126, 130–36, 139f, 142f, 146–49, 159f, 173, 177–80, 184–86, 189f, 209, 282n173; and Heidegger's Nazism, 173–82, 281n165, 282n172, 285n210; and religious views, 146f, 159, 191–205, 284n196, 284n187, 285n204, 285n207, 285n208, 285n218, 286n229, 288n248; and weak thought, 6, 12–16, 28, 123, 125–209, 213, 245n1, 263n104, 266n27, 270n51, 273n75, 293n75; and Western history, 154, 192, 197, 201f; *Addio alla verità*, 176, 180, 188,

283n184; *The Adventure of Difference*, 129, 152, 156, 175f, 179; *After Christianity*, 199, 201f, 204; "Apology for Nihilism," 234; *Belief*, 191f, 201; *Beyond Interpretation*, 147f, 163, 173, 185; "Dialectic, Difference, Weak Thought," 129f; *Ecce comu: Come si ridiventa ciò che si era*, 15f, 134, 154, 206–209, 265n23; *The End of Modernity*, 127, 131, 140, 152, 168, 179, 293n76; "Il comunismo ritrovato," 206; *Lightening as Responsibility*, 139; *Nihilism and Emancipation*, 150, 154, 159, 179, 185, 187, 189; *The Transparent Society*, 13, 127, 137, 140, 142, 144, 152, 168, 170, 179, 189, 207; *Vocation and Responsibility of the Philosopher*, 185; with Pier Aldo Rovatti, *Weak Thought*, 13, 125, 129, 142, 157. *See also* exchange value
Veltroni, Walter, 50, 54
Versace, Gianni, 49
Via Veneto, 41
Viano, Carlo Augusto, 126, 128, 143f, 270n51
Vico, Giambattista, 149, 190, 267n31, 284n195; *La scienza nuova*, 190
Vidal, Gore, 289n258
Virno, Paolo, 16
Visconti, Luchino, 11, 48, 59, 246n8; *The Earth Trembles*, 59; *Rocco and His Brothers*, 48

Vittorini, Elio, 34, 249n44
Voltaire (pen name of François-Marie Arouet), 99; and Candide (character), 99; *Candide* (novel), 110

Waco, Texas, 208, 289n258
Warhol, Andy, 232f, 293n69, 293n74; "Brillo Box," 233; "Campbell's Soup Cans," 233
Weber, Max, 128, 183, 201; *The Protestant Ethic and the Spirit of Capitalism*, 201
Weill, Kurt, 26; "The Ballad of Mack the Knife," 26
Welles, Orson, 40; *The Trial*, 40
Williams, Raymond, 27, 247n22
Wölfflin, Heinrich, 218
Wolin, Richard, 13, 280n153
Woolf, Virginia, 247n22
World War One, 229
World War Two, 2, 28, 35, 48, 73, 83f, 99, 145, 175, 178

Yale University, 84
Yom Kippur War, 212
Young, Julian, 280n153

Zabala, Santiago, 138f
Zavattini, Cesare, 29, 59
Žižek, Slavoj, 70, 78

Cultural Memory in the Present

Daniel Innerarity, *The Future and Its Enemies: In Defense of Political Hope*

Pisters, Patricia, *The Neuro-Image: A Deleuzian Film-Philosophy of Digital Screen Culture*

François-David Sebbah, *Testing the Limit: Derrida, Henry, Levinas, and the Phenomenological Tradition*

Erik Peterson, *Theological Tractates*, edited by Michael J. Hollerich

Feisal G. Mohamed, *Milton and the Post-Secular Present: Ethics, Politics, Terrorism*

Pierre Hadot, *The Present Alone Is Our Happiness, Second Edition: Conversations with Jeannie Carlier and Arnold I. Davidson*

Yasco Horsman, *Theaters of Justice: Judging, Staging, and Working Through in Arendt, Brecht, and Delbo*

Jacques Derrida, *Parages*, edited by John P. Leavey

Henri Atlan, *The Sparks of Randomness, Volume 1: Spermatic Knowledge*

Rebecca Comay, *Mourning Sickness: Hegel and the French Revolution*

Djelal Kadir, *Memos from the Besieged City: Lifelines for Cultural Sustainability*

Stanley Cavell, *Little Did I Know: Excerpts from Memory*

Jeffrey Mehlman, *Adventures in the French Trade: Fragments Toward a Life*

Jacob Rogozinski, *The Ego and the Flesh: An Introduction to Egoanalysis*

Marcel Hénaff, *The Price of Truth: Gift, Money, and Philosophy*

Paul Patton, *Deleuzian Concepts: Philosophy, Colonialization, Politics*

Michael Fagenblat, *A Covenant of Creatures: Levinas's Philosophy of Judaism*

Stefanos Geroulanos, *An Atheism that Is Not Humanist Emerges in French Thought*

Andrew Herscher, *Violence Taking Place: The Architecture of the Kosovo Conflict*

Hans-Jörg Rheinberger, *On Historicizing Epistemology: An Essay*

Jacob Taubes, *From Cult to Culture*, edited by Charlotte Fonrobert and Amir Engel

Peter Hitchcock, *The Long Space: Transnationalism and Postcolonial Form*

Lambert Wiesing, *Artificial Presence: Philosophical Studies in Image Theory*

Jacob Taubes, *Occidental Eschatology*

Freddie Rokem, *Philosophers and Thespians: Thinking Performance*

Roberto Esposito, *Communitas: The Origin and Destiny of Community*

Vilashini Cooppan, *Worlds Within: National Narratives and Global Connections in Postcolonial Writing*

Josef Früchtl, *The Impertinent Self: A Heroic History of Modernity*

Frank Ankersmit, Ewa Domanska, and Hans Kellner, eds., *Re-Figuring Hayden White*

Michael Rothberg, *Multidirectional Memory: Remembering the Holocaust in the Age of Decolonization*

Jean-François Lyotard, *Enthusiasm: The Kantian Critique of History*

Ernst van Alphen, Mieke Bal, and Carel Smith, eds., *The Rhetoric of Sincerity*

Stéphane Mosès, *The Angel of History: Rosenzweig, Benjamin, Scholem*

Pierre Hadot, *The Present Alone Is Our Happiness: Conversations with Jeannie Carlier and Arnold I. Davidson*

Alexandre Lefebvre, *The Image of the Law: Deleuze, Bergson, Spinoza*

Samira Haj, *Reconfiguring Islamic Tradition: Reform, Rationality, and Modernity*

Diane Perpich, *The Ethics of Emmanuel Levinas*

Marcel Detienne, *Comparing the Incomparable*

François Delaporte, *Anatomy of the Passions*

René Girard, *Mimesis and Theory: Essays on Literature and Criticism, 1959-2005*

Richard Baxstrom, *Houses in Motion: The Experience of Place and the Problem of Belief in Urban Malaysia*

Jennifer L. Culbert, *Dead Certainty: The Death Penalty and the Problem of Judgment*

Samantha Frost, *Lessons from a Materialist Thinker: Hobbesian Reflections on Ethics and Politics*

Regina Mara Schwartz, *Sacramental Poetics at the Dawn of Secularism: When God Left the World*

Gil Anidjar, *Semites: Race, Religion, Literature*

Ranjana Khanna, *Algeria Cuts: Women and Representation, 1830 to the Present*

Esther Peeren, *Intersubjectivities and Popular Culture: Bakhtin and Beyond*

Eyal Peretz, *Becoming Visionary: Brian De Palma's Cinematic Education of the Senses*

Diana Sorensen, *A Turbulent Decade Remembered: Scenes from the Latin American Sixties*

Hubert Damisch, *A Childhood Memory by Piero della Francesca*

José van Dijck, *Mediated Memories in the Digital Age*

Dana Hollander, *Exemplarity and Chosenness: Rosenzweig and Derrida on the Nation of Philosophy*

Asja Szafraniec, *Beckett, Derrida, and the Event of Literature*

Sara Guyer, *Romanticism After Auschwitz*

Alison Ross, *The Aesthetic Paths of Philosophy: Presentation in Kant, Heidegger, Lacoue-Labarthe, and Nancy*

Gerhard Richter, *Thought-Images: Frankfurt School Writers' Reflections from Damaged Life*

Bella Brodzki, *Can These Bones Live? Translation, Survival, and Cultural Memory*

Rodolphe Gasché, *The Honor of Thinking: Critique, Theory, Philosophy*

Brigitte Peucker, *The Material Image: Art and the Real in Film*

Natalie Melas, *All the Difference in the World: Postcoloniality and the Ends of Comparison*

Jonathan Culler, *The Literary in Theory*

Michael G. Levine, *The Belated Witness: Literature, Testimony, and the Question of Holocaust Survival*

Jennifer A. Jordan, *Structures of Memory: Understanding German Change in Berlin and Beyond*

Christoph Menke, *Reflections of Equality*

Marlène Zarader, *The Unthought Debt: Heidegger and the Hebraic Heritage*

Jan Assmann, *Religion and Cultural Memory: Ten Studies*

David Scott and Charles Hirschkind, *Powers of the Secular Modern: Talal Asad and His Interlocutors*

Gyanendra Pandey, *Routine Violence: Nations, Fragments, Histories*

James Siegel, *Naming the Witch*

J. M. Bernstein, *Against Voluptuous Bodies: Late Modernism and the Meaning of Painting*

Theodore W. Jennings, Jr., *Reading Derrida / Thinking Paul: On Justice*

Richard Rorty and Eduardo Mendieta, *Take Care of Freedom and Truth Will Take Care of Itself: Interviews with Richard Rorty*

Jacques Derrida, *Paper Machine*

Renaud Barbaras, *Desire and Distance: Introduction to a Phenomenology of Perception*

Jill Bennett, *Empathic Vision: Affect, Trauma, and Contemporary Art*

Ban Wang, *Illuminations from the Past: Trauma, Memory, and History in Modern China*

James Phillips, *Heidegger's Volk: Between National Socialism and Poetry*

Frank Ankersmit, *Sublime Historical Experience*

István Rév, *Retroactive Justice: Prehistory of Post-Communism*

Paola Marrati, *Genesis and Trace: Derrida Reading Husserl and Heidegger*

Krzysztof Ziarek, *The Force of Art*

Marie-José Mondzain, *Image, Icon, Economy: The Byzantine Origins of the Contemporary Imaginary*

Cecilia Sjöholm, *The Antigone Complex: Ethics and the Invention of Feminine Desire*

Jacques Derrida and Elisabeth Roudinesco, *For What Tomorrow . . . : A Dialogue*

Elisabeth Weber, *Questioning Judaism: Interviews by Elisabeth Weber*

Jacques Derrida and Catherine Malabou, *Counterpath: Traveling with Jacques Derrida*

Martin Seel, *Aesthetics of Appearing*

Nanette Salomon, *Shifting Priorities: Gender and Genre in Seventeenth-Century Dutch Painting*

Jacob Taubes, *The Political Theology of Paul*

Jean-Luc Marion, *The Crossing of the Visible*

Eric Michaud, *The Cult of Art in Nazi Germany*

Anne Freadman, *The Machinery of Talk: Charles Peirce and the Sign Hypothesis*

Stanley Cavell, *Emerson's Transcendental Etudes*

Stuart McLean, *The Event and Its Terrors: Ireland, Famine, Modernity*

Beate Rössler, ed., *Privacies: Philosophical Evaluations*

Bernard Faure, *Double Exposure: Cutting Across Buddhist and Western Discourses*

Alessia Ricciardi, *The Ends of Mourning: Psychoanalysis, Literature, Film*

Alain Badiou, *Saint Paul: The Foundation of Universalism*

Gil Anidjar, *The Jew, the Arab: A History of the Enemy*

Jonathan Culler and Kevin Lamb, eds., *Just Being Difficult? Academic Writing in the Public Arena*

Didier Maleuvre, *Museum Memories: History, Technology, Art*
Jacques Derrida, *Monolingualism of the Other; or, The Prosthesis of Origin*
Andrew Baruch Wachtel, *Making a Nation, Breaking a Nation:*
    Literature and Cultural Politics in Yugoslavia
Niklas Luhmann, *Love as Passion: The Codification of Intimacy*
Mieke Bal, ed., *The Practice of Cultural Analysis:*
    Exposing Interdisciplinary Interpretation
Jacques Derrida and Gianni Vattimo, eds., *Religion*

The authorized representative in the EU for product safety and compliance is:
Mare Nostrum Group
B.V Doelen 72
4831 GR Breda
The Netherlands

www.ingramcontent.com/pod-product-compliance
Lightning Source LLC
Chambersburg PA
CBHW020331240426
43665CB00043B/218